# THE ROLE OF THEORY IN
# COMPUTER SCIENCE

**Essays Dedicated to Janusz Brzozowski**

# THE ROLE OF THEORY IN COMPUTER SCIENCE

## Essays Dedicated to Janusz Brzozowski

Edited by

**Stavros Konstantinidis**
Saint Mary's University, Halifax, Canada

**Nelma Moreira**
University of Porto, Portugal

**Rogério Reis**
University of Porto, Portugal

**Jeffrey Shallit**
Waterloo University, Canada

**World Scientific**

NEW JERSEY · LONDON · SINGAPORE · BEIJING · SHANGHAI · HONG KONG · TAIPEI · CHENNAI · TOKYO

*Published by*

World Scientific Publishing Co. Pte. Ltd.

5 Toh Tuck Link, Singapore 596224

*USA office:* 27 Warren Street, Suite 401-402, Hackensack, NJ 07601

*UK office:* 57 Shelton Street, Covent Garden, London WC2H 9HE

**British Library Cataloguing-in-Publication Data**
A catalogue record for this book is available from the British Library.

**THE ROLE OF THEORY IN COMPUTER SCIENCE**
**Essays Dedicated to Janusz Brzozowski**

ISBN 978-981-3148-19-2

Janusz Brzozowski
(photography by Maria Brzozowski)

Group photo from Brzozowski 80, June 24, 2015

Janusz Brzozowski with some students, June 24, 2015

# Preface

Janusz (John) A. Brzozowski has made fundamental contributions to many areas of theoretical computer science, including finite automata, regular expressions, semigroup theory, asynchronous circuits and networks, verification, and descriptional complexity of regular languages.

He is a pioneer in automata theory, with applications in digital circuits and testing. He is renowned for his work on regular languages and on syntactic semigroups of formal languages, with several concepts carrying Brzozowski's name in honour of his contributions. Many of these are automata theory notions now widely taught in introductory courses, but also still the subject of research and generalizations.

In his Ph.D. thesis, he introduced the notion of derivative of a regular expression, now called the Brzozowski derivative, which allows the conversion of regular expressions to deterministic finite automata [Brz64a]. More than 50 years later, the use of derivatives for efficiently deciding equivalence and membership problems in regular languages and extended models is still a major topic of research. Brzozowski's algorithm [Brz63a] for obtaining a minimal deterministic finite automaton by double reversal is surprisingly simple: starting with a finite automaton (possibly nondeterministic), one reverses its transitions, makes it deterministic, trims the result and repeats these operations once more. Although it has exponential worst-case running time, it is nevertheless useful for small examples. Recently, it was generalized in the context of studying minimization of nondeterministic finite automata [BT14]. The state elimination method for converting a finite automaton into an equivalent regular expression is due to Brzozowski and McCluskey [BM63], and again has the advantage of leading to simple computations.

Star-free languages are languages denoted by regular expressions involving only Boolean operations and concatenation. Cohen and Brzozowski introduced a hierarchy of star-free languages, known as the dot-depth or Brzozowski hierarchy [CB71]. This hierarchy and its generalizations had a great influence in the development of automata theory. In particular, the Brzozowski hierarchy corresponds, level by level, to the quantifier alternation hierarchy of first-order logical formulas. Several subhierarchies of star-free languages were also studied by Brzozowski. An important subclass is the class of locally testable languages. With Imre Simon, he gave an algebraic characterization of locally testable languages analogous to Schützenberger's characterization of the star-free languages [BS73].

In the 1990s, Brzozowski worked mostly in the development of mathematical models for the design and verification of asynchronous networks, and in particular for deterministic and random testing. Him and his collaborators introduced mathematical definitions for basic concepts such as fault model, testing, fault diagnosis and fault detection. They also proved fundamental bounds on the required random test length for certain important types of faults. Much of this work is accounted for quite thoroughly in Chapter 4 by Helmut Jürgensen.

In the last decade his research interests have focused largely on the state complexity of regular languages. His contributions in this area have been impressive. He introduced the notion of quotient complexity that, although for regular languages it coincides with state complexity, has several interesting algebraic properties [Brz10b,BJL10,BL12b,BJZ14,BJLS14,BJL13,BBMR14]. With several coauthors, he proceeded to a thorough study of the syntactic complexity of several subregular languages [BLY12b,BLL12,BL14,BS14b,BS15c]. He introduced the notion of universal witnesses for operational state complexities and, with collaborators studied the characterization of the most complex regular languages [Brz13,BD14b,Brz16]. In this context, with Tamm et al., he defined the notion of atom, studied several related complexity measures, and introduced atomic automata and the so-called átomata [BT14,BT12,BD14a,BD15].

A 1-day conference in honour of the 80th birthday of Janusz Brzozowski took place in the School of Computer Science at the University of Waterloo, Waterloo, Ontario, Canada, on June 24, 2015. Invited speakers were distinguished researchers, colleagues and former students. This book contains contributions of selected invited speakers, as well as some contributions by other renowned researchers. For the choice of title of the conference and of this volume *The Role of Theory in Computer Science* we quote Janusz Brzozowski:

> *Any problem we attack, we should try to look to a mathematical model and some known results in mathematics and very often we will succeed.*

This book is a tribute to his work and achievements and an inspiration for future research. The volume consists of eleven chapters. Several chapters survey and account for the impact and new developments of his results. In Chapters 7 and 8, Jean-Éric Pin revisits several open problems about regular languages selected by Janusz Brzozowski in 1980 [Brz80b], which proved to be most influential in the last thirty-five years. In Chapter 4, Helmut Jürgensen recounts his journey with Janusz Brzozowski from 1984 to 1999, on formal modeling of circuit testing and software specification and verification using automata theory. In the 1980s, Ernst Leiss introduced with Janusz Brzozowski the notion of boolean automata and studied related systems of equations. In Chapter 5, Leiss re-examines the complementation operation on formal languages. In Chapter 3, Markus Holzer and Martin Kutrib present a survey on the complexity of subregular languages, and in particular consider star-free languages and the Brzozowski (or dot-depth) hierarchy. Janusz Brzozowski studied several aspects of closures in formal languages. Arto Salomaa, in Chapter 9, investigates the depth of closed classes of functions. In Chapter 6, Timothy Ng, David Rappaport and Kai Salomaa characterize distances between regular languages. Finally, in Chapter 10, Bruce Watson and his co-authors focus on the problem of developing parallel versions of the algorithm to convert regular expressions to deterministic finite automata using Brzozowski derivatives. The remaining chapters also reflect the role of theory for modelling systems. Chapter 1 by Andrzej Ehrenfeucht, Ion Peter, and Grzegorz Rozenberg is an introductory tutorial to reaction systems, which are a model of computation for formalizing interactions between biochemical reactions taking place within the living cell. The late Zoltán Ésik and Werner Kuich study solutions of systems of polynomial fixed-point equations in Chapter 2. And, in Chapter 11, Andrew Szilard gives programming examples of graphical interpretations of L-systems which provide a variety of space-filling curves.

All the papers were refereed according to the standards of World Scientific. We would like to thank the authors for their contributions and also for their help with the reviewing process.

Financial support for the conference was supplied by the Fields Institute and by the School of Computer Science at the University of Waterloo.

We wish to thank World Scientific for supporting this project and Chelsea Chin for her valuable help in the edition of this volume. We are grateful to Saint Mary's University, Centro de Matemática da Universidade do Porto (CMUP) and the School of Computer Science, University of Waterloo, for their kind sponsorship.

August 2016
Stavros Konstantinidis
Nelma Moreira
Rogério Reis
Jeffrey Shallit

# Short Biography for Janusz A. Brzozowski

Janusz A. (John) Brzozowski was born on May 10, 1935 in Warsaw, Poland. He received the BASc and MASc degrees in electrical engineering from the University of Toronto in 1957 and 1959, respectively. In 1962, he received the MA and PhD degrees in electrical engineering from Princeton University under Edward J. McCluskey. The title of the thesis was *Regular Expression Techniques for Sequential Circuits*.

He was Assistant Professor from 1962 to 1965 and Associate Professor from 1965 to 1967 in the Department of Electrical Engineering, University of Ottawa. From 1967 to 1996 he was Professor in the Department of Computer Science, University of Waterloo. In the periods 1978-1983 and 1987-1989 he was chair of that department. He has had visiting appointments at the University of California, Berkeley (1965-1966), University of Paris (1974-1975), University of São Paulo (1983), Kyoto University (1984), and Eindhoven University (1989-1990). In 1996 he received the title Distinguished Professor Emeritus from the University of Waterloo, where he is currently an Adjunct Professor.

Brzozowski has published more than 200 papers in the areas of regular languages, finite automata, asynchronous circuits, and testing. He is co-author of Digital Networks (Prentice-Hall, 1976), and of Asynchronous Circuits (Springer-Verlag, 1995). His present research interests include state complexity of operations on regular languages, general complexity measures for regular languages, and nondeterministic finite automata.

## Awards

He received the following academic awards:

- NSERC Scientific Exchange Award to France (1974–1975)
- Japan Society for the Promotion of Science Research Fellowship (1984)

- Distinguished Professor Emeritus, University of Waterloo, Canada (1996)
- Medal of Merit, Catholic University of Lublin, Poland (2001)
- Canadian Pioneer in Computing (2005)

## PhD Theses Supervised

- Wayne Alton Davis, 1966, *Contributions to Structure Theory of Sequential Machines*, PhD Thesis, Department of Electrical Engineering, University of Ottawa, Ottawa, ON, Canada (External Examiner: H. P. Zeiger, University of Colorado)
- Lansun Lee, 1967, *Grade of Service of a Telephone Exchange*, PhD Thesis, Department of Electrical Engineering, University of Ottawa, Ottawa, ON, Canada (External Examiner: H. Frank, UC Berkeley)
- Rina Sara Cohen, 1968, *Cycle Rank of Transition Graphs and the Star Height of Regular Events*, PhD Thesis, Department of Mathematics, University of Ottawa, Ottawa, ON, Canada (External Examiner: R. McNaughton, Renssealer Polytechnic Institute)
- Shanker Singh, 1968, *Design of Asynchronous Sequential Circuits with Asynchronous Unit Delays*, PhD Thesis, Department of Electrical Engineering, University of Ottawa, Ottawa, ON, Canada (External Examiner: E. B. Eichelberger, IBM, White Plains, NY)
- Bobby Otis Nash, 1970, *Context-Free Parallel Leveled Languages*, PhD Thesis, Department of Applied Analysis and Computer Science, University of Waterloo, Waterloo, ON, Canada (External Examiner: M. A. Harrison, UC Berkeley)
- Dilip Kumar Banerji, 1971, *Residue Arithmetic in Computer Design*, PhD Thesis, Department of Applied Analysis and Computer Science, University of Waterloo, Waterloo, ON, Canada (External Examiner: A. Avizienis, UCLA)
- Ina Pamela McWhirter, 1971, *Substitution Expressions for Context-Free Languages*, PhD Thesis, Department of Applied Analysis and Computer Science, University of Waterloo, Waterloo, ON, Canada (External Examiner: A. Aho, then at Bell Telephone Laboratories)
- Imre Simon, 1972, *Hierarchies of Events with Dot-Depth One*, PhD Thesis, Department of Applied Analysis and Computer Science, University of Waterloo, Waterloo, ON, Canada (External Examiner: R. McNaughton, Renssealer Polytechnic Institute)

- Luigi Logrippo, 1974, *Renamings in Parallel Program Schemas*, PhD Thesis, Department of Applied Analysis and Computer Science, University of Waterloo, Waterloo, ON, Canada. Jointly supervised with E. A. Ashcroft (External Examiner: R. E. Miller, then at IBM Watson Research Center)
- Denis Therien, 1980, *Classification of Regular Languages by Congruences*, PhD Thesis, Department of Computer Science, University of Waterloo, Waterloo, ON, Canada (External Examiner: D. Perrin, then at University of Rouen)
- Carl-Johan Henry Seger, 1988, *Models and Algorithms for Race Analysis in Asynchronous Circuits*, PhD Thesis, Department of Computer Science, University of Waterloo, Waterloo, ON, Canada (External Examiner: R. E. Bryant, Carnegie Mellon University)
- Bruce Fordyce Cockburn, 1990, *Fault Models and Tests for Coupling Faults in Random-Access Memories*, PhD Thesis, Department of Computer Science, University of Waterloo, Waterloo, ON, Canada (External Examiner: V. K. Agarwal, then at McGill University)
- Chuan-Jin (Richard) Shi, 1994, *Optimum Logic Encoding and Layout Wiring for VLSI Design: A Graph-Theoretic Approach*, PhD Thesis, Department of Computer Science, University of Waterloo, Waterloo, ON, Canada (External Examiner: E. S. Kuh, UC Berkeley)
- Radu Negulescu, 1998, *Process Spaces and Formal Verification of Asynchronous Circuits*, PhD Thesis, Department of Computer Science, University of Waterloo, Waterloo, ON, Canada (External Examiner: D. L. Dill, Stanford University)
- Piotr R. Sidorowicz, 2000, *A Formal Framework for Modeling and Testing Memories*, PhD Thesis, Department of Computer Science, University of Waterloo, Waterloo, ON, Canada (External Examiner: Y. Zorian, LogicVision, San Jose, CA)

**Master's Theses Supervised**

- Wayne Alton Davis, 1963, *On the Linearity of Sequential Machines*, MSc Thesis, Department of Electrical Engineering, University of Ottawa, Ottawa, ON, Canada
- Peter Hawtrey, 1966, *Logic-Free Realizations of Sequential Machines*, MSc Thesis, Department of Electrical Engineering, University of Ottawa, Ottawa, ON, Canada

- Dilip Kumar Banerji, 1967, *Sign Detection in Residue Number Systems*, MSc Thesis, Department of Electrical Engineering, University of Ottawa, Ottawa, ON, Canada
- Vinod Kumar Batra, 1967, *Design of Asynchronous Unit Delays*, MSc Thesis, Department of Electrical Engineering, University of Ottawa, Ottawa, ON, Canada
- Zaw-Sing Su, 1968, *Some Families of Star-Free Events*, MSc Thesis, Department of Electrical Engineering, University of Ottawa, Ottawa, ON, Canada
- John Gear McEntyre, 1968, *Maximal Sequences from Non-Linear Shift Registers*, MSc Thesis, Department of Electrical Engineering, University of Ottawa, Ottawa, ON, Canada
- Chung-Wo Chiu, 1969, *A Study of Universal Switching Circuit Modules*, MASc Thesis, Department of Electrical Engineering, University of Waterloo, Waterloo, ON, Canada
- Eric Bierman, 1971, *Realization of Star-Free Events*, MASc Thesis, Department of Electrical Engineering, University of Waterloo, Waterloo, ON, Canada
- Faith Ellen Fich , 1978, *Languages of R-Trivial and Related Monoids*, MMath Thesis, Department of Computer Science, University of Waterloo, Waterloo, ON, Canada
- Carl-Johan Henry Seger, 1985, *Ternary Simulation of Asynchronous Gate Networks*, MMath Thesis, Department of Computer Science, University of Waterloo, Waterloo, ON, Canada
- Hao Zhang, 1997, *Delay-Insensitive Networks*, MMath Thesis, Department of Computer Science, University of Waterloo, Waterloo, ON, Canada
- Jay Jie Lou, 1998, *Decomposition of Multi-Valued Functions*, MMath Thesis, Department of Computer Science, University of Waterloo, Waterloo, ON, Canada
- Signe Silver, 1999, *True Concurrency in Models of Asynchronous Circuit Behavior*, MMath Thesis, Department of Computer Science, University of Waterloo, Waterloo, ON, Canada
- Mihaela Gheorghiu, 2002, *Circuit Simulation Using a Hazard Algebra*, MMath Thesis, Department of Computer Science, University of Waterloo, Waterloo, ON, Canada
- Elad Lahav, 2006, *An Automaton-Theoretic View of Algebraic Specifications*, MMath Thesis, David R. Cheriton School of Computer Science, University of Waterloo, Waterloo, ON, Canada

- Baiyu Li, 2012, *Syntactic Complexities of Nine Subclasses of Regular Languages*, MMath Thesis, David R. Cheriton School of Computer Science,University of Waterloo, Waterloo, ON, Canada

## Selected Publications

### Theses

[Brz59]  Janusz A. Brzozowski. *Sensitivity of Transfer Matrices in Multivariable Control Systems*. Master's thesis, Department of Electrical Engineering University of Toronto, Toronto, Ontario, March 1959. Thesis supervisors: J. M. Ham and R. J. Kavanagh

[Brz62a]  Janusz A. Brzozowski. *Regular Expression Techniques for Sequential Circuits*. PhD thesis, Department of Electrical Engineering, Princeton University, Princeton, NJ, June 1962. Thesis supervisor: E. J. McCluskey

### Books

[BY76a]  Janusz A. Brzozowski and Michael Yoeli. *Digital Networks*. Prentice Hall, Englewood Cliffs, NJ, 1976

[BS95]  Janusz A. Brzozowski and Carl-Johan H. Seger. *Asynchronous Circuits*. Monographs in Computer Science. Springer, New York, NY, 1995

### Chapters in Books

[Brz06b]  Janusz A. Brzozowski. Topics in asynchronous circuit theory. In Zoltán Ésik, Carlos Martín-Vide, and Victor Mitrana, editors, *Recent Advances in Formal Languages and Applications*, volume 25 of *Studies in Computational Intelligence*, pages 11–42. Springer, 2006

### Articles in Journals

[Brz62b]  Janusz A. Brzozowski. A survey of regular expressions and their applications. *IRE Trans. Electron. Comput.*, EC-11(3):324–335, 1962

[BP63]  Janusz A. Brzozowski and J. F. Poage. On the construction of sequential machines from regular expressions. *IEEE Trans. Electron. Comput.*, EC-12(4):402–403, 1963

[BM63]  Janusz A. Brzozowski and E. J. McCluskey. Signal flow graph techniques for sequential circuit state diagrams. *IEEE Trans. Electron. Comput.*, EC-12(2):67–76, 1963

[Brz64a]  Janusz A. Brzozowski. Derivatives of regular expressions. *J. ACM*, 11(4):481–494, 1964

[Brz64b]  Janusz A. Brzozowski. Regular expressions from sequential circuits. *IEEE Trans. Electron. Comput.*, EC-13(6):741–744, 1964

[BD64]  Janusz A. Brzozowski and Wayne A. Davis. On the linearity of autonomous sequential machines. *IEEE Trans. Electron. Comput.*, EC-13(6):673–679, 1964

[Brz65c]  Janusz A. Brzozowski. Some problems in relay circuit design. *IEEE Trans. Electron. Comput.*, EC-14(4):630–634, 1965

[Brz65b]  Janusz A. Brzozowski. Regular expressions for linear sequential circuits. *IEEE Trans. Electron. Comput.*, EC-14(2):148–156, 1965

[LB66a]  Lansun Lee and Janusz A. Brzozowski. An approximate method for computing blocking probability in switching networks. *IEEE Trans. Commun. Tech.*, COM-14(2):85–93, 1966

[DB66]  Wayne A. Davis and Janusz A. Brzozowski. On the linearity of sequential machines. *IEEE Trans. Electron. Comput.*, EC-15(1):21–29, 1966

[Brz67a]  Janusz A. Brzozowski. On single-loop realizations of sequential machines. *Information and Control*, 10(3):292–314, 1967

[Brz67b]  Janusz A. Brzozowski. Roots of star events. *J. ACM*, 14(3):466–477, 1967

[BS68]  Janusz A. Brzozowski and Shanker Singh. Definite asynchronous sequential circuits. *IEEE Trans. Computers*, C17(1):18–26, 1968

[BC69]  Janusz A. Brzozowski and Rina S. Cohen. On decompositions of regular events. *J. ACM*, 16(1):132–144, 1969

[BB69]  Dilip K. Banerji and Janusz A. Brzozowski. Sign detection in residue number systems. *IEEE Trans. Computers*, C18(4):313–320, 1969

[CB70]  Rina S. Cohen and Janusz A. Brzozowski. General properties of star height of regular events. *J. Comput. Syst. Sci.*, 4(3):260–280, 1970

[BIG71]  Janusz A. Brzozowski, Karel Culik II, and Armen Gabrielian. Classification of noncounting events. *J. Comput. Syst. Sci.*, 5(1):41–53, 1971

[CB71]  Rina S. Cohen and Janusz A. Brzozowski. Dot-depth of star-free events. *J. Comput. Syst. Sci.*, 5(1):1–16, 1971

[BB72] Dilip K. Banerji and Janusz A. Brzozowski. On translation algorithms in residue number systems. *IEEE Trans. Computers*, C21(12):1281–1285, 1972

[BS73] Janusz A. Brzozowski and Imre Simon. Characterizations of locally testable events. *Discrete Math.*, 4(3):243–271, 1973

[Brz76a] Janusz A. Brzozowski. Hierarchies of aperiodic languages. *ITA*, 10(2):33–49, 1976

[Brz76b] Janusz A. Brzozowski. Run languages. *Discrete Math.*, 16(4):299–307, 1976

[BY76b] Janusz A. Brzozowski and Michael Yoeli. Practical approach to asynchronous gate networks. *IEE Proceedings*, 123(6):495–498, 1976

[Brz77] Janusz A. Brzozowski. A generalization of finiteness. *Semigroup Forum*, 13(3):239–251, 1977

[BK78] Janusz A. Brzozowski and Robert Knast. The dot-depth hierarchy of star-free languages is infinite. *J. Comput. Syst. Sci.*, 16(1):37–55, 1978

[BY79] Janusz A. Brzozowski and Michael Yoeli. On a ternary model of gate networks. *IEEE Trans. Computers*, 28(3):178–184, 1979

[BF80] Janusz A. Brzozowski and Faith E. Fich. Languages of R-trivial monoids. *J. Comput. Syst. Sci.*, 20(1):32–49, 1980

[BL80] Janusz A. Brzozowski and Ernst L. Leiss. On equations for regular languages, finite automata, and sequential networks. *Theor. Comput. Sci.*, 10:19–35, 1980

[BF84] Janusz A. Brzozowski and Faith E. Fich. On generalized locally testable languages. *Discrete Math.*, 50:153–169, 1984

[BM85] Janusz A. Brzozowski and Shojiro Muro. On serializability. *Int. J. Parallel Program*, 14(6):387–403, 1985

[BK86] Janusz A. Brzozowski and Robert Knast. Graph congruences and pair testing. *ITA*, 20(2):129–147, 1986

[BY87] Janusz A. Brzozowski and Michael Yoeli. Combinational static CMOS networks. *Integration*, 5(2):103–122, 1987

[BS87] Janusz A. Brzozowski and Carl-Johan H. Seger. A characterization of ternary simulation of gate networks. *IEEE Trans. Computers*, 36(11):1318–1327, 1987

[Brz87a] Janusz A. Brzozowski. Detection of timing problems in VLSI circuits. *Congressus Numerantium*, 56:7–18, 1987

[SB88] Carl-Johan H. Seger and Janusz A. Brzozowski. An optimistic ternary simulation of gate races. *Theor. Comput. Sci.*, 61:49–66, 1988

[Brz89]  Janusz A. Brzozowski. Minimization by reversal is not new. *Bulletin of the European Association for Theoretical Computer Science*, 37:130, 1989

[BS89]  Janusz A. Brzozowski and Carl-Johan H. Seger. A unified framework for race analysis of asynchronous networks. *J. ACM*, 36(1):20–45, 1989

[BC90]  Janusz A. Brzozowski and Bruce F. Cockburn. Detection of coupling faults in RAMs. *J. Electronic Testing*, 1(2):151–162, 1990

[BS90]  Janusz A. Brzozowski and Carl-Johan H. Seger. Advances in asynchronous circuit theory Part I: Gate and unbounded inertial delay models. *Bulletin of the European Association for Theoretical Computer Science*, 42:198–249, 1990

[CB90]  Bruce F. Cockburn and Janusz A. Brzozowski. Switch-level testability of the dynamic CMOS PLA. *Integration*, 9(1):49–80, 1990

[BGM91]  Janusz A. Brzozowski, Tony Gahlinger, and Farhad Mavaddat. Consistency and satisfiability of waveform timing specifications. *Networks*, 21(1):91–107, 1991

[BS91]  Janusz A. Brzozowski and Carl-Johan H. Seger. Advances in asynchronous circuit theory Part II: Bounded inertial delay models, MOS circuits, design techniques. *Bulletin of the European Association for Theoretical Computer Science*, 43:199–263, 1991

[BJ92c]  Janusz A. Brzozowski and Helmut Jürgensen. A model for sequential machine testing and diagnosis. *J. Electronic Testing*, 3(3):219–234, 1992

[CB92]  Bruce F. Cockburn and Janusz A. Brzozowski. Near-optimal tests for classes of write-triggered coupling faults in RAMs. *J. Electronic Testing*, 3(3):251–264, 1992

[BE92]  Janusz A. Brzozowski and Jo C. Ebergen. On the delay-sensitivity of gate networks. *IEEE Trans. Computers*, 41(11):1349–1360, 1992

[SB93]  Chuan-Jin Richard Shi and Janusz A. Brzozowski. An efficient algorithm for constrained encoding and its applications. *IEEE Trans. Computer-Aided Design*, 12(12):1813–1836, 1993

[SB94]  Carl-Johan H. Seger and Janusz A. Brzozowski. Generalized ternary simulation of sequential circuits. *ITA*, 28(3-4):159–186, 1994

[BJ96]  Janusz A. Brzozowski and Helmut Jürgensen. An algebra of multiple faults in RAMs. *J. Electronic Testing*, 8(2):129–142, 1996

[DBJ97]  René David, Janusz A. Brzozowski, and Helmut Jürgensen. Testing for bounded faults in RAMs. *J. Electronic Testing*, 10(3):197–214, 1997

[BLN97]  Janusz A. Brzozowski, Jay J. Lou, and Radu Negulescu. A characterization of finite ternary algebras. *IJAC*, 7(6):713–722, 1997

[SB98a]  Chuan-Jin Richard Shi and Janusz A. Brzozowski. Cluster-cover a theoretical framework for a class of VLSI-CAD optimization problems. *ACM Trans. Design Autom. Electr. Syst.*, 3(1):76–107, 1998

[NB98]  Radu Negulescu and Janusz A. Brzozowski. Relative liveness: From intuition to automated verification. *Formal Methods in System Design*, 12(1):73–115, 1998

[SB99]  Chuan-Jin Richard Shi and Janusz A. Brzozowski. A characterization of signed hypergraphs and its applications to VLSI via minimization and logic synthesis. *Discrete Appl. Math.*, 90(1-3):223–243, 1999

[BZ00]  Janusz A. Brzozowski and Hao Zhang. Delay-insensitivity and semi-modularity. *Formal Methods in System Design*, 16(2):191–218, 2000

[Brz00b]  Janusz A. Brzozowski. Delay-insensitivity and ternary simulation. *Theor. Comput. Sci.*, 245(1):3–25, 2000

[BN00]  Janusz A. Brzozowski and Radu Negulescu. Automata of asynchronous behaviors. *Theor. Comput. Sci.*, 231(1):113–128, 2000

[Brz01]  Janusz A. Brzozowski. A characterization of De Morgan algebras. *IJAC*, 11(5):525–528, 2001

[SB02]  Piotr R. Sidorowicz and Janusz A. Brzozowski. A framework for testing special-purpose memories. *IEEE Trans. on CAD of Integrated Circuits and Systems*, 21(12):1459–1468, 2002

[SB03]  Signe J. Silver and Janusz A. Brzozowski. True concurrency in models of asynchronous circuit behavior. *Formal Methods in System Design*, 22(3):183–203, 2003

[BÉ03]  Janusz A. Brzozowski and Zoltán Ésik. Hazard algebras. *Formal Methods in System Design*, 23(3):223–256, 2003

[GB03b]  Mihaela Gheorghiu and Janusz A. Brzozowski. Simulation of feedback-free circuits in the algebra of transients. *Int. J. Found. Comput. Sci.*, 14(6):1033–1054, 2003

[BL03]  Janusz A. Brzozowski and Tadeusz Luba. Decomposition of Boolean functions specified by cubes. *Multiple-Valued Logic and Soft Computing*, 9(4):377–417, 2003

[Brz04] Janusz A. Brzozowski. Involuted semilattices and uncertainty in ternary algebras. *IJAC*, 14(3):295–310, 2004

[BJ05] Janusz A. Brzozowski and Helmut Jürgensen. Representation of semiautomata by canonical words and equivalences. *Int. J. Found. Comput. Sci.*, 16(5):831–850, 2005

[BG05] Janusz A. Brzozowski and Mihaela Gheorghiu. Gate circuits in the algebra of transients. *ITA*, 39(1):67–91, 2005

[YB06] Yuli Ye and Janusz A. Brzozowski. Covering of transient simulation of feedback-free circuits by binary analysis. *Int. J. Found. Comput. Sci.*, 17(4):949–974, 2006

[Brz06a] Janusz A. Brzozowski. Representation of a class of nondeterministic semiautomata by canonical words. *Theor. Comput. Sci.*, 356(1-2):46–57, 2006

[BJ07] Janusz A. Brzozowski and Helmut Jürgensen. Representation of semiautomata by canonical words and equivalences, part II: specification of software modules. *Int. J. Found. Comput. Sci.*, 18(5):1065–1087, 2007

[AB09] Thomas Ang and Janusz A. Brzozowski. Languages convex with respect to binary relations, and their closure properties. *Acta Cybernet.*, 19(2):445–464, 2009

[BK09] Janusz A. Brzozowski and Stavros Konstantinidis. State-complexity hierarchies of uniform languages of alphabet-size length. *Theor. Comput. Sci.*, 410(35):3223–3235, 2009

[BS09] Janusz A. Brzozowski and Nicolae Santean. Predictable semiautomata. *Theor. Comput. Sci.*, 410(35):3236–3249, 2009

[Brz10b] Janusz A. Brzozowski. Quotient complexity of regular languages. *Journal of Automata, Languages and Combinatorics*, 15(1/2):71–89, 2010

[BY10] Janusz A. Brzozowski and Yuli Ye. Gate circuits with feedback in finite multivalued algebras of transients. *Multiple-Valued Logic and Soft Computing*, 16(1-2):155–176, 2010

[BSX11] Janusz A. Brzozowski, Jeffrey Shallit, and Zhi Xu. Decision problems for convex languages. *Inform. and Comput.*, 209(3):353–367, 2011

[BGS11] Janusz A. Brzozowski, Elyot Grant, and Jeffrey Shallit. Closures in formal languages and Kuratowski's theorem. *Int. J. Found. Comput. Sci.*, 22(2):301–321, 2011

[BLY12a] Janusz A. Brzozowski, Baiyu Li, and Yuli Ye. On the complexity of the evaluation of transient extensions of Boolean functions. *Int. J. Found. Comput. Sci.*, 23(1):21–35, 2012

[BL12b]  Janusz A. Brzozowski and Bo Liu. Quotient complexity of star-free languages. *Int. J. Found. Comput. Sci.*, 23(6):1261–1276, 2012

[BLL12]  Janusz A. Brzozowski, Baiyu Li, and David Liu. Syntactic complexities of six classes of star-free languages. *Journal of Automata, Languages and Combinatorics*, 17(2-4):83–105, 2012

[BLY12b]  Janusz A. Brzozowski, Baiyu Li, and Yuli Ye. Syntactic complexity of prefix-, suffix-, bifix-, and factor-free regular languages. *Theor. Comput. Sci.*, 449:37–53, 2012

[BJL13]  Janusz A. Brzozowski, Galina Jirásková, and Baiyu Li. Quotient complexity of ideal languages. *Theor. Comput. Sci.*, 470:36–52, 2013

[BT13]  Janusz A. Brzozowski and Hellis Tamm. Complexity of atoms of regular languages. *Int. J. Found. Comput. Sci.*, 24(7):1009–1028, 2013

[Brz13]  Janusz A. Brzozowski. In search of most complex regular languages. *Int. J. Found. Comput. Sci.*, 24(6):691–708, 2013

[BL14]  Janusz A. Brzozowski and Baiyu Li. Syntactic complexity of R- and J-trivial regular languages. *Int. J. Found. Comput. Sci.*, 25(7):807–822, 2014

[BJZ14]  Janusz A. Brzozowski, Galina Jirásková, and Chenglong Zou. Quotient complexity of closed languages. *Theory Comput. Syst.*, 54(2):277–292, 2014

[BJLS14]  Janusz A. Brzozowski, Galina Jirásková, Baiyu Li, and Joshua Smith. Quotient complexity of bifix-, factor-, and subword-free languages. *Acta Cybernet.*, 21(4):505–527, 2014

[BT14]  Janusz A. Brzozowski and Hellis Tamm. Theory of átomata. *Theor. Comput. Sci.*, 539:13–27, 2014

[BS15b]  Janusz A. Brzozowski and Marek Szykuła. Large aperiodic semigroups. *Int. J. Found. Comput. Sci.*, 26(7):913–932, 2015

[BD15]  Janusz A. Brzozowski and Sylvie Davies. Quotient complexities of atoms in regular ideal languages. *Acta Cybernet.*, 22(2):293–311, 2015

### Articles in Conferences

[AB62]  Saul Amarel and Janusz A. Brzozowski. Theoretical considerations on reliability properties of recursive triangular switching networks.

In R. H. Wilcox and W. C. Mann, editors, *Redundancy Techniques for Computing Systems, Washington, DC., 1962*, pages 70–128. Spartan Books, 1962

[Brz63a] Janusz A. Brzozowski. Canonical regular expressions and minimal state graphs for definite events. In J. Fox, editor, *Mathematical Theory of Automata. New York, NY, April 24-26, 1962*, volume 12 of *MRI Symposia Series*, pages 529–561. Polytechnic Press of the Polytechnic Institute of Brooklyn, 1963

[Brz63b] Janusz A. Brzozowski. Regular expressions for linear sequential circuits. In J. B. Cruz and J. C. Hofer, editors, *First Allerton Conference on Circuit and System Theory. Monticello, IL, November 15-17, 1963*, pages 406–426. University of Illinois, Urbana, 1963

[DB64] Wayne A. Davis and Janusz A. Brzozowski. On the linearity of sequential machines. In *5th Annual Symposium on Switching Circuit Theory and Logical Design, Princeton, New Jersey, USA, November 11-13, 1964*, pages 197–208. IEEE Computer Society, 1964

[Brz65a] Janusz A. Brzozowski. On single-loop realizations of automata. In *6th Annual Symposium on Switching Circuit Theory and Logical Design, Ann Arbor, Michigan, USA, October 6-8, 1965*, pages 84–93. IEEE Computer Society, 1965

[Brz67c] Janusz A. Brzozowski. Synthesis of sequential machines. In J. F. Hart and S. Takasu, editors, *Systems and Computer Science. London, ON, September 10-11, 1965*, pages 14–26. University of Toronto Press, 1967

[LB66b] Lansun Lee and Janusz A. Brzozowski. An approximate method for computing blocking probability in switching networks. In *IEEE Communication Conference*, 1966

[Brz66] Janusz A. Brzozowski. Roots of star events. In *7th Annual Symposium on Switching and Automata Theory, Berkeley, California, USA, October 23-25, 1966*, pages 88–95. IEEE Computer Society, 1966

[BC67] Janusz A. Brzozowski and Rina S. Cohen. On decompositions of regular events. In *8th Annual Symposium on Switching and Automata Theory, Austin, Texas, USA, October 18-20, 1967*, pages 255–264. IEEE Computer Society, 1967

[CB67] Rina S. Cohen and Janusz A. Brzozowski. On the star height of regular events. In *8th Annual Symposium on Switching and Automata Theory, Austin, Texas, USA, October 18-20, 1967*, pages 265–279. IEEE Computer Society, 1967

[Brz68] Janusz A. Brzozowski. Regular-like expressions for some irregular languages. In *9th Annual Symposium on Switching and Automata Theory, Schenectady, New York, USA, October 15-18, 1968*, pages 278–286. IEEE Computer Society, 1968

[CB68] R. Cohen and Janusz A. Brzozowski. On star-free events. In B. K. Kinariwala and Franklin F. Kuo, editors, *Hawaii International Conference on System Sciences. Honolulu, HI, January 29-31, 1968*, pages 1–4, Honolulu, HI, 1968. University of Hawaii Press

[BS71] Janusz A. Brzozowski and Imre Simon. Characterizations of locally testable events. In *12th Annual Symposium on Switching and Automata Theory, East Lansing, Michigan, USA, October 13-15, 1971*, pages 166–176. IEEE Computer Society, 1971

[BY74] Janusz A. Brzozowski and Michael Yoeli. Models for analysis of races in sequential networks. In Andrzej Blikle, editor, *Mathematical Foundations of Computer Science, 3rd Symposium at Jadwisin near Warsaw, June 17-22, 1974, Proceedings*, volume 28 of *Lecture Notes in Computer Science*, pages 26–32. Springer, 1974

[YB77] Michael Yoeli and Janusz A. Brzozowski. Ternary simulation of binary gate networks. In J. Michael Dunn and George Epstein, editors, *Modern Uses of Multiple-Valued Logic. Fifth International Symposium on Multiple-Valued Logic. Bloomington, IN, May 13-16, 1975*, pages 39–50, Dordrecht, Holland, 1977. D. Reidel Publishing Company

[FB79] Faith E. Fich and Janusz A. Brzozowski. A characterization of a dot-depth two analogue of generalized definite languages. In Hermann A. Maurer, editor, *Automata, Languages and Programming, 6th Colloquium, Graz, Austria, July 16-20, 1979, Proceedings*, volume 71 of *Lecture Notes in Computer Science*, pages 230–244. Springer, 1979

[Brz80a] Janusz A. Brzozowski. Developments in the theory of regular languages. In Simon H. Lavington, editor, *Information Processing 80, Proceedings of IFIP Congress 80, Tokyo, Japan - October 6-9, 1980 and Melbourne, Australia - October 14-17, 1980*, pages 29–40. North-Holland/IFIP, 1980

[Brz80b] Janusz A. Brzozowski. Open problems about regular languages. In Ronald V. Book, editor, *Formal Language Theory - Perspectives and Open Problems. Symposium on Formal Language Theory, Santa Barbara, CA, December 10-14, 1979*, pages 23–47. Academic Press, 1980

[BS85]  Janusz A. Brzozowski and Mokbel Sayed. Design of testable CMOS cells. In *Canadian Conference on VLSI. Toronto, Ontario, November 4-5, 1985*, pages 225–228, 1985

[YB85]  Michael Yoeli and Janusz A. Brzozowski. A mathematical model of digital CMOS networks. In Jerome Fox, editor, *Canadian Conference on VLSI. Toronto, Ontario, November 4-5, 1985*, pages 117–120, 1985

[Brz86b]  Janusz A. Brzozowski. On the testability of static CMOS latches. In *Technical Digest of the Canadian Conference on VLSI. Montreal, Quebec, October 27-28, 1986*, pages 153–158, 1986

[Brz86a]  Janusz A. Brzozowski. Detection of timing problems in VLSI circuits. In *Sixteenth Manitoba Conference on Numerical Mathematics and Computing. Winnipeg, Manitoba, October 2-4*, 1986

[Brz87c]  Janusz A. Brzozowski. Testability of combinational networks of CMOS cells. In D. Michael Miller, editor, *Developments in Integrated Circuit Testing: International Workshop on New Directions in IC Testing Victoria, British Columbia, March 18-20, 1986*, New York, 1987. Academic Press

[SB86]  Carl-Johan Seger and Janusz A. Brzozowski. An optimistic ternary simulation of gate races. In *Technical Digest of the Canadian Conference on VLSI. Montreal, Quebec, October 27-28, 1986*, pages 67–72, 1986

[BY86]  Janusz A. Brzozowski and Michael Yoeli. Combinatorial static CMOS networks (extended summary). In Fillia Makedon, Kurt Mehlhorn, Theodore S. Papatheodorou, and Paul G. Spirakis, editors, *VLSI Algorithms and Architectures, Aegean Workshop on Computing, Loutraki, Greece, July 8-11, 1986, Proceedings*, volume 227 of *Lecture Notes in Computer Science*, pages 271–282. Springer, 1986

[BS86]  Janusz A. Brzozowski and Carl-Johan H. Seger. Correspondence between ternary simulation and binary race analysis in gate networks (extended summary). In Laurent Kott, editor, *Automata, Languages and Programming, 13th International Colloquium, ICALP86, Rennes, France, July 15-19, 1986, Proceedings*, volume 226 of *Lecture Notes in Computer Science*, pages 69–78. Springer, 1986

[Brz87b]  Janusz A. Brzozowski. A model for sequential machine testing. In *International Workshop on New Directions in IC Testing. Winnipeg, Manitoba, April 8-10*, 1987

[CB88] Bruce F. Cockburn and Janusz A. Brzozowski. Switch-level testability of the dynamic CMOS PLA. In *Third Technical Workshop on New Directions in IC Testing. Halifax, Nova Scotia, October 26-27*, 1988

[BJ88c] Janusz A. Brzozowski and Helmut Jürgensen. Probabilistic diagnosis of sequential machines. In *Third Technical Workshop on New Directions in IC Testing. Halifax, Nova Scotia, October 26-27*, 1988

[BJ88a] Janusz A. Brzozowski and Helmut Jürgensen. Deterministic diagnosis of sequential machines. In *Third Technical Workshop on New Directions in IC Testing. Halifax, Nova Scotia, October 26-27*, 1988

[BJ88b] Janusz A. Brzozowski and Helmut Jürgensen. Deterministic diagnosis of sequential machines. In Ferenc Gécseg and István Peák, editors, *Second Conference on Automata Languages and Programming Systems. Salgotarjan, Hungary, May 23-26, 1988*, pages 35–49. Department of Mathematics, Karl Marx University of Economics, Budapest, Hungary, 1988

[BJ88d] Janusz A. Brzozowski and Helmut Jürgensen. Probabilistic diagnosis of sequential machines. In Ferenc Gécseg and István Peák, editors, *Second Conference on Automata Languages and Programming Systems. Salgotarjan, Hungary, May 23-26, 1988*, pages 51–66. Department of Mathematics, Karl Marx University of Economics, Budapest, Hungary, 1988

[BE89] Janusz A. Brzozowski and Jo C. Ebergen. Recent developments in the design of asynchronous circuits. In János Csirik, János Demetrovics, and Ferenc Gécseg, editors, *Fundamentals of Computation Theory, International Conference FCT'89, Szeged, Hungary, August 21-25, 1989, Proceedings*, volume 380 of *Lecture Notes in Computer Science*, pages 78–94. Springer, 1989

[CB91a] Bruce F. Cockburn and Janusz A. Brzozowski. Near-optimal tests for classes of coupling faults in RAMs. In *Poster Paper, International Test Conference. Nashville, TN, October 28 - November 1*, 1991

[CB91b] Bruce F. Cockburn and Janusz A. Brzozowski. Near-optimal tests for classes of coupling faults in RAMs. In *Fifth Technical Workshop on New Directions in IC Testing. Ottawa, Ontario, August 1-2*, 1991

[BJ92a] Janusz A. Brzozowski and Helmut Jürgensen. Automaton-theoretic considerations in circuit testing. In *Second Theoriedag. Kiel, Germany, October 2-3*, page 4, 1992

[SB92] Chuan-Jin Richard Shi and Janusz A. Brzozowski. Efficient constrained encoding for VLSI sequential logic synthesis. In *European Design Automation Conference. Hamburg, Germany, September 7-10*, pages 266–271. IEEE Computer Society Press, 1992

[BJ92b] Janusz A. Brzozowski and Helmut Jürgensen. Component automata and RAM faults. In *Second International Colloquium on Words, Languages and Combinatorics. Kyoto, Japan, August 25-28*, pages 6–10, 1992

[Brz93] Janusz A. Brzozowski. Asynchronous behaviours and fundamental-mode realizations. In *Seminar on Automata Theory: Distributed Models. Dagstuhl, Germany, January 11-15, 1993*, volume 54 of *Dagstuhl Seminar Report*, pages 4–5, 1993

[BJ93] Janusz A. Brzozowski and Helmut Jürgensen. An automaton theoretic approach to circuit testing. In *7th International Conference on Automata and Formal Languages. Salgotarjan, Hungary, May 18 – 21*, 1993

[DBJ93] René David, Janusz A. Brzozowski, and Helmut Jürgensen. Random test length for bounded faults in RAMs. In *European Test Conference. Rotterdam, The Netherlands, April 19-24, 1993*, pages 149–158. IEEE Computer Society Press, 1993

[SB95] Chuan-Jin Richard Shi and Janusz A. Brzozowski. A framework for the analysis and design of algorithms for a class of VLSI-CAD optimization problems. In Isao Shirakawa, editor, *Proceedings of the 1995 Conference on Asia Pacific Design Automation, Makuhari, Massa, Chiba, Japan, August 29 - September 1, 1995*. ACM, 1995

[NB95] Radu Negulescu and Janusz A. Brzozowski. Relative liveness: from intuition to automated verification. In *Second Working Conference on Asynchronous Design Methodologies, May 30-31, 1995, London, England, UK*, pages 108–117. IEEE Computer Society, 1995

[BR95] Janusz A. Brzozowski and Kaamran Raahemifar. Testing C-elements is not elementary. In *Second Working Conference on Asynchronous Design Methodologies, May 30-31, 1995, London, England, UK*, pages 150–159. IEEE Computer Society, 1995

[Brz96] Janusz A. Brzozowski. Some applications of ternary algebras. In *8th International Conference on Automata and Formal Languages. Salgótarján, Hungary, July 29 – August 2*, 1996

[Brz97b] Janusz A. Brzozowski. Delay-insensitivity and ternary simulation. In *First International Conference on Semigroups and Algebraic Engineering, Aizu-Wakamatsu City, Japan, March 24-28, 1997*

[BN98] Janusz A. Brzozowski and Radu Negulescu. Automata of asynchronous behaviors. In Derick Wood and Sheng Yu, editors, *Automata Implementation, Second International Workshop on Implementing Automata, WIA '97, London, Ontario, Canada, September 18-20, 1997, Revised Papers*, volume 1436 of *Lecture Notes in Computer Science*, pages 29–45. Springer, 1998

[Brz97a] Janusz A. Brzozowski. Blanket algebra for multiple-valued function decomposition. In *International Workshop on Formal Languages and Computer Systems, Kyoto, Japan, March 18–21*, 1997

[SB98b] Piotr R. Sidorowicz and Janusz A. Brzozowski. An approach to modeling and testing memories and its application to CAMs. In *16th IEEE VLSI Test Symposium (VTS '98), 28 April - 1 May 1998, Princeton, NJ, USA*, pages 411–417. IEEE Computer Society, 1998

[BJ99] Janusz A. Brzozowski and Helmut Jürgensen. Semilattices of fault semiautomata. In Juhani Karhumäki, Hermann A. Maurer, Gheorghe Păun, and Grzegorz Rozenberg, editors, *Jewels are Forever, Contributions on Theoretical Computer Science in Honor of Arto Salomaa*, pages 3–15. Springer, 1999

[LB99] Jay J. Lou and Janusz A. Brzozowski. A generalization of Shestakov's function decomposition method. In *ISMVL*, pages 66–71, 1999

[BÉ01] Janusz A. Brzozowski and Zoltán Ésik. Hazard algebras (extended abstract). In Arto Salomaa, Derick Wood, and Sheng Yu, editors, *A Half-Century of Automata Theory: Celebration and Inspiration*, pages 1–19. World Scientific, 2001

[Brz00a] Janusz A. Brzozowski. De Morgan bisemilattices. In *ISMVL*, pages 173–178, 2000

[Brz00c] Janusz A. Brzozowski. Sequential machines. In Anthony Ralston, Edwin D. Reilly, and David Hemmendinger, editors, *Encyclopedia of Computer Science, 4th ed*, pages 1565–1569, Nw York, 2000. Grove's Dictionaries, Inc

[BÉI01] Janusz A. Brzozowski, Zoltán Ésik, and Yaacov Iland. Algebras for hazard detection. In *ISMVL*, page 3, 2001

[Brz02] Janusz A. Brzozowski. Partially ordered structures for hazard detection. In *Joint Mathematics Meetings, Special Session: The many lives of lattice theory. San Diego, CA, Jan. 6–9*, page 3, 2002

[BG03] Janusz A. Brzozowski and Mihaela Gheorghiu. Simulation of gate circuits in the algebra of transients. In Jean-Marc Champarnaud and Denis Maurel, editors, *Implementation and Application of Automata, 7th International Conference, CIAA 2002, Tours, France, July 3-5, 2002, Revised Papers*, volume 2608 of *Lecture Notes in Computer Science*, pages 57–66. Springer, 2003

[GB03a] Mihaela Gheorghiu and Janusz A. Brzozowski. Feedback-free circuits in the algebra of transients. In Jean-Marc Champarnaud and Denis Maurel, editors, *Implementation and Application of Automata, 7th International Conference, CIAA 2002, Tours, France, July 3-5, 2002, Revised Papers*, volume 2608 of *Lecture Notes in Computer Science*, pages 106–116. Springer, 2003

[BÉI03] Janusz A. Brzozowski, Zoltán Ésik, and Yaacov Iland. Algebras for hazard detection. In Melvin Fitting and Ewa Orłowska, editors, *Beyond Two - Theory and Applications of Multiple-Valued Logic*, pages 3–24, Heidelberg, 2003. Springer-Verlag

[BN04] Janusz A. Brzozowski and Radu Negulescu. Duality for three: Ternary symmetry in process spaces. In Juhani Karhumäki, Hermann A. Maurer, Gheorghe Păun, and Grzegorz Rozenberg, editors, *Theory Is Forever, Essays Dedicated to Arto Salomaa on the Occasion of His 70th Birthday*, volume 3113 of *Lecture Notes in Computer Science*, pages 1–14. Springer, 2004

[BJ04] Janusz A. Brzozowski and Helmut Jürgensen. Representation of semiautomata by canonical words and equivalences. In Lucian Ilie and Detlef Wotschke, editors, *6th International Workshop on Descriptional Complexity of Formal Systems - DCFS 2004, London, Ontario, Canada, July 26 - 28, 2004. Pre-proceedings*, volume Report No. 619, pages 13–27. Department of Computer Science, The University of Western Ontario, Canada, 2004

[BY07] Janusz A. Brzozowski and Yuli Ye. Simulation of gate circuits with feedback in multi-valued algebras. In *37th International Symposium on Multiple-Valued Logic, ISMVL 2007, 13-16 May 2007, Oslo, Norway*, page 46. IEEE Computer Society, 2007

[AB08] Thomas Ang and Janusz A. Brzozowski. Continuous languages. In Erzsébet Csuhaj-Varjú and Zoltán Ésik, editors, *Automata and Formal Languages, 12th International Conference, AFL 2008, Balatonfüred, Hungary, May 27-30, 2008, Proceedings.*, pages 74–85, 2008

[BK08] Janusz A. Brzozowski and Stavros Konstantinidis. State-complexity hierarchies of uniform languages of alphabet-size length. In Cezar Câmpeanu and Giovanni Pighizzini, editors, *10th Interna-*

*tional Workshop on Descriptional Complexity of Formal Systems, DCFS 2008, Charlottetown, Prince Edward Island, Canada, July 16-18, 2008.*, pages 97–108. University of Prince Edward Island, 2008

[BS08] Janusz A. Brzozowski and Nicolae Santean. Determinism without determinization. In Cezar Câmpeanu and Giovanni Pighizzini, editors, *10th International Workshop on Descriptional Complexity of Formal Systems, DCFS 2008, Charlottetown, Prince Edward Island, Canada, July 16-18, 2008.*, pages 109–120. University of Prince Edward Island, 2008

[BSX09] Janusz A. Brzozowski, Jeffrey Shallit, and Zhi Xu. Decision problems for convex languages. In Adrian Horia Dediu, Armand-Mihai Ionescu, and Carlos Martín-Vide, editors, *Language and Automata Theory and Applications, Third International Conference, LATA 2009, Tarragona, Spain, April 2-8, 2009. Proceedings*, volume 5457 of *Lecture Notes in Computer Science*, pages 247–258. Springer, 2009

[BGS09] Janusz A. Brzozowski, Elyot Grant, and Jeffrey Shallit. Closures in formal languages and Kuratowski's theorem. In Volker Diekert and Dirk Nowotka, editors, *Developments in Language Theory, 13th International Conference, DLT 2009, Stuttgart, Germany, June 30 - July 3, 2009. Proceedings*, volume 5583 of *Lecture Notes in Computer Science*, pages 125–144. Springer, 2009

[Brz09] Janusz A. Brzozowski. Quotient complexity of regular languages. In Jürgen Dassow, Giovanni Pighizzini, and Bianca Truthe, editors, *Proceedings Eleventh International Workshop on Descriptional Complexity of Formal Systems, DCFS 2009, Magdeburg, Germany, July 6-9, 2009.*, volume 3 of *EPTCS*, pages 17–28, 2009

[BJL10] Janusz A. Brzozowski, Galina Jirásková, and Baiyu Li. Quotient complexity of ideal languages. In Alejandro López-Ortiz, editor, *LATIN 2010: Theoretical Informatics, 9th Latin American Symposium, Oaxaca, Mexico, April 19-23, 2010. Proceedings*, volume 6034 of *Lecture Notes in Computer Science*, pages 208–221. Springer, 2010

[Brz10a] Janusz A. Brzozowski. Complexity in convex languages. In Adrian Horia Dediu, Henning Fernau, and Carlos Martín-Vide, editors, *Language and Automata Theory and Applications, 4th International Conference, LATA 2010, Trier, Germany, May 24-28, 2010. Proceedings*, volume 6031 of *Lecture Notes in Computer Science*, pages 1–15. Springer, 2010

[BJZ10]  Janusz A. Brzozowski, Galina Jiráskóva, and Chenglong Zou. Quotient complexity of closed languages. In Farid M. Ablayev and Ernst W. Mayr, editors, *Computer Science - Theory and Applications, 5th International Computer Science Symposium in Russia, CSR 2010, Kazan, Russia, June 16-20, 2010. Proceedings*, volume 6072 of *Lecture Notes in Computer Science*, pages 84–95. Springer, 2010

[BLY10]  Janusz A. Brzozowski, Baiyu Li, and Yuli Ye. On the complexity of the evaluation of transient extensions of Boolean functions. In Ian McQuillan and Giovanni Pighizzini, editors, *Proceedings Twelfth Annual Workshop on Descriptional Complexity of Formal Systems, DCFS 2010, Saskatoon, Canada, 8-10th August 2010.*, volume 31 of *EPTCS*, pages 27–37, 2010

[BLY11]  Janusz A. Brzozowski, Baiyu Li, and Yuli Ye. Syntactic complexity of prefix-, suffix-, and bifix-free regular languages. In Markus Holzer, Martin Kutrib, and Giovanni Pighizzini, editors, *Descriptional Complexity of Formal Systems - 13th International Workshop, DCFS 2011, Gießen/Limburg, Germany, July 25-27, 2011. Proceedings*, volume 6808 of *Lecture Notes in Computer Science*, pages 93–106. Springer, 2011

[BT11]  Janusz A. Brzozowski and Hellis Tamm. Theory of átomata. In Giancarlo Mauri and Alberto Leporati, editors, *Developments in Language Theory - 15th International Conference, DLT 2011, Milan, Italy, July 19-22, 2011. Proceedings*, volume 6795 of *Lecture Notes in Computer Science*, pages 105–116. Springer, 2011

[BY11]  Janusz A. Brzozowski and Yuli Ye. Syntactic complexity of ideal and closed languages. In Giancarlo Mauri and Alberto Leporati, editors, *Developments in Language Theory - 15th International Conference, DLT 2011, Milan, Italy, July 19-22, 2011. Proceedings*, volume 6795 of *Lecture Notes in Computer Science*, pages 117–128. Springer, 2011

[BJLS11]  Janusz A. Brzozowski, Galina Jiráskóva, Baiyu Li, and Joshua Smith. Quotient complexity of bifix-, factor-, and subword-free regular languages. In Pál Dömösi and Szabolcs Iván, editors, *Automata and Formal Languages, 13th International Conference, AFL 2011, Debrecen, Hungary, August 17-22, 2011, Proceedings.*, pages 123–137, 2011

[BL11]  Janusz A. Brzozowski and Bo Liu. Quotient complexity of star-free languages. In Pál Dömösi and Szabolcs Iván, editors, *Automata* and Formal Languages, 13th International Conference, AFL 2011, Debrecen, Hungary, August 17-22, 2011, Proceedings., pages 138–152, 2011 [[BL12a]]

[BL12a] Janusz A. Brzozowski and Baiyu Li. Syntactic complexities of some classes of star-free languages. In Martin Kutrib, Nelma Moreira, and Rogério Reis, editors, *Descriptional Complexity of Formal Systems - 14th International Workshop, DCFS 2012, Braga, Portugal, July 23-25, 2012. Proceedings*, volume 7386 of *Lecture Notes in Computer Science*, pages 117–129. Springer, 2012

[Brz12] Janusz A. Brzozowski. In search of most complex regular languages. In Nelma Moreira and Rogério Reis, editors, *Implementation and Application of Automata - 17th International Conference, CIAA 2012, Porto, Portugal, July 17-20, 2012. Proceedings*, volume 7381 of *Lecture Notes in Computer Science*, pages 5–24. Springer, 2012

[BT12] Janusz A. Brzozowski and Hellis Tamm. Quotient complexities of atoms of regular languages. In Hsu-Chun Yen and Oscar H. Ibarra, editors, *Developments in Language Theory - 16th International Conference, DLT 2012, Taipei, Taiwan, August 14-17, 2012. Proceedings*, volume 7410 of *Lecture Notes in Computer Science*, pages 50–61. Springer, 2012

[BL13c] Janusz A. Brzozowski and David Liu. Universal witnesses for state complexity of Boolean operations and concatenation combined with star. In Helmut Jürgensen and Rogério Reis, editors, *Descriptional Complexity of Formal Systems - 15th International Workshop, DCFS 2013, London, ON, Canada, July 22-25, 2013. Proceedings*, volume 8031 of *Lecture Notes in Computer Science*, pages 30–41. Springer, 2013

[BL13a] Janusz A. Brzozowski and Baiyu Li. Syntactic complexity of R- and J-trivial regular languages. In Helmut Jürgensen and Rogério Reis, editors, *Descriptional Complexity of Formal Systems - 15th International Workshop, DCFS 2013, London, ON, Canada, July 22-25, 2013. Proceedings*, volume 8031 of *Lecture Notes in Computer Science*, pages 160–171. Springer, 2013

[BL13b] Janusz A. Brzozowski and David Liu. Universal witnesses for state complexity of basic operations combined with reversal. In Stavros Konstantinidis, editor, *Implementation and Application of Automata - 18th International Conference, CIAA 2013, Halifax, NS, Canada, July 16-19, 2013. Proceedings*, volume 7982 of *Lecture Notes in Computer Science*, pages 72–83. Springer, 2013

[BD14a] Janusz A. Brzozowski and Gareth Davies. Maximally atomic languages. In Zoltán Ésik and Zoltán Fülöp, editors, *Proceedings 14th International Conference on Automata and Formal Languages, AFL 2014, Szeged, Hungary, May 27-29, 2014.*, volume 151 of *EPTCS*, pages 151–161, 2014

[BBMR14] Jason Bell, Janusz A. Brzozowski, Nelma Moreira, and Rogério Reis. Symmetric groups and quotient complexity of Boolean operations. In Javier Esparza, Pierre Fraigniaud, Thore Husfeldt, and Elias Koutsoupias, editors, *Automata, Languages, and Programming - 41st International Colloquium, ICALP 2014, Copenhagen, Denmark, July 8-11, 2014, Proceedings, Part II*, volume 8573 of *Lecture Notes in Computer Science*, pages 1–12. Springer, 2014

[BS14a] Janusz A. Brzozowski and Marek Szykuła. Large aperiodic semigroups. In Markus Holzer and Martin Kutrib, editors, *Implementation and Application of Automata - 19th International Conference, CIAA 2014, Giessen, Germany, July 30 - August 2, 2014. Proceedings*, volume 8587 of *Lecture Notes in Computer Science*, pages 124–135. Springer, 2014

[BD14b] Janusz A. Brzozowski and Gareth Davies. Most complex regular right-ideal languages. In Helmut Jürgensen, Juhani Karhumäki, and Alexander Okhotin, editors, *Descriptional Complexity of Formal Systems - 16th International Workshop, DCFS 2014, Turku, Finland, August 5-8, 2014. Proceedings*, volume 8614 of *Lecture Notes in Computer Science*, pages 90–101. Springer, 2014

[BS14b] Janusz A. Brzozowski and Marek Szykuła. Upper bounds on syntactic complexity of left and two-sided ideals. In Arseny M. Shur and Mikhail V. Volkov, editors, *Developments in Language Theory - 18th International Conference, DLT 2014, Ekaterinburg, Russia, August 26-29, 2014. Proceedings*, volume 8633 of *Lecture Notes in Computer Science*, pages 13–24. Springer, 2014

[BS15c] Janusz A. Brzozowski and Marek Szykuła. Upper bound on syntactic complexity of suffix-free languages. In Jeffrey Shallit and Alexander Okhotin, editors, *Descriptional Complexity of Formal Systems - 17th International Workshop, DCFS 2015, Waterloo, ON, Canada, June 25-27, 2015. Proceedings*, volume 9118 of *Lecture Notes in Computer Science*, pages 33–45. Springer, 2015

[BS15a] Janusz A. Brzozowski and Marek Szykuła. Complexity of suffix-free regular languages. In Adrian Kosowski and Igor Walukiewicz, editors, *Fundamentals of Computation Theory - 20th International Symposium, FCT 2015, Gdańsk, Poland, August 17-19, 2015, Proceedings*, volume 9210 of *Lecture Notes in Computer Science*, pages 146–159. Springer, 2015

[Brz16]  Janusz A. Brzozowski. Unrestricted state complexity of binary operations on regular languages. In *Descriptional Complexity of Formal Systems - 18th IFIP WG 1.2 International Conference, DCFS 2016, Bucharest, Romania, July 5-8, 2016. Proceedings*, pages 60–72, 2016

[BJL⁺16]  Janusz A. Brzozowski, Galina Jirásková, Bo Liu, Aayush Rajasekaran, and Marek Szykuła. On the state complexity of the shuffle of regular languages. In *Descriptional Complexity of Formal Systems - 18th IFIP WG 1.2 International Conference, DCFS 2016, Bucharest, Romania, July 5-8, 2016. Proceedings*, pages 73–86, 2016

**Other Articles**

[BSY15]  Janusz A. Brzozowski, Marek Szykuła, and Yuli Ye. Syntactic complexity of regular ideals. *CoRR*, abs/1509.06032, 2015

[BDL15]  Janusz A. Brzozowski, Sylvie Davies, and Bo Yang Victor Liu. Most complex regular ideals. *CoRR*, abs/1511.00157, 2015

[BS16]  Janusz A. Brzozowski and Corwin Sinnamon. Complexity of prefix-convex regular languages. *CoRR*, abs/1605.06697, 2016

# Contents

# Chapter 1

# Reaction Systems: A Model of Computation Inspired by the Functioning of the Living Cell

Andrzej Ehrenfeucht

*University of Colorado, Department of Computer Science*
*Boulder CO 80309-0347 USA*

Ion Petre

*Computational Biomodeling Laboratory*
*Åbo Akademi University and Turku Centre for Computer Science*
*Turku 20500, Finland*

Grzegorz Rozenberg

*Leiden Institute of Advanced Computer Science, Leiden University*
*Niels Bohrweg 1, 2333 CA Leiden, The Netherlands*
*and*
*University of Colorado, Department of Computer Science*
*Boulder CO 80309-0347 USA*

Reaction systems are a model of computation inspired by the functioning of the living cell. They formalize the interactions between biochemical reactions that form the basic mechanism (the skeleton) underlying this functioning. This paper is a tutorial-style introduction to reaction systems – it introduces the basic notions, and reviews a number of research directions which are motivated either by biological considerations, or by the need to understand the basic formal processes (computations) underlying the dynamic behavior of reaction systems.

## Contents

## 1.1. Introduction

Natural Computing (see, e.g., [27, 37]) is concerned with models of computation, computational techniques, and computing technologies (referred to as *human-designed computing*) inspired by nature, as well as with investigating, in terms of information processing, phenomena taking place in nature (referred to as *computing taking place in nature*).

Well-known examples of the former strand of research include evolutionary computation (inspired by Darwinian evolution of species), neural computation (inspired by the functioning of the central nervous system and the brain), artificial immune systems (inspired by the natural immune system), quantum computing (inspired by quantum mechanics), and molecular computing (inspired by molecular biology). Examples of the latter strand include investigations into the computational nature of self-assembly, the computational nature of brain processes, the computational nature of developmental processes, and the computational nature of biochemical reactions.

A research line which has attracted a lot of attention in natural computing is the functioning of the living cell. It is a central research topic for biology and biochemistry, while at the same time it is very attractive for computer science because, for example, it leads to novel models of computation.

This paper belongs to this research line. The methodology underlying the model presented in this paper is to first propose the basic mechanism underlying the functioning of the living cell, and then to attempt (first) to understand this mechanism only. It consists of the interactions between biochemical reactions taking place in the living cell. These interactions form the bare skeleton of the functioning of the living cell. It will still require many additional levels (on top of the skeleton) to achieve a basic understanding of how the living cell functions.

A key property of interactions between biochemical reactions is that they are based on two mechanisms: *facilitation* and *inhibition*. The product of one reaction may contain reactants of some reactions (and hence facilitate these reactions) and it may contain inhibitors of some reactions (and hence inhibit these reactions).

The model of *reaction systems* (introduced in [19]; also see, e.g., [6, 14, 15]) formalizes biochemical reactions in such a way that dynamic processes taking place in reaction systems formalize these interactions. Moreover, because this model is concerned with interactions taking place *within the living cell*, the formal notion of a dynamic process in reaction systems also captures the interactions with an environment, reflecting the fact that the living cell is an open system.

This paper is a tutorial-style introduction to reaction systems. It introduces basic notions together with the underlying intuition and motivation, and then it presents a number of representative research directions. The paper is organized as follows.

In Section 1.3 we first introduce the basic (formal) notion of a *reaction* and define its effect on the current state of a (biochemical) system. Each reaction $b$ is of the form $b = (R_b, I_b, P_b)$, where $R_b$ are all *reactants* $b$ needs to take place, $I_b$ is the set of all *inhibitors* of $b$ (if any of them is present in the current state $T$, then $b$ will not take place in $T$), and $P_b$ is the *product* set of $b$ (if $b$ takes place in the current state $T$, then it contributes its product set $P_b$ to the successor state of $T$). Then we present *reaction systems* as a model of interactions between biochemical reactions in the living cell, where the dynamic processes induced by such interactions (also involving interactions with the environment) are formalized as so-called *interactive processes*.

From a formal, mathematical point of view, a reaction system is an implementation (through the cumulative effect of all reactions of the system) of a function from the set of states (of the system) into itself. This point of view is explored in Section 1.4, where the focus is on the understanding of minimal implementations, i.e., implementations through reaction systems which use reactions with the minimal number of reactants or reactions with the minimal number of inhibitors.

Although the model of reaction systems was inspired by biology, the topics guiding research on reaction systems are motivated by both biological motivations and by the need to understand the underlying computations (the dynamic processes taking place in reaction systems). In fact, reaction systems turns out to be a novel model of computation. From this point of view it is important to understand the relationship of reaction systems to other models of computation. In Section 1.5 we discuss the relationship of reaction systems to finite transition systems, one of the classic models of computation.

The basic model of reaction systems abstracts from many technical (numerical) properties of biochemical reactions, so that it is a qualitative, rather than a quantitative, model. Consequently, there is no counting in reaction systems (the basic data structure used here are sets rather than multisets). However, it is very common in biology to assign quantitative parameters to states (e.g., the numbers of specific kinds of molecules present in the given state). To account for this, the basic model of reaction systems is equipped with a finite number of the so-called *measurement functions*, where each such function measures a specific (numerical) property, i.e., it assigns numerical values (real numbers) to the states of a reaction system. The so-obtained extensions of reaction systems are called *reaction systems with measurements* and they are discussed in Section 1.6. Of special interest in modeling biological systems (the living cell) is the case when the values of measurements (the values given by the measurement functions) for the given state influence the identity of the successor state. Although this case seems to be very quantitative, we demonstrate that it can be implemented (modeled) by ordinary (qualitative) reaction systems.

One of the basic properties of reaction systems is *non-permanency*: an entity $x$ present in the current state $T$ of the reaction system will *vanish* (i.e., it will *not* be present in the successor state $T'$) unless it is produced by a reaction of the system (which is enabled/active in $T$) or it is "thrown into" $T'$ by the environment. The non-permanency property reflects the basic bioenergetics of the living cell. This vanishing in reaction systems is instantaneous ($x$ is present in $T$ but not present in the successor state $T'$). However biochemical entities do not vanish instantly, but rather decay within a certain time interval. To account for this decay, reaction systems are extended by duration functions which assign a decay time (a positive integer) to each entity of a reaction system. The so-obtained *reaction systems with durations* are discussed in Section 1.7. In particular, we demonstrate that the phenomenon of durations/decay may be implemented (modeled) by ordinary reaction systems.

In Sections 1.8 and 1.9 we present two examples of modeling of bio-processes by reaction systems. More specifically, we discuss reaction systems modeling of the self-assembly of intermediate filaments and of the eukaryotic heat shock response, respectively. In both models we show that dynamic behavior typically explained in standard modeling frameworks through a numerical interplay driven by kinetic rate constants may also be explained qualitatively through intricate sequences of facilitation and inhibition between biochemical reactions.

Finally, in the last section we review topics covered in the paper and then provide a brief review of some research topics not covered here.

## 1.2. Preliminaries

Throughout the paper we use standard mathematical terminology and notation. In particular:

(1) We use $\mathbb{Z}^+$ and $\mathbb{R}$ to denote the sets of positive integers and real numbers, respectively.

(2) The empty set is denoted by $\emptyset$. For a set $X$, its cardinality is denoted by $|X|$ and $2^X$ denotes the power set of $X$. For sets $X$ and $Y$, $X - Y$, $X \cup Y$, and $X \cap Y$ denote set difference, set union, and set intersection, respectively, while $X \subseteq Y$ denotes set inclusion. For a family $\mathcal{L}$ of sets, $\bigcup \mathcal{L}$ denotes the union of sets from $\mathcal{L}$.

(3) For a sequence of sets $\zeta = Z_0, \ldots, Z_n$ and a set $Q$, the $Q$-projection of $\zeta$, denoted $\mathsf{proj}_Q(\zeta)$, is the sequence of sets $Z_0 \cap Q, Z_1 \cap Q, \ldots, Z_n \cap Q$.

## 1.3. Basic Notions

The basic intuition behind a biochemical reaction is that its functioning is based on two mechanisms, facilitation and inhibition, with the former represented by the reactants and the latter represented by the inhibitors. Accordingly, the formal notion of a reaction is defined as follows.

**Definition 1.** *A reaction is a triplet $b = (R, I, P)$ such that $R$, $I$, $P$ are finite nonempty sets with $R \cap I = \emptyset$.*

The sets $R$, $I$, and $P$ are called the *reactant set of $b$*, the *inhibitor set of $b$*, and the *product set of $b$*, respectively. They are also written as $R_b$, $I_b$, and $P_b$. The set $M_b = R_b \cup I_b$ is the *set of resources of $b$*. If $S$ is a set such that $R_b, I_b, P_b \subseteq S$, then $b$ is a *reaction in $S$*. The set of all reactions in $S$ is denoted by $\mathsf{rac}(S)$.

A biochemical reaction can take place (in a given biochemical state/environment) if all of its reactants are present and none of its inhibitors is present; moreover, if it takes place then it produces its product. This intuition underlies the following formal definition.

**Definition 2.** *Let $S$ be a finite set and $T \subseteq S$. A reaction $b \in \mathsf{rac}(S)$ is enabled by $T$, denoted by $\mathsf{en}_b(T)$, if and only if $R_b \subseteq T$ and $I_b \cap T = \emptyset$. The result of $b$ on $T$, denoted by $\mathsf{res}_b(T)$, is defined by: $\mathsf{res}_b(T) = P_b$ if $\mathsf{en}_b(T)$, and $\mathsf{res}_b(T) = \emptyset$ otherwise.*

A set $T$ formalizes here a state of a biochemical system which is simply a set of currently present biochemical entities. The first part of the above definition says indeed that $b$ can take place in a state $T$ ($b$ is enabled by $T$) if *all* reactants from $R_b$ are present in $T$ and *none* of the inhibitors from $I_b$ is present in $T$; hence $T$ separates $R_b$ from $I_b$. The second part of the definition says that if $b$ is enabled by $T$, then the result of $b$ on $T$ is the product $P_b$ of $b$; however if $b$ is not enabled by $T$, then it will produce "nothing" ($\emptyset$) on $T$. We will consider finite sequences of states where each state (except for the final state) has a successor. Then $\mathsf{res}_b(T) = P_b$ means that $b$ will contribute $P_b$ to the successor of $T$, while $\mathsf{res}_b(T) = \emptyset$ means that $b$ will not contribute to the successor of $T$.

In considering the functioning of a living cell we are interested in the effects (on the current state) of *sets* of reactions taking place. This is formalized as follows.

**Definition 3.** *Let $S$ be a finite set and $T \subseteq S$. The result of a set of reactions $B \subseteq \mathsf{rac}(S)$ on $T$, denoted by $\mathsf{res}_B(T)$, is defined by $\mathsf{res}_B(T) = \bigcup\{\mathsf{res}_b(T) : b \in B\}$.*

Thus the result of a set of reactions $B$ is cumulative: it is the union of results of all individual reactions from $B$. Since $\mathsf{res}_b(T) = \emptyset$ if $b$ is not enabled by $T$, $\mathsf{res}_B(T)$ can be obtained by considering only the results of all reactions enabled by $T$. Consequently, $\mathsf{res}_B(T) = \bigcup\{\mathsf{res}_b(T) : b \in B \text{ and } \mathsf{en}_b(T)\}$.

Note that an entity $x \in \mathsf{res}_B(T)$ if and only if $x \in P_b$ for a reaction $b$ enabled by $T$. For $x \in T$ we say that $x$ is *sustained* by $B$ in $T$ if $x \in \mathsf{res}_B(T)$. Thus $x$ is sustained by $B$ in $T$ if and only if $x$ is produced by a reaction from $B$ enabled by $T$. This holds even if $x \notin \bigcup\{R_b : b \in B\}$, i.e., $x$ is not "touched" (not processed) by any reaction in $B$. This is very different from standard models of computation in computer science, where typically if an element from the current state is not processed, then it also belongs to the successor state. This implies *non-permanency* in reaction systems: in the transition from the current state $T$ to its successor $\mathsf{res}_B(T)$ an entity from $T$ vanishes unless it is sustained by a reaction from $B$. This non-permanency property reflects the basic bioenergetics of the living cell: without the supply of energy living cells disintegrate. However, the absorption of energy by the living cell is achieved through biochemical reactions (see [30]).

If $b$, $c$ are two reactions from $B$ enabled by $T$, then both $P_b \subseteq \mathsf{res}_B(T)$ and $P_c \subseteq \mathsf{res}_B(T)$ even if $R_b \cap R_c \neq \emptyset$. This means that there is no conflict of resources: both $b$ and $c$ use $R_b \cap R_c$ to produce their products. Thus a nonempty intersection of sets of reactants of enabled reactions does not constitute a conflict. This is an important difference with standard models of concurrent systems such as, e.g., Petri nets (see, e.g., [36]), and it is implied by our *threshold assumption*: either a resource is present and then it is present in a sufficient amount, or it is not present. This reflects the level of abstraction that we have adopted in our basic model of reaction systems – we do not count concentrations/amounts of entities to decide which reactions are enabled in a given state. Our model is formulated on a higher level of abstraction. Thus there is no counting in reaction systems and we deal with sets rather than multisets. Our model is a qualitative (rather than a quantitative) model.

With the notion of a reaction (and its effects on the current state) defined, we are ready to recall the formal notion of a reaction system which was originally proposed as a formal model of (the "skeleton" of) the functioning of the living cell.

**Definition 4.** *A reaction system, abbreviated* rs, *is an ordered pair* $\mathcal{A} = (S, A)$, *where $S$ is a finite nonemtpy set and $A \subseteq \mathsf{rac}(S)$.*

The set $A$ is called the *set of reactions of* $\mathcal{A}$. Since $S$ is finite, so is $A$. The set $S$ is called the *background set of* $\mathcal{A}$ and its elements are called *entities*; they represent molecular entities present in the states of biochemical systems.

The subsets of $S$ are called the *states of* $\mathcal{A}$. Thus, all states of $\mathcal{A}$ are finite with the cardinality of each state limited by an a priori fixed number, viz., $|S|$.

For a state $T$ of $\mathcal{A}$, the *result of $\mathcal{A}$ on $T$*, denoted by $\mathsf{res}_{\mathcal{A}}(T)$, is defined by $\mathsf{res}_{\mathcal{A}}(T) = \mathsf{res}_A(T)$. We will refer to $\mathsf{res}_{\mathcal{A}}$ as the *result function of* $\mathcal{A}$. In fact, $\mathsf{res}_{\mathcal{A}}$ is a function from $2^S$ into itself.

The dynamic behavior of a reaction system is expressed through interactive processes that take place within it. They are defined as follows.

**Definition 5.** *Let $\mathcal{A} = (S, A)$ be an* rs *and let $n \geq 1$ be an integer. An (n-step) interactive process in $\mathcal{A}$ is a pair $\pi = (\gamma, \delta)$ of finite sequences such*

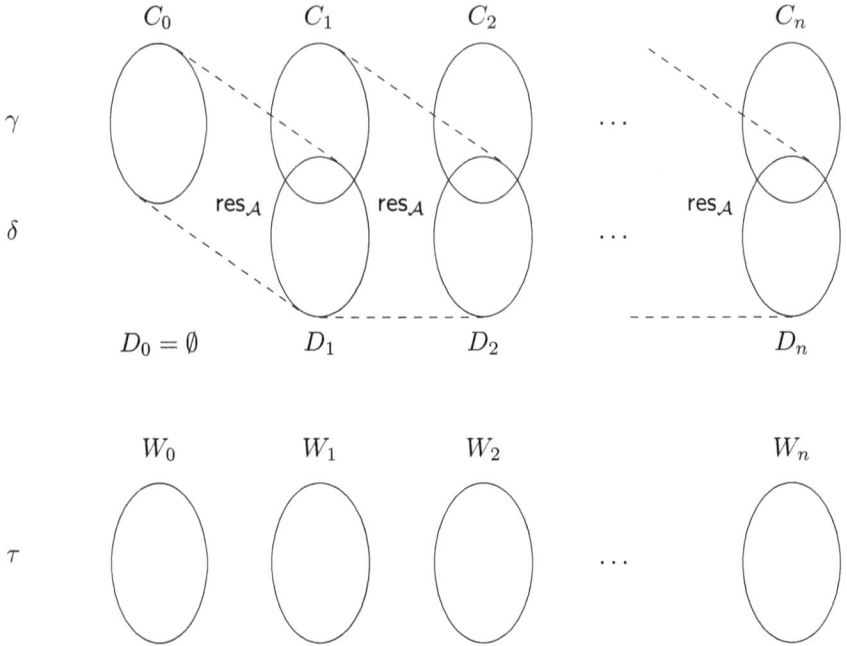

Fig. 1.1.   An interactive process.

*that* $\gamma = C_0, \ldots, C_n$ *and* $\delta = D_0, \ldots, D_n$, *where* $C_0, \ldots, C_n, D_0, \ldots, D_n \subseteq S$, $D_0 = \emptyset$, *and* $D_i = \mathsf{res}_A(D_{i-1} \cup C_{i-1})$ *for all* $i \in \{1, \ldots, n\}$.

The sequence $\gamma$ is the *context sequence* of $\pi$, the sequence $\delta$ is the *result sequence* of $\pi$, and the sequence $\tau = W_0, \ldots, W_n$ such that $W_0 = C_0$ and $W_i = C_i \cup D_i$ for all $i \in \{1, \ldots, n\}$ is the *state sequence* of $\pi$, where $W_0$ is called the *initial state of* $\pi$.

The interactive process $\pi$ begins in the initial state $W_0$, and the reactions from $A$ which are enabled by $W_0$ produce result $D_1$, which together with context $C_1$, forms state $W_1 = D_1 \cup C_1$. The state sequence $\tau$ is formed by the iteration of this procedure: for each state $W_i$ with $i \in \{0, \ldots, n-1\}$ its *successor* is $W_{i+1} = D_{i+1} \cup C_{i+1}$, where $D_{i+1} = \mathsf{res}_A(W_i)$. This is illustrated in Figure 1.1.

The context sequence $\gamma$ formalizes the fact that *the living cell is an open system* in the sense that it interacts with its environment (i.e., with the rest of the bigger system).

The first element $C_0$ of the context sequence is just the initial state and so the rest of the sequence $C_1, \ldots, C_n$ is called the *proper context sequence.* Note that if the current proper context set $C_i$ is such that $C_i \subseteq D_i$, then this context does not influence the current state $W_i$ (all entities from $C_i$ are already contributed by the reactions of the system, because $D_i = \text{res}_A(D_{i-1})$). Accordingly, the sequence $C_1 - D_1, \ldots, C_n - D_n$ is called the *significant context sequence.* In fact, for computing the result sequence and the state sequence, one can replace the proper context sequence by the significant context sequence.

If the significant context sequence consists of empty sets only, then $\pi$ is *context-independent.* In this case, whatever the environment adds to the current state $W_i$ is already included in the result $D_i$, hence already produced by $\text{res}_A$ from the previous state. Hence, if $\pi$ is context-independent, then it is determined by its initial state $W_0 = C_0$ and the number of steps $n$.

Note that if $\pi$ is context-independent and

$$\tau = W_0, \ldots, W_i, W_{i+1}, \ldots, W_n$$

is its state sequence, then during the transition of $W_i$ to $W_{i+1}$ all entities from $W_i - \text{res}_A(W_i)$ vanish (they are not present in $W_{i+1}$). This reflects the non-permanency property of reaction systems discussed above. For a general (not necessarily context-independent) interactive process, the non-permanency property says that in transition from $W_i$ to $W_{i+1}$ an entity $x \in W_i$ will vanish (will not be present in $W_{i+1}$) unless it is produced by the system ($x \in \text{res}_A(W_i)$) or it is thrown in by the context ($x \in C_{i+1}$).

We will use $\text{IP}(A)$ to denote the set of all interactive processes of $A$, $\text{STS}(A)$ to denote the set of all state sequences of all interactive processes of $A$, and $\text{CISTS}(A)$ to denote the set of all state sequences of all context-independent interactive processes of $A$.

## 1.4. Power Set Functions

The state sequence $\tau$ of an interactive process $\pi = (\gamma, \delta)$ is formed as a combination of an *internal* effect (given by the result function $\text{res}_A$) and an *external* effect (given by the context sequence $\gamma$). In the case of context-independent processes, $\tau$ is formed by $\text{res}_A$ only. In either case the understanding of $\text{res}_A$ is crucial for the understanding of the dynamics of reaction systems. Since states of a reaction system are sets, the result function is a power set function which is defined as follows.

**Definition 6.** *Let $S$ be a finite set. A function $f : 2^S \to 2^S$ is called a power set function (over $S$).*

In the context of reaction systems, we are interested in power set functions that are implementable by reaction systems. They are defined as follows.

**Definition 7.** *A power set function $f$ over a set $S$ is a reaction system power set function, abbreviated a* rs *power set function, if there exists a reaction system $\mathcal{A} = (S, A)$ such that $f = \text{res}_{\mathcal{A}}$.*

We note that for each reaction system $\mathcal{A} = (S, A)$ we have $\text{res}_{\mathcal{A}}(S) = \emptyset$ (because for each $b \in A$, $I_b$ is a nonempty subset of $S$) and $\text{res}_{\mathcal{A}}(\emptyset) = \emptyset$ (because for each $b \in A$, $R_b \neq \emptyset$, and so no $b \in A$ is enabled by $\emptyset$). Since we are interested in rs power set functions, we have to restrict ourselves to power set functions satisfying the above two conditions.

**Definition 8.** *A power set function over a set $S$ is* boundary *if $f(S) = f(\emptyset) = \emptyset$.*

It turns out that reaction systems are powerful implementations of power set functions: almost all of them are rs power set functions.

**Theorem 1** ([19]). *Let $S$ be a finite set and let $f$ be a power set function over $S$. Then $f$ is an* rs *power set function if and only if $f$ is a boundary power set function.*

An important research topic concerning reaction systems is the power of resources. In a general definition of an rs $\mathcal{A}$ one does not restrict either the cardinalities of the sets of reactants or the cardinalities of the sets of inhibitors of reactions of $\mathcal{A}$. One way to understand the role/power of resources is to consider reactions with the minimal number of reactants and reactions with the minimal number of inhibitors. This leads to the following definition.

**Definition 9.** *Let $\mathcal{A} = (S, A)$ be an* rs.

*(i) $\mathcal{A}$ is* reactant-minimal *if $|R_a| = 1$ for each $a \in A$.*
*(ii) $\mathcal{A}$ is* inhibitor-minimal *if $|I_a| = 1$ for each $a \in A$.*
*(iii) $\mathcal{A}$ is* resource-minimal *if $|M_a| = 2$ for each $a \in A$.*

The above definition translates naturally into the following definition for rs power set functions.

**Definition 10.** *Let $f$ be an* rs *power set function.*

*(1) f is* reactant-minimal *if there exists a reactant-minimal* rs $\mathcal{A}$ *such that* $f = \text{res}_{\mathcal{A}}$.

*(2) f is* inhibitor-minimal *if there exists an inhibitor-minimal* rs $\mathcal{A}$ *such that* $f = \text{res}_{\mathcal{A}}$.

*(3) f is* resource-minimal *if there exists a resource-minimal* rs $\mathcal{A}$ *such that* $f = \text{res}_{\mathcal{A}}$.

We will state now a characterization (from [13]) of reactant-minimal, inhibitor-minimal, and resource-minimal rs power set functions. First we need an auxiliary definition.

**Definition 11.** *Let $S$ be a finite set and let $f$ be a power set function over $S$.*

*(1) f is* union-subadditive *if $f(X \cup Y) \subseteq f(X) \cup f(Y)$ for all $X, Y \subseteq S$.*

*(2) f is* intersection-subadditive *if $f(X \cap Y) \subseteq f(X) \cup f(Y)$ for all $X, Y \subseteq S$.*

The basic intuition behind the notion of a union-subadditive function $f$ is that of a set-theoretical union related constraint in defining $f$ on $2^S$. For all subsets $X$, $Y$ of $S$, once the values of $f$ on $X$ and on $Y$ (hence $f(X)$ and $f(Y)$) are defined, the value of $f$ on the union $X \cup Y$ (hence $f(X \cup Y)$) must be a subset of $f(X) \cup f(Y)$. In other words, each element of $S$ included in $f(X \cup Y)$ is already included in either $f(X)$ or in $f(Y)$. Similarly, if $f$ is intersection-subadditive, then each element of $S$ included in $f(X \cap Y)$ is already included in either $f(X)$ or in $f(Y)$.

**Example 1.** Let $S = \{x, y, z, u\}$.

(1) Let $f_1 : 2^S \rightarrow 2^S$ be such that $f_1(\{x\}) = \{x, y\}$, $f_1(\{y\}) = \{x\}$, and $f_1(\{x, y\}) = \{z\}$. Then $f_1$ is *not* union-subadditive, as $z \in f_1(\{x\} \cup \{y\}) = f_1(\{x, y\})$, while $z \notin f_1(\{x\})$ and $z \notin f_1(\{y\})$.

(2) Let $f_2 : 2^S \rightarrow 2^S$ be such that $f_2(\{u, z\}) = \{u, z\}$, $f_2(\{u, y\}) = \{u\}$, and $f_2(\{u\}) = \{y\}$. Then $f_2$ is *not* intersection-subadditive, as $y \in f_2(\{u, z\} \cap \{u, y\}) = f_2(\{u\})$, while $y \notin f_2(\{u, z\})$ and $y \notin f_2(\{u, y\})$.

**Theorem 2** ([13]). *Let $f$ be an rs power set function. Then*

(1) *$f$ is reactant-minimal if and only if $f$ is union-subadditive.*

(2) *$f$ is inhibitor-minimal if and only if $f$ is intersection-subadditive.*

(3) *$f$ is resource-minimal if and only if $f$ is both union-subadditive and intersection-subadditive.*

**Corollary 3** ([13]). *Let $f$ be an rs power set function. If $f$ is reactant-minimal and intersection-minimal, then $f$ is resource-minimal.*

The research on minimal systems is by now rich and broader than what we could cover in this section. Typical research topics in this area include simulation of state sequences [44]; functions defined by minimal reaction systems [42]; computational complexity of various problems in such systems [41, 25]; normal forms [33]; and connections to Boolean lattices [32].

## 1.5. Relationship to Transition Systems

A standard (and natural) research problem about models of computation is concerned with their computational power, and this problem is often resolved by relating the given model to already existing, preferably "traditional", models of computation. In this section we demonstrate a close relationship between reaction systems and finite transition systems (see, e.g., [1]) by showing how to simulate finite transition systems by reaction systems and how to simulate reaction systems by finite transition systems.

(I) Let's begin with finite transition systems. For didactic reasons we will first consider *deterministic* finite transition systems.

Recall that a deterministic finite transition system is a 3-tuple $\mathcal{T} = (Q, \Sigma, \delta)$, where $Q$ is a finite nonempty set of *states*, $\Sigma$ is a finite nonempty set of *symbols* (the *input alphabet*), and $\delta : Q \times \Sigma \to Q$ is the *state transition function* (in general, $\delta$ is a partial function).

For $n \geq 1$, an *n-step transition process* in $\mathcal{T}$ is a pair $\mu = (\rho, \alpha)$, where $\rho = q_0, \ldots, q_n$ is a sequence of *states*, and $\alpha = x_1, \ldots, x_n$ is a sequence of *symbols* such that $\delta(q_{i-1}, x_i) = q_i$ for each $i \in \{1, \ldots, n\}$.

We will now construct (see [6]) an rs $\mathcal{A}_{\mathcal{T}} = (S_{\mathcal{T}}, A_{\mathcal{T}})$, which simulates $\mathcal{T}$ in the sense that transition processes of $\mathcal{T}$ will be in one-to-one correspondence with certain kinds of interactive processes of $\mathcal{A}_{\mathcal{T}}$. To simplify the construction we will assume that $Q \cap \Sigma = \emptyset$ and $|Q \cup \Sigma| > 2$. More specifically, $\mu = (\rho, \alpha)$ with $\rho = q_0, \ldots, q_n$ and $\alpha = x_1, \ldots, x_n$ is a transition process in $\mathcal{T}$ if and only if $\pi_\mu = (\gamma, \delta)$ is an interactive process in $\mathcal{A}_{\mathcal{T}}$, where $\gamma = (\{q_0, x_1\}, \{x_2\}, \ldots, \{x_n\}, \emptyset)$ and $\delta = (\emptyset, \{q_1\}, \ldots, \{q_n\})$. The state sequence of $\pi$ is then $W = \{q_0, x_1\}, \{q_1, x_2\}, \ldots, \{q_n\}$. Thus the initial state of $\pi$ is $W_0 = \{q_0, x_1\}$ corresponding to $\mathcal{T}$ reading symbol $x_1$ in state $q_0$, the successor state of $W_0$ is $W_1 = \{q_1, x_2\}$, which corresponds to $\mathcal{T}$ reading symbol $x_2$ in state $q_1 = \delta(q_0, x_1), \ldots$, and finally the last state $W_n = \{q_n\}$ is the state of $\mathcal{T}$ after reading the last symbol $x_n$ of $\alpha$ in state $q_{n-1}$.

The rs $\mathcal{A}_{\mathcal{T}} = (S_{\mathcal{T}}, A_{\mathcal{T}})$, where $S_{\mathcal{T}} = Q \cup \Sigma$ and

$$A_{\mathcal{T}} = \{(\{q,x\}, S_{\mathcal{T}}-\{q,x\}, \{\delta(q,x)\}) : q \in Q, x \in \Sigma, \text{ and } \delta(q,x) \text{ is defined}\}.$$

It is easily seen that indeed the so-constructed rs $\mathcal{A}_{\mathcal{T}}$ simulates the given transition system $\mathcal{T}$ in the sense explained above. Also, this simulation is "natural", as the prime intuition for the dynamic behavior of a transition system is that it is currently in a specific state $q$ (an *internal* parameter of the transition system) and the current symbol $x$ to be read is provided *externally* (by the "outside world"). Then, for the provided symbol $x$, $\mathcal{T}$ computes internally (by its transition function $\delta$) the successor state $\delta(q,x)$. Hence the behavior of $\mathcal{T}$ results from the interaction of its internal structure (function $\delta$) and the external environment (providing the sequence of input symbols). It is exactly this interaction that is simulated by the rs $\mathcal{A}_{\mathcal{T}}$.

For the above construction we have assumed that $|Q \cup \Sigma| > 2$, as otherwise we would get reactions with empty inhibitor sets. Then, however, we could use an additional entity serving only as a "formal inhibitor" for reactions with the empty inhibitor sets. We also required that $Q \cap \Sigma = \emptyset$. If this is not the case then we could, e.g., use a coding which "primes" the states from $Q$ creating $Q'$ disjoint with $\Sigma$. Then the correspondence between $\mathcal{T}$ and (the modified) $\mathcal{A}_{\mathcal{T}}$ is expressed through this coding.

Above, we have considered *deterministic* finite transition systems. For a general (possibly nondeterministic) finite transition system $\mathcal{T} = (Q, \Sigma, \delta)$, $\delta \subseteq Q \times \Sigma \times Q$ is a relation, meaning that for a given state $q$ and a given symbol $x$, if $\delta(q,x)$ is defined, then one may have several states $p_1, \ldots, p_m$ such that $(q,x,p_1), \ldots, (q,x,p_m) \in \delta$: reading $x$ in state $q$ may nondeterministically lead to any of the states $p_1, \ldots, p_m$.

This nondeterminism in transitions can be simulated by reaction systems through the use of context sequences as follows. First, for each $q \in Q$ and $x \in \Sigma$ such that $\delta(q,x)$ is defined, let $m_{q,x}$ be the number of different transitions in $\delta$ of the form $(q,x,p)$ where $p \in Q$. This is the *degree of nondeterminism* for $x$ in $q$. Then let $m_\delta$ be the maximal number among all $m_{q,x}$; this is the *degree of nondeterminism* of $\delta$. Then, for each such $q \in Q$ and $x \in \Sigma$, we fix an (arbitrary) order, $\mathrm{ord}(q,x)$, of all transitions of the form $(q,x,p)$ from $\delta$. Now we modify the construction of $\mathcal{A}_{\mathcal{T}}$ to $\mathcal{A}'_{\mathcal{T}}$ in such a way that each nonempty context set provides not a symbol $x \in \Sigma$, but rather a symbol of the form $(x,i)$, where $i \in \{1, \ldots, m_\delta\}$. Consequently, in an interactive process $\pi'_\mu$, an intermediate state $W_k$ will be of the form $W_k = \{q_k, (x_{k+1}, i)\}$ (where $C_k = \{(x_{k+1}, i)\}$ and $D_k = \{q_k\}$) and so $D_{k+1} = \{p\}$, where if $i \leq m_{q_k, x_{k+1}}$, then $(q_k, x_{k+1}, p)$ is the $i$'th transition of $\mathsf{ord}(q_k, x_{k+1})$ and if $i > m_{q_k, x_{k+1}}$, then $(q_k, x_{k+1}, p)$ is the last transition of $\mathsf{ord}(q_k, x_{k+1})$.

Thus nondeterministic finite transition systems can also be simulated by reaction systems in a "natural way", meaning that both the choice of the current input symbol and the choice of the transition to be applied are taken care of by the context sequence (while the computation of the consecutive result sets is taken care of by the result sequence).

(II) Now we demonstrate how to simulate reaction systems by finite transition systems. Let $\mathcal{A} = (S, A)$ be an rs. Let $\mathcal{T}_{\mathcal{A}} = (Q, \Sigma, \delta)$ be a finite transition system such that $Q = 2^S$, $\Sigma = 2^S$, and let $\delta : Q \times \Sigma \to Q$ be defined by: for all $U, X, T \subseteq S$, $\delta(U, X) = T$ if and only if $T = \mathsf{res}_A(U) \cup X$, where $X \cap \mathsf{res}_A(U) = \emptyset$.

To see that transition processes in $\mathcal{T}_{\mathcal{A}}$ simulate interactive processes in $\mathcal{A}$, recall that when $\pi = (\gamma, \delta)$ is an interactive process with $\gamma = C_0, \ldots, C_n$, $\delta = D_0, \ldots, D_n$, and $\tau = W_0, \ldots, W_n$, then, for each $i \in \{0, \ldots, n-1\}$, $D_{i+1} = \mathsf{res}_A(W_i)$ and $W_{i+1} = \mathsf{res}_A(W_i) \cup X_{i+1}$, where $X_1, \ldots, X_n$ is the significant context sequence of $\pi$. Moreover, any subset of $S$ appears as the context set on position $i + 1$ in some interactive process of $\mathcal{A}$. These two observations explain the above definition of the transition function $\delta$ of the transition system $\mathcal{T}_{\mathcal{A}}$ simulating $\mathcal{A}$.

It follows directly from the definition of $\mathcal{T}_{\mathcal{A}}$ that the precise relationship between the interactive processes in $\mathcal{A}$ and the transition processes in $\mathcal{T}_{\mathcal{A}}$ (hence the definition of the way that $\mathcal{T}_{\mathcal{A}}$ simulates $\mathcal{A}$) is as follows.

(1) Let $\pi = (\gamma, \delta)$ be an interactive process in $\mathcal{A}$ with $\gamma = C_0, C_1, \ldots, C_n$ and $\delta = D_0, \ldots, D_n$ for some $n \geq 1$, let $\eta = X_1, \ldots, X_n$ be the significant context sequence of $\pi$, and let $\tau = W_0, \ldots, W_n$ be the state sequence of $\pi$. Then $\mu = (\tau, \eta)$ is a transition process in $\mathcal{T}_{\mathcal{A}}$.

(2) Let $\mu = (\rho, \alpha)$ be a transition process in $\mathcal{T}_{\mathcal{A}}$ with $\rho = q_0, \ldots, q_n$ and $\alpha = x_1, \ldots, x_n$ for some $n \geq 1$. Then $\pi = (\gamma, \delta)$ such that $\gamma = C_0, C_1, \ldots, C_n$ and $\delta = D_0, D_1, \ldots, D_n$, where $C_0 = q_0, C_1 = x_1, \ldots, C_n = x_n$, $D_0 = \emptyset$, and $D_i = q_i - x_i$ for each $i \in \{1, \ldots, n\}$, is an interactive process in $\mathcal{A}$.

We end this section by observing that one can represent state sequences of $\mathcal{A}$ by finite *unlabeled* transition systems. Such a system is of the form $\mathcal{U} = (Q, \mu)$ where $\mu \subseteq Q \times Q$. Here, for states $q, q' \in Q$, $q'$ is a *successor* of $q$ if and only if $(q, q') \in \mu$. The transition from $q$ to $q'$ is unlabeled, i.e., there is no symbol marking/labeling/causing this transition. As a matter of fact, there is no set of symbols ($\Sigma$) here (which is the case for finite transition systems).

For $n \geq 1$, an *n-step transition process* in $\mathcal{U}$ is a sequence of states $q_0, q_1, \ldots, q_n$ such that, for each $i \in \{0, \ldots, n-1\}$, $(q_i, q_{i+1}) \in \mu$.

For a given rs $\mathcal{A} = (S, A)$, as above, let $\mathcal{U}_\mathcal{A} = (Q, \mu)$ be the finite unlabeled transition system such that $Q = 2^S$ and $\mu \subseteq Q \times Q$ is defined by: for all $T, Z \subseteq S$, $(T, Z) \in \mu$ if and only if $\mathsf{res}_\mathcal{A}(T) \subseteq Z$. We note that

(1) It follows directly from the definition of the state sequence $\tau$ of an interactive process in $\mathcal{A}$ that, if $W, W'$ are two consecutive states of $\tau$, then $(W, W') \in \mu$.

(2) Since for each ordered pair $(C, C')$ with $C, C' \subseteq S$ there is an interactive process $\pi$ for which $C, C'$ are two consecutive context sets of the context sequence of $\pi$, it follows that for each $(q, q') \in \mu$ there exists an interactive process of $\mathcal{A}$ such that $q, q'$ are two consecutive states of the state sequence of this process.

It follows from (1) and (2) that $\mathcal{U}_\mathcal{A}$ simulates the state sequences of $\mathcal{A}$. More precisely, for $n \geq 1$, a sequence $\tau = q_0, q_1, \ldots, q_n$ is an $n$-step transition process in $\mathcal{U}_\mathcal{A}$ if and only if there exists an interactive process $\pi$ in $\mathcal{A}$ such that $\tau$ is the state sequence of $\pi$.

Note that the unlabeled transition system $\mathcal{U}_\mathcal{A}$ simulates *only* the state sequences of interactive processes in $\mathcal{A}$, while the transition system $\mathcal{T}_\mathcal{A}$ discussed above simulates (through the use of symbols from $\Sigma$ as labels of transitions) interactive processes in $\mathcal{A}$ *together* with their state sequences. Clearly, one can obtain the *graph* of $\mathcal{U}_\mathcal{A}$ (where $2^S$ is the set of nodes and there is a directed edge from a node $T$ to a node $Z$ if and only if $(T, Z) \in \mu$) from the *labeled graph* of $\mathcal{T}_\mathcal{A}$ (where $2^S$ is the set of nodes and there is a directed edge labeled by $X$ from a node $T$ to a node $Z$ if and only if $\delta(T, X) = Z$) by simply removing the labels of edges.

For an rs $\mathcal{A}$, the (graph of the) unlabeled transition system $\mathcal{U}_\mathcal{A}$ provides the basic structure of transitions between states of $\mathcal{A}$. In particular it illustrates the "inclusion feature" of these transitions very well: if a state $Z$ is a successor of a state $T$ (i.e., $(T, Z)$ is a state sequence of $\mathcal{A}$) and state $Z$ is a subset of a state $W$, then $W$ is also a successor of $T$.

## 1.6. Measurement Functions

As discussed already, the basic model of reaction systems satisfies the threshold assumption, and so it is a qualitative model. On the other hand, it is a common practice in biology (reflected in various formal models) to assign quantitative/numerical parameters to states. To account for this, the basic model of reaction systems was extended in [20] to reaction systems with measurements.

The basic idea here is that a numerical value assigned to a state reflects a measurement performed on this state, where the intuitive notion of a measurement is formalized through the formal notion of a measurement function, which assigns a real number to each state of a reaction system.

**Definition 12.** *Let $\mathcal{A} = (S, A)$ be an* rs. *A measurement function for $\mathcal{A}$ is a function $f : 2^S \to \mathbb{R}$ such that, for all $X, Y \in 2^S$ with $X \cap Y = \emptyset$, $f(X \cup Y) = f(X) + f(Y)$.*

Note that the *additive property* of $f$ required in the above definition implies that $f(\emptyset) = 0$. The additive property is natural here, as states of an rs are abstract sets (in general, we do not know the nature of the entities from the background set), while the value of a measurement function for a set $Z$ should be obtainable from the values of this function for the singleton sets containing individual elements of $Z$.

We are ready now to extend the notion of an rs by a finite set of measurement functions (with each of them assigning a numerical parameter to each state of an rs).

**Definition 13.** *A reaction system with measurements, abbreviated* rsm, *is a triplet $\mathcal{A} = (S, A, F)$, where $(S, A)$ is an* rs *and $F$ is a finite set of measurement functions for $(S, A)$.*

The rs $(S, A)$ is the *underlying reaction system of $\mathcal{A}$*, denoted by und($\mathcal{A}$). The *result function of $\mathcal{A}$* is simply the result function of und($\mathcal{A}$); hence the dynamics of $\mathcal{A}$ are determined by the dynamics of und($\mathcal{A}$). In particular, interactive processes of $\mathcal{A}$ are just the interactive processes of und($\mathcal{A}$). The measurement functions from $F$ can be seen as annotations of the state sequences of $\mathcal{A}$. These annotations are global (in general, for a measurement function $f$ and a state $T$, the value $f(T)$ depends on the whole state $T$) and they are computed externally (outside of und($\mathcal{A}$)), i.e., not given as parts of the states of state sequences of interactive processes of und($\mathcal{A}$). This is illustrated in Figure 1.2 for a rsm $\mathcal{A} = (S, A, F)$, where $F = \{f_1, \ldots, f_n\}$.

All of the notation and terminology of reaction systems carry over to reaction systems with measurements through their underlying reaction systems.

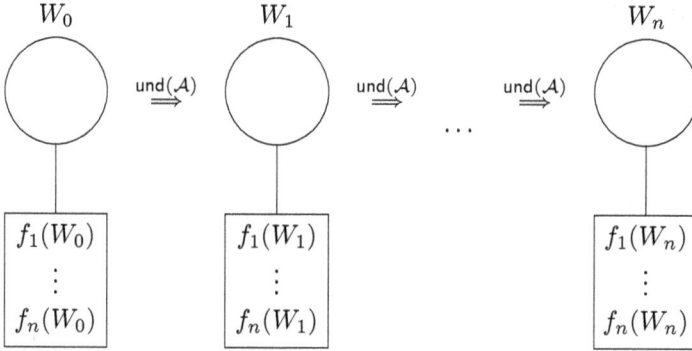

Fig. 1.2.   Annotating state sequences by measurement functions.

In quantitative models of biochemical processes, the numerical values assigned to the current state (such as, e.g., the number of molecules or concentrations) do influence the state transitions, i.e., the successor state $q'$ of state $q$ depends on, e.g., the concentrations of molecules in $q$. This is not the case for reaction systems with measurements; the measurement function just yields the values (of various numerical parameters) for each state, but these values do not influence the successor state.

We will demonstrate now how to make state transitions dependent on the values of measurement functions (see [14]). This is achieved through the use of generalized reactions where the intuition behind them is as follows.

Let $S$ be a finite set and let $b \in \mathrm{rac}(S)$. Then, for each $T \subseteq S$, $\mathrm{res}_b(T) = P_b$ if $\mathrm{en}_b(T)$ and $\mathrm{res}_b(T) = \emptyset$ otherwise. The crucial point of this definition is the partition of $2^S$ into the set $\Delta_b = \{X \in 2^S : \mathrm{en}_b(X)\}$ of subsets of $S$ which enable $b$ and the set $2^S - \Delta_b$ of subsets of $S$ which do not enable $b$. With this in mind we can rewrite the definition of $\mathrm{res}_b$ as follows: for each $T \subseteq S$, $\mathrm{res}_b(T) = P_b$ if $T \in \Delta_b$ and $\mathrm{res}_b(T) = \emptyset$ if $T \notin \Delta_b$. In this definition we use explicitly the set $\Delta_b$ of all subsets of $S$ enabling $b$. Here one does not have to know *why* a subset $T$ belongs to $\Delta_b$, while the original definition of $\mathrm{res}_b$ tells us explicitly why $\mathrm{en}_b(T)$ for a subset $T$. This leads us to the notion of a generalized reaction.

**Definition 14.** *Let $S$ be a finite nonempty set. A generalized reaction in $S$ is an ordered pair $d = (\Delta, P)$, where $\Delta \subseteq 2^S$ and $P \in 2^S - \{\emptyset\}$.*

The set $\Delta$ is called the *condition* of $d$ and the set $P$ is called the *product* of $d$. They are also written as $\Delta_b$ and $P_b$, respectively.

**Definition 15.** *Let $S$ be a finite nonempty set and $T \subseteq S$. A generalized reaction $b$ in $S$ is* enabled *by $T$, denoted* $\mathrm{en}_b(T)$, *if and only if $T \in \Delta_b$. The* result *of $b$ on $T$, denoted by* $\mathrm{res}_b(T)$, *is defined by* $\mathrm{res}_b(T) = P_b$ *if* $\mathrm{en}_b(T)$ *and* $\mathrm{res}_b(T) = \emptyset$ *otherwise.*

As follows from the discussion preceding Definition 14, the notion of a generalized reaction generalizes the notion of a reaction. The notion of the result function is extended to sets of generalized reactions in the same (cumulative) way as it was done for sets of ordinary reactions.

**Definition 16.** *Let $S$ be a finite nonempty set and $T \subseteq S$. The* result *of a set $B$ of generalized reactions in $S$ on $T$, denoted by* $\mathrm{res}_B(T)$, *is defined by* $\mathrm{res}_B(T) = \bigcup \{\mathrm{res}_b(T) : b \in B\}$.

As it was the case for ordinary reactions, also here $\mathrm{res}_B(T)$ can be restated by $\mathrm{res}_B(T) = \bigcup \{\mathrm{res}_b(T) : b \in B \text{ and } \mathrm{en}_b(T)\}$.

Since we are developing the framework of reaction systems, we are interested in generalized reactions that can be explained/implemented by ordinary reactions. Accordingly, we call a generalized reaction $d$ in $S$ *acceptable* if there exists a finite set of reactions $A \in \mathrm{rac}(S)$ such that $\mathrm{res}_d = \mathrm{res}_A$. It turns out that generalized reactions are acceptable providing that they do not violate the boundary condition.

**Theorem 4** ([14]). *Let $S$ be a finite nonemtpy set. A generalized reaction $d$ in $S$ is acceptable if and only if neither $\emptyset \in \Delta_d$ nor $S \in \Delta_d$.*

We are ready now to formulate the notion of "a reaction driven by a measurement function" as a special case of a generalized reaction. For didactical reasons, here we consider a single measurement function, but our reasoning easily carries over to finite sets of measurement functions.

Let $f : 2^S \to \mathbb{R}$ be a measurement function and let $Y \subseteq \mathrm{range}(f)$. The intuition behind the set $Y$ is that we want a generalized reaction $d$ to be enabled on a state $T$ if and only if $f(T)$ equals to one of the values specified by $Y$, for only then will $d$ contribute its product $P_d$ to the successor state of $T$. In particular, if $Y$ is a singleton, $Y = \{y\}$, then $d$ is enabled on $T$ only if $f(T) = y$.

Let $\Delta_{f,Y} = \{T \in 2^S : T \neq \emptyset, T \neq S, \text{ and } f(T) \in Y\}$ and let $d$ be the generalized reaction defined by $d = (\Delta_{f,Y}, P)$. Clearly, for each $T \in 2^S - \{\emptyset, S\}$, $d$ is enabled by $T$ if and only if $f(T)$ belongs to a prescribed set $Y$ of "good values" of $f$. Hence, indeed, $d$ is a generalized reaction driven by $f$, as illustrated in Figure 1.3.

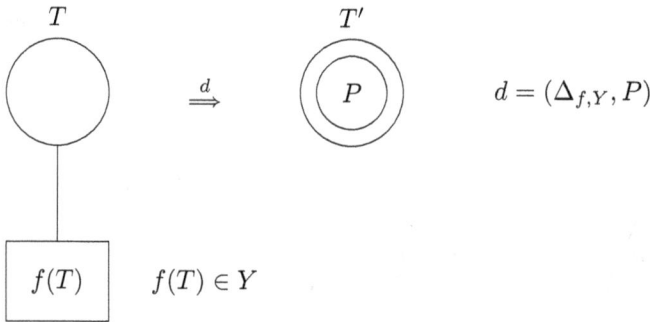

Fig. 1.3. Generalized reaction $d$ is driven by $f$.

## 1.7. Reaction Systems with Duration

The non-permanency feature of reaction systems implies that an entity $x$ from the current state will vanish (will not be present in the successor state) unless it is produced by a reaction enabled in the current state or it is introduced by the context of the successor state. This vanishing of $x$ is *instant*: $x$ is present in the current state but it is not present in its successor. However, in organic chemistry entities do not vanish instantly, but rather they have a decay time, meaning that they vanish within a certain time period. To take this into account one considers reaction systems with duration (introduced in [8]).

**Definition 17.** *A* reaction system with duration, *abbreviated* rsd, *is a triplet* $\mathcal{A} = (S, A, d)$, *where* $(S, A)$ *is a reaction system and* $d : S \to \mathbb{Z}^+$.

The rs $(S, A)$ is called the *underlying* rs *of* $\mathcal{A}$, denoted und($\mathcal{A}$), and $d$ is called the *duration function of* $\mathcal{A}$. The *result function of* $\mathcal{A}$, denoted res$_\mathcal{A}$, is the result function of und($\mathcal{A}$).

For $x \in S$, $d(x)$ is the *duration of* $x$ (in $\mathcal{A}$). The intuition behind $d(x)$ is that when $x$ is produced by res$_\mathcal{A}$ in an interactive process, its lifetime is $d(x)$ consecutive states (where the count begins in the state where $d$ is produced by res$_\mathcal{A}$).

The notion of an interactive process for a reaction system with duration $\mathcal{A}$ is then modified in order to take into account the durations of entities of $\mathcal{A}$.

**Definition 18.** *Let* $\mathcal{A} = (S, A, d)$ *be a* rsd *and let* $n \geq 1$ *be an integer. An* ($n$-step) interactive process in $\mathcal{A}$ *is a triplet* $\pi = (\gamma, \delta, \rho)$ *of finite sequences* *of sets such that* $\gamma = C_0, \ldots, C_n$, $\delta = D_0, \ldots, D_n$, *and* $\rho = G_0, \ldots, G_n$, *where* $C_0, \ldots, C_n, D_0, \ldots, D_n, G_0, \ldots, G_n \subseteq S$, $D_0 = \emptyset$, $G_0, G_1 = \emptyset$, $D_i = \mathsf{res}_A(D_{i-1} \cup C_{i-1} \cup G_{i-1})$ *for all* $i \in \{2, \ldots, n\}$, *and* $G_i = \{x \in S : d(x) \geq 2 \text{ and } x \in D_j, \text{ for some } j \in \{i - (d(x) - 1), \ldots, i - 1\}\}$.

The terminology and notation of reaction systems carry over to reaction systems with duration (through their underlying reaction systems). The sequence $\rho$ is called the *duration sequence of* $\mathcal{A}$. The *state sequence of* $\pi$ is now defined by $\tau = W_0, W_1, \ldots, W_n$ where, for each $i \in \{0, \ldots, n\}$, $W_i = C_i \cup D_i \cup G_i$. Note that if $d(x) = 1$ for all $x \in S$, then $G_i = \emptyset$ for all $i \in \{0, \ldots, n\}$ and in fact $\mathcal{A}$ behaves just as an ordinary rs.

To incorporate the notion of decay into reaction systems we have extended the notion of rs by adding a duration function to it, which is a "numerical function" assigning to each entity its duration, which is a positive integer. It turns out that one can incorporate the notion of duration in a "non-numerical" way, by extending a given rs $\mathcal{A}$ to a "bigger" rs $\mathcal{A}'$ which will ensure that the entities from $\mathcal{A}$ will have the durations required by a specific duration function. This is formalized as follows.

**Definition 19.** *Let* $\mathcal{A} = (S, A)$ *and* $\mathcal{A}' = (S', A')$ *be reaction systems. We say that* $\mathcal{A}'$ *is an* extension *of* $\mathcal{A}$ *if* $S \subseteq S'$ *and* $A \subseteq A'$; *we also say then that* $\mathcal{A}$ *is* embedded *in* $\mathcal{A}'$.

The notion of extension provides a convenient formalization of an environment of an rs: if $\mathcal{A}'$ is an extension of $\mathcal{A}$, then $\mathcal{A}'$ provides an environment for $\mathcal{A}$. Since $\mathcal{A}$ "knows" only the entities from its own background set $S$, its basic behavior *within* (the environment) $\mathcal{A}'$ is expressed by the projection $\mathsf{proj}_S(\mathsf{CISTS}(\mathcal{A}'))$. In this way we can investigate the behavior of $\mathcal{A}$ within different environments.

As announced already, the notion of an extension can also account for the phenomenon of duration/decay, as expressed by the following result.

**Theorem 5** ([8])**.** *For every* rsd $\mathcal{A} = (S, A, d)$ *there exists a reaction system* $\mathcal{A}' = (S', A')$ *such that* $\mathcal{A}'$ *is an extension of* $(S, A)$ *and* $\mathsf{proj}_S(\mathsf{CISTS}(\mathcal{A}')) = \mathsf{CISTS}(\mathcal{A})$.

The construction of $\mathcal{A}'$ is dependent on $d$, and so this result interprets the phenomenon of duration as an interaction with an environment.

Another area of research on reaction systems with duration is applications of the Chinese remainder theorem; see [43].

## 1.8. A Reaction Systems Model for the Self-Assembly of Intermediate Filaments

Intermediate filaments (IFs) form, alongside microtubules and actin filaments, the cytoskeleton of eukaryotic cells, found in the vast majority of cells of multicellular organisms; see [45]. The main function of intermediate filaments is structural: they form the cellular network of "girders" and "ropes" that give cells mechanical strength and helps maintain their shapes; see [31]. They have an essential contribution to durable structures such as hair, claws, and fingernails. Intermediate filaments form through the self-assembly of specific proteins. We focus in this section on the self-assembly of vimentin proteins (the most widely distributed of all IF proteins), following the model proposed in [28] and further investigated in [9]. Because of restrictions on the size of the paper we only present very briefly some of the main biological aspects of the self-assembly of intermediate filaments. For details we refer the reader to [26] for a review on this topic.

Vimentin proteins are $\alpha$-helical rods and they rapidly assemble parallelly into *dimers* (complexes consisting of two vimentins). Then two dimers form (antiparallel, half-staggered) vimentin *tetramers* (complexes consisting of four vimentins). Eight tetramers undergo a fast lateral aggregation forming a thick block of tetramers, so-called *unit-length filament* (ULF). These filaments get then *elongated* through longitudinal annealing with other forming filaments. The model proposed in [28] explains the self-assembly of vimentin IFs through the progressive assembly of tetramers ($T$) into octamers ($O$), then into hexadecamers ($H$) and ULFs ($U$). It consists of the biochemical reactions in Table 1.1; the emerging filaments are denoted by $F$ in this model.

Table 1.1.  The molecular model of [28] for the self-assembly of vimentin IFs.

| | | |
|---|---|---|
| (1) $2T \to O$; | (3) $2H \to U$; | (5) $F + U \to F$; |
| (2) $2O \to H$; | (4) $2U \to F$; | (6) $2F \to F$. |

The numerical properties of this model were analyzed in [28] and [29], by associating with it a mass-action-based mathematical model expressed as a set of ordinary differential equations. It turns out that the model is versatile — depending on its kinetic constants, the model may show both the formation of stable short filaments, as well as the formation of longer and longer filaments. This is in line with experimental observations of [29] that the chemical properties of the environment (such as ionic strength and pH) may change the dynamics of the IF self-assembly.

The dynamic, context-dependent self-assembly of intermediate filaments can also be followed through reaction systems models. Several such models were introduced in [5]; we discuss one of them here.

To distinguish between (the formation of) two types of filaments, we introduce two species/entities, $F_s$ and $F_l$, denoting short and long filaments, respectively. Tetramers, octamers, hexadecamers and unit-length filaments are modeled through species/entities $T$, $O$, $H$, $U$, respectively; for them we use the same names as in the molecular model. We also add to the background set species/entities short and long to be used as a signal from the environment regarding the type of filaments to be formed in the model; we assume that the environment adds, in each step of an interactive process, either short or long, possibly in addition to other species/entities. Finally, we add $f$ to the background set, to be used as a "formal inhibitor" for reactions that need no explicit inhibitor.

Table 1.2.  A reaction systems model for the self-assembly of vimentin IFs.

| | | | |
|---|---|---|---|
| (i) | $(\{T\}, \{f\}, \{O\})$; | (v.1) | $(\{U, F_s, \text{long}\}, \{\text{short}\}, \{F_l\})$; |
| (ii) | $(\{O\}, \{f\}, \{H\})$; | (v.2) | $(\{U, F_l, \text{long}\}, \{\text{short}\}, \{F_l\})$; |
| (iii) | $(\{H\}, \{f\}, \{U\})$; | (vi.1) | $(\{F_s, \text{long}\}, \{\text{short}\}, \{F_l\})$; |
| (iv) | $(\{U\}, \{F_l\}, \{F_s\})$; | (vi.2) | $(\{F_s, F_l, \text{long}\}, \{\text{short}\}, \{F_l\})$; |
| | | (vi.3) | $(\{F_l, \text{long}\}, \{\text{short}\}, \{F_l\})$. |

Reactions (i)–(iii) in the reaction system in Table 1.2 correspond to the reactions (1)–(3) in the molecular model in Table 1.1; they stand for the sequence of self-assemblies of tetramers to octomers to hexadecamers to unit-length filaments. This part of the reaction systems model is obtained from the molecular model in a straightforward way: for each reaction in the molecular model we create a reaction in the reaction systems model that uses the same reactants and products as its molecular correspondent. Note that even though each of the molecular reactions (1)–(3) has a reactant with multiplicity 2, we ignore the multiplicity in reactions (i)–(iii) based on the *threshold assumption* discussed in Section 1.3.

The molecular reaction (4) explaining the longitudinal annealing of two unit-length filaments to form the shortest proper filament is translated to reaction (iv) in the reaction systems model. Its product set is $\{F_s\}$, i.e., a *short* filament; we set $F_l$ as the inhibitor of this reaction to indicate that in the case when the formation of long filaments is favored over the formation of short ones, the unit-length filaments will have a preference to extend existing long filaments rather than start new short ones.

The molecular reaction (5) explaining the elongation of existing filaments with unit-length filaments is captured in our reaction systems model through reactions (v.1) and (v.2). To ensure that this reaction will take place only if the context favors the formation of long filaments, we add long to the set of reactants, in addition to $U, F_s$ in (v.1) and $U, F_l$ in (v.2). The product set in each case is $\{F_l\}$.

The molecular reaction (6) explaining the longitudinal annealing of two existing filaments and the formation of a longer filament is captured in the reaction systems model through reactions (vi.1)-(vi.3). The three reactions differ in the type of filaments (short or long) involved in the elongation, and they all take place only if the context indicates that the formation of long filaments is favored by throwing in the species long.

The reaction systems model successfully captures the dynamic context-dependent formation of short and long filaments in the following sense. For a constant context $\{T, \text{short}\}$, providing in each step of the interactive process more tetramers to support the formation of more filaments and short, the interactive process quickly arrives at a self-loop on state $\{O, H, U, F_s\}$, which corresponds to the situation when only short filaments are being self-assembled, along with the intermediary steps of the assembly from tetramers to filaments. On the other hand, for a constant context $\{T, \text{long}\}$, the interactive process arrives at a self-loop on state $\{U, H, U, F_l\}$, which corresponds to the situation where only existing filaments are being elongated, and new ones are not started. Moreover, the interactive process may cycle between these states by changing the context from $\{T, \text{short}\}$ to $\{T, \text{long}\}$ and the other way around. Generating all these interactive processes may be done through the online reaction system simulator at [48].

## 1.9. A Reaction Systems Model for the Heat Shock Response

The heat shock response is a cellular defense mechanism against stress-induced protein misfolding. The mechanisms is present in roughly the same form throughout all eukaryotes; even prokaryotes have a similar heat shock response. Because of restrictions on the size of the paper we only present some of the main biological aspects of the heat shock response very briefly. For more details, we refer the reader to [47] for a review of the heat shock response.

Exposure to elevated temperatures (and other types of stress such as oxidative stress or exposure to heavy metals) leads, among others, to highly accelerated protein misfolding. Misfolded proteins tend to form aggregates that may eventually lead to cell death. The cellular response to accumulating misfolded proteins is to accelerate the synthesis of protein chaperones (in our case, the heat shock proteins) which help misfolded proteins regain their native fold and block them from binding to other misfolded proteins. If the cell returns to physiological temperatures, then eventually the synthesis of heat shock proteins is decreased, as a consequence of a lower level of misfolded proteins.

The heat shock response is about the genetic regulation of the heat shock proteins in the presence as well as in the absence of heat stress. Here we follow a simplified version of the molecular model proposed in [35]; its molecular reactions are listed in Table 1.3. The main focus of this model is on the transcription regulation of the heat shock protein-encoding gene. This gene is transcribed with the help of a transcription factor called the *heat shock factor* (hsf); the gene's promoter is called the *heat shock element* (hse). The heat shock factors form homologous trimers (hsf$_3$) through reaction (1.3), which are able to bind to the heat shock element forming complex hsf$_3$: hse (in reaction (1.3)), and thus promote the transcription of the gene and subsequent synthesis of additional heat shock proteins, through reaction (1.3).

The heat shock proteins have an affinity for binding to heat shock factors in all of their forms (hsf, hsf$_3$, and hsf$_3$: hse); this is modeled through reactions (1.3)–(1.3). They have a much higher affinity to bind to misfolded proteins, through reaction (1.3), and help them get refolded through reaction (1.3). The model also includes the degradation of heat shock proteins, reaction (1.3) and the protein misfolding reaction (1.3); this latter reaction has a flux that depends exponentially on the temperature (see [35]).

Table 1.3.  A simplified version of the molecular model of [35] for the heat shock response.

| | |
|---|---|
| (7) 3 hsf → hsf$_3$; | (12) hsp + hsf$_3$: hse → hsp: hsf +2 hsf + hse; |
| (8) hsf$_3$ + hse → hsf$_3$: hse; | (13) hsp → $\emptyset$; |
| (9) hsf$_3$: hse → hsf$_3$: hse + hsp; | (14) prot → mfp; |
| (10) hsp + hsf $\rightleftarrows$ hsp: hsf; | (15) hsp + mfp → hsp: mfp; |
| (11) hsp + hsf$_3$ → hsp: hsf +2 hsf; | (16) hsp: mfp → hsp + prot. |

The numerical properties of the heat shock response model were analyzed in [35] by associating with it a mass-action model based on ordinary differential equations. The model was able to explain all the available quantitative and qualitative data, including the quick temperature-induced transactivation of the heat shock gene and its silencing in the absence of heat stress. These properties were explained through the numerical contributions of the kinetic rate constants of the various reactions in the model. The same basic interplay between temperature and the transactivation of the gene can, however, also be demonstrated through a reaction systems model, i.e., through a *qualitative* interplay between the reactions of the model. We discuss this in the following reaction systems model for the heat shock response proposed in [4] and shown in Table 1.4.

Table 1.4. A reaction systems model for the heat shock response.

| (vii.1) | $(\{\mathsf{hsf}\}, \{\mathsf{hsp}\}, \{\mathsf{hsf}_3\})$; |
|---------|-----------------------------------------------------------|
| (vii.2) | $(\{\mathsf{hsf}, \mathsf{hsp}, \mathsf{mfp}\}, \{f\}, \{\mathsf{hsf}_3\})$; |
| (viii.1) | $(\{\mathsf{hsf}_3, \mathsf{hse}\}, \{\mathsf{hsp}\}, \{\mathsf{hsf}_3\colon \mathsf{hse}\})$; |
| (viii.2) | $(\{\mathsf{hsf}_3, \mathsf{hse}, \mathsf{hsp}, \mathsf{mfp}\}, \{f\}, \{\mathsf{hsf}_3\colon \mathsf{hse}\})$; |
| (ix.1) | $(\{\mathsf{hsf}_3\colon \mathsf{hse}\}, \{\mathsf{hsp}\}, \{\mathsf{hsf}_3\colon \mathsf{hse}, \mathsf{hsp}\})$; |
| (ix.2) | $(\{\mathsf{hsf}_3\colon \mathsf{hse}, \mathsf{hsp}, \mathsf{mfp}\}, \{f\}, \{\mathsf{hsf}_3\colon \mathsf{hse}, \mathsf{hsp}\})$; |
| (x.1) | $(\{\mathsf{hsp}, \mathsf{hsf}\}, \{\mathsf{mfp}\}, \{\mathsf{hsp}\colon \mathsf{hsf}\})$; |
| (x.2) | $(\{\mathsf{hsp}\colon \mathsf{hsf}, \mathsf{stress}\}, \{\mathsf{nostress}\}, \{\mathsf{hsp}, \mathsf{hsf}\})$; |
| (x.3) | $(\{\mathsf{hsp}\colon \mathsf{hsf}, \mathsf{nostress}\}, \{\mathsf{stress}\}, \{\mathsf{hsp}\colon \mathsf{hsf}\})$; |
| (xi) | $(\{\mathsf{hsp}, \mathsf{hsf}_3\}, \{\mathsf{mfp}\}, \{\mathsf{hsp}\colon \mathsf{hsf}\})$; |
| (xii) | $(\{\mathsf{hsp}, \mathsf{hsf}_3\colon \mathsf{hse}\}, \{\mathsf{mfp}\}, \{\mathsf{hsp}\colon \mathsf{hsf}, \mathsf{hse}\})$; |
| (xiv.1) | $(\{\mathsf{prot}, \mathsf{stress}\}, \{\mathsf{nostress}\}, \{\mathsf{prot}, \mathsf{mfp}\})$; |
| (xiv.2) | $(\{\mathsf{prot}, \mathsf{nostress}\}, \{\mathsf{stress}\}, \{\mathsf{prot}\})$; |
| (xv) | $(\{\mathsf{hsp}, \mathsf{mfp}\}, \{f\}, \{\mathsf{hsp}\colon \mathsf{mfp}\})$; |
| (xvi) | $(\{\mathsf{hsp}\colon \mathsf{mfp}\}, \{f\}, \{\mathsf{hsp}, \mathsf{prot}\})$; |
| (hse.1) | $(\{\mathsf{hse}\}, \{\mathsf{hsf}_3\}, \{\mathsf{hse}\})$; |
| (hse.2) | $(\{\mathsf{hse}, \mathsf{hsf}_3, \mathsf{hsp}\}, \{\mathsf{mfp}\}, \{\mathsf{hse}\})$; |
| (mfp) | $(\{\mathsf{mfp}\}, \{\mathsf{hsp}\}, \{\mathsf{mfp}\})$. |

In the reaction systems model we use the same species names as in the molecular model. We add to the background set the species **stress** and **nostress**, and assume that in each step of an interactive process, the context adds either one of them, indicating whether the model is under heat stress or not. We also add species $f$ serving as a "formal inhibitor" for reactions that need no explicit inhibitor.

Building the reaction system corresponding to the molecular reactions in Table 1.3 takes into account the implicit, kinetic rate-driven competition on resources between molecular reactions, and makes it explicit through the inhibition mechanism. Whereas in the molecular model a reaction $b$ could block another reaction $a$ simply through a faster access to the common reactants driven by its higher kinetic rate constant, in the reaction systems model we explicitly introduce inhibitors such that in states where both reactions would have their reactants available, the reaction corresponding to $a$ would not be enabled.

An example of this situation is in the modeling of the trimer formation reaction (1.3). We introduce two reactions in our reaction systems model, (vii.1)–(vii.2) corresponding to this situation. In (vii.1) we indicate through the set of reactants and products that hsf trimerizes into $hsf_3$. We indicate through the inhibitor hsp that reaction (1.3) has a higher kinetic rate constant and competes for the same resource hsf and so, if hsp is present in the current state, then (vii.1) is not enabled. On the other hand, even if hsp were present in the current state, hsf could still be left free to trimerize, if hsp is 'hijacked' by reaction (1.3) that has a higher kinetic rate constant than (1.3); this is the case if both hsp and mfp are present in the current state. Hence, we also introduce reaction (vii.2) showing that hsf may get trimerized into $hsf_3$ in the presence of both hsp and mfp.

Using similar reasoning, the molecular reaction (1.3) is translated into reactions (viii.1) and (viii.2). In the former one, the reactant and the product sets are $\{hsf_3, hse\}$ and $\{hsf_3 : hse\}$, respectively. We set hsp as an inhibitor to indicate that it may block this reaction by starving it of $hsf_3$ through the molecular reaction (1.3) that has a higher kinetic rate constant than (1.3). However, hsp may be itself 'hijacked' by reaction (1.3) that has an even higher kinetic rate constant than (1.3), and thus it will leave $hsf_3$ and hse able to produce $hsf_3 : hse$ if both hsp and mfp are present in the current state. This situation is captured in reaction (viii.2).

The other reactions of our reaction systems model are deduced in a similar way. Note the additional reactions (hse.1), (hse.2), and (mfp): their role is to make sure that the species hse and mfp do not disappear from the current state if they are not handled by any reaction, as would otherwise be the case due to the *non-permanency principle* discussed in Section 1.1. Note also that the degradation of hsp (reaction (1.3)) need not be explicitly modeled because of the non-permanency principle. We refer to [4] for a detailed discussion about building this model.

The reaction system model obtained in this way successfully captures the temperature-induced dynamics of the transactivation of the heat shock gene in the following sense. Starting from a context $\{hsp, prot, hse, nostress\}$ introducing the main species into the interactive process, and continuing with constant context $\{nostress\}$, the interactive process eventually enters into a self-loop on state $\{hse, hsp : hsf, prot\}$. As discussed above, this is a good qualitative description of the state of the molecular model in the absence of stress: the heat shock factors are bound in complexes with the heat shock proteins, the gene is not transcribed (i.e., the heat shock element is free), and there are 'no' (or very few) misfolded proteins. On the other hand, if one continues after the first context set with a constant context {stress}, the interactive process eventually enters into a self-loop on state {hsf$_3$: hse, hsp, hsp: mfp, mfp, prot}. This is indeed a good qualitative description of the state of the molecular model in the presence of stress: the gene is transcribed (i.e., the heat shock element is occupied by heat shock factor trimers), there are misfolded proteins both free and bound to heat shock proteins, and also free heat shock proteins. Moreover, the interactive process may eventually switch between these states if the (constant) context switches between {stress} and {nostress}. These interactive processes may be automatically generated online through the simulator at [48].

## 1.10. Discussion

In this paper we introduced (in a tutorial fashion) the framework of reaction systems. We first presented (along with the underlying intuition and motivation) the formal notions of a reaction and its effect (as well as the effect of a set of reactions) on the current state of a system and then introduced the formal notion of a reaction system which is the central technical notion of the framework. We discussed two lines of research concerning reaction systems: reaction systems as definitions ("implementations") of power set functions and the relationship between reaction systems and finite transition systems.

Sometimes a research theme leads to a need to add additional components to the basic construct of reaction systems. Reaction systems, together with such extensions, form a broad framework of reaction systems. We have presented two such extensions: reaction systems with measurements and reaction systems with durations. Reaction systems are a qualitative model — there are no numerical parameters (there is no counting) in reaction systems. Extending reaction systems by measurement functions allows to assign numerical parameters to states, something that is often done in biology. We have demonstrated that the dynamic behavior of reaction systems with measurements can be also implemented by ordinary reaction systems using so-called generalized reactions (which are simply macros for finite sets of ordinary reactions). Non-permanence of entities is a basic feature of reaction systems (motivated by bioenergetics of the living cell). It causes an *instant* vanish of an entity from the current state unless it is sustained either by reactions or by a context. However, biochemical entities decay in nature within a certain period of time. To take this into account reaction systems were extended with duration functions (defining the decay time for each entity). Also in this case it turned out that the duration function can be implemented by ordinary reaction systems (in fact, the phenomenon of duration/delay can be explained as an interaction of the reaction system with its environment).

We also presented two reaction system models, for self-assembly of intermediate filaments and for eukaryotic heat shock response. In both cases, the models were constructed starting from molecular reaction models in such a way that their qualitative dynamic behavior (in terms of interactive processes) captures key aspects of the quantitative dynamic behavior of the corresponding mass-action-based ordinary differential equations models. This demonstrates that reaction systems are a versatile framework capable of capturing sophisticated dynamic behavior and explaining it through cause-effect relationships in terms of facilitation and inhibition between biochemical reactions.

In this paper we have presented only few research lines from the framework of reaction systems. To provide a better perspective we will give now a brief overview of some other research topics.

State sequences are the main (and traditional) "manifestation" of dynamic processes, and they are a central topic of research in the framework of reaction systems. Representative topics for this line of research are 'life and death' properties, stability and chaos, and estimates of the lengths of state sequences; see, e.g., [16, 17, 39, 42, 40, 38, 25, 24, 23].

Structural properties of consecutive states of state sequences are important in understanding the dynamics of reaction systems. In particular, formalization of the so-called *modules* (motivated by research in biochemistry and biology, see [46]) has been investigated in [18].

Understanding causalities in dynamic processes is a classic research topic in computer science. It is also well-motivated, from both the biological and computational points of view, in the framework of reaction systems. Static and dynamic causalities (influences) between entities in reaction systems were investigated in [7].

The topic of time in models of biological processes ("What is time?", "How to assign time to states of biochemical systems?") is both important and fascinating. It turns out that one can introduce time in reaction systems using measurement functions satisfying certain properties (see [20]). In this way one can introduce and investigate important concepts such as reaction times and time distances between consecutive states.

A recent popular topic of research is that of model checking for reaction systems. Results along this line include computational complexity of checking various properties [24, 23, 2, 12, 10, 11], importing standard modeling concepts (such as steady states and mass conservations) to reaction systems [2, 3], and temporal logic for reaction systems [34].

Finally we want to mention the use of reaction systems within so-called *exploration systems*: a formal framework for exploring a discipline of science. Reaction systems captured two important features of the functioning of the living cell: the fact that the living cell is an open system and the non-permanency of its entities. Another important feature of biological systems is the presence of hierarchical structures on both the physical and the methodological levels. This feature is not addressed by reaction systems but it is addressed by zoom structures (see [21, 22]). Reaction systems together with zoom structures form exploration systems ([21]). An exploration system consists of a depository of knowledge provided by a zoom structure and of dynamic processes (exploring this depository of knowledge) provided by a finite set of reaction systems.

## Dedication and Acknowledgments

This paper is dedicated to Janusz Brzozowski, in recognition of his outstanding contributions to computer science. The authors are indebted to Robert Brijder and Sepinoud Azimi for valuable comments concerning the working version of this paper.

## References

1. A. ARNOLD, *Finite Transition Systems: Semantics of Communicating Systems*, Prentice Hall International (UK) Ltd., Hertfordshire, UK, 1994.

2. S. AZIMI, C. GRATIE, S. IVANOV, L. MANZONI, I. PETRE AND A. E. PORRECA, Complexity of model checking for reaction systems, *Theoret. Comput. Sci.* **623** (2016), 103–113.

3. S. AZIMI, C. GRATIE, S. IVANOV AND I. PETRE, Dependency graphs and mass conservation in reaction systems, *Theoret. Comput. Sci.* **598** (2015), 23–39.

4. S. AZIMI, B. IANCU AND I. PETRE, Reaction system models for the heat shock response, *Fund. Inform.* **131** (2014), 1–14.

5. S. AZIMI, C. PANCHAL, E. CZEIZLER AND I. PETRE, Reaction systems models for the self-assembly of intermediate filaments, *Annals of University of Bucharest* **LXII**,2 (2015), 9–24.

6. R. BRIJDER, A. EHRENFEUCHT, M. MAIN AND G. ROZENBERG, A tour of reaction systems, *Int. J. Found. Comput. Sci.* **22**,07 (Nov. 2011), 1499–1517.

7. R. BRIJDER, A. EHRENFEUCHT AND G. ROZENBERG, A note on causalities in reaction systems, *Electronic Communications of the EASST* **30** (2010), 1–9.

8. R. BRIJDER, A. EHRENFEUCHT AND G. ROZENBERG, Reaction Systems with Duration, in *Computation, Cooperation, and Life*, J. Kelemen and A. Kelemenová (eds.), pp. 191–202, *LNCS* vol. 6610, Springer Berlin Heidelberg, 2011.

9. E. CZEIZLER, A. MIZERA, E. CZEIZLER, R. J. BACK, J. E. ERIKSSON AND I. PETRE, Quantitative analysis of the self-assembly strategies of intermediate filaments from tetrameric vimentin, *IEEE/ACM Transactions on Computational Biology and Bioinformatics* **9**,3 (May 2012), 885–898.

10. A. DENNUNZIO, E. FORMENTI, L. MANZONI AND A. E. PORRECA, Ancestors, descendants, and gardens of eden in reaction systems, *Theor. Comput. Sci.* **608** (2015), 16–26.

11. A. DENNUNZIO, E. FORMENTI, L. MANZONI AND A. E. PORRECA, Preimage problems for reaction systems, in *9th LATA 2015*, A. H. Dediu, E. Formenti, C. Martín-Vide and B. Truthe (eds.), pp. 537–548, *LNCS* vol. 8977, Springer, 2015.

12. A. DENNUNZIO, E. FORMENTI, L. MANZONI AND A. E. PORRECA, Reachability in resource-bounded reaction systems, in *10th LATA 2016*, A. Dediu, J. Janousek, C. Martín-Vide and B. Truthe (eds.), pp. 592–602, *LNCS* vol. 9618, Springer, 2016.

13. A. EHRENFEUCHT, J. KLEIJN, M. KOUTNY AND G. ROZENBERG, Minimal reaction systems, in *Transactions on Computational Systems Biology XIV SE-5*, C. Priami, I. Petre and E. de Vink (eds.), pp. 102–122, *LNCS* vol. 7625, Springer Berlin Heidelberg, 2012.

14. A. EHRENFEUCHT, J. KLEIJN, M. KOUTNY AND G. ROZENBERG, Qualitative and quantitative aspects of a model for processes inspired by the functioning of the living cell, in *Biomolecular Information Processing: From Logic Systems to Smart Sensors and Actuators*, E. Katz (ed.), ch. 16, pp. 303–322, Wiley-VCH Verlag GmbH & Co. KGaA, Weinheim, Germany, July 2012.

15. A. EHRENFEUCHT, J. KLEIJN, M. KOUTNY AND G. ROZENBERG, Reaction systems: A natural computing approach to the functioning of living cells, in *A Computable Universe: Understanding and Exploring Nature as Computation*, Z. Hector (ed.), ch. 10, pp. 189–208, World Scientific, Singapore, 2012.

16. A. EHRENFEUCHT, M. MAIN AND G. ROZENBERG, Combinatorics of life and death for reaction systems, *Int. J. Found. Comput. Sci.* **21**,03 (June 2010), 345–356.

17. A. EHRENFEUCHT, M. MAIN, G. ROZENBERG AND A. T. BROWN, Stability and chaos in reaction systems, *Int. J. Found. Comput. Sci.* **23**,05 (2012), 1173–1184.

18. A. EHRENFEUCHT AND G. ROZENBERG, Events and modules in reaction systems, *Theoret. Comput. Sci.* **376**,1-2 (May 2007), 3–16.
19. A. EHRENFEUCHT AND G. ROZENBERG, Reaction systems, *Fund. Inform.* **75**,1 (Jan. 2007), 263–280.
20. A. EHRENFEUCHT AND G. ROZENBERG, Introducing time in reaction systems, *Theoret. Comput. Sci.* **410**,4-5 (Feb. 2009), 310–322.
21. A. EHRENFEUCHT AND G. ROZENBERG, Zoom structures and reaction systems yield exploration systems, *Int. J. Found. Comput. Sci.* **25** (2014), 275–305.
22. A. EHRENFEUCHT AND G. ROZENBERG, Standard and ordered zoom structures, *Theoret. Comput. Sci.* **608** (2015), 4–15.
23. E. FORMENTI, L. MANZONI AND A. E. PORRECA, Cycles and global attractors of reaction systems, in *16th DCFS 2014*, H. Jürgensen, J. Karhumäki and A. Okhotin (eds.), pp. 114–125, *LNCS* vol. 8614, Springer International Publishing, 2014.
24. E. FORMENTI, L. MANZONI AND A. E. PORRECA, Fixed points and attractors of reaction systems, in *Language, Life, Limits*, A. Beckmann, E. Csuhaj-Varjú and K. Meer (eds.), pp. 194–203, *LNCS* vol. 8493, Springer International Publishing, 2014.
25. E. FORMENTI, L. MANZONI AND A. E. PORRECA, On the complexity of occurrence and convergence problems in reaction systems, *Natural Computing* **14**,1 (2015), 185–191.
26. H. HERRMANN, H. BÄR, L. KREPLAK, S. V. STRELKOV AND U. AEBI, Intermediate filaments: from cell architecture to nanomechanics, *Nature Reviews Mol Cell Biol* **8** (2007), 562–573.
27. L. KARI AND G. ROZENBERG, The many facets of natural computing, *Communications of the ACM* **51**,10 (Oct. 2008), 72–83.
28. R. KIRMSE, S. PORTET, N. MÜCKE, U. AEBI, H. HERRMANN AND J. LANGOWSKI, A quantitative kinetic model for the in vitro assembly of intermediate filaments from tetrameric vimentin, *J. Biol. Chem.* **282**,52 (2007), 18563–18572.
29. L. KREPLAK, U. AEBI AND H. HERRMANN, Molecular mechanisms underlying the assembly of intermediate filaments, *Experimental Cell Research*, 2004.
30. A. LEHNINGER, *Bioenergetics: The Molecular Basis of Biological Energy Transformations*, Addison-Wesley Pub (Sd), 1971.
31. H. LODISH, A. BERK, L. S. ZIPURSKY, P. MATSUDAIRA, D. BALTIMORE AND J. DARNELL, *Molecular Cell Biology (4th edition)*, W.H.Freeman, 2000.
32. L. MANZONI, D. POCAS AND A. E. PORRECA, Simple reaction systems and their classification, *Int. J. Found. Comput. Sci.* **25**,04 (2014), 441–457.
33. L. MANZONI AND A. E. PORRECA, Reaction systems made simple, in *Unconventional Computation and Natural Computation*, G. Mauri, A. Dennunzio, L. Manzoni and A. E. Porreca (eds.), Berlin, Heidelberg, 2013, pp. 150–161, *LNCS* vol. 7956, Springer Berlin Heidelberg.
34. A. MĘSKI, W. PENCZEK AND G. ROZENBERG, Model checking temporal properties of reaction systems, *Inform. Sciences*, 2015.

35. I. PETRE, A. MIZERA, C. L. HYDER, A. MEINANDER, A. MIKHAILOV, R. I. MORIMOTO, L. SISTONEN, J. E. ERIKSSON AND R.-J. BACK, A simple mass-action model for the eukaryotic heat shock response and its mathematical validation, *Natural Computing* **10**,1 (2011), 595–612.

36. W. REISIG, *Understanding Petri Nets*, Springer Berlin Heidelberg, 2013.

37. G. Rozenberg, T. H. W. Bäck and J. N. Kok (eds.), *Handbook of Natural Computing*, Springer Heidelberg, 2010.

38. A. SALOMAA, Functions and sequences generated by reaction systems, *Theor. Comput. Sci.* **466** (2012), 87–96.

39. A. SALOMAA, On state sequences defined by reaction systems, in *Logic and Program Semantics*, R. L. Constable and A. Silva (eds.), pp. 271–282, *LNCS* vol. 7230, Springer-Verlag, 2012.

40. A. SALOMAA, Functional constructions between reaction systems and propositional logic, *Int. J. Found. Comput. Sci.* **24**,1 (2013), 147–160.

41. A. SALOMAA, Minimal and almost minimal reaction systems, *Natural Computing* **12**,3 (2013), 369–376.

42. A. SALOMAA, Minimal reaction systems defining subset functions, in *Computing with New Resources*, C. Calude, R. Freivalds and K. Iwama (eds.), pp. 436–446, *LNCS* vol. 8808, Springer, 2014.

43. A. SALOMAA, Applications of the chinese remainder theorem to reaction systems with duration, *Theoret. Comput. Sci.* **598** (2015), 15–22.

44. A. SALOMAA, Two-step simulations of reaction systems by minimal ones, *Acta Cybernetica* **22**,2 (2015), 393–311.

45. M. SCHLIWA, *The Cytoskeleton, Cell Biology Monographs* vol. 13, Springer-Verlag, Vienna, Austria, 1986.

46. G. Schlosser and G. P. Wagner (eds.), *Modularity in Development and Evolution*, University of Chicago Press Books, 2004.

47. R. VOELLMY, Transduction of the stress signal and mechanisms of transcriptional regulation of heat shock/stress protein gene expression in higher eukaryotes, *Critical reviews in eukaryotic gene expression* **4**,4 (1994), 357—401.

48. The web interface of the reaction system simulator. `http://combio.abo.fi/research/reaction-systems/reaction-system-simulator`, Accessed 01/06/2016.

# Chapter 2

# Solving Fixed Point Equations over Complete Semirings

Zoltán Ésik

*Dept. of Computer Science*
*University of Szeged*
*Szeged, Hungary*

Werner Kuich

*Inst. of Discrete Mathematics and Geometry*
*Technical University of Vienna*
*Vienna, Austria*

We prove that any system of polynomial fixed point equations with coefficients in a complete commutative semiring has a canonical solution. In fact, our result also applies to systems of fixed point equations involving arbitrary formal series. When the semiring is continuous, the canonical solution is the least solution. Moreover, we prove that the canonical fixed point operation over series satisfies the standard identities of fixed point operations as described by the axioms of iteration theories.

## Contents

## 2.1. Introduction

Suppose that $X$ is a set and $S$ is a complete semiring. It is well-known that the semiring $S\langle\!\langle X^* \rangle\!\rangle$ of power series over $X$ with coefficients in $S$ is also a complete semiring. We characterize the semirings $S\langle\!\langle X^* \rangle\!\rangle$ by a universal property and use this property to define a category $\mathbf{Ser}_S$ of power series over $S$ when $S$ is additionally commutative. The objects of $\mathbf{Ser}_S$ are sets $X, Y, \ldots$, and a morphism $f : X \to Y$ is a family $f = (f_x)_{x \in X}$ of power series, where $f_x \in S\langle\!\langle Y^* \rangle\!\rangle$ for all $x \in X$. It will be clear from the definition that each category $\mathbf{Ser}_S$ has finite (actually all) coproducts. In fact, the coproduct $X \oplus Y$ of $X$ and $Y$ is given by a disjoint union.

In computer science, it is common to define the semantics of recursion by fixed point operations. It has been shown in [5] that all major fixed point operations used in computer science share the same equational properties. These equational properties define iteration theories, or iteration categories. Iteration categories include the categories of monotonic or continuous functions over complete lattices or cpo's equipped with the least fixed point operation, the categories of continuous functors over categories with initial object and colimits of directed diagrams equipped with the initial fixed point operation, and many others. For a recent account of iteration categories, the reader is referred to [12].

In our main contribution, we define a natural fixed point or dagger operation $^\dagger$ on $\mathbf{Ser}_S$, for any complete commutative semiring $S$. When $f : X \to X \oplus Y$ in $\mathbf{Ser}_S$, $f^\dagger : X \to Y$ provides a canonical solution of the fixed point equation $\xi = f \circ \langle \xi, \mathrm{id}_Y \rangle$ associated with $f$. We show that equipped with this operation, $\mathbf{Ser}_S$ is also an iteration category. Moreover, we prove that $\mathbf{Ser}_S$ satisfies the 'weak functoriality axiom' of [5].

It is well-known that each continuous semiring is a complete semiring. We prove that when $S$ is a continuous commutative semiring, then for each $f : X \to X \oplus Y$, $f^\dagger$ is the least solution of the fixed point equation associated with $f$. Hence our main result extends the known fact that when $S$ is a continuous commutative semiring, then $\mathbf{Ser}_S$, equipped with the least fixed point operation, is an iteration category.

## 2.2. Complete and Continuous Semirings

Recall that a monoid $V = (V, +, 0)$ is *complete* if the sum $\sum_{i \in I} x_i$ of any family $x_i$, $i \in I$ of elements of $V$ exists; moreover,

$$\sum_{i \in F} x_i = x_{i_1} + \cdots + x_{i_n}$$

for all finite families $x_i \in V$, $i \in F = \{i_1, \ldots, i_n\}$, and

$$\sum_{j \in J} \sum_{i \in I_j} x_i = \sum_{i \in I} x_i$$

whenever $I$ is the disjoint union of the sets $I_j$, $j \in J$ and $x_i \in V$ for all $i \in I$. It follows that

$$\sum_{i \in I} x_i = \sum_{i \in I} x_{h(i)}$$

for all families $x_i$, $i \in I$, and for all permutations $h : I \to I$. In particular, every complete monoid $V$ is commutative: $x + y = y + x$ for all $x, y \in V$. Moreover, if $\sum_{i \in I} x_i = 0$, then $x_i = 0$ for all $i \in I$.

Let $V$ and and $V'$ be complete monoids. We call a function $h : V \to V'$ *completely additive* if $h(\sum_{i \in I} x_i) = \sum_{i \in I} h(x_i)$ for all $x_i \in V$, $i \in I$, where $I$ is any set. In particular, $h(0) = 0$ and $h(x + y) = h(x) + h(y)$, so that $h$ is a monoid homomorphism.

A subclass of complete monoids is given by the *continuous monoids*. We say that a commutative monoid $V = (V, +, 0)$ is continuous[1] if it is equipped with a partial order $\leq$ such that the supremum $\bigvee C$ of any nonempty directed set (or equivalently, nonempty chain [17]) $C \subseteq V$ exists and 0 is the least element of $V$. (Thus, 0 is the supremum of the empty set.) Moreover, the operation $+$ is continuous, i.e., it preserves the supremum of all nonempty directed sets (or chains) in either argument. It follows that $+$ is monotonic: if $x \leq y$ in $V$, then $x + z \leq y + z$ for all $z \in V$. Moreover, $x \leq x + y$ for all $x, y \in V$.

Suppose that $V$ is a continuous monoid and $x_i \in V$ for all $i \in I$. We define $\sum_{i \in I} x_i$ as the supremum of all finite sums $x_{i_1} + \cdots + x_{i_n}$ where $i_1, \ldots, i_n$, $n \geq 0$ are pairwise different elements of $I$. It is well-known that, equipped with this summation operation, $V$ is a complete monoid, cf. Section 2.2 of [13]. For later use, we note the following lemma.

**Lemma 2.1.** *Let $V$ be a continuous monoid and $I$ be a set. Suppose that for each $i \in I$, $D_i$ is a nonempty directed subset of $V$. Let $\Delta$ denote the*

---

[1]More generally, one could define continuous monoids without the commutativity requirement; however, the present definition is more convenient here.

set of all families $(x_i)_{i \in I}$ with $x_i \in D_i$ for all $i \in I$. Then the supremum $\bigvee_{(x_i)_{i \in I} \in \Delta} \sum_{i \in I} x_i$ of the set $\{\sum_{i \in I} x_i : (x_i)_{i \in I} \in \Delta\}$ exists and

$$\bigvee_{(x_i)_{i \in I} \in \Delta} \sum_{i \in I} x_i = \sum_{i \in I} \bigvee D_i.$$

**Proof.** The sum on the right-hand side of the above equality exists. We show that it is the supremum of the set $\{\sum_{i \in I} x_i : (x_i)_{i \in I} \in \Delta\}$. Indeed, using the fact that $+$ is continuous in the second equality,

$$\sum_{i \in I} \bigvee D_i = \bigvee_{F \subseteq I} \sum_{i \in F} \bigvee D_i$$

$$= \bigvee_{F \subseteq I} \bigvee_{(x_i)_{i \in F} \in \Delta_F} \sum_{i \in F} x_i$$

$$= \bigvee_{(x_i)_{i \in I} \in \Delta} \bigvee_{F \subseteq I} \sum_{i \in F} x_i$$

$$= \bigvee_{(x_i)_{i \in I} \in \Delta} \sum_{i \in I} x_i,$$

where $F$ ranges over the finite subsets of $I$ and for each $F$, the elements of the set $\Delta_F$ are all families $(x_i)_{i \in F}$ with $x_i \in D_i$ for all $i \in F$.            □

Suppose that $V$ and $V'$ are continuous monoids. We say that a monoid homomorphism $V \to V'$ is continuous if it preserves the supremum of all nonempty directed sets (or nonempty chains). Clearly, every continuous homomorphism is completely additive.

Complete and continuous monoids are closed under several constructions including direct product. Suppose that $V_i$ is a complete monoid for each $i \in I$. Then $V = \prod_{i \in I} V_i$ is also a complete monoid in which the sum of any family of elements is defined pointwise. And if each $V_i$ is a continuous monoid, then $V = \prod_{i \in I} V_i$, equipped with the pointwise $+$ operation and the pointwise ordering, is also a continuous monoid. It follows that the sum of any family of elements is the pointwise sum. In particular, if $V$ is a complete or a continuous monoid, then so is $V^I$ for any set $I$.

Now suppose that $S = (S, +, \cdot, 0, 1)$ is a semiring. Following [8], we say that $S$ is a *complete semiring* if $(S, +, 0)$ is a complete monoid and

$$\left(\sum_{i \in I} x_i\right)y = \sum_{i \in I} x_i y$$

$$y\left(\sum_{i \in I} x_i\right) = \sum_{i \in I} y x_i$$

whenever $y \in S$ and $x_i \in S$ for all $i \in I$, where $I$ is any set. Moreover, we say that $S$ is a *continuous semiring* if $(S, +, 0)$ is a continuous monoid equipped with a partial order $\leq$ and the product operation is continuous, i.e., it preserves the supremum of nonempty chains (or nonempty directed subsets) in either argument:

$$\left(\bigvee_{i \in I} x_i\right)y = \bigvee_{i \in I} x_i y$$

$$y\left(\bigvee_{i \in I} x_i\right) = \bigvee_{i \in I} y x_i$$

for all $x_i \in S$ and $y \in S$ such that the set $\{x_i : i \in I\}$ is a nonempty directed set (or nonempty chain). Since each continuous monoid is a complete monoid, it follows that every continuous semiring is a complete semiring (also see Section 2.2 of [13]).

We now describe two constructions on complete (or continuous) semirings.

## 2.3. Formal Power Series Semirings over Complete Semirings

Complete and continuous semirings are closed under the formation of *formal power series semirings*. Suppose that $S$ is a complete semiring and $X$ is a set. As usual, let $X^*$ denote the free monoid of all words over $X$ including the empty word $\epsilon$, and let $S\langle\!\langle X^* \rangle\!\rangle$ denote the semiring of all formal power series [4, 14, 16] $s = \sum_{u \in X^*} \langle s, u \rangle u$ over $X$ with coefficients in $S$. Each series $s$ may be viewed as a function $X^* \to S$ mapping a word $u \in X^*$ to $\langle s, u \rangle$. The sum of any family of series is the pointwise sum

$$\langle s + s', u \rangle = \langle s, u \rangle + \langle s', u \rangle,$$

for all $s, s' \in S\langle\!\langle X^* \rangle\!\rangle$ and $u \in X^*$, and

$$\left\langle \sum_{i \in I} s_i, u \right\rangle = \sum_{i \in I} \langle s_i, u \rangle$$

for all families of series $s_i \in S\langle\!\langle X^* \rangle\!\rangle$, $i \in I$, and words $u \in X^*$. The product operation is the usual *convolution*

$$\langle sr, u \rangle = \sum_{u = vw} \langle s, v \rangle \langle r, w \rangle$$

for all $s, r \in S\langle\!\langle X^* \rangle\!\rangle$ and $u \in X^*$.

The *support* of a series $s \in S\langle\!\langle X^* \rangle\!\rangle$ is the set $\{ u \in X^* : \langle s, u \rangle \neq 0 \}$. A *polynomial* is a series with finite support. The polynomials in $S\langle\!\langle X^* \rangle\!\rangle$ form a subsemiring that we denote by $S\langle X^* \rangle$. Note that $S\langle X^* \rangle$ is not necessarily a complete semiring, since the sum of an infinite number of polynomials may not have finite support.

As usual, we identify each element $s \in S$ with the series (in fact, a polynomial) which, as a function, maps $\epsilon$ to $s$ and and all other words in $X^*$ to 0. Similarly, we identify each word $u \in X^*$ with a series which, as a function, maps $u$ to 1 and and all other words in $X^*$ to 0. Thus, the identity element of $S\langle\!\langle X^* \rangle\!\rangle$ that we usually denote 1 is both the series corresponding to the identity element of $S$ and the series corresponding to $\epsilon$. The zero series is denoted by 0.

It is known that when $S$ is a continuous semiring, then so is $S\langle\!\langle X^* \rangle\!\rangle$, equipped with the pointwise order relation, cf. Section 2.2 of [13]. The complete semiring structure determined by the continuous semiring structure is the same as above.

We end this section with a characterization of the power series semirings $S\langle\!\langle X^* \rangle\!\rangle$, for complete semirings $S$.

**Theorem 2.1.** *Suppose that $S$ is a complete semiring. Then for each set $X$, the complete semiring $S\langle\!\langle X^* \rangle\!\rangle$ has the following universal property. Given a complete semiring $S'$, a completely additive semiring morphism $h_S : S \to S'$, and any function $h_X : X \to S'$ such that the elements of $h_S(S)$ commute with the elements of $h_X(X)$, there is a unique completely additive semiring morphism $h^\sharp : S\langle\!\langle X^* \rangle\!\rangle \to S'$ extending $h_S$ and $h_X$.*

**Proof.** First extend $h_X$ to a monoid morphism $X^* \to S'$, denoted just by $h$. Note that the elements of $h_S(S)$ commute with those of $h(X^*)$. Then, for a series $s \in S\langle\!\langle X^* \rangle\!\rangle$, define $h^\sharp(s) = \sum_{u \in X^*} h_S(\langle s, u \rangle) h(u)$. It is clear that $h^\sharp$ extends $h_S$ and $h_X$ and preserves the constants 0 and 1. We prove that $h^\sharp$ is completely additive. Suppose that $s_i \in S\langle\!\langle X^* \rangle\!\rangle$ for all $i \in I$. Let $s = \sum_{i \in I} s_i$. Then

$$h^\sharp(s) = \sum_{u \in X^*} h_S(\langle s, u \rangle) h(u)$$

$$= \sum_{u \in X^*} (\sum_{i \in I} h_S(\langle s_i, u \rangle)) h(u)$$

$$= \sum_{u \in X^*} \sum_{i \in I} h_S(\langle s_i, u \rangle) h(u)$$

$$= \sum_{i \in I} \sum_{u \in X^*} h_S(\langle s_i, u \rangle) h(u)$$

$$= \sum_{i \in I} h^\sharp(s_i),$$

proving that $h^\sharp$ is completely additive. Next we prove that $h^\sharp$ preserves the product operation. To this end, let $s, r \in S\langle\!\langle X^* \rangle\!\rangle$. Then

$$h^\sharp(sr) = \sum_{u \in X^*} h_S(\langle sr, u \rangle) h(u)$$

$$= \sum_{u \in X^*} h_S(\sum_{u=vv'} \langle s, v \rangle \langle r, v' \rangle) h(u)$$

$$= \sum_{u \in X^*} \sum_{u=vv'} h_S(\langle s, v \rangle \langle r, v' \rangle) h(v) h(v')$$

$$= \sum_{u \in X^*} \sum_{u=vv'} h_S(\langle s, v \rangle) h_S(\langle r, v' \rangle) h(v) h(v')$$

$$= \sum_{u \in X^*} \sum_{u=vv'} h_S(\langle s, v \rangle) h(v) h_S(\langle r, v' \rangle) h(v')$$

$$= (\sum_{v \in X^*} h_S(\langle s, v \rangle) h(v)) (\sum_{v' \in X^*} h_S(\langle r, v' \rangle) h(v'))$$

$$= h^\sharp(s) h^\sharp(r),$$

where in the fifth equality we used that the elements of $h_S(S)$ commute with the elements of $h(X^*)$.

Since the definition of $h^\sharp$ was forced, $h^\sharp$ is unique. $\qquad\square$

For continuous semirings, we have an analogous result.

**Theorem 2.2.** *Suppose that $S$ is a continuous semiring. Then for each set $X$, the continuous semiring $S\langle\!\langle X^* \rangle\!\rangle$ has the following universal property.*

*Given a continuous semiring $S'$, a continuous semiring morphism $h_S$ :
$S \to S'$ and any function $h_X : X \to S'$ such that the elements of $h_S(S)$
commute with the elements of $h_X(X)$, there is a unique continuous semiring
morphism $h^{\sharp} : S\langle\!\langle X^* \rangle\!\rangle \to S'$ extending $h_S$ and $h_X$.*

**Proof.** By the previous theorem, there is a unique completely additive
semiring morphism $h^{\sharp}$ extending $h_S$ and $h$. To complete the proof, we
show that $h^{\sharp}$ is continuous. We use the notation of the previous proof.

Suppose that $s_i \in S\langle\!\langle X^* \rangle\!\rangle$ for all $i \in I$, where $(I, \leq)$ is a nonempty
directed partially ordered set. Moreover, suppose that $s_i \leq s_j$ whenever
$i \leq j$ in $I$ and let $s = \bigvee_{i \in I} s_i$. Using Lemma 2.1 we have

$$
\begin{aligned}
h^{\sharp}(s) &= \sum_{u \in X^*} h_S(\langle s, u \rangle) h(u) \\
&= \sum_{u \in X^*} h_S(\bigvee_{i \in I} \langle s_i, u \rangle) h(u) \\
&= \sum_{u \in X^*} \bigvee_{i \in I} h_S(\langle s_i, u \rangle) h(u) \\
&= \bigvee_{i \in I} \sum_{u \in X^*} h_S(\langle s_i, u \rangle) h(u) \\
&= \bigvee_{i \in I} h^{\sharp}(s_i),
\end{aligned}
$$

proving that $h^{\sharp}$ is continuous. $\qquad\qquad\qquad\qquad\qquad\qquad\square$

## 2.4. Matrix Semirings over Complete Semirings

Suppose that $S$ is a complete semiring and $I$ is a set. Then the *matrix
semiring* $S^{I \times I}$, equipped with the pointwise sum operation and the usual
matrix product operation, is also complete. Let $M, M' \in S^{I \times I}$. Then
$M + M'$ and $MM'$ are defined so that for all $i, j \in I$,

$$
(M + M')_{ij} = M_{ij} + M'_{ij}
$$
$$
(MM')_{ij} = \sum_{k \in I} M_{ik} M'_{kj}.
$$

Moreover,

$$
(\sum_{j \in J} M_j)_{k\ell} = \sum_{j \in J} (M_j)_{k\ell}
$$

for all families of matrices $M_j \in S^{I \times I}$, $j \in J$ and all $k, \ell \in I$. The sum in the definition of the product is meaningful since the sum of any $J$-indexed family of elements of $S$ exists. We let $0_I$ (or just $0$) and $E_I$, respectively, denote the zero matrix and the identity matrix in $S^{I \times I}$.

When $S$ is a continuous semiring, we may equip $S^{I \times I}$ with the pointwise order relation. The following result is well-known for finite matrices, but we could not locate it for infinite matrices.

**Proposition 2.1.** *If $S$ is a continuous semiring and $I$ is a set, then, equipped with the pointwise order relation, $S^{I \times I}$ is also a continuous semiring.*

**Proof.** Since the order relation on $S^{I \times I}$ is pointwise, the supremum of any nonempty directed set of matrices exists and is the pointwise supremum.

Since the ordering is pointwise and $+$ is also defined pointwise, it follows easily that the operation $+$ is continuous on matrices. We still need to show that the product operation is continuous.

Suppose that $\{M_j : j \in J\}$ is a nonempty directed set of matrices in $S^{I \times I}$ and $M' \in S^{I \times I}$. Then for all $k, \ell \in I$,

$$
\begin{aligned}
((\bigvee_{j \in J} M_j) M')_{k\ell} &= \sum_{t \in I} (\bigvee_{j \in J} M_j)_{kt} M'_{t\ell} \\
&= \sum_{t \in I} (\bigvee_{j \in J} (M_j)_{kt} M'_{t\ell}) \\
&= \bigvee_{j \in J} (\sum_{t \in I} (M_j)_{kt} M'_{t\ell}) \\
&= \bigvee_{j \in J} (M_j M')_{k\ell},
\end{aligned}
$$

where in the third equality we used Lemma 2.1. This proves that $(\bigvee_{j \in J} M_j) M' = \bigvee_{j \in J} M_j M'$. In the same way, $M'(\bigvee_{j \in J} M_j) = \bigvee_{j \in J} M' M_j$. $\square$

Suppose that $S$ is a continuous semiring. Then, as shown above, so is $S^{I \times I}$. Thus, $S^{I \times I}$ is a complete semiring in two ways. First, $S^{I \times I}$ is a complete semiring since $S$ is continuous and hence complete. Second, $S^{I \times I}$ is complete since it is continuous. However, the two complete semiring structures are identical, as the reader may easily verify.

### 2.5.  Categories of Formal Power Series over Complete Semirings

For basic notions from category theory we refer to [2]. We say that a semiring $S$ is *commutative* if $xy = yx$ for all $x, y \in S$.

Suppose that $S$ is a complete commutative semiring. We define a category whose objects are sets $X, Y, \ldots$ and a morphism $f : X \to Y$ is a family $(f_x)_{x \in X}$ of formal power series in $S\langle\langle Y^* \rangle\rangle$, or alternatively, a function $X \to S\langle\langle Y^* \rangle\rangle$. For convenience, we identify $S$ and $S\langle\langle \emptyset^* \rangle\rangle$, so that a morphism $X \to \emptyset$ is a function $X \to S$.

Composition is defined in the following way. Suppose that $f : X \to Y$ and $g : Y \to Z$. Then since $S$ is commutative, by Theorem 2.1 we may extend $g$ to a completely additive semiring morphism $g^\sharp : S\langle\langle Y^* \rangle\rangle \to S\langle\langle Z^* \rangle\rangle$ in a unique way. We define $f \circ g : X \to Z$ as the composition of the functions $f : X \to S\langle\langle Y^* \rangle\rangle$ and $g^\sharp : S\langle\langle Y^* \rangle\rangle \to S\langle\langle Z^* \rangle\rangle$. Note that composition corresponds to substitution and is completely additive in its first argument.

It is a routine matter to verify that composition is associative. Indeed, if $f : X \to Y$, $g : Y \to Z$ and $h : Z \to V$, then both $f \circ (g \circ h) : X \to V$ and $(f \circ g) \circ h : X \to V$ are equal to the composition of the functions $f$, $g^\sharp$ and $h^\sharp$. Moreover, for each set $X$, the embedding of $X$ into $S\langle\langle X^* \rangle\rangle$ serves as the identity morphism $\mathrm{id}_X : X \to X$.

Let $\mathbf{Ser}_S$ denote the category of series described above. For any pair of objects $X, Y$, let $X \oplus Y$ denote the disjoint union of $X$ and $Y$ with canonical embeddings $\iota_X : X \to X \oplus Y$ and $\iota_Y : Y \to X \oplus Y$. Note that both $\iota_X$ and $\iota_Y$ may be seen as morphisms, in fact coproduct injections in $\mathbf{Ser}_S$: given any $f : X \to Z$ and $g : Y \to Z$ in $\mathbf{Ser}_S$, there is a unique $h : X \oplus Y \to Z$ in $\mathbf{Ser}_S$ with $\iota_X \circ h = f$ and $\iota_Y \circ h = g$. Indeed, $h$ is defined by $h_x = f_x$ for all $x \in X$ and $h_y = f_y$ for all $y \in Y$. We let $\langle f, g \rangle$ denote $h$. More generally, when $f_i : X_i \to Y$ for all $i \in \{1, \ldots, n\}$, $n \geq 0$, there is a unique $h = \langle f_1, \ldots, f_n \rangle : \bigoplus_{i=1}^n X_i \to Y$ with $\iota_{X_j} \circ h = f_j$ for all $j = 1, \ldots, n$. (Here, the coproduct injection $\iota_j : X_j \to \bigoplus_{i=1}^n X_i$ is the natural embedding.) In particular, for each $Y$, the empty family of series in $S\langle\langle Y^* \rangle\rangle$ is the unique morphism $\emptyset \to Y$ (or $0 \to Y$). We denote it by $0_Y$. Thus, $\mathbf{Ser}_S$ is a *co-cartesian category*. It follows that for any $f : X \to X'$ and $g : Y \to Y'$ there is a unique $h : X \oplus Y \to X' \oplus Y'$ with

$$f \circ \iota_{X'} = \iota_X \circ h \quad \text{and} \quad g \circ \iota_{Y'} = \iota_Y \circ h.$$

We denote $h$ by $f \oplus g$. Indeed, $f \oplus g$ is the morphism with $(f \oplus g)_x = f_x$ for all $x \in X$ and $h_y = g_y$ for all $y \in Y$, where $f_x$ and $g_y$ are now considered as series in $S\langle\langle (X' \oplus Y')^* \rangle\rangle$.

For each $X$, let $0^X$ denote the morphism $X \to 0$ mapping each $x \in X$ to $0 \in S$. Given sets $X, Y$, we define $0_{X,Y} = 0^X \circ 0_Y$.

We now equip $\mathbf{Ser}_S$ with a *dagger* (or *fixed point*) *operation* [5]. Suppose that $f : X \to X \oplus Y$ in $\mathbf{Ser}_S$. We define $f^\dagger : X \to Y$. To this end, consider the system of fixed point equations

$$x = f_x, \quad x \in X. \tag{2.1}$$

For each $k \geq 1$ and $x \in X$, we define $x^{(k)} \in S\langle\!\langle Y^* \rangle\!\rangle$ by induction on $k$ as follows.

$$x^{(1)} = \sum_{u \in Y^*} \langle f_x, u \rangle u$$

$$x^{(k+1)} = \sum_{w = u_0 x_1 \cdots x_m u_m,\, m > 0,\, j_1 + \cdots + j_m = k} \langle f_x, w \rangle u_0 x_1^{(j_1)} \cdots x_m^{(j_m)} u_m$$

where $k \geq 1$, $u_0, \ldots, u_m \in Y^*$ and $x_1, \ldots, x_m \in X$. Finally, for all $x \in X$, let

$$x^{(\infty)} = \sum_{k \geq 1} x^{(k)}.$$

Moreover, we define $f^\dagger : X \to Y$ by $f_x^\dagger = x^{(\infty)}$ for all $x \in X$. Sometimes we write $f_x^{(k)}$ instead of $x^{(k)}$, and define $f^{(k)} : X \to Y$ as the morphism $(f_x^{(k)})_{x \in X}$ for all $k \geq 1$.

**Theorem 2.3.** *Suppose that $S$ is a complete commutative semiring. For each $f : X \to X \oplus Y$ in $\mathbf{Ser}_S$, $f^\dagger$ is a solution of the fixed point equation*

$$\xi = f \circ \langle f^\dagger, \mathrm{id}_Y \rangle, \tag{2.2}$$

*i.e., the fixed point identity holds:*

$$f^\dagger = f \circ \langle f^\dagger, \mathrm{id}_Y \rangle, \quad f : X \to X \oplus Y.$$

**Proof.** We use the notation introduced above. For each $x \in X$,

$(f \circ \langle f^\dagger, \mathrm{id}_Y \rangle)_x$

$$= \sum_{u \in Y^*} \langle f_x, u \rangle u + \sum_{w = u_0 x_1 \cdots x_m u_m, \; m > 0} \langle f_x, w \rangle u_0 x_1^{(\infty)} \cdots x_m^{(\infty)} u_m$$

$$= x^{(1)} + \sum_{w = u_0 x_1 \cdots x_m u_m, \; m > 0, \; j_1, \ldots, j_m \geq 1} \langle f_x, w \rangle u_0 x_1^{(j_1)} \cdots x_m^{(j_m)} u_m$$

$$= x^{(1)} + \sum_{k \geq 1} x^{(k+1)}$$

$$= x^{(\infty)}$$

$$= f_x^\dagger,$$

where $x_1, \ldots, x_m \in X$ and $u_0, \ldots, u_m \in Y^*$. $\qquad \square$

We call the system $(x^{(\infty)})_{x \in X}$ the *canonical solution* of (2.1), and $f^\dagger$ the canonical solution of (2.2), or the *canonical fixed point* of $f$.

For continuous commutative semirings, the canonical fixed point can be characterized as the least fixed point. Suppose that $S$ is a continuous commutative semiring with order relation $\leq$. Then, equipped with the pointwise order, also denoted $\leq$, each hom-set of $\mathbf{Ser}_S$ is a cpo and composition is continuous, cf. Proposition 2.1. It follows that for each $f : X \to X \oplus Y \in \mathbf{Ser}_S$, the function mapping each $g : X \to Y$ to $f \circ \langle g, \mathrm{id}_Y \rangle$ is also continuous so that it has a least fixed point. Below we show that the least fixed point agrees with the canonical fixed point.

**Theorem 2.4.** *Suppose that $S$ is a continuous commutative semiring. Then for each $f : X \to X \oplus Y$ in $\mathbf{Ser}_S$, $f^\dagger$ is the least solution of (2.2).*

**Proof.** Consider the system of equations (2.1). Suppose that $g = (g_x)_{x \in X} : X \to Y$ is a solution. Our aim is to prove that for each $x \in X$, $x^{(\infty)} \leq g_x$.

We prove by induction on $k$ that $\sum_{j=1}^{k} x^{(j)} \leq g_x$ for all $i$. When $k = 1$ this is clear:

$$x^{(1)} = \sum_{u \in Y^*} \langle f_x, u \rangle u$$

$$\leq \sum_{u \in Y^*} \langle f_x, u \rangle u + \sum_{w = u_0 x_1 \cdots x_m u_m, \; m > 0, \; j_1, \ldots, j_m \geq 1} \langle f_x, w \rangle u_0 g_{x_1} \cdots g_{x_m} u_m$$

$$= (f \circ \langle g, \mathrm{id}_Y \rangle)_x$$

$$= g_x,$$

where $x_1, \ldots, x_m \in X$ and $u_0, \ldots, u_m \in Y^*$. Now suppose that $k \geq 1$ and our claim holds for all integers less than or equal to $k$. Then, using the notation introduced above, by the induction hypothesis we have

$$\sum_{j=1}^{k+1} x^{(j)}$$

$$= \sum_{u \in \Sigma^*} \langle f_x, u \rangle u$$

$$+ \sum_{j=1}^{k} \sum_{w = u_0 x_1 \cdots x_m u_m,\ m>0,\ j_1 + \cdots + j_m = j} \langle f_x, w \rangle u_0 x_1^{(j_1)} \cdots x_m^{(j_m)} u_m$$

$$\leq \sum_{u \in \Sigma^*} \langle f_x, u \rangle u$$

$$+ \sum_{w = u_0 x_1 \cdots x_m u_m,\ m>0,\ 1 \leq j_1, \ldots, j_m \leq k} \langle f_x, w \rangle u_0 x_1^{(j_1)} \cdots x_m^{(j_m)} u_m$$

$$= \sum_{u \in \Sigma^*} \langle f_x, u \rangle u$$

$$+ \sum_{w = u_0 x_1 \cdots x_m u_m,\ m>0} \langle f_x, w \rangle u_0 \Big( \sum_{j_1=1}^{k} x_1^{(j_1)} \Big) \cdots \Big( \sum_{j_m=1}^{k} x_m^{(j_m)} \Big) u_m$$

$$\leq \sum_{u \in \Sigma^*} \langle f_x, u \rangle u + \sum_{w = u_0 x_1 \cdots x_m u_m,\ m>0} \langle f_x, w \rangle u_0 g_{x_1} \cdots g_{x_m} u_m$$

$$= g_x,$$

for all $x \in X$. Thus,

$$x^{(\infty)} = \sum_{k \geq 1} x^{(k)}$$

$$= \bigvee_{k \geq 1} \sum_{j=1}^{k} x^{(j)}$$

$$\leq g_x$$

for all $x \in X$, proving that $f_x^\dagger = x^{(\infty)} \leq g_x$. $\qquad\square$

### 2.5.1. Generalized Context-Free Grammars

Let $S$ be a complete commutative semiring and let us consider the system of fixed point equations (2.1) again. We may view (2.1) as a generalized *(weighted) context-free grammar* $G = G_f$ whose set of variables is $X$ and set of terminal letters is $Y$. The rules of the grammar are of the form

$$x \rightarrow \langle f_x, w \rangle w, \quad \langle f_x, w \rangle \neq 0.$$

We call $\langle f_x, w \rangle$ the weight of the rule.

Consider an ordinary derivation tree $T$ of this grammar with root labeled $x$ all of whose leaves are labeled in $Y \cup \{\epsilon\}$. Let $u$ denote the frontier of $T$, i.e., the word in $Y^*$ formed by the labels of the leaves of $T$. We can associate a weight $s \in S$ with each vertex of the tree so that each leaf carries the weight 1 and such that if $s_1, \ldots, s_n$ is the (left–to–right) sequence of the weights of the immediate successors of a vertex then the weight of that vertex is $ss_1 \cdots s_n$, where $s$ is the weight of the corresponding rule. The weight of the root is called the weight of $T$. We define $\mathsf{yd}(T) = su$, where $s$ is the weight of $T$, and call it the *monomial determined by $T$*.

**Theorem 2.5.** *Under the above assumptions, for each $x \in X$, $x^{(\infty)}$ is the sum of all monomials determined by the derivation trees rooted $x$:*

$$x^{(\infty)} = \sum (\mathsf{yd}(T) : T \text{ is a derivation tree rooted at } x).$$

**Proof.** Let $x \in X$ and consider a derivation tree $T$ rooted $x$. Define the *rank* of $T$ as the number of vertices of $T$ labeled by a variable. It is a routine matter to show by induction on $k \geq 1$ that $x^{(k)}$ is the sum of all $\mathsf{yd}(T)$, where $T$ ranges over the set of derivation trees of rank $k$ rooted $x$. $\qquad\square$

Conversely, we may define weighted context-free grammars $G$ over $S$ and a set $X$ of variables and a set $Y$ of terminals, and assign a system of fixed point equations to $G$.

When $G$ is a grammar whose set of variables is $X$, then for each $x \in X$, let $(G, x)$ denote the grammar $G$ with initial variable $x$. The *series generated by* $(G, x)$ is the $x$-component of the canonical solution of the corresponding system of equations, or equivalently, the sum of the yields of all derivation trees rooted $x$. We say that $(G, x)$ is *equivalent* to $(G', x')$ if $(G, x)$ and $(G', x')$ generate the same series. Moreover, when $G$ and $G'$ have the same terminals and $X$ is included in the intersection of the sets of variables of the two grammars, then we say that $G$ and $G'$ are equivalent with respect to $X$ if $(G, x)$ is equivalent to $(G', x)$ for each $x \in X$. In particular, when $X$ is the common set of variables of $G$ and $G'$, we simply say that $G$ and $G'$ are equivalent.

**Remark 2.1.** The above grammar associated with $f : X \to X \oplus Y$ has the special property that for each $x \in X$ and $w \in (X \cup Y)^*$, there is at most one rule whose left side is $x$ and whose right side involves $w$. We may easily generalize the notion of grammar to allow several, even an infinite number of such rules. Given such a generalized grammar $G$, one can construct an equivalent ordinary grammar by replacing for each $x \in X$ and $w \in (X \cup Y)^*$, the set of rules of the sort $x \to s_i w$, where $i$ ranges over some index set $I$, by the single rule $x \to sw$, where $s = \sum_{j \in I} s_i$.

**Remark 2.2.** Let $\Sigma$ denote a fixed set. All results of this section carry over to categories of series with functions $X \to S \langle\!\langle (Y \cup \Sigma)^* \rangle\!\rangle$ as morphisms $X \to Y$, where $S$ is a complete or continuous commutative semiring.

## 2.6. Equational Properties of Dagger

*Iteration categories* [5] are cartesian categories equipped with a dagger operation satisfying certain equational axioms. It has been shown that the axioms of iteration categories are sound and complete for the equational theory of all major point operations used in computer science including the (parametrized) fixed point operation over monotonic or continuous functions of complete lattices or cpo's. In this section our aim is to show that when $S$ is a complete semiring, then $\mathbf{Ser}_S$, equipped with the canonical fixed point operation, is an iteration category.

In this section, we assume that $S$ is a complete commutative semiring.

**Lemma 2.2.** *The parameter identity holds in* $\mathbf{Ser}_S$. *Suppose that* $f : X \to X \oplus Y$ *and* $g : Y \to Z$ *in* $\mathbf{Ser}_S$. *Then*

$$(f \circ (\mathrm{id}_X \oplus g))^\dagger = f^\dagger \circ g. \tag{2.3}$$

**Proof.** Let $h = f \circ (\mathrm{id}_X \oplus g)$. We prove by induction on $k$ that $f_x^{(k)} \circ g = h_x^{(k)}$ for all $x \in X$. (Note that $f_x^{(k)}$ can be seen as a morphism $\{x\} \to Y$, so that $f_x^{(k)} \circ g = g^\sharp(f_x^{(k)})$ is defined.)

First we consider the case $k = 1$.

$$
\begin{aligned}
f_x^{(1)} \circ g &= f_x \circ \langle 0_{X,Y}, \mathrm{id}_Y \rangle \circ g \\
&= f_x \circ \langle 0_{X,Z}, g \rangle \\
&= f_x \circ (\mathrm{id}_X \oplus g) \circ \langle 0_{X,Z}, \mathrm{id}_Z \rangle \\
&= h_x^{(1)}.
\end{aligned}
$$

Suppose that $k > 1$ and we have proved the claim for all $1 \leq j < k$. Then

$$f_x^{(k)} \circ g$$

$$= \Big( \sum_{w=u_0 x_1 \cdots x_m u_m, \ m>0, \ j_1+\cdots+j_m=k-1} \langle f_x, w \rangle u_0 f_{x_1}^{(j_1)} \cdots f_{x_m}^{(j_m)} u_m \Big) \circ g$$

$$= \sum_{w=u_0 x_1 \cdots x_m u_m, \ m>0, \ j_1+\cdots+j_m=k-1} \langle f_x, w \rangle u_0' (f_{x_1}^{(j_1)} \circ g) \cdots (f_{x_m}^{(j_m)} \circ g) u_m'$$

$$= \sum_{w=u_0 x_1 \cdots x_m u_m, \ m>0, \ j_1+\cdots+j_m=k-1} \langle f_x, w \rangle u_0' h_{x_1}^{(j_1)} \cdots h_{x_m}^{(j_m)} u_m'$$

$$= \sum_{w'=v_0 x_1 \cdots x_m v_m, \ m>0, \ j_1+\cdots+j_m=k-1} \langle h_x, w' \rangle v_0 h_{x_1}^{(j_1)} \cdots h_{x_m}^{(j_m)} v_m$$

$$= h_x^{(k)},$$

where $u_i \in Y^*$, $v_i \in Z^*$ and $u_i' = u_i \circ g = g^\sharp(u_i)$, $i = 0, \ldots, m$, moreover, $x_1, \ldots, x_m \in X$. We conclude that

$$f_x^\dagger \circ g = \Big( \sum_{k \geq 1} f_x^{(k)} \Big) \circ g$$

$$= \sum_{k \geq 1} f_x^{(k)} \circ g$$

$$= \sum_{k \geq 1} h_x^{(k)}$$

$$= h_x^\dagger.$$

Since this holds for all $x$, the proof is complete. $\qquad\square$

**Lemma 2.3.** *The* double dagger identity *holds in* $\mathbf{Ser}_S$:

$$f^{\dagger\dagger} = (f \circ (\langle \mathrm{id}_X, \mathrm{id}_X \rangle \oplus \mathrm{id}_Z))^\dagger$$

*for all* $f : X \to X \oplus X \oplus Z$.

**Proof.** Let $X' = \{x' : x \in X\}$ be a disjoint copy of $X$. Given $f : X \to X \oplus X \oplus Z$, we represent the set $X \oplus X$ as $X \cup X'$. Thus $f_x \in S \langle\!\langle (X \cup X' \cup Z)^* \rangle\!\rangle$ for all $x \in X$. Also $\langle f, f \rangle : X \oplus X \to X \oplus X \oplus Y$, so that $f_x = \langle f, f \rangle_x = \langle f, f \rangle_{x'}$ for all $x \in X$.

Define $h = f \circ (\langle \mathrm{id}_X, \mathrm{id}_X \rangle \oplus \mathrm{id}_Z) : X \to X \oplus Z$. Thus $\langle h_x, u \rangle = \langle f_x, u \rangle$ for all $x \in X$ and $u \in Z^*$, and

$$\langle h_x, u_0 x_1 \cdots x_m u_m \rangle = \sum_{y_i \in \{x_i, x_i'\}} \langle f_x, u_0 y_1 \cdots y_m u_m \rangle$$

for all $x \in X$, $x_1, \ldots, x_m \in X$, $u_0, \ldots, u_m \in Z^*$, $m > 0$.

First we show that

$$\langle f, f \rangle^\dagger = \langle h^\dagger, h^\dagger \rangle,$$

i.e.,

$$\langle f, f \rangle^\dagger_x = h^\dagger_x = \langle f, f \rangle^\dagger_{x'}$$

for all $x \in X$. We prove by induction on $k$ that

$$\langle f, f \rangle^{(k)}_x = h^{(k)}_x = \langle f, f \rangle^{(k)}_{x'}$$

for all $x \in X$ and $k \geq 1$. First consider the case $k = 1$. Then

$$\langle f, f \rangle^{(1)}_x = f^{(1)}_x$$
$$= \sum_{u \in Z^*} \langle f_x, u \rangle u$$
$$= \sum_{u \in Z^*} \langle h_x, u \rangle u$$
$$= h^{(1)}_x.$$

In a similar way, $\langle f, f \rangle^{(1)}_{x'} = h^{(1)}_x$. Now suppose that $k > 1$ and our claim holds for all $1 \leq j < k$. Then

$$\langle f, f \rangle^{(k)}_x$$

$$= \sum_{w = u_0 y_1 \cdots y_m u_m, u_i \in Z^*, y_j \in X \cup X', \sum_{j=1}^m j_i = k-1} \langle f_x, w \rangle u_0 \langle f, f \rangle^{(j_1)}_{y_1} \cdots \langle f, f \rangle^{(j_m)}_{y_m} u_m$$

$$= \sum_{w = u_0 x_1 \cdots x_m u_m, u_i \in Z^*, x_j \in X, \sum_{i=1}^m j_i = k-1}$$
$$\sum_{y_j \in \{x_j, x_j'\} w' = u_0 y_1 \cdots y_m u_m} \langle f_x, w' \rangle u_0 \langle f, f \rangle^{(j_1)}_{y_1} \cdots \langle f, f \rangle^{(j_m)}_{y_m} u_m$$

$$= \sum_{w = u_0 x_1 \cdots x_m u_m, u_i \in Z^*, x_j \in X, \sum_{i=1}^m j_i = k-1} \langle h_x, w \rangle u_0 h^{(j_1)}_{x_1} \cdots h^{(j_m)}_{x_m} u_m$$

$$= h^{(k)}_x.$$

The same argument proves that $\langle f, f \rangle^{(k)}_{x'} = h^{(k)}_x$ for all $x \in X$ and $k \geq 1$.

Since $\langle f, f \rangle^\dagger = \langle h^\dagger, h^\dagger \rangle$, the grammar $G_{\langle f, f \rangle}$ associated with $\langle f, f \rangle$ is equivalent to the grammar $G_h$ associated with $h$ with respect to $X$. Note that $G_{\langle f, f \rangle}$ can be constructed from $G_f$ by adding the rule $x' \to p$ for each rule $x \to p$ of $G_f$, and $G_h$ can be constructed by replacing each occurrence of a variable $x'$ on the right hand side of a rule of $G_f$ by $x$. (Also see Remark 2.1). The equivalence of $(G_{\langle f, f \rangle}, x)$ and $(G_h, x)$ for each $x \in X$ can also be seen by noting that for every derivation tree $T$ of $G_h$ rooted $x$ there is a unique corresponding derivation tree $T'$ of $G_{\langle f, f \rangle}$ rooted $x$ and a unique derivation tree $T''$ of $G_{\langle f,f \rangle}$ rooted $x'$ such that $T$ can be obtained from both $T'$ and $T''$ by replacing each node labeled $y'$ for some $y \in X$ by $y$. This correspondence creates a bijection between the derivation trees of $G_h$ rooted $x$ and the derivation trees of $G_{\langle f,f \rangle}$ rooted $x$ on the one hand, and the derivation trees of $G_{\langle f,f \rangle}$ rooted $x'$ on the other hand.

To complete the proof, it suffices to show that $(G_{f^\dagger}, x')$ and $(G_{\langle f,f \rangle}, x')$ are equivalent for each selection of a start symbol $x' \in X'$. (Here, we consider $f^\dagger$ as morphism $X' \to X' \oplus Z$.)

Consider a rule $y' \to su$ of $G_{f^\dagger}$, where $y \in X$, $s \in S$ and $u \in (X' \cup Z)^*$. (The set of variables of $G_{f^\dagger}$ is the disjoint copy $X'$ of $X$.) Then $s$ is the sum of all $s_i$ such that $s_i u$ is the monomial of a derivation tree $T_i$ of $G_f$ rooted $y$. By replacing the root label $y$ with $y'$, each $T_i$ becomes a derivation tree $T'_i$ of $G_{\langle f,f \rangle}$ rooted $y'$. Consider now a derivation tree of $G_{f^\dagger}$ rooted $x'$ whose frontier is a word in $Z^*$. By the above remark, for each branch corresponding to a rule $y' \to su$ ($s \in S$, $u \in (X' \cup Z)^*$) it holds that $s$ is the sum of all $s_i$ such that $s_i u$ is the monomial of a derivation tree $T'_i$ of $G_{\langle f,f \rangle}$ rooted $y'$ constructed above. Moreover, by replacing each branch of each derivation tree of $G_{f^\dagger}$ rooted in $x'$ by the corresponding derivation trees $T'_i$ in all possible ways, we obtain exactly the derivation trees of $G_{\langle f,f \rangle}$ rooted $x'$ with frontier in $Z^*$. Hence, $(G_{f^\dagger}, x')$ and $(G_{\langle f,f \rangle}, x')$ are equivalent for each selection of a start symbol $x' \in X'$. $\qquad \square$

**Lemma 2.4.** *The composition identity holds in* $\mathbf{Ser}_S$:

$$(f \circ \langle g, 0_X \oplus \mathsf{id}_Z \rangle)^\dagger = f \circ \langle (g \circ \langle f, 0_Y \oplus \mathsf{id}_Z \rangle)^\dagger, \mathsf{id}_Z \rangle$$

*for all* $f : X \to Y \oplus Z$ *and* $g : Y \to X \oplus Z$.

**Proof.** Let $G$ denote the grammar with variables $X \cup Y$, terminal alphabet $Z$ and rules

$$x \to \langle f_x, u \rangle u \quad \text{and} \quad y \to \langle g_y, v \rangle v$$

for all $u \in (Y \cup Z)^*$ and $v \in (X \cup Z)^*$ such that $\langle f_x, u \rangle \neq 0$ and $\langle g_y, v \rangle \neq 0$. It is not difficult to prove that $G$ is equivalent to $G_{f \circ \langle g, 0_X \oplus \mathsf{id}_Z \rangle}$ with respect to $X$ and $G$ is equivalent to $G_{g \circ \langle f, 0_Y \oplus \mathsf{id}_Z \rangle}$ with respect to $Y$. Indeed, consider a derivation tree $T$ of $G_{f \circ \langle g, 0_X \oplus \mathsf{id}_Z \rangle}$ rooted $x \in X$. For each vertex of $T$ labeled by a variable such that the label sequence of its successors is a word $w$, replace the branch rooted at this vertex, in all possible ways, by derivation trees of $G$ with the same root label of depth at most 2 whose frontier is $w$. The derivation trees of $G$ so obtained have the same frontier as $T$ and the sum of the weights of all these trees is equal to the weight of $T$. Since all derivation trees of $G$ rooted $x$ can be obtained from some derivation tree of $G_{f \circ \langle g, 0_X \oplus \mathrm{id}_Z \rangle}$ rooted $x$, it follows that $(G_{f \circ \langle g, 0_X \oplus \mathrm{id}_Z \rangle}, x)$ is equivalent to $(G, x)$. Similarly, for each $y \in Y$, $(G_{g \circ \langle f, 0_Y \oplus \mathrm{id}_Z \rangle}, y)$ is equivalent to $(G, y)$. In particular, for each $x \in X$, the series generated by $(G, x)$ is $(f \circ \langle g, 0_X \oplus \mathrm{id}_Z \rangle)^\dagger_x$ and for each $y \in Y$, the series generated by $(G_{g \circ \langle f, 0_Y \oplus \mathrm{id}_Z \rangle}, y)$ is $(g \circ \langle f, 0_Y \oplus \mathrm{id}_Z \rangle)^\dagger_y$.

Now let $X' = \{ x' : x \in X \}$ be a disjoint copy of $X$ and consider the grammar $G'$ whose set of variables is $X' \cup X \cup Y$ and whose terminal alphabet is $Z$. The rules are those of $G$ together with a rule $x' \to p$ for each rule $x \to p$ of $G$. For each $x \in X$, the derivation trees of $G'$ rooted $x'$ can be constructed as follows. First consider a rule $x' \to su = su_0 y_1 \cdots y_m u_m$ of $G'$ with $s \in S$, $u_0, \ldots, u_m \in Z^*$ and $y_1, \ldots, y_m \in Y$ and consider the corresponding depth 1 tree with root labeled $x'$ whose monomial is $su$. Then replace each leaf labeled $y_i$ by a derivation tree of $G$ rooted $y_i$. Since the trees so obtained are exactly the derivation trees of $G'$ rooted $x'$, it follows that for each $x \in X$, the series generated by $(G', x')$ is $(f \circ \langle (g \circ \langle f, 0_Y \oplus \mathrm{id}_Z \rangle)^\dagger, \mathrm{id}_Z \rangle)_x$.

Consider a derivation tree of $G'$ rooted $x'$. Then by replacing the root label by $x$, we obtain a derivation tree of $G$ rooted $x$. And in fact this correspondence between the derivation trees of $G'$ rooted $x'$ and the derivation trees of $G$ rooted $x$ is bijective, so that for each $x \in X$, $(G', x')$ is equivalent to $(G, x)$. It follows now that

$$((f \circ \langle g, 0_X \oplus \mathrm{id}_Z \rangle)^\dagger)_x = (f \circ \langle (g \circ \langle f, 0_Y \oplus \mathrm{id}_Z \rangle)^\dagger, \mathrm{id}_Z \rangle)_x$$

for all $x \in X$. □

**Lemma 2.5.** *Suppose that $f : X \to X \oplus Z$ and $g : Y \to Y \oplus Z$, and suppose that $\rho : X \to Y$ is a function viewed as a morphism. If $f \circ (\rho \oplus \mathrm{id}_Z) = \rho \circ g$, then $f^\dagger = \rho \circ g^\dagger$.*

**Proof.** Note that the assumption is that $f_x \circ (\rho \oplus \mathrm{id}_Z) = g_{x\rho}$ for all $x \in X$. Hence, $\langle f_x, u \rangle = \langle g_{x\rho}, u \rangle$ for all $x \in X$ and $u \in Z^*$. Moreover,

$$\langle g_{x\rho}, u_0 y_1 \cdots y_m u_m \rangle = \sum_{x_i \rho = y_i} \langle f_x, u_0 x_1 \cdots x_m u_m \rangle$$

for all $x \in X$, $y_1, \ldots, y_m \in Y$, $u_0, \ldots, u_m \in Z^*$, where $m > 0$.

One proves by induction on $k$ that $f_x^{(k)} = g_{x\rho}^{(k)}$, for all $x \in X$ and $k \geq 1$.

Let $k = 1$. Then

$$
\begin{aligned}
f_x^{(1)} &= f_x \circ \langle 0_{X,Z}, \mathrm{id}_Z \rangle \\
&= f_x \circ (\rho \oplus \mathrm{id}_Z) \circ \langle 0_{Y,Z}, \mathrm{id}_Z \rangle \\
&= g_{x\rho} \circ \langle 0_{Y,Z}, \mathrm{id}_Z \rangle \\
&= g_{x\rho}^{(1)}.
\end{aligned}
$$

Now suppose that $k \geq 1$ and our claim holds for all integers $1 \leq j \leq k$. Let $x \in X$ be arbitrary. Then, using the induction hypothesis,

$f_x^{(k+1)}$

$$
\begin{aligned}
&= \sum_{w = u_0 x_1 \cdots x_m u_m, \ m > 0, \ j_1 + \cdots + j_m = k} \langle f_x, w \rangle u_0 f_{x_1}^{(j_1)} \cdots f_{x_m}^{(j_m)} u_m \\
&= \sum_{w = u_0 x_1 \cdots x_m u_m, \ m > 0, \ j_1 + \cdots + j_m = k} \langle f_x, w \rangle u_0 g_{x_1\rho}^{(j_1)} \cdots g_{x_m\rho}^{(j_m)} u_m \\
&= \sum_{w = u_0 y_1 \cdots y_m u_m, \ m > 0, \ j_1 + \cdots + j_m = k} \langle g_{x\rho}, w \rangle u_0 g_{y_1}^{(j_1)} \cdots g_{y_m}^{(j_m)} u_m \\
&= g_{x\rho}^{(k+1)}.
\end{aligned}
$$

$\square$

In the terminology of [5], Lemma 2.5 asserts that the *weak functoriality axiom* holds in $\mathbf{Ser}_S$.

In [5, 9, 10], an *iteration category* has been axiomatized by the parameter, double dagger and composition identities, together with an identity associated with each finite group, or the commutative identities. In the category $\mathbf{Ser}_S$, where $S$ is a complete semiring, the group identities can be formulated as follows.

Suppose that $G$ is a finite group of order $n$. Without loss of generality we may assume that the elements of $G$ are the integers $\{1, \ldots, n\}$. Let $X, Y$ be any sets and $f : X \to X\mathbf{n} \oplus Y$, where $X\mathbf{n}$ denotes the $n$-fold coproduct $X \oplus \cdots \oplus X$. Below we will represent the elements of $X\mathbf{n}$ as ordered pairs $(x, i)$ with $i \in \{1, \ldots, n\}$, as usual.

Before formulating the identity associated with $G$, we explain its meaning informally. For each $x \in X$ and $i \in \{1, \ldots, n\}$, let $g_{x,i} \in S\langle\!\langle (X\mathbf{n} \oplus Y)^* \rangle\!\rangle$ denote the series obtained from $f_x$ by substituting $(y, i \cdot j)$ for each $(y, j)$, where $y \in X$, $j \in \{1, \ldots, n\}$ and $i \cdot j$ denotes the product of $i$ and $j$ in the group $G$. Also, let $h_x$ denote the series in $S\langle\!\langle (X \oplus Y)^* \rangle\!\rangle$ obtained from $f_x$ by substituting $y$ for each $(y, j)$ with $y \in X$ and $j \in \{1, \ldots, n\}$. Then consider the system of fixed point equations

$$
(x, i) = g_{x,i}, \quad x \in X, \ i \in \{1, \ldots, n\}. \tag{2.4}
$$

Moreover, consider the system of equations

$$x = h_x, \quad x \in X. \tag{2.5}$$

The group identity associated with $G$ asserts that for each $x$ and $i$, the $(x, i)$-component of the canonical solution of (2.4) is equal to the $x$-component of the canonical solution of (2.5). Formally, for each $i = 1, \ldots, n$, define

$$\rho_i^X : \mathbf{Xn} \to \mathbf{Xn}$$

to be the morphism in $\mathbf{Ser}_S$ corresponding to the function mapping $(x, j)$ to $(x, i \cdot j)$, for all $x \in X$ and $j \in \{1, \ldots, n\}$. Then, given $f : X \to \mathbf{Xn} \oplus Y$, let $g = \langle g_1, \ldots, g_n \rangle : \mathbf{Xn} \to \mathbf{Xn} \oplus Y$ where

$$g_i = f \circ (\rho_i^X \oplus \mathsf{id}_Y)$$

for all $i \in \{1, \ldots, n\}$. Moreover, let $h = f \circ (\tau_n^X \oplus \mathsf{id}_Y) : X \to X \oplus Y$, where $\tau_n^X = \langle \mathsf{id}_X, \ldots, \mathsf{id}_X \rangle$. Then the group identity associated with $G$ asserts that

$$g^\dagger = \tau_n^X \circ h^\dagger,$$

i.e., $g^\dagger$ is the tupling $\langle h^\dagger, \ldots, h^\dagger \rangle$ of $n$ copies of $h^\dagger$.

**Lemma 2.6.** *All group identities hold in* $\mathbf{Ser}_S$.

**Proof.** Consider the group identity associated with the above group $G$ of order $n$. Then we have $g \circ (\tau_n^X \otimes \mathsf{id}_Y) = \tau_n^X \circ h$, since $f \circ (\rho_i^X \oplus \mathsf{id}_Y) \circ (\tau_n^X \oplus \mathsf{id}_Y) = f \circ ((\rho_i^X \circ \tau_n^X) \oplus \mathsf{id}_Y) = f \circ (\tau_n^X \oplus \mathsf{id}_Y)$ for all $i$. It follows now from Lemma 2.5 that $g^\dagger = \tau_n^X \circ h^\dagger$. $\qquad\square$

We now summarize the above results.

**Theorem 2.6.** *Suppose that $S$ is a complete semiring. Then $\mathbf{Ser}_S$ is an iteration category satisfying the weak functoriality axiom.*

**Proof.** By the previous sequence of lemmas, the parameter, double dagger, composition and group identities all hold in $\mathbf{Ser}_S$, as does the weak functoriality axiom. $\qquad\square$

Thus, all identities of iteration categories hold in $\mathbf{Ser}_S$. This includes the *pairing identity*, found independently by Bekić [3] and De Bakker and Scott [1].

Suppose that $f : X \to X \oplus Y \oplus Z$ and $g : Y \to X \oplus Y \oplus Z$, so that $\langle f, g \rangle : X \oplus Y \to X \oplus Y \oplus Z$. Then the pairing identity asserts that

$$\langle f, g \rangle^\dagger = \langle f^\dagger \circ \langle h^\dagger, \mathrm{id}_Z \rangle, h^\dagger \rangle,$$

where

$$h = g \circ \langle f^\dagger, \mathrm{id}_{Y \oplus Z} \rangle : Y \to Y \oplus Z.$$

**Remark 2.3.** When $S$ is a nontrivial complete semiring, $\mathbf{Ser}_S$ is also non-trivial. It follows from a result proved in [18] that an identity involving the cartesian category operations (and constants) and dagger holds in $\mathbf{Ser}_S$ iff it holds in all iteration categories. A direct proof of this fact is also possible using the representation of free iteration categories by regular trees [5].

### 2.7. Embedding Matrix Categories in Power Series Categories

In this section, we assign the *category* $\mathbf{Mat}_S$ *of matrices over $S$* to any complete semiring $S$ and equip it with a dagger operation. We then show that $\mathbf{Mat}_S$ can be embedded into $\mathbf{Ser}_S$, at least when $S$ is commutative.

Suppose that $S$ is a complete semiring. We define the following category $\mathbf{Mat}_S$. The objects are sets $I, J, \ldots$ and a morphism $I \to J$ is an $I \times J$ matrix over $S$. The composition of matrices $M : I \to J$ and $M' : J \to K$ is defined by matrix product, so that

$$(M \circ M')_{ik} = \sum_{j \in J} M_{ij} M'_{jk},$$

for all $i \in I$ and $k \in K$. For any set $I$, the identity morphism $I \to I$ is the identity matrix $E_I$.

$\mathbf{Mat}_S$ is a co-cartesian category. Indeed, for any sets $I$ and $J$, let $I \oplus J$ denote the disjoint union of $I$ and $J$ and let $\iota_I : I \to I \oplus J$ and $\iota_J : J \to I \oplus J$ be the natural embeddings. Then, considered as 0-1 matrices, $\iota_I$ and $\iota_J$ are coproduct injections. Note that for any $M : I \to K$ and $M' : J \to K$, the matrix $\langle M, M' \rangle : I \oplus J \to K$ is $\begin{pmatrix} M \\ M' \end{pmatrix}$. Moreover, the empty set $\emptyset$, also denoted $0$, is initial in $\mathbf{Mat}_S$. When $M : I \to J$ and $M' : I' \to J'$, then $M \oplus M' : I \oplus J \to I' \oplus J'$ is the block diagonal matrix $\begin{pmatrix} M & 0 \\ 0 & M' \end{pmatrix}$.

Each hom-set of $\mathbf{Mat}_S$ possesses an additive structure defined by

$$(M + M')_{ij} = M_{ij} + M'_{ij}, \quad i \in I, \ j \in J,$$

for all $M, M' : I \to J$, or more generally,

$$(\sum_{k \in K} M_k)_{ij} = \sum_{k \in K} (M_k)_{ij}, \quad i \in I, \ j \in J,$$

for all $M_k : I \to J$, $k \in K$. It is clear that each hom-set of morphisms $I \to J$ is a complete monoid, and composition distributes over all sums on either side:

$$M \circ (\sum_{k \in K} M_k) = \sum_{k \in K} M \circ M_k$$

$$(\sum_{k \in K} M_k) \circ M' = \sum_{k \in K} M_k \circ M',$$

for all $M_k : I \to J$, $k \in K$, and $M : I' \to I$ and $M' : J \to J'$. In particular, the zero matrices $0_{I,J} : I \to J$ satisfy the expected identities: $0_{I,J} \circ M = 0_{I,K}$ for all $M : J \to K$ and $M \circ 0_{I,J} = 0_{K,J}$ for all $M : K \to I$.

In what follows, we denote the composition of two matrices $M : I \to J$ and $M' : J \to K$ by just $MM'$.

If $S$ is any complete semiring, we define a *star operation* on $S$ by $x^* = \sum_{n \geq 0} x^n$, for all $x \in S$. Since for each set $I$, $S^{I \times I}$ is also a complete semiring, we also obtain a star operation on $S^{I \times I}$. Thus, $\mathbf{Mat}_S$ is equipped with a star operation mapping a morphism $I \to I$ to a morphism $I \to I$. Given the star operation on $\mathbf{Mat}_S$, we define a dagger operation. To this end, let $M : I \to I \oplus J$ in $\mathbf{Mat}_S$, say $M = (A\ B)$, where $A$ is an $I \times I$ matrix and $B$ is an $I \times J$ matrix. We define

$$M^\dagger = A^* B : I \to J.$$

We show that when $S$ is commutative, $\mathbf{Mat}_S$ can be embedded into $\mathbf{Ser}_S$ such that the embedding preserves the co-cartesian structure and dagger. Let $X, Y$ be sets. Then to each matrix $M : X \to Y$ in $\mathbf{Mat}_S$, we assign the morphism $\psi(M) : X \to Y$ in $\mathbf{Ser}_S$ such that $\psi(M)_x = \sum_{y \in Y} M_{xy} y$.

It is a routine matter to verify:

**Proposition 2.2.** *Let $S$ be a complete commutative semiring. The assignment $M : X \to Y \mapsto \psi(M) : X \to Y$ defines an embedding of $\mathbf{Mat}_S$ into $\mathbf{Ser}_S$ which preserves coproduct, the sum operation, and dagger.*

**Proof.** We only prove that dagger is preserved. To this end, let $M = (A\ B) : X \to X \oplus Y$ in $\mathbf{Mat}_S$ as above and let $f = \psi(M)$. It is easy to show by induction that $\psi(A^k B) = f^{(k+1)}$ for all $k \geq 0$. Hence, $\psi(M^\dagger) = \psi(A^* B) = \psi(\sum_{k \geq 0} A^k B) = \sum_{k \geq 0} \psi(A^k B) = \sum_{k \geq 1} f^{(k)} = f^\dagger$. $\qquad \square$

It was shown in [5] that the equational properties of the dagger operation are reflected by corresponding properties of the star operation and vice versa. For example, the fixed point identity corresponds to the identity

$$M^* = MM^* + E_I, \quad M : I \to I,$$

while the double dagger and composition identities correspond to

$$(A + B)^* = (A^*B)^*A^*, \quad A, B : I \to I$$
$$(AB)^* = E_I + A(BA)^*B, \quad A : I \to J, B : J \to I.$$

Moreover, the pairing identity corresponds to

$$\begin{pmatrix} A & B \\ C & D \end{pmatrix}^* = \begin{pmatrix} (A + BD^*C)^* & (A + BD^*C)^*BD^* \\ (D + CA^*B)^*CA^* & (D + CA^*B)^* \end{pmatrix}$$

where $A : I \to I, B : I \to J, C : J \to I, D : J \to J$. Hence, these identities hold in $\mathbf{Mat}_S$; also see [5, 15].

**Remark 2.4.** Suppose that $S$ is a complete commutative semiring. Then one can extend the star operation on $\mathbf{Mat}_S$ to the whole of $\mathbf{Ser}_S$. Indeed, let $f : X \to X$ in $\mathbf{Ser}_S$. Represent $X \oplus X$ as the disjoint union $X \cup X'$ with the embeddings $\iota_X : X \to X \cup X'$ and $\iota_{X'} : X \to X \cup X'$ as coproduct injections $X \to X \oplus X$. (Note that we consider $\iota_{X'}$ as a morphism with source $X$.) Define $\widehat{f} = (f \circ \iota_X) + \iota_{X'}$. Finally let $f^* = (\widehat{f})^\dagger : X \to X$. This operation also satisfies the above identities.

## 2.8. Algebraic Series

Suppose that $S$ is a complete commutative semiring. In this section we consider the subcategory $\mathbf{Ser}_S^f$ of $\mathbf{Ser}_S$ spanned by the finite sets as objects. Note that $\mathbf{Ser}_S^f$ has finite coproducts and is closed under dagger and hence also by star. Thus $\mathbf{Ser}_S^f$ is an iteration category.

Call a morphism $f : X \to Y$ in $\mathbf{Ser}_S^f$ a *polynomial morphism* if each component of $f$ is a polynomial in $S\langle Y^* \rangle$. The polynomial morphisms determine a subcategory of $\mathbf{Ser}_S^f$. Let $\mathbf{Alg}_S$ denote the smallest subcategory of $\mathbf{Ser}_S^f$ containing the polynomial morphisms which is closed under dagger. Clearly, $\mathbf{Alg}_S$ is also an iteration category. We call a morphism $f : X \to Y$ of $\mathbf{Ser}_S^f$ an *algebraic morphism* if it belongs to $\mathbf{Alg}_S$. In this case, we call the components of $f$ *algebraic series*.

Since $\mathbf{Ser}_S^f$ is an iteration category, the following result follows from Theorem 1.4 of Chapter 11 in [5].

**Theorem 2.7.** *Let $S$ be a complete commutative semiring. A series in $S\langle\!\langle Y^* \rangle\!\rangle$, where $Y$ is a finite set, is algebraic iff there is some polynomial morphism $g : X \to X \oplus Y$ such that it is equal to a component of $g^\dagger$.*

More accurately, this means that a series in $S\langle\!\langle Y^* \rangle\!\rangle$ is algebraic iff there is some polynomial morphism $g : X \to X \oplus Y$ such that it is equal to $g^\dagger_x$ for some $x \in X$.

Suppose that $X$ is a finite set. Let $S^{\mathrm{alg}}\langle\!\langle X^* \rangle\!\rangle$ denote the collection of all algebraic series in $S\langle\!\langle X^* \rangle\!\rangle$.

**Corollary 2.1.** *Let $S$ be a complete commutative semiring and let $X$ be a finite set. Then $S^{\mathrm{alg}}\langle\!\langle X^* \rangle\!\rangle$ is a semiring closed under the star operation.*

**Proof.** It is immediate from Theorem 2.7 that $S^{\mathrm{alg}}\langle\!\langle X^* \rangle\!\rangle$ contains $S$ and is closed under $+$, $\cdot$ and $*$. $\qquad\square$

## 2.9. Conclusion

We showed that formal power series with coefficients in a commutative semiring $S$ form a cartesian category **Ser**$_S$ and defined a fixed point (or dagger) operation on **Ser**$_S$ in a natural way. We proved that when $S$ is continuous, this fixed point operation agrees with the familiar least fixed point operation. Then we proved that the operation satisfies the standard identities of fixed point operations captured by the notion of iteration theories. Hence one can manipulate fixed point equations over formal power series in the usual way.

## Acknowledgments

The first author received support from NKFI grant no. ANN 110883. The second author was partially supported by Austrian Science Fund (FWF): grant no. I1661 - N25.

## References

1. J. D. BAKKER AND D. SCOTT, A theory of programs. IBM Seminar, 1968.
2. M. BARR AND C. WELLS, *Category Theory for Computing Science*, Prentice Hall, ed. 2nd, 1995.
3. H. BEKIĆ, Definable operation in general algebras, and the theory of automata and flowcharts. IBM seminar, 1969.

4. J. BERSTEL AND C. REUTENAUER, *Noncommutative Rational Series with Applications*, Cambridge University Press, 2010.
5. S. BLOOM AND Z. ÉSIK, *Iteration Theories*, Springer, 1993.
6. S. BLOOM AND Z. ÉSIK, Axiomatizing rational power series over natural numbers, *Inform. Comput.* **207**, 793–811 (2009).
7. J. CONWAY, *Regular Algebra and Finite Machines*, Chapman and Hall, Ltd., 1971.
8. S. EILENBERG, *Automata, Languages, and Machines*, Academic Press, 1973.
9. Z. ÉSIK, Identities in iterative and rational algebraic theories, in *Computational Linguistics and Computer Languages*, vol. XIV, pp. 183–207, 1980.
10. Z. ÉSIK, Group axioms for iteration, vol. 148, pp. 131–180, Inform. Comput., 1999.
11. Z. ÉSIK, Equational properties of fixed point operations in cartesian categories: An overview, in *40th MFCS 2015*, pp. 18–37, *LNCS* vol. 9234, Springer, 2015.
12. Z. ÉSIK, Equational axioms associated with finite automata for fixed point operations in cartesian categories, *Mathematical Structures in Computer Science*, To appear.
13. Z. ÉSIK AND W. KUICH, Modern Automata Theory. `http://www.dmg.tuwien.ac.at/kuich/`.
14. J. GOLAN, *Semirings and their Applications*, Springer, 1999.
15. U. HEBISCH, The Kleene theorem in countably complete semirings, *Bayreuther Math. Schriften* **31** (1990), 55–66.
16. W. KUICH AND A. SALOMAA, *Semirings, Automata, Languages*, Springer, 1986.
17. G. MARKOWSKY, Chain complete posets and directed sets with applications, *Algebra Universalis* **6** (1976), 53–68.
18. A. SIMPSON AND G. PLOTKIN, Complete axioms for categorical fixed-point operators, in *15th LICS 2000*, pp. 30–41, IEEE Press, 2000.

# Chapter 3

# Structure and Complexity of Some Subregular Language Families

Markus Holzer

Martin Kutrib

*Institut für Informatik, Universität Giessen,*
*Arndtstr. 2, 35392 Giessen, Germany,*
{holzer,kutrib}@informatik.uni-giessen.de

We consider several subregular language families such as, for example, finite and co-finite languages, definite languages and variants, star-free languages, deterministic regular expression languages, union-free languages, and concatenation-free languages. In particular, we give definitions and structural characterizations in terms of (deterministic) finite automata. Moreover, we emphasize the computational complexity of deciding whether a regular language belongs to one of the aforementioned subregular language families. Obviously, this summary lacks completeness, as subregular language families fall short of exhausting the large selection of this problem area in the literature.

## Contents

## 3.1. Introduction

The history of regular languages dates back to the early days of automata theory; see, for example, Kleene [31]. Since then, a significant theory of subfamilies of regular languages has been developed in the literature. Examples of such early-studied classes are finite languages, definite languages and variants, star-free languages, etc. Some of these regular subfamilies were motivated by particular issues such as, for instance, nerve nets or circuit design. A list of some of these early regular subfamilies, their structure, and their properties was already given by Havel [24, 25]. Since then, new developments in the theory of computer science triggered the study of new subregular language families. For instance, deterministic expression languages or one-unambiguous regular languages [3] are motivated from the document type definitions (DTDs) used in the standard generalized markup language (SGML) and extensible markup language (XML) schemes.

In this paper we give a brief overview of some of the classical subregular language families such as, for example, finite and co-finite languages, definite languages and variants, and star-free languages, as well as some recently introduced ones such as, for example, deterministic regular expression languages, union-free languages, and concatenation-free languages (see Figure 3.1). Most of these classes are well understood. An overview of their descriptional complexity is given, for example, by Gao, Moreira, Reis, and Yu [14]. In particular, the determinization of NFAs that accept certain subregular languages was investigated in detail [2]. In most cases it turns out that the conversion problem is nearly as costly (in terms of the number of states) as in the general case. Here we focus on characterizations in terms of automata and on the computational complexity on deciding whether a regular language belongs to the subregular family under consideration. Our tour of the subject obviously lacks completeness, and gives a very personal view on some of the issues discussed here.

We recall some definitions about finite automata as contained, for example, in Harrison [22]. A *nondeterministic finite automaton* (NFA) is a system $M = \langle Q, \Sigma, \delta, q_0, F \rangle$, where $Q$ is the finite set of *internal states*, $\Sigma$ is the alphabet of *input symbols*, $q_0 \in Q$ is the *initial state*, $F \subseteq Q$ is the set of *accepting states*, and $\delta \colon Q \times \Sigma \to 2^Q$ is the *transition function*. As usual, the transition function is extended to $\delta \colon Q \times \Sigma^* \to 2^Q$ reflecting sequences of inputs: $\delta(q, \lambda) = \{q\}$, where $\lambda$ refers to the empty word, and $\delta(q, aw) = \bigcup_{q' \in \delta(q,a)} \delta(q', w)$, for $q \in Q$, $a \in \Sigma$, and $w \in \Sigma^*$. A word $w \in \Sigma^*$ is *accepted* by $M$ if $\delta(q_0, w) \cap F \neq \emptyset$. The *language accepted* by $M$ is $L(M) = \{\, w \in \Sigma^* \mid w \text{ is accepted by } M \,\}$.

A finite automaton is *deterministic* (DFA) if and only if $|\delta(q, a)| = 1$, for every $q \in Q$ and $a \in \Sigma$. In this case we simply write $\delta(q, a) = p$ for

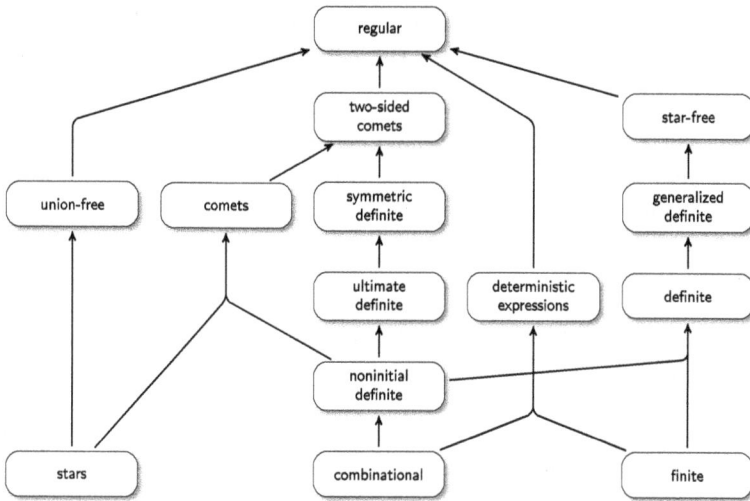

Fig. 3.1. Hierarchy of some subregular language families under investigation. The inclusions are strict, where for stars the inclusion does not apply to the language $\{\lambda\}$. Language families that are not linked by a path are not necessarily incomparable.

$\delta(q, a) = \{p\}$, assuming that the transition function is a mapping of the form $\delta : Q \times \Sigma \to Q$. So, unless otherwise stated, we consider complete DFAs, that is, the transition function is total, whereas for NFAs it is possible that $\delta$ maps to the empty set.

A finite automaton is said to be *minimal* if there is no finite automaton of the same type with fewer states, accepting the same language. Note that a sink state is counted for complete DFAs, whereas it is not counted for NFAs. In the following, two devices are said to be *equivalent* if they accept the same language.

## 3.2. Some Classical Subregular Language Families

### 3.2.1. *Finite and Co-Finite Languages*

One of the simplest (and non-trivial) language families are the finite and co-finite languages. A language $L \subseteq \Sigma^*$ is *co-finite* if its complement language $\overline{L} = \Sigma^* \setminus L$ is finite. Finite and co-finite languages are the basis of the Brzozowski hierarchy that exhausts the star-free languages, which will be discussed in detail in the forthcoming.

The given characterization of finite and co-finite languages is folklore and reads as follows—a state for an automaton is *useless* if it is either not reachable from the initial state of the automaton or no final state can be reached from it.

**Theorem 3.1.** *Let $M$ be a minimal deterministic finite automaton. Then the following holds: (1) The language $L(M)$ is finite if and only if the automaton obtained by removing useless states is acyclic. (2) The language $L(M)$ is co-finite if and only if $M$ contains an accepting sink state and the (partial) automaton obtained after removing it is acyclic.*

This characterization can be utilized to obtain the following exact complexity result.

**Theorem 3.2.** *Deciding whether a given deterministic finite automaton accepts a finite or co-finite language is* NL-*complete.*

It is worth mentioning that the previous two theorems generalize to NFAs. Asking for particular properties such as being the empty set or being universal, these problems are NL-complete, too, regardless of whether the automaton is deterministic or nondeterministic [30], except for the universality of NFAs, which is known to be PSPACE-complete [37].

### 3.2.2. *Definite Languages and Friends*

In this section we are going to discuss definite languages and several variants thereof that were introduced and first investigated by Brzozowski [4], Ginzburg [16], and Paz and Peleg [39].

Basically, whether or not a word belongs to a given definite language can be determined by inspecting the last $k$ symbols, where $k$ is a constant only depending on the language. In particular, two words whose lengths exceed $k$ having the same suffix either both belong to the language, or both do not. More precisely, a language $L \subseteq \Sigma^*$ is said to be *definite* if and only if $L = E \cup \Sigma^* H$, for some finite languages $E, H \subseteq \Sigma^*$. Definite languages were introduced by Brzozowski [4]. We note that an alternative definition of definite languages was given by Perles, Rabin, and Shamir [40], which turned out to be equivalent. This alternative definition reads as follows. Let $k \geq 0$ and $L \subseteq \Sigma^*$. A language $L$ is said to be *weakly $k$-definite* if an arbitrary $x \in \Sigma^*$ with $|x| \geq k$ belongs to $L$ if and only if the $k$-suffix of $x$ belongs to $L$. A language $L$ is said to be *$k$-definite* if $L$ is weakly $k$-definite but not weakly $(k-1)$-definite. For $k = 0$, $L$ is 0-definite if and only if it is weakly 0-definite. Finally, $L$ is *definite* if it is $k$-definite for some $k \geq 0$.

It follows immediately that the empty set and $\Sigma^*$ are the only 0-definite languages.

As many other subregular language families, definite languages are well motivated from a practical point of view: they can be realized by a register and a combinational circuit. They have also been intensively studied by Perles, Rabin, and Shamir [40]. Their canonical expressions were described by Brzozowski [4]. For a characterization of definite languages by finite automata, let us introduce the following notation. We call a DFA *definite* if it accepts a definite language. Such automata have the property that their decision depends only on the last $k$ input symbols, where $k$ is some constant. They are driven by a *definite transition function*.

An interesting structural property of definite minimal DFAs is that the initial state, as well as the set of accepting states, can be arbitrarily changed without leaving the class of definite languages [16]. That is, if $M$ is a definite minimal DFA with state set $Q$, then $M' = \langle Q, \Sigma, \delta, q, F \rangle$ still accepts a definite language, for any $q \in Q$ and $F \subseteq Q$. We give an example illustrating this property.

**Example 3.1.** The minimal DFA $M$ depicted in Figure 3.2 accepts the definite language $\{a, b, c\}^* \{aa, ca\}$.

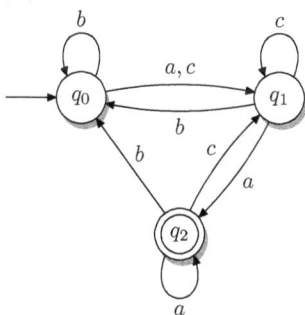

Fig. 3.2.   A minimal deterministic finite automaton accepting a definite language over the alphabet $\{a, b, c\}$.

Consider the automaton $M'$ constructed from $M$ by choosing the initial state $q_1$ and set of accepting states $\{q_2\}$. It accepts the language $E \cup \Sigma^* H$ with $\Sigma = \{a, b, c\}$, $E = \{a\}$, and $H = \{aa, ca\}$. If $M'$ is constructed from $M$ by choosing the initial state $q_0$ and set of accepting states $\{q_0, q_1\}$, it accepts the language $(E \cup \Sigma^* H) \cup (E' \cup \Sigma^* H')$ with $\Sigma = \{a, b, c\}$, $E = \{\lambda\}$, $H = \{b\}$, and $E' = \{a\}$, $H' = \{c, ba\}$. Since the family of definite languages is closed under union, it is definite as well.                                   ∎

In order to derive the critical property that determines whether a given DFA $M = \langle Q, \Sigma, \delta, q_0, F \rangle$ accepts a definite language, the 1-equivalence of states is defined as follows. Two states $q_1, q_2 \in Q$ are said to be 1-*equivalent* if $\delta(q_1, a) = \delta(q_2, a)$, for all $a \in \Sigma$. It is worth mentioning that this definition of 1-equivalence differs from the one that is, for example, used in DFA minimization, since here 1-equivalent states are not required to be equivalent. With the help of 1-equivalent states, next, the transition function $\delta$ is compressed. So, let $q_1, q_2 \in Q$ be two different 1-equivalent states. Then $\delta_{q_1, q_2} : (Q \setminus \{q_1\}) \times \Sigma \to (Q \setminus \{q_1\})$ is the *compressed transition function* which is defined as follows:

$$
\delta_{q_1, q_2}(q, x) = \begin{cases} \delta(q, x), & \text{if } \delta(q, x) \neq q_1; \\ q_2, & \text{if } \delta(q, x) = q_1. \end{cases}
$$

for all $q \in Q \setminus \{q_1\}$ and $x \in \Sigma$. Note that $\delta_{q_1, q_2}$ is defined only if $q_1$ and $q_2$ are different and 1-equivalent. Moreover, a compressed transition function is definite if and only if its uncompressed transition function is definite. Now the next theorem gives a characterization of definite languages in terms of finite automata [40].

**Theorem 3.3.** *Let $M = \langle Q, \Sigma, \delta, q_0, F \rangle$ be a minimal deterministic finite automaton. Then $L(M)$ is definite if and only if there is some $m \geq 0$ such that $|Q_m| = 1$, where $Q_m$ is the state set of the $m$-fold compressed transition function.*

Next, we give an example of this compression procedure.

**Example 3.2.** Consider the minimal deterministic finite automaton $M$ depicted in Figure 3.2, where the edges labeled by $c$ are removed. The states $q_1$ and $q_2$ are 1-equivalent. Compressing $\delta$ to $\delta_1$ yields state set $Q_1 = \{r_0, r_1\}$ and $\delta_1(r_0, a) = r_1$, $\delta_1(r_0, b) = r_0$, $\delta_1(r_1, a) = r_1$, and $\delta_1(r_1, b) = r_0$. Now, the states $r_0$ and $r_1$ are 1-equivalent. Compressing $\delta_1$ to $\delta_2$ yields state set $Q_2 = \{s_0\}$ and $\delta_2(s_0, a) = s_0 = \delta_2(s_0, b)$. Since $|Q_2| = 1$, we conclude that the language $L(M)$ is definite.                       ∎

With the help of Theorem 3.3 one derives a decidability procedure. However, applied to $k$-definite DFAs (devices that accept $k$-definite languages), this procedure does not give the degree $k$ of definiteness. Nevertheless, a generalization of the procedure that yields the degree as well was provided by Perles, Rabin, and Shamir [40]. A careful inspection of the decidability procedure for definiteness shows that it can be implemented on a nondeterministic logspace bounded Turing machine. To this end, the Turing machine implementation for DFA minimization as given by Cho and Huynh [11] is modified. Moreover, by an easy reduction from graph reachability, one can derive the NL-hardness of the problem. Thus, the next theorem is obtained:

**Theorem 3.4.** *Deciding whether a given deterministic finite automaton accepts a definite language is* NL*-complete.*

We conclude this section by mentioning some variants of definite languages. A language $L \subseteq \Sigma^*$ is *noninitial definite* if and only if $L = \Sigma^* H$ and *generalized definite* if and only if $L = E \cup \bigcup_{i=1}^m G_i \Sigma^* H_i$, for some finite languages $E, H, G_i, H_i \subseteq \Sigma^*$, $1 \leq i \leq m$. If the condition of finiteness is relaxed to arbitrary regular languages, we obtain the following families. A language $L \subseteq \Sigma^*$ is *ultimate definite* if and only if $L = \Sigma^* H$, and *symmetric definite* if and only if $L = G\Sigma^* H$, for some regular languages $G, H \subseteq \Sigma^*$.

It follows immediately from the definitions that every noninitial definite language is also definite and ultimate definite. On the other hand, there are, for example, finite definite languages that are not noninitial definite, so that the inclusion of the language families is proper. Similarly, a language $L = \Sigma^* H$ with $H = \{\, ba^n b \mid n \geq 0 \text{ and } a, b \in \Sigma \,\}$ is ultimate definite but not noninitial definite. The additional inclusions depicted in Figure 3.1 are easily derived as well.

Representation theorems for ultimate and symmetric definite languages were obtained by Paz and Peleg [39]. The representation $L = \Sigma^* H$ of a ultimate definite language is *canonical* if $H$ is a suffix-free language. Moreover, the representation $L = G\Sigma^* H$ of a symmetric definite language is *canonical* if $G$ is a prefix-free and $H$ is a suffix-free language. In both cases the canonical representation is unique and can effectively be constructed [39]—in case of symmetric definite languages only nonempty languages are considered.

The structural property of minimal definite deterministic finite automata that the initial state, as well as the set of accepting states, can be changed arbitrarily without leaving the class of definite languages nicely carries over to the generalized definite case. Ginzburg [16] showed the following: let $M$ be some minimal generalized definite deterministic finite automaton with state set $Q$, and construct $M'$ from $M$ by choosing an arbitrary initial state $q_0 \in Q$ and an arbitrary set of accepting states $F \subseteq Q$. Then $M'$ accepts a generalized definite language.

Finally, we turn to structural properties of minimal DFAs that permit an effective procedure to decide whether the language accepted is ultimate definite or symmetric definite. For ultimate definite languages the automaton characterization reads as follows [39].

**Theorem 3.5.** *Let $M = \langle Q, \Sigma, \delta, q_0, F \rangle$ be a minimal deterministic finite automaton. Then $L(M)$ is ultimate definite if and only if, for all $w \in L(M)$ with $|w| \leq |Q| \cdot (|Q| - 1)$, and all $q \in Q$, the inclusion $\delta(q, w) \in F$ holds.*

Basically, the theorem says that all accepted words whose lengths do not exceed $|Q| \cdot (|Q| - 1)$ drive any state into an accepting state. For symmetric definite languages we find the situation described next [39].

**Theorem 3.6.** *Let $M = \langle Q, \Sigma, \delta, q_0, F \rangle$ be a minimal deterministic finite automaton. Then $L(M)$ is symmetric definite if and only if there is some $q \in Q$ with the following property: for all $a_1 a_2 \cdots a_n \in L(M)$ with $a_i \in \Sigma$, for $1 \leq i \leq n$, and $n \leq |Q| - 1$ there is a $0 \leq j \leq n$ so that $\delta(q_0, a_1 a_2 \cdots a_j) = q$, and the deterministic finite automaton $\langle Q, \Sigma, \delta, q, F \rangle$ is ultimate definite.*

With other words, the theorem requires that $M$ runs through a certain state $q$ while processing any accepted word whose length is at most $|Q| - 2$. Moreover, if the initial state of $M$ is replaced by $q$, then the resulting DFA has to be ultimate definite. But this essentially means that $M$ processes words from $G$ until it reaches state $q$, where $L(M) = G\Sigma^* H$ is a symmetric definite language with regular languages $G, H \subseteq \Sigma^*$.

By standard arguments we can conclude an NL upper bound on the complexity of deciding ultimate definiteness and symmetric definiteness utilizing the above given two theorems. NL-hardness follows by a reduction from graph reachability. Thus we have

**Theorem 3.7.** *Deciding whether a given deterministic finite automaton accepts an ultimate definite or a symmetric definite language is NL-complete.*

### 3.2.3. Star-Free Languages: A Hierarchy in the Hierarchy

Regular languages can be constructed from letters by Boolean operations (union and complement) together with concatenation and Kleene star. A language $L \subseteq \Sigma^*$ is *star-free* if the language can be constructed like described above but with the restriction that the Kleene star operation is *not* allowed (and complementation is done with respect to $\Sigma^*$). Thus, alternatively star-free languages can be defined by classical regular expressions for which the Kleene star operation is traded for the complementation operation—hence, the allowed set of operations is $op = \{\cdot, +, ^-\}$. These languages are very well studied and early results on them can be found, for example, in work of McNaughton and Papert [35] and Schützenberger [47]. By some of the results obtained there, it follows that checking whether a regular language is star-free is decidable. The exact complexity of this problem is determined by Cho and Huynh [10].

**Theorem 3.8.** *Deciding whether a given deterministic finite automaton accepts a star-free language is* PSPACE-*complete.*

In fact, this result (at the least the upper bound) is based on a structural characterization of star-free languages in terms of DFAs. To this end, we need the following notation: a DFA $M$ is *permutation-free* if there is no word $w$ that makes a non-trivial permutation (not the identity) of any subset of states, that is, there are distinct states $q_1, q_2, \ldots, q_n$, for some $n \geq 2$, such that $M$ moves from $q_i$ to $q_{i+1}$ on $w$, for every $1 \leq i \leq n$, assuming $q_{n+1} = q_1$. Then the characterization of star-free languages reads as follows—cf. [35] and [47].

**Theorem 3.9.** *A language $L \subseteq \Sigma^*$ is star-free if and only if the minimal deterministic finite automaton $M$ of $L$ is permutation-free.*

The following simple example shows that star-free languages induce a language family that is strictly included in the regular languages.

**Example 3.3.** Consider the regular expression $r = (aa)^*$ and $s = (ab)^*$. See Figure 3.3 for a drawing of the corresponding minimal DFAs.

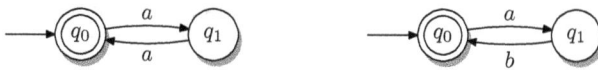

Fig. 3.3. Two minimal DFAs (the sink states are not shown) for the regular expression $r = (aa)^*$ (left) and $s = (ab)^*$ (right). Note, that the left automaton is *not* permutation-free, while the right one is permutation-free, and hence describes a star-free language.

The language denoted by the regular expression $r$ is not star-free, since the word $w = a$ induces a non-trivial permutation on the state set $\{q_0, q_1\}$, while the language described by $s$ is star-free, since the corresponding automaton is permutation-free. An equivalent star-free description for the language over the alphabet $\Sigma = \{a, b\}$ described by $s$ is

$$\overline{b\Sigma^* + \Sigma^*a + \Sigma^*aa\Sigma^* + \Sigma^*bb\Sigma^*},$$

where $\overline{\Sigma^*} = \overline{\emptyset}$. ∎

The significance of star-free languages is supported by a host of various characterizations from different research areas such as, for instance, finite model theory [53], the theory of finite semigroups, topology, Boolean circuits [52], etc., to mention just a few of them.

Altering the Boolean operations together with concatenation in the definition of star-free languages, as we have seen in the previous example, leads to the definition of at least two hierarchies, namely to the *Brzozowski hierarchy* (BH) (also known as *dot-depth hierarchy*) and the *Straubing-Thérien hierarchy* (STH). The first level of the former hierarchy is named $\mathcal{B}_0$ and contains all finite and co-finite languages, while the first level of the latter hierarchy is referred to $\mathcal{L}_0$ and consists of $\emptyset$ and $\Sigma^*$. In general the levels $\mathcal{B}_{n/2}$ and $\mathcal{L}_{n/2}$ are inductively built as follows: one defines level $n + \frac{1}{2}$, for $n \geq 0$, as the polynomial closure of level $n$, and level $n+1$ is the Boolean closure of level $n + \frac{1}{2}$. Thus,

$$\mathcal{B}_0 = \{\, L \subseteq \Sigma^+ \mid L \text{ is finite or co-finite} \,\} \quad \text{and} \quad \mathcal{B}_{n+\frac{1}{2}} = \mathrm{POL}(\mathcal{B}_n),$$

$$\mathcal{B}_{n+1} = \mathrm{BC}(\mathcal{B}_{n+\frac{1}{2}})$$

and

$$\mathcal{L}_0 = \{\emptyset, \Sigma^*\} \quad \text{and} \quad \mathcal{L}_{n+\frac{1}{2}} = \mathrm{POL}(\mathcal{L}_n), \quad \mathcal{L}_{n+1} = \mathrm{BC}(\mathcal{L}_{n+\frac{1}{2}})$$

for $n \geq 0$. Here the polynomial closure $\mathrm{POL}(\mathcal{C})$ of a class $\mathcal{C}$ is the set of languages that are finite unions of products of the form $L_0 a_1 L_1 a_2 \cdots a_n L_n$, where the $a_i$ are letters and the $L_i$ are languages from $\mathcal{C}$. Moreover, BC refers to Boolean closure. It is well known that both hierarchies are infinite for languages over an alphabet of at least two letters [8]. Note that a unary language is star-free if and only if it is finite or co-finite [6, 26].

What about the decidability of the membership problem for these levels? It is shown that both hierarchies are related such that $\mathcal{B}_{n/2}$ is decidable if and only if $\mathcal{L}_{n/2}$ is decidable [42, 50]. This does not answer the question on the decidability of the individual levels, but for some lower levels the decidability is known. To be more precise, the levels 0, 1/2, 1, and 3/2 of both hierarchies are decidable [18, 32, 41, 48]. Partial results are known for levels 2 and 5/2 of the STH for binary alphabets [17, 51], which were recently improved by the decidability of the corresponding levels 2 and 5/2 of the BH in general [44]—also see, for example, [43]. To our knowledge, the question of decidability is still open for other levels.

Next, we recall what is known about the the exact complexity of these decidability problems. Level 0 of both hierarchies is decidable for the reasons stated in Subsection 3.2.1. The decidability results for levels 1/2 and 3/2 share an interesting property: namely, both levels obey a "forbidden-pattern" characterization. That is, a language $L$ belongs to the level under consideration if and only if the minimal DFA for $L$ does not have a certain structural pattern. Since the patterns for the higher levels $3/2$ are quite involved, we only give the characterization for the level $1/2$ of both hierarchies, which reads as follows [41]:

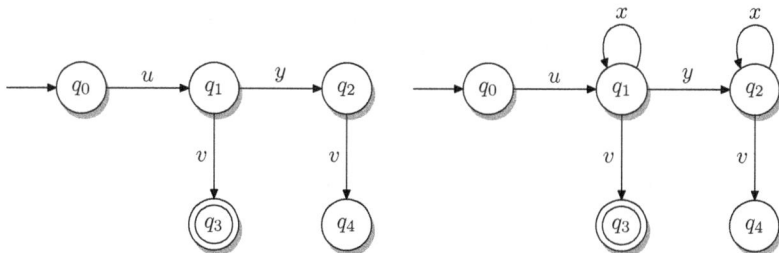

Fig. 3.4.　Forbidden patterns for level $1/2$ of the STH (left) and the BH (right). For the words in the left pattern the inclusion $u, y, v \in \Sigma^*$ must hold, while for the words in the right pattern we must have $u, v \in \Sigma^*$ and $x, y \in \Sigma^+$.

**Theorem 3.10.** *A language $L \subseteq \Sigma^*$ belongs to level $1/2$ of the Straubing-Thérien hierarchy (Brzozowski hierarchy, respectively) if and only if the minimal deterministic automaton $M$ of $L$ does not contain the pattern shown in Figure 3.4 on the left (right, respectively).*

To decide whether a DFA contains one of the specified patterns, one has to verify the respective graph reachability conditions in the automaton's transition graph. For both patterns depicted in Figure 3.4 this results in an on-the-fly guess-and-check NL algorithm. For a more general discussion on the relation between forbidden patterns and decision complexity we refer to Schmitz [45]. In fact, for both decision problems NL-completeness was shown by Schmitz, Wagner [46] and Glaßer, Schmitz, Selivanov [13].

**Theorem 3.11.** *Deciding whether a given deterministic finite automaton accepts a language from level $1/2$ of the Straubing-Thérien or the Brzozowski hierarchy is NL-complete.*

Next we climb up both hierarchies to the next full level. Languages from the level 1 of the STH hierarchy are also called *piecewise testable languages*. Recall that by definition these languages are Boolean combinations of languages of the form

$$\Sigma^* a_1 \Sigma^* a_2 \cdots \Sigma^* a_n \Sigma^*.$$

An automata-based characterization of these languages was provided by Simon [48]. It reads as follows:

**Theorem 3.12.** *Let $L \subseteq \Sigma^*$ and $M$ be its the minimal deterministic finite automaton. Then $L$ is piecewise testable if and only if (1) every strongly connected component of the automaton $M$ is a singleton set and for any subset $\Gamma$ of $\Sigma$, each component[1] of $M$ restricted to transitions which correspond to letters in $\Gamma$ contains a unique maximal state.[2]*

For languages on level 1 of the BH, a structural characterization in terms of automata is even more involved. To this end we need some more notation. An automaton $M$ with transition function $\delta$ is $k$-*stable*, whenever $p$ and $q$ are states and the word $w$ is of length $k$ such that $p$, $q$, $\delta(p, w)$, and $\delta(q, w)$ belong to the same strongly connected component (SCC) of $M$, then $\delta(p, w) = \delta(q, w)$. Two words $x$ and $y$ are *co-initial* if they have the same first $k$ letters, for some $k$. Now we are ready to state the characterization of languages on level 1 of the BH given by Stern [49]:

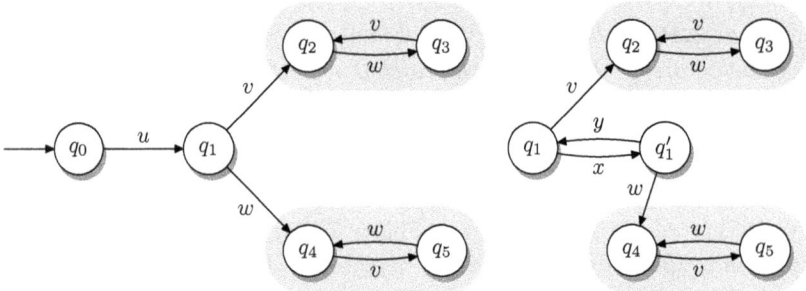

Fig. 3.5.   Forbidden patterns for the level 1 of the BH. For the words in the left pattern the inclusion $u, v, w \in \Sigma^*$ must hold, where $v$ and $w$ are co-initial and both gray shaded areas are distinct SCCs. The conditions for the words in the right pattern (the connection between $q_0$ and $q_1$ with the word $u$ is not shown) are as follows: $u \in \Sigma^*$, $x, v, y, w \in \Sigma^{\geq k}$, where $x$ and $v$ are co-initial as well as $y$ and $w$, and the gray shaded areas on the top and bottom are distinct SCCs.

**Theorem 3.13.** *A language $L \subseteq \Sigma^*$ if of dot-depth one if and only if its*

---

[1]A *component* of a state $q$ of the automaton $M$ with transition function $\delta$ is the set of states $\{ p \mid \exists w \in \Sigma^* : \delta(q, w) = p \}$.

[2]A finite automaton where every strongly connected component is a singleton set is acyclic and, thus, can be partially ordered by $p \leq q$ if and only if either $p = q$ or there is a path from $p$ to $q$. Therefore we can define a state to be maximal with respect to this ordering.

*minimal deterministic finite automaton is $k$-stable and does not contain any of the structures depicted in Figure 3.5, for some $k$.*

Both aforementioned characterizations were used by Cho and Huynh [10] to obtain the following result on the complexity of checking membership for piecewise testable languages and languages on level 1 of the BH.

**Theorem 3.14.** *Deciding whether a given deterministic finite automaton accepts a piecewise testable language or a language on level 1 of the BH is* NL-*complete.*

There are legions of further results on the STH and BH and subhierarchies within. We think that the presented results are only an appetizer for further reading on this subject.

## 3.3. Families Defined by Restricted Regular Expressions

### 3.3.1. *Deterministic Regular Expressions*

Deterministic regular expressions were introduced by Brüggemann-Klein and Wood [3]. Alternatively, these expressions are also called one-unambiguous in the literature. These expressions are motivated from document type definitions (DTDs) used in the standard generalized markup language (SGML) and extensible markup language (XML) schemes.

The idea behind deterministic regular expressions is that if we read a word from left to right without look-ahead, it is always clear where in the expression the next symbol can be matched. This property is modeled in terms of the *position automaton*, also known as *Glushkov automaton* [19]—see also McNaughton and Yamada [36]. Intuitively, the states of this automaton correspond to the alphabetic symbols or, in other words, to positions between subsequent symbols in the regular expression. Let us be more precise: assume that $r$ is a regular expression over $\Sigma$ with $n$ occurrences of letters from $\Sigma$ in $r$. In $r$ we attach subscripts to each letter referring to its position (counted from left to right) in $r$. This yields a *marked* expression $\bar{r}$ with distinct input symbols over an alphabet $\bar{\Sigma}$ that contains all letters that occur in $\bar{r}$. To simplify our presentation we assume that the same notation is used for unmarking, that is, $\bar{\bar{r}} = r$. Then in order to describe the position automaton we need to define the following sets of positions on the marked expression. Let $\mathsf{Pos}(r) = \{1, 2, \ldots, n\}$ and

$\mathsf{Pos}_0(r) = \mathsf{Pos}(r) \cup \{0\}$. The position set First takes care of the possible prefixes of words in $L(\overline{r})$, and is defined as follows:

$$\mathsf{First}(r) = \{\, i \mid \text{there is a } w \in \overline{\Sigma}^* \text{ such that } a_i w \in L(\overline{r}) \,\}.$$

Accordingly the position set Last takes care of the possible suffixes of words in $L(\overline{r})$, that is

$$\mathsf{Last}(r) = \{\, i \mid \text{there is a } v \in \overline{\Sigma}^* \text{ such that } v a_i \in L(\overline{r}) \,\}.$$

Finally, the set Follow takes care about the possible continuations in the words in $L(\overline{r})$. It is defined by

$$\mathsf{Follow}(r) = \{\, (i,j) \mid \text{there are } v, w \in \overline{\Sigma}^* \text{ such that } v a_i a_j w \in L(\overline{r}) \,\}.$$

Then the *position automaton* for the regular expression $r$ is defined as $M_{pos}(r) = (\mathsf{Pos}_0(r), \Sigma, \delta_{pos}, 0, F_{pos})$, where

$$\delta(0, a) = \{\, j \in \mathsf{First}(\overline{r}) \mid a = \overline{a_j} \,\},$$

for every $a \in \Sigma$, and the transition function

$$\delta(i, a) = \{\, j \mid (i,j) \in \mathsf{Follow}(\overline{r}) \text{ and } a = \overline{a_j} \,\},$$

for every $i \in \mathsf{Pos}(r)$ and $a \in \Sigma$, and $F_{pos} = \mathsf{Last}(\overline{r})$, if $\lambda \notin L(r)$, and $F_{pos} = \mathsf{Last}(\overline{r}) \cup \{0\}$ otherwise.

In general, the position automaton for a regular expression is nondeterministic. An interesting special case is formed by those regular expressions $r$ whose position automaton $M_{pos(r)}$ is a partial deterministic finite automaton. These expressions are referred to as *deterministic* regular expressions [3]. A language $L \subseteq \Sigma^*$ is a *deterministic regular expression language* if it can be described by a deterministic regular expression $r$, that is, $L = L(r)$. Observe that Brüggemann-Klein and Wood [3] already showed that $r$ is a deterministic regular expression over $\Sigma$ if and only if for all $a \in \Sigma$ and all marked words $u, v, w \in \overline{\Sigma}$ the inclusion $u a_i v \in L(\overline{r})$ holds, and $u a_j w \in L(\overline{r})$ implies $i = j$. This is where the alternative name *one-unambiguous regular expression* comes from.

**Example 3.4.** The following examples are from [3]. Consider the regular expression $r = (a+b)^* a$. The marked version of $r$ is $\overline{r} = (a_1 + b_2)^* a_3$. Taking $u = b_1$, $v = a_3$, and $w = \lambda$, the words $u a_1 v = b_1 a_1 a_3$ and $u a_2 w = b_1 a_3$ are both in $L(\overline{r})$. Thus $r$ is not deterministic. The expression $s = b^* a (b^* a)^*$ denotes the same language as $r$ and is deterministic. See Figure 3.6 for a drawing of the corresponding position automata. ∎

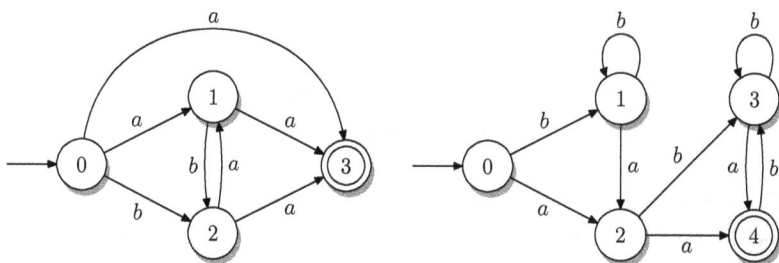

Fig. 3.6. Two position automata for the equivalent regular expressions $r = (a + b)^*a$ (left) and $s = b^*a(b^*a)^*$ (right). Observe that the left automaton is nondeterministic, while the automaton on the right is a partial deterministic finite automaton.

The languages denoted by the regular expressions $(a + b)^*a(a + b)^n$, for $n \geq 1$, are the canonical examples of languages that are regular but not deterministic. Thus, while deterministic finite automata capture the full class of regular languages, this notion of determinism for regular expressions is strictly less expressive, and the deterministic expression languages form a proper subclass of the regular languages. The minimal DFA accepting a deterministic expression language obeys certain structural restrictions, which are given next, and can be used to give a rigorous proof that the languages mentioned above are not deterministic. Before we state the characterization result we need some notation. Let $M$ be a finite automaton. The *orbit* of a state $q$ in an automaton $M$ is the set of all states that belong to the same strongly connected component as $q$. This set is denoted by $O(q)$. Moreover, a state $q$ of the automaton $M$ is a *gate* of its orbit $O(q)$ if $q$ is a final state or $q$ has a transition to a state outside of its orbit. Then an automaton $M$ satisfies the *orbit property* if all gates of each orbit have identical connections to the outside of their orbits. Finally, the languages $L(M_q)$ are referred to as *orbit languages*, where $M_q$ is built from $M$ by restricting $M$ to the orbit states $O(q)$, setting the initial state to $q$, and the gates of $O(q)$ to final states. Now we are ready to state the characterization of deterministic regular expression languages [3]:

**Theorem 3.15.** *A language $L \subseteq \Sigma^*$ is a deterministic expression language if and only if (i) the minimal deterministic finite automaton of $L$ obeys the orbit property and (ii) all orbit languages are deterministic expression languages.*

There is a linear-time algorithm that decides whether a given regular expression is deterministic, and these expressions admit very fast regular expression matching algorithms [20]. Furthermore, the equivalence problem of deterministic regular expressions, as well as the decision problem whether the language denoted by a regular expression is contained in the language denoted by a deterministic regular expression, are both solvable efficiently [27].

For deterministic regular expression definability, that is the problem of deciding whether a given regular language can be expressed by a deterministic regular expression, the following result is known [3], which is based on the previously-given characterization that gives rise to a recursive algorithm.

**Theorem 3.16.** *The deterministic regular expression definability problem is contained in* P *if the regular language is given by a deterministic finite automaton.*

To our knowledge, the exact computational complexity of the deterministic regular expression definability problem is not known, but it was mentioned by Czerwinski, David, Losemann, and Martens [12] that this problem is at least NL-hard. If the input is changed from a DFA to an NFA or a regular expression, the deterministic regular expression definability becomes PSPACE-complete [12].

Finally, we note in passing that several approaches to generalize the notion of deterministic regular expressions have been considered; see, for example, Giammarresi, Montalbano, and Wood [15] and Han and Wood [21]. The generalizations are called *k-unambiguous* and *k-block deterministic* regular expressions, respectively. In both cases the idea is to generalize the look-ahead of deterministic regular expressions to $k$ letters instead of only one letter. For more on these expressions, their corresponding language classes, and a proper hierarchy with respect to the parameter $k$ we refer to [15, 21] and especially to [9], which repairs a subtle flaw in the latter paper.

### 3.3.2. Union-Free Languages

A regular language is *union-free* if it can be described by a regular expression that does not contain the union operation, that is, if the allowed set of operations is $op = \{\cdot, {}^*\}$. Note, that there is a significant difference in the definition of union-free and star-free languages. While for union-free languages it is forbidden to use the union operation, for star-free languages the Kleene star operation is replaced by the complementation operation.

Union-free languages obey a nice characterization in terms of one-cycle-free-path NFAs. Here a finite automaton has the *one-cycle-free-path* property if there is a unique accepting cycle-free path from each of its states. The following result is due to Nagy [38].

**Theorem 3.17.** *A language $L \subseteq \Sigma^*$ is union-free if and only if $L$ is accepted by a* one-cycle-free-path *nondeterministic finite automaton.*

Since by definition one-cycle-free-path automata have exactly *one* accepting state, the class of union-free languages is a strict subfamily of all regular languages. Moreover, it is worth mentioning that one-cycle-free-path partial deterministic finite automata induce a language class called *deterministic union-free languages* that is a strict subset of all union-free languages [29]. An example of a language that cannot be accepted by any one-cycle-free path partial deterministic finite automaton, but which is union-free is $(aa + ab + ba + bb)^*$.

**Example 3.5.** Consider the automaton drawn in Figure 3.7, which is used by Jirásková and Nagy [29] to show some non-closure properties of deterministic union-free languages. Further investigations on union-free

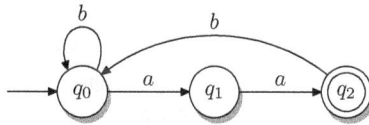

Fig. 3.7. One-cycle-free-path *nondeterministic* finite automaton accepting a union-free language over the alphabet $\{a, b\}$.

languages (in particular, descriptional complexity issues) were studied by Jirásková and Masopust [28].

Although the automaton depicted contains a self-loop and a non-trivial cycle, the device obeys the one-cycle-free-path property, since from every state there is a cycle-free accepting path to the final state $q_2$. Structurally, a one-cycle-free-path automaton consists of a so-called "backbone" together with self-loops and cycles. The *backbone* is formed by the (unique) shortest word of the language which is equal to the word that is accepted by a cycle-free path from the initial state. In our case, the word $aa$ induces the backbone of the automaton, and the remaining parts are the self-loop and the cycle. This special structure gives rise to the fact that every word of a union-free language contains the word of the backbone as a scattered subword [38]. It is easy to see that the union-free regular expression $b^*aa(bb^*aa)^*$ is equivalent to the automaton shown in Figure 3.7. There the subword $aa$ is easily identified in the regular expression.   ∎

One of the most important results on union-free regular languages is that every regular language can be written as a finite union of union-free languages [38]—this result is basically related to the identity $(r+s)^* = (r^*s^*)^*$ on regular expressions. Such a representation of a regular language is called *union-free decomposition*. The minimal number of union operations required in a union-free decomposition of a regular language is computable [1]. Note that the union-free decomposition of a regular language implies that for each regular language $L$ the language $L^*$ is a union-free language, too. This result is somehow nicely related to the star languages investigated by Brzozowski and Cohen [7].

Whether the structural characterization of union-free languages in terms of one-cycle-free-path NFAs can be utilized to show decidability of union-free language membership is not clear. Nevertheless, from Afonin and Golomazov [1] one deduces that union-freeness of regular languages is decidable. In fact, this is part of a more general result due to Hashiguchi [23], which reads as follows:

**Theorem 3.18.** *Let* $op \subseteq \{\cdot, +, ^*\}$ *and* $\mathcal{F}$ *be any finite class of languages. Then it is decidable whether a regular language can be described only by operations from the set* $op$ *starting from languages from* $\mathcal{F}$.

Thus, the decidability of union-freeness follows by taking $op = \{\cdot, ^*\}$ and $\mathcal{F} = \{\, \{a\} \mid a \in \Sigma^* \,\} \cup \{\emptyset, \{\lambda\}\}$. To our knowledge the *exact* complexity of the algorithm that decides $op$-representation over $\mathcal{F}$ is not known. Since the proof by Hashiguchi [23] reduces the problem under consideration to the limitedness problem on distance automata, at least an upper bound can be given. A distance automaton is an ordinary NFA whose transitions are additionally equipped with a distance 0 or 1. As usual, the distance of a path is defined as the sum of distances on the transitions taken, and the distance of an accepted word as the minimum of the distances over all accepting paths of the word. Finally, the distance of the automaton is the supremum over all distances of accepted words. Then the *limitedness problem* asks whether for a given distance automaton there exists a $d$ such that the distance of the automaton is at most $d$. This problem was shown to be **PSPACE**-complete by Leung and Podolskiy [34].

### 3.3.3. *Concatenation-Free Languages*

Similar as for star-free languages that are defined by classical regular expressions for which the star is traded for complementation, *concatenation-free* languages are defined by regular expressions for which concatenation is traded for complementation, that is, the set of allowed operations is $op = \{+, {}^*, {}^-\}$. Since in the presence of concatenation, every word in an initial finite set can be obtained by concatenating letters from $\Sigma$, the set can be created for free. In the absence of concatenation initially such a *finite set* of words is provided in order to allow non-trivial languages to be expressed.

Concatenation-free languages were introduced and studied by Kutrib and Wendlandt [33], where the results are mainly in terms of unary languages.

**Example 3.6.** Let $L \subseteq \{a, b\}^*$ be the language of words that either begin with an $a$ and have at least two consecutive $b$, or begin with a $b$. The language $L$ is described by the concatenation-free expression $r = \overline{(a + ab)^*}$. The subexpression $(a + ab)^*$ gives all words over the alphabet $\{a, b\}$ beginning with an $a$ that do not have the factor $bb$. The complement of $r$ describes $L$. ∎

A first natural question in connection with concatenation-free expressions is whether they capture the regular languages or define a proper subregular family. The question has been answered by characterizing the unary concatenation-free languages by the Boolean closure of certain sets of languages as follows [33].

A *co-finite unary* language $L$ is stretched in the following sense. We define $L_{(m)} = \{ w \mid |w| = m \cdot |v|,$ for some $v \in L \}$, for $m \geq 1$. Now the family of all unary languages that are either finite or have a representation as a co-finite language stretched by $m \geq 1$ joined with a finite language is denoted by $\mathcal{U}_{(m)}$. The union of all of these families is $\mathcal{U} = \bigcup_{m \geq 1} \mathcal{U}_{(m)}$. The Boolean closure of $\mathcal{U}$ is denoted by UKF. So, UKF is the *least family of languages which contains all members of $\mathcal{U}$ and is closed under complementation and union (and, thus, under intersection)*. Then Kutrib and Wendlandt [33] have shown the next result.

**Theorem 3.19.** *A unary language is concatenation-free if and only if it belongs to the family UKF, that is, to the Boolean closure of $\mathcal{U}$.*

Whether this characterization can be utilized to decide the

concatenation-freeness of unary regular languages is open, which is also true for the general case. Nevertheless, the above characterization is exploited to derive regular languages that are not concatenation-free—again, see, [33].

**Lemma 3.1.** *Let $1 \leq x < y$ be two integers with $x \neq \frac{y}{2}$. Then the language $L = \{\, a^n \mid n \equiv x \pmod{y} \,\}$ is not concatenation-free.*

The next example shows that the conditions on $x$ and $y$ in Lemma 3.1 are in fact necessary.

**Example 3.7.** (i) Let $y \geq 1$ be an integer. Then the concatenation-free regular expression $r = (a^y)^*$ represents the language
$$L(r) = \{\, a^n \mid n \equiv 0 \pmod{y} \,\}.$$

(ii) Let $1 \leq x < y$ be two integers with $x = \frac{y}{2}$. Then the concatenation-free regular expression $r = \overline{(a^x)^*} + (a^y)^*$ represents the language
$$L(r) = \{\, a^n \mid n \equiv x \pmod{y} \,\}. \qquad \blacksquare$$

In particular, Lemma 3.1 immediately implies the next theorem.

**Theorem 3.20.** *The (unary) concatenation-free languages are strictly included in the (unary) regular languages.*

Once the strict inclusion of the previous theorem is known, the question arises, how many applications of concatenations are necessary to obtain all regular languages. Is the number bounded or unbounded? For unary languages it is, in fact, bounded by one [33].

**Theorem 3.21.** *Every unary regular language can be represented by a (generalized) concatenation-free expression that contains one occurrence of a concatenation operation.*

Finally, the position of the family in the subregular hierarchy has been settled for the *unary* case [33]. On the right branch of Figure 3.1 the family of concatenation-free languages lies properly in between the regular and star-free languages. Since a unary language is star-free if and only if it is either finite or co-finite [6, 26], the unary concatenation-free regular expressions are strictly more expressive than the unary star-free regular expressions.

**Theorem 3.22.** *The family of unary star-free languages is strictly included in the family of unary concatenation-free languages.*

A language $L \subseteq \Sigma^*$ is a *star language* if and only if it can be written as $L = H^*$, for some regular language $H \subseteq \Sigma^*$, and $L \subseteq \Sigma^*$ is a *comet language* if and only if it can be represented as concatenation $G^*H$ of a regular star language $G^* \subseteq \Sigma^*$ and a regular language $H \subseteq \Sigma^*$, such that $G \neq \{\lambda\}$ and $G \neq \emptyset$. Star languages and comet languages were introduced by Brzozowski [5] and Brzozowski and Cohen [7], respectively. Next, a language $L \subseteq \Sigma^*$ is a *two-sided comet language* if and only if $L = EG^*H$, for a regular star language $G^* \subseteq \Sigma^*$ and regular languages $E, H \subseteq \Sigma^*$, such that $G \neq \{\lambda\}$ and $G \neq \emptyset$. Clearly, every star language not equal to $\{\lambda\}$ is also a comet language and every comet is a two-sided comet language, but the converse is not true in general.

It follows immediately from the definitions that any (two-sided) comet language that contains at least one nonempty word is infinite. On the other hand, any finite language is concatenation-free. Conversely, by Lemma 3.1 the language $L = \{\, a^n \mid n \equiv 1 \pmod 3 \,\}$ is not concatenation-free. On the other hand, it is described by $\{a^3\}^*\{a\}$ and, thus, a comet language. This implies the next theorem.

**Theorem 3.23.** *The families of unary concatenation-free languages and unary (two-sided) comet languages are incomparable.*

The family of concatenation-free languages and, therefore, UKF are closed under star. With this observation it is shown that the star of any unary language is even concatenation-free [33]. Finite languages yield the proper inclusion in the next theorem.

**Theorem 3.24.** *The family of unary star languages is strictly included in the family of unary concatenation-free languages.*

Concerning the middle branch of the hierarchy, we already know that the family of concatenation-free languages is incomparable with the family of (two-sided) comet languages. However, let $L = G\{a\}^*H$ be symmetric definite. If $G$ or $H$ is empty, then $L$ is empty and, thus, concatenation-free. Otherwise, $L$ contains all words whose length is at least the sum of the lengths of the shortest words in $G$ and $H$. So, $L$ is co-finite and, therefore, concatenation-free.

**Theorem 3.25.** *The family of unary symmetric definite languages is strictly included in the family of unary concatenation-free languages.*

The results show that unary concatenation-free expressions are very powerful, though they are not as expressive as general regular expressions.

# References

1. S. AFONIN AND D. GOLOMAZOV, Minimal union-free decompositions of regular languages, in *3rd LATA 2009*, A. H. Dediu, A. Ionescu and C. Martín-Vide (eds.), pp. 83–92, *LNCS* vol. 5457, Springer, 2009.

2. H. BORDIHN, M. HOLZER AND M. KUTRIB, Determinization of finite automata accepting subregular languages, *Theoret. Comput. Sci.* **410** (2009), 3209–3222.

3. A. BRÜGGEMANN-KLEIN AND D. WOOD, One-unambiguous regular languages, *Inform. Comput.* **140** (1998), 229–253.

4. J. A. BRZOZOWSKI, Canonical regular expressions and minimal state graphs for definite events, in *Mathematical Theory of Automata*, pp. 529–561, Polytechnic Institute of Brooklyn, 1962.

5. J. A. BRZOZOWSKI, Roots of star events, *J. ACM* **14** (1967), 466–477.

6. J. A. BRZOZOWSKI, Hierarchies and aperiodic languages, *RAIRO Inform. Théor.* **10** (1976), 33–50.

7. J. A. BRZOZOWSKI AND R. S. COHEN, On decompositions of regular events, *J. ACM* **16** (1969), 132–144.

8. J. A. BRZOZOWSKI AND R. KNAST, The dot-depth hierarchy of star-free languages is infinite, *J. Comput. System Sci.* **16** (1978), 37–55.

9. P. CARON, L. MIGNOT AND C. MIKLARZ, On the hierarchy of block deterministic languages, in *20th CIAA 2015*, F. Drewes (ed.), pp. 63–75, *LNCS* vol. 9223, Springer, 2015.

10. S. CHO AND D. T. HUYNH, Finite-automaton aperiodicity is PSPACE-complete, *Theoret. Comput. Sci.* **88** (1991), 99–116.

11. S. CHO AND D. T. HUYNH, The parallel complexity of finite-state automata problems, *Inform. Comput.* **97** (1992), 1–22.

12. W. CZERWINSKI, C. DAVID, K. LOSEMANN AND W. MARTENS, Deciding definability by deterministic regular expressions, in *16th FOSSACS, ETAPS 2013*, F. Pfenning (ed.), pp. 289–304, *LNCS* vol. 7794, Springer, 2013.

13. C. G. ER, H. SCHMITZ AND V. SELIVANOV, Efficient algorithms for membership in Boolean hierarchies of regular languages, in *STACS 2008*, S. Albers and P. Weil (eds.), pp. 337–348, *LIPIcs* vol. 1, Dagstuhl, 2008.

14. Y. GAO, N. MOREIRA, R. REIS AND S. YU, A survey on state complexity. Submitted for publication, 2013.

15. D. GIAMMARRESI, R. MONTALBANO AND D. WOOD, Block-deterministic regular languages, in *7th ICTCS 2001*, A. Restivo, S. R. D. Rocca and L. Roversi (eds.), pp. 184–196, *LNCS* vol. 2202, Springer, 2001.

16. A. GINZBURG, About some properties of definite, reverse-definite and related automata, *IEEE Trans. Elect. Comput.* **EC-15** (1966), 806–810.

17. C. GLASSER AND H. SCHMITZ, Level 5/2 of the Straubing-Thérien hierarchy for two-letter alphabets, in *5th DLT 2001*, W. Kuich, G. Rozenberg and A. Salomaa (eds.), pp. 251–261, *LNCS* vol. 2295, Springer, 2001.

18. C. GLASSER AND H. SCHMITZ, Languages of dot-depth 3/2, *Theory Comput. Syst.* **42** (2008), 256–286.

19. V. M. GLUSHKOV, The abstract theory of automata, *Russian Mathematics*

*Surveys* **16** (1961), 1–53.

20. B. GROZ, S. MANETH AND S. STAWORKO, Deterministic regular expressions in linear time, in *31st ACM SIGMOND-SIGACT-SIGART Symposium on Principles of Database Systems*, pp. 49–60, ACM, 2012.

21. Y.-S. HAN AND D. WOOD, Generalizations of 1-deterministic regular languages, *Inform. Comput.* **206** (2008), 1117–1125.

22. M. A. HARRISON, *Introduction to Formal Language Theory*, Addison-Wesley, 1978.

23. K. HASHIGUCHI, Representation theorems on regular languages, *J. Comput. System Sci.* **27** (1983), 101–115.

24. I. M. HAVEL, The theory of regular events I, *Kybernetika* **5** (1969), 400–419.

25. I. M. HAVEL, The theory of regular events II, *Kybernetika* **6** (1969), 520–544.

26. M. HOLZER, M. KUTRIB AND K. MECKEL, Nondeterministic state complexity of star-free languages, *Theoret. Comput. Sci.* **450** (2012), 68–80.

27. D. HOVLAND, The inclusion problem for regular expressions, *J. Comput. System Sci.* **78** (2012), 1795–1813.

28. G. JIRÁSKOVÁ AND T. MASOPUST, Complexity in union-free languages, in *14th DLT 2010*, Y. Gao, H. Lu, S. Seki and S. Yu (eds.), pp. 255–266, *LNCS* vol. 6224, Springer, 2010.

29. G. JIRÁSKOVÁ AND B. NAGY, On union-free and deterministic union-free languages, in *Theoretical Computer Science - 7th IFIP TC 1/WG 2.2 International Conference (TCS 2012)*, J. C. M. Baeten, T. Ball and F. S. de Boer (eds.), pp. 179–192, *LNCS* vol. 7604, 2012.

30. N. JONES, Space-bounded reducibility among combinatorial problems, *J. Comput. System Sci.* **11** (1975), 68–85.

31. S. C. KLEENE, Representation of events in nerve nets and finite automata, in *Automata studies*, pp. 2–42, *Annals of mathematics studies* vol. 34, Princeton University Press, 1956.

32. R. KNAST, A semigroup characterization of dot-depth one languages, *RAIRO Inform. Théor.* **17** (1983), 321–330.

33. M. KUTRIB AND M. WENDLANDT, Expressive capacity of concatenation freeness, in *20th CIAA 2015*, F. Drewes (ed.), pp. 199–210, *LNCS* vol. 9223, Springer, 2015.

34. H. LEUNG AND V. PODOLSKIY, The limitedness problem on distance automata: Hashiguchi's method revisited, *Theoret. Comput. Sci.* **310** (2004), 147–158.

35. R. MCNAUGHTON AND S. PAPERT, *Counter-free automata, Research monographs* n° 65, MIT Press, 1971.

36. R. MCNAUGHTON AND H. YAMADA, Regular expressions and state graphs for automata, *IRE Transactions on Electronic Computers* **EC-9** (1960), 39–47.

37. A. R. MEYER AND L. J. STOCKMEYER, The equivalence problem for regular expressions with squaring requires exponential time, in *Symposium on Switching and Automata Theory (SWAT 1972)*, pp. 125–129, IEEE Society Press, 1972.

38. B. NAGY, Union-fee regular languages and 1-cycle-free-path automata, *Publicationes Mathematicae Debrecen* **68** (2006), 183–197.

39. A. Paz and B. Peleg, Ultimate-definite and symmetric-definite events and automata, *J. ACM* **12** (1965), 399–410.
40. M. Perles, M. O. Rabin and E. Shamir, The theory of definite automata, *IEEE Trans. Elect. Comput.* **EC-12** (1963), 233–243.
41. J.-É. Pin and P. Weil, Polynomial closure and unambiguous product, *Theory Comput. Syst.* **30** (1997), 383–422.
42. J.-É. Pin and P. Weil, The wreath product principle for ordered semigroups, *Communications in Algebra* **30** (2002), 5677–5713.
43. T. Place and M. Zeitoun, Going higher in the first-order quantifier alternation hierarchy on words, in *41st ICALP 2014*, J. Esparza, P. Fraigniaud, T. Husfeldt and E. Koutsoupias (eds.), pp. 342–353, *LNCS* vol. 8573, Springer, 2014.
44. T. Place and M. Zeitoun, Separation and successor relation, in *STACS 2015*, E. W. Mayr and N. Ollinger (eds.), pp. 662–675, *LIPIcs* vol. 30, 2015.
45. H. Schmitz, *The Forbidden Pattern Approach to Concatenation Hierarchies*, PhD thesis, Universität Würzburg, Fakultät für Mathematik und Informatik, 2001.
46. H. Schmitz and K. W. Wagner, The Boolean hierarchy over level 1/2 of the Straubing-Thérien hierarchy. http://arxiv.org/abs/cs/9809118, 1998.
47. M. P. Schützenberger, On finite monoids having only trivial subgroups, *Inform. Control* **8** (1965), 190–194.
48. I. Simon, Piecewise testable events, in *Automata Theory and Formal Languages*, pp. 214–222, *LNCS* vol. 33, Springer, 1975.
49. J. Stern, Characterizations of some classes of regular events, *Theoret. Comput. Sci.* **35** (1985), 17–42.
50. H. Straubing, Finite semigroup varieties of the form $\mathbf{V} * \mathbf{D}$, *Journal of Pure and Applied Algebra* **36** (1985), 53–94.
51. H. Straubing, Semigroups and languages of dot-depth two, *Theoret. Comput. Sci.* **58** (1988), 361–378.
52. H. Straubing, *Finite Automata, Formal Logic, and Circuit Complexity*, Birkhäuser, 1994.
53. W. Thomas, Languages, automata, and logic, in *Handbook of Formal Languages*, vol. 3, pp. 389–455, Springer, 1997.

# Chapter 4

# The Arduous Road of Modelling:
# Excerpts from Records of an
# Enjoyable Co-operation of Nearly 20 Years

Helmut Jürgensen

*Department of Computer Science, The University of Western Ontario,*
*London, Ontario, Canada N6A 5B7*
`hjj@csd.uwo.ca`

Theoretical computer science, like theoretical physics, differs from pure mathematics in that the former is guided by real-world issues into the investigation of mathematical problems, while the latter investigates such problems, regardless of their nature, for mere fundamental insights. Sometimes, fortunately, these goals coincide.

From about 1984 until about 1999 John Brzozowski and I worked on establishing a formal model for circuit testing. It was a long journey from understanding what practitioners in the field proposed as a reason for their success to proving that their conclusions were justified. Later, we also applied our modelling experience to software specification and verification.

I retrace our work to exhibit why finding really adequate mathematical models for real-world issues is such an intrinsically difficult task and why, on the other hand, it is immensely important for the application area in establishing a solid foundation. On the basis of this experience I state some "lessons" for computer science in general and also for the teaching of computer science.

## Contents

## 4.1. Beginnings

I believe that John and I may have first met at the predecessor of the ICALP meetings in Haifa in 1971 [54]. Most likely, we both attended a party at Michael Yoeli's house — I have photographs of the party, but none showing him. I also have many other photographs taken in Israel during the 1971 trip — but those were taken of antiquities.

We met again in 1975 at the *École de Printemps d'Informatique Théorique* on syntactic monoids that was organized by Jean-François Perrot and held in Vic-sur-Cère; Marcel-Paul Schützenberger and Samuel Eilenberg were discussing the successors to Eilenberg's two volumes on automaton theory [42] at that time. Our next meeting was in 1976 in Waterloo. I visited Gabriel Thierrin in London — my very first journey to North America — and John invited me to Waterloo, where I gave a talk on the enumeration of semigroups; that first visit also took me to Bowling Green, Ohio, meeting Motupalli Satyanarayana, to Purdue University to meet Michael Drazin and Richard Büchi, and to Pennsylvania State University, meeting Gérard Lallement and Haskell Curry, and to an unexpected and very first encounter with cockroaches, albeit the small European kind, in a downtown hotel in New York.

I do not remember other specific meetings between then and 1982, as most of my correspondence files have been sacrificed to moving from one office to other ones on several occasions. It is likely that we met many more times, as I was frequently visiting Derick Wood at McMaster University in Hamilton, Gabriel Thierrin at The University of Western Ontario in London, and Karel Culik II and David Matthews at the University of Waterloo. John visited me in the early eighties in Darmstadt, from where he had a rather eventful railway journey, worth the pen of Mark Twain, together with a famous colleague. In 1982 I spent a sabbatical in Waterloo, working with Karel Culik II, Jozsef Gruska, David Matthews, Arto Salomaa, Derick Wood, and John. Well, John had just again assumed his regular job as chair of Computer Science. We were looking at syntactic monoids of languages with certain solvable groups as maximal subgroups; we did not get very far on that topic.

In 1983 I moved to London, and it was during one of my frequent visits to Waterloo after that, probably in 1985, that John suggested that we look at modelling the testing of electronic circuits. This is when our more intensive co-operation started.

We worked on modelling circuit testing and also later on modelling software specification and verification using automaton theory. Some details of this research are explained further below. Our co-operation lasted for nearly twenty years. Sometimes it was impeded by my holding two positions simultaneously, one in London in Canada and one in Potsdam in Germany. This made me commute frequently between continents. Despite these obstacles, this was a most enjoyable and fruitful co-operation.

The main theme of our joint work was to model technical processes mathematically in such a way that one could prove properties of these processes. We started out with circuit testing and later moved on to software specification and verification. In both cases a tentative theory existed, but without a solid mathematical foundation. We established the latter. There are many more applied areas in computer science or engineering that could benefit from a sound mathematical foundation similar to what we achieved. When explaining our work, I suggest that our methods, appropriately modified, be used to model those fields. In practice, unfortunately, many researchers in the applied areas attempt to re-invent the basics — often badly — instead of applying the huge knowledge that already exists.

As the present conference in honour of John Brzozowski carries, in its title, the rôle of theoretical computer science, I shall also comment on this more general theme.

As mentioned, most of my written records have been lost to several office moves. Beyond my rather incomplete memory I rely on a huge number of computer files reflecting the process and progress of our thinking about the topics. Fortunately, I hardly ever cleaned up the computer directories, but just moved them untouched between generations of computers and operating systems. It is also worth noting that TEX was around and just about to replace typewriting or *troff* when John and I started working together — initially we did not use LATEX, but my own plain TEX set of macros written before LATEX was around; these macros still exist and are being used. Otherwise even those early documents might not be available or readable today.

## 4.2. Computer Science?

The theme of the present conference is the rôle of theory in computer science. In this spirit, before entering into the details I mention a few points regarding computer science, which might help in understanding statements made further below.

In 1991 Jozsef Gruska and I worked on a position paper regarding the rôle of informatics as a science. The essence of this paper was later published in a volume dedicated to the late A. P. Ershov [47]. We stated what, in our view, distinguished informatics from other sciences and what the main focus of informatics was to be. Moreover, we recommended ideas on how to accomplish these goals. The manuscript, unfinished as it was, provided one of the highly controversial discussion points, leading to IFIP recognizing theoretical computer science as a field in the form of SG14 and later as TC1. This happened during ICALP 1990 in Warwick, UK.

In a reflection paper [52] I wrote that informatics still has to find its real focus and not to spread itself thinly among all kinds of interesting applications. As scientists, we cannot go on with just navigating the opportunities of popularity or funding. Researchers need to learn this, but, more importantly, governments and research funding organizations have to accept this too. "It is not surprising that informatics is still looked down upon with some suspicion by the established fields ... There is still a great deal of basic misunderstanding around — informatics as *working with computers* — that undermines the credibility of our field. To convince others, we ought to agree on what informatics is about; this seems to be more difficult now than it was some thirty years ago. In this context the rôle of theoretical informatics is by no means clear. The gap between the experimental research in informatics and theory is huge ... In fact, we seem to be moving further and further away from a consensus about the essence of the field and the rôles of its components. Informatics still has to establish itself according to lines familiar from physics" [52].

I maintain that computer science has a legitimate and special position among the sciences and that it spans areas that would otherwise never have been in contact with each other. However, in doing that, it over-extends itself so as to be unidentifiable. Computer scientists themselves, not just everyone around them (like application areas, university administration, or political opportunism), have to agree on what their core field is about, and what is application, albeit wonderfully attractive, but not central. In research funding, this disastrous trend for the field, triggered by its own peers who look for fashionable subjects rather than the core, results in basic research in computer science being starved nearly into extinction.

The discussion about computer science as a discipline on its own keeps re-surfacing. In most of Europe, instead of "computer science" the discipline is called "informatics" or "cybernetics" or "datalogi". These names were chosen to avoid the implied linkage to a specific technology about 65 years ago. Unfortunately, the naming difference did not change attitudes. Nearly everywhere in the world, computer science or informatics or cybernetics or datalogi play the game of "Clue": "There is something new! Let's all run for it! Forget the left-over hard problems of the past!"[1]

## 4.3. Scientific Background of Our Work

In the 1980s, several papers on randomized testing had recently been published, and one of the important claims in them was *Allowing for a small probability of an existing fault not being detected, random tests are significantly faster in most relevant situations than deterministic (targeted) tests.* Extensive simulations and case-by-case analyses supported this conjecture (see, for example, [1, 36, 40, 41, 43, 44]). A proof of this claim was impossible without a rigorous formal model. On the engineering side, a formal proof might have been replaced by an equivalently convincing argument. The work mentioned above and related material were later evaluated and presented by R. David in a monograph entitled *Random Testing of Digital Circuits* [35].

We started with the early publications among these. There are also some later papers related to the general theme of randomized testing including [51, 55, 58, 70]. Our point was not, however, to prove specific results for specific kinds of circuits, but to establish fundamental insights into the testing process itself. Thus particular technological issues, such as peculiarities of CMOS circuits, entered the discussions only when they were inevitable.

The general testing scenario is as follows: A *test sequence generator (TG)* sends a finite string of test patterns (symbols) to both a reference circuit[2] (the 'good' circuit) and the *circuit under test (CUT)*. The outputs

---

[1]Our Canadian granting agency NSERC seems to play this game as well. Once considered to be among the best in the world in supporting fundamental research and a broad research base, over the last few years it has managed to deteriorate by discouraging long-term visions and disregarding established records and their consequent research requirements. They have even managed to introduce a negative feed-back loop: if you have little money you cannot support many graduate students; if you have few graduate students you get less money. Actually the system, most likely copied from south of the border, is even more devastating as, within a given granting period of five years one can responsibly accept graduate students at most twice.

[2]Of course, the good circuit need not be an actual circuit, but could be a simulator or a behaviour specification, for example.

of these circuits are compared by a device, which we called the *observer*. The presence of a fault is *detected* when different outputs are observed. The CUT passes the test if the output sequences are identical. A CUT passing the test may still contain faults. In *deterministic testing* the TG sends a single test sequence; in *random testing* a randomly generated test sequence is used. In either case, the cost of testing is measured in terms of the length of the test sequence; the success is measured in terms of *fault coverage*.

A skeptic might doubt the merits of randomized testing, arguing that testing ought to guarantee that the circuit contain no fault at all. However, even with deterministic testing there is a non-zero probability that a fault that is present in the circuit remains undetected. A test result, regardless of the testing method, cannot affirm that the CUT is correct, but only that no faults have been detected. Thus, even in a critical system, like an airplane or a nuclear reactor, one has to accept that a fault may be present, albeit with a very low probability. Whether to use the system ultimately depends on a risk analysis.

The claim of the early papers — that random testing is more economical than deterministic testing while being no less reliable — felt right. Certainly one would want to prove such a very important statement. The mathematics of the original papers was far from clear.

After a very brief attempt at modelling testing in its full generality as suggested in [36], for instance, we soon followed the lead of the papers that we had started to study in detail, [43, 44] in particular, in restricting our discussions to sequential circuits and, especially, to random-access memories (RAMs).

The reasoning presented further below requires some background knowledge: for automaton theory I use [63] and [62]; for circuit testing I refer to [67] and [45].

I briefly review some basic concepts of automaton theory as needed to explain the testing problem in abstract terms, and I introduce the corresponding notation. A *(finite deterministic Mealy) automaton*[3] is a construct $A = (Q_A, X, Y, \delta_A, \lambda_A)$ with the following properties and meanings: $Q_A$ is a finite, non-empty set of *states;* $X$ and $Y$ are finite non-empty sets, the *input and output alphabets,* respectively; $\delta_A : Q_A \times X \to Q_A$ is the *(state) transition function;* and $\lambda_A : Q_A \times X \to Y$ is the *output function.*

---

[3]Throughout this paper I simplify the terminology by omitting restrictive terms written in parentheses unless there is a risk of confusion: thus, for example, 'automaton' means 'finite deterministic Mealy automaton'.

The intuition is as follows: upon input $x \in X$, the automaton moves from its present state $q \in Q_A$ to the state $\delta_A(q, x)$ and simultaneously outputs the symbol $\lambda_A(q, x)$. As usual, the transition and output functions are extended to input words $w \in X^*$ such that $\delta_A(q, w)$ is the state reached, when the input $w$ has been read completely, and $\lambda_A(q, w)$ is the output word obtained during the transitions. The Mealy automaton $A$ can be considered as *initialized* to a state $q \in Q_A$, written as $A_q$ or $(A, q)$, implying that all computations will start at state $q$. Occasionally I omit the output alphabet and the output function; the resulting construct is called a *semiautomaton*.

Let $A$ and $B$ be automata with the same input and output alphabets $X$ and $Y$. Let $q_A \in Q_A$ and $q_B \in Q_B$ be states of $A$ and $B$, respectively. These states are said to be *equivalent*, $q_A \sim q_B$, if and only if $\lambda_A(q_A, w) = \lambda_B(q_B, w)$ for all $w \in X^*$. Equivalently, $q_A \sim q_B$ if and only if $\lambda_A(q_A, x) = \lambda_B(q_B, x)$ and $\delta_A(q_A, x) \sim \delta_B(q_B, x)$ for all $x \in X$. One proves that the states $q_A$ and $q_B$ are equivalent if and only if $\lambda_A(q_A, w) = \lambda_B(q_B, w)$ for all words $w \in X^*$ with $|w| = |Q_A| + |Q_B| - 1$ [63, Folgerung 2.8]. This bound is tight.

The automaton $A$ can be *equivalently embedded* in the automaton $B$, $A \subsetneqq B$, if and only if, for every state $q_A$ of $A$ there is an equivalent state $q_B$ of $B$. The automata are equivalent when each of them can be equivalently embedded in the other one. The initialized automaton $A_p$ can be embedded equivalently into the initialized automaton $B_q$ if and only if $A \subsetneqq B$ and $p \sim q$.

**Observation 1** *Let $A_p$ and $B_q$ be initialized automata such that every state of $A$ is reachable from the initial state $p$. If $p \sim q$ then $A_p$ is equivalent to the subautomaton of $B_q$, which consists of the states of $B$ that are reachable from $q$.*

**Proof.** Let $p' \in Q_A$. Then there is a word $w$ such that $\delta_A(p, w) = p'$. As $p \sim q$, one has $\delta_A(p, w) \sim \delta_B(q, w)$. $\qquad\square$

When there is no risk of confusion I omit the subscript referring to the associated automaton.

The good sequential circuit can be modelled as an automaton $A$; one may assume that $A$ is strongly connected[4] and that it can be reset[5] to some fixed state $q_0^A$. This state will be treated as the initial state of $A$.

---

[4] For each pair of states $q$ and $q'$ of $A$ there is an input word $w$ such that $\delta(q, w) = q'$.
[5] There is an input word $w$, a *reset word*, such that $\delta_A(q, w) = q_0^A$ for all $q \in Q_A$ where $q_0^A$ is a fixed (initial) state.

Assuming that the CUT is also sequential, it is also modelled by an automaton $B$ which, however, may neither be resettable nor strongly connected; moreover, the current state of $B$ may be unknown. The input and output alphabets, respectively, of $A$ and $B$ can be assumed to be the same. Testing $B$ amounts to checking whether $A$ and $B$ are equivalent or, at least, whether $A$ can be equivalently embedded in $B$. For this reason it is important that the good circuit $A$ be resettable. Let $w$ be a reset word for $A$. Applying $w$ to the CUT $B$, which is in an unknown state initially, will set $B$ to a state $q_0^B$. This state need not be unique if $B$ is not equivalent to $A$. After initialization with the reset word $w$, the states $q_0^A$ and $q_0^B$ would be equivalent if $A$ and $B$ are equivalent.

To check whether $A$ and $B$ are equivalent, a simple procedure would compare every state $q_A$ of $A$ with every state $q_B$ of $B$. This amounts to $|Q_A| \cdot |Q_B|$ comparisons. Each of these requires one to consider all inputs of length $|Q_A| + |Q_B| - 1$. Thus, checking the equivalence of $A$ and $B$ in this way takes time proportional to

$$|Q_A| \cdot |Q_B| \cdot |X|^{|Q_A|+|Q_B|-1}.$$

This bound is tight, but can be reduced when only special types of sequential circuits (like RAMs) are considered[6]. More importantly, however, the set of states $Q_B$ of the CUT and their number is unknown. Hence, this simple procedure will not work[7].

To avoid this issue one applies the reset word $w$ first, and then compares the resulting automata initialized to the known state $q_0^A$ and the unknown state $q_0^B$, respectively. One needs to test only whether $q_0^A \sim q_0^B$. This holds if and only if the initialized automaton $A$ can be equivalently embedded into the initialized automaton $B$ with fixed initial states established by the reset word. It does not exclude the possibility of $B$ having states that cannot be reached from $q_0^B$. A naive procedure would iterate the following steps:

(1) Apply the reset word[8] $w$ to $A$ and $B$.
(2) Apply the next input $v$ of length $|Q_A| + |Q_B| - 1$.
(3) If the outputs differ, $q_0^A$ and $q_0^B$ are not equivalent; indicate that an error is present. Otherwise, continue with Step 1 and the next input

---

[6]The taxonomy of [69] does not include optimized algorithms for automaton equivalence.
[7]Of course, there are improvements to this naive algorithm. However, for large numbers of states, the improvements are negligible.
[8]The length of a shortest reset word for a resettable $n$-state automaton is conjectured to be no more than $(n-1)^2/2$ [31, 30] and has been proven to be no more than $(n^3-n)/6$ [60]. For a survey of this issue see [68].

word.

In Step 1, the state reached by $A$ is $q_0^A$, whereas the state reached by $B$ could vary. Thus, this seemingly convincing algorithm is not guaranteed to perform its task unless both $A$ and $B$ can be reset using the same input word. In general, this cannot be expected.

A typical sequential circuit has a huge number of states. For example, a 1 GB-RAM, neglecting the states of the peripheral logic, has $|Q_A| = 2^{38}$ bits, thus $2^{76}$ states. In view of such numbers it is obvious that a complete equivalence test requiring more than linear time in terms of the number of state variables — in the case of the 1 GB-RAM this is $2^{38}$ — is not going to finish within anyone's life.

Obviously, the general approach to equivalence testing is useless. One needs to exploit the specific structure of the good circuit and the likely properties of the CUT to achieve reasonable test lengths[9].

To avoid the complexity issues, there is only one way: reduce the length of test sequences. This means exploiting the special properties of the good circuit and of the likely faults of the CUTs. Instead of looking for non-equivalence one would look only for faults within a given fault model with the implicit assumption that other faults would either be very unlikely to be present or would be found accidentally. Alternatively, rely on random testing. In either case, there will be errors that are undetected. The probability of this happening must be controlled and be provably very small.

Using automaton-based concepts for testing sequential circuits was not a new idea. It dates back to at least Moore's work on *gedanken-experiments* [57]. Poage and McCluskey proposed an automaton-based technique for testing sequential circuits with respect to a given fault model [61]. Similar methods were investigated by Hennie [49, 50], and Gössel and Graf [46]. An explicit early application of this technique to memory testing was proposed by Hayes [48]. A fault model defines which faults one should be looking for. It must be justified by the physical properties of the circuit.

The essential simplification of the testing problem comprises two complementary ideas:

(1) Fault Model: the CUT is assumed to be in a class $\mathcal{F}_A$ of versions of $A$, including $A$. Each member of $\mathcal{F}_A$ is obtained from $A$ by changes implied by the "likely" faults in the model.

---

[9]In reality, several CUTs are tested in parallel. This does not change the time complexity by more than a constant factor.

(2) Instead of all potential test inputs, only such inputs are applied for which the probability is high that faults from the model, if present, will be detected.

### 4.3.1. *The Special Case of Memory Testing*

In contrast to arbitrary sequential circuits including even central processing units (CPUs), memories have a highly regular structure that can be exploited. Disregarding the access logic, a memory is the direct sum of a very large number of very small isomorphic automata, the *memory cells*. Each cell is a 2-state automaton as shown in Fig. 4.1. The automaton has three input symbols, $r^i$, $w_0^i$, and $w_1^i$, where $i$ is the number (or address) of the cell, $r$ means reading the cell, and $w_0$ and $w_1$ mean writing a 0 or 1 into the cell[10]. The corresponding output $x$ is indicated in the form $/x$: read operations give the current state as output; write operations yield a 'dummy' symbol \$ as output. Thus, an $n$-bit memory would consist of $n$ copies of this 2-state automaton, having the input alphabet $\{r^i, w_0^i, w_1^i \mid i = 1, 2, \ldots, n\}$.

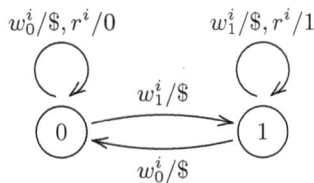

Fig. 4.1. A good memory cell with address $i$.

In a faulty memory some cells misbehave. A general convincing assumption is that detecting a fault in a memory with many faulty cells is easier than detecting a fault in a memory with few faulty cells. I assume this as a trusted conjecture, but with some reservations and should like to see a proof of this.

Testing assumes a *fault model*, that is, as explained above, a collection of faulty behaviours that are deemed likely to occur for physical reasons. For memory testing, these are usually expressed as behaviours of a small number of memory cells. One distinguishes between pattern-sensitive faults in which the behaviour of certain cells depends on the contents of certain other cells, and pattern-insensitive faults. Suppose, for example, that the only likely faults are that the value of a cell might be stuck at the value

---

[10]One cannot, in general make any assumption about the topology of a memory circuit based on the cell addresses.

of 0. In this case, a test of the following form would detect the presence of a fault: for each cell $i$ with $i = 1, \ldots, n$, do $w_0^i r^i w_1^i r^i$. The last read operation $r^i$ would reveal the presence of a fault in cell $i$. Hence a test input of only $4n$ operations is needed for this fault model. Faults in memories can be far more complicated than the stuck-at faults: the operation on one memory cell may influence other cells (coupling faults) and depend on the contents of other cells (pattern-sensitive faults).

In testing one might be satisfied if the result just says that the CUT is faulty — detection; or one may want to know the kind of error detected — diagnosis. The automaton-theoretic procedures are similar. If no error is detected, the CUT may still be faulty. On the other hand, a fault may be detected even if it is not part of the fault model. *Fault coverage* concerns the faults that are detected by tests for a given fault model. An abstract, comprehensive formal definition of fault coverage was proposed in [53].

A typical fault model for memory testing might include the following types of faults:

- *Stuck-at faults:* a memory cell contains the same value, regardless of what is written to it.
- *Transition faults:* a memory cell, which may contain either value, but fails to make the transition, when the other value is written to it.
- *Coupling faults:* writing to a memory cell influences the value in another memory cell.
- *Destructive reading:* reading a memory cell changes its contents.

The first three types form the model proposed by Thatte and Abraham [64]. There are many important variants of these fault types, such as toggling faults and stuck-equal faults. A deterministic test of an $n$-bit RAM for general coupling faults requires at least $2n^2 + 3n$ read-write operations, and a test for this purpose exists, which uses $2n^2 + 4n$ such operations (see [33, 34]). As expected, the deterministic test length for general coupling faults is quadratic in $n$. Surprisingly, and contrary to intuition, a linear test length suffices for a large class of coupling faults. The work by Courtois, David, Foesse, Fuentes, Thévenod-Fosse [40, 41, 43, 44] suggests that random testing for all faults in this model takes only linear time.

Another important distinction between faults concerns *pattern sensitivity:* a pattern-sensitive fault may or may not manifest itself as the faulty behaviour of some memory cells depending on the contents of some other cells. For example, considering two distinct cells $i$ and $j$, cell $i$ may behave correctly when cell $j$ contains a 0 and may be stuck at its current value otherwise. One expects that deterministic testing for pattern-sensitive faults is even more time consuming than testing for coupling faults (see [67]). A general theoretical analysis of pattern-sensitive faults does not seem to exist.

Other fault classifications may have to be considered as well. Our basic assumption was that faults are non-transient. Transient faults are even harder to catch than pattern-sensitive faults. A formal model for these would most likely have to impose severe observability requirements[11] on the good circuit and on the CUT.

Research on circuit testing relies on the *single-fault assumption:* in the CUT there is at most one fault of the fault model present affecting the same set of cells. Multiple faults, that is the presence of more than one fault captured by the fault model, may result in several situations ranging from harmless to disaster:

- The faults affect disjoint sets of memory cells; for testing this causes no problem.
- The faults affect non-disjoint sets of memory cells.
    - The joint effect of the faults is equivalent to a fault in the model: for testing this causes no problem.
    - The joint effect of the faults is impossible (like a cell stuck at 0 and stuck at 1); this requires thoughtful modelling.
    - The joint effect of the faults is outside the fault model; testing procedures have to be analysed to understand how they deal with this new fault type.

John and I established a *fault algebra* with which to handle the conflicting ones among these situations in a systematic fashion [20].

### 4.4. Scientific Expectations

Commonly one under-estimates the scope and theoretical difficulties of a problem that arises from a seemingly well-understood technical procedure. It took us about ten years to arrive at a mathematically rigorous model of a small, but important, part of the problem at hand. Some of the insights we gained helped us to address a similar problem in software specification and verification later. We identified a set of notions, well understood at an intuitive or semi-formal level by specialists in the field of circuit testing, but lacking a formal definition required for rigorous proofs. This set includes, but is not limited to the following:

---

[11] *Observability* in the formal sense of automaton theory.

(1) fault model;
(2) single faults, multiple faults;
(3) pattern-sensitive faults;
(4) testing;
(5) deterministic versus random testing;
(6) fault coverage;
(7) diagnosis versus detection;
(8) the 'most difficult' fault.

Some of these have been explained above or below. The list indicates the tasks undertaken to create a formal theory of circuit testing.

### 4.5. Winnipeg 1987

While our aim was to model the testing, both deterministic and random, of arbitrary sequential machines, we focussed quite early on the testing of RAMs. In terms of automaton theory a fault-free RAM is a huge direct sum of very small automata. As is common in the testing literature, the RAM is considered at the bit level, that is, the operations on the RAM concern single bits[12]. The Mealy automaton modelling a single fault-free memory cell is shown in Fig. 4.1.

A fault type is modelled by a Mealy automaton showing the behaviour of a number $k$ of memory cells where $k$ is exactly the number of cells involved. To illustrate the idea I show four examples.

**Example 1** *The fault type* $\uparrow i \Rightarrow \updownarrow j$ *involves two cells, $i$ and $j$. When $i$ contains 0 and 1 is written into $i$, then $i$ gets contents 1 and the contents of $j$ changes. This is called a toggling fault. The transition diagram, with read operations and outputs omitted is shown in Fig. 4.2 along with the model for the fault-free 2-cell RAM.*

**Example 2** *Consider two memory cells $i$ and $j$ such that $j$ behaves normally when $i$ contains 0 and is stuck at its current value when $i$ contains 1. Such a fault is called a pattern-sensitive transition fault. The automaton, with read operations and outputs omitted, is shown in Fig. 4.3 on the left.*

---

[12]Working at the byte or word levels leads to complications without affecting the essence of the results.

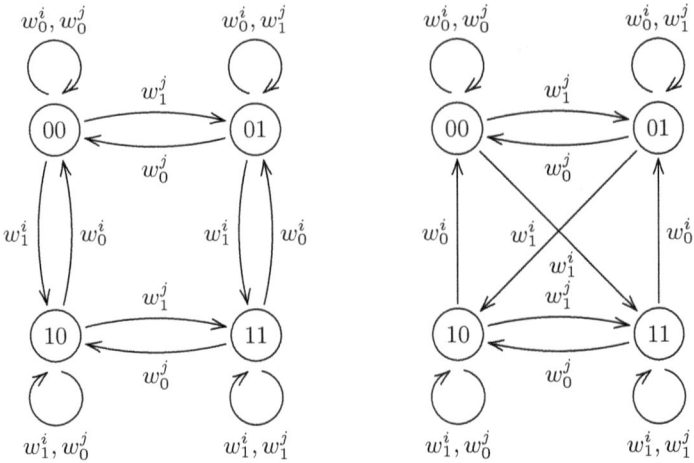

Fig. 4.2.   Two-cell memory: fault-free (left) and $\uparrow i \Rightarrow \updownarrow j$ (right).

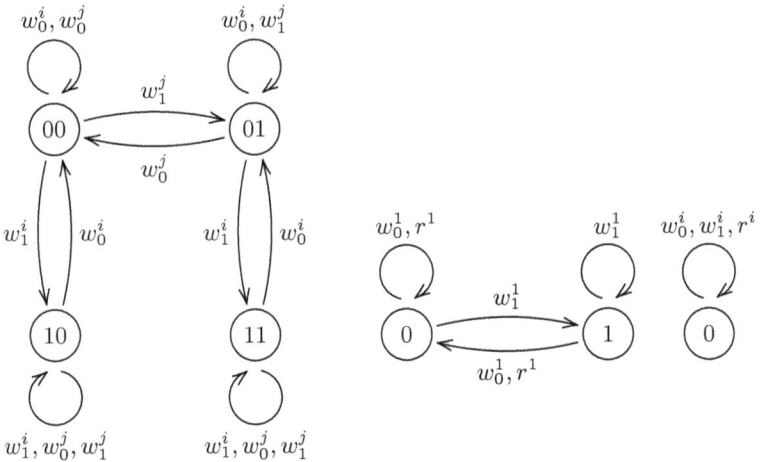

Fig. 4.3.   Pattern-sensitive transition fault (left); destructive read (middle); stuck-at-0 (right).

**Example 3** *If cell $i$ contains 1, the read operation $r^i$ will give the correct output, but also change the contents of the cell to 0. When the cell contains 0 the read operation behaves normally. In all cases, the write operations act correctly. This is a destructive read fault. The automaton, with outputs omitted, is shown in Fig. 4.3 in the middle.*

**Example 4** *The fault of a cell being stuck at the value of 0 is shown in Fig. 4.3 on the right.*

The first version of our model was described in *A Model for Sequential Machine Testing*, presented at *The Second Workshop on IC Testing* in April of 1997 in Winnipeg [7]. In the sequel I refer to this model as MODEL 1. It concerns both deterministic and random testing. The Winnipeg paper gives a very brief exposition of ideas for arbitrary sequential machines and, after that, deals only with memory testing; in particular, we attempted to explain and systematize the procedures leading to the transition diagrams and Markov chains obtained by Fuentes et al. in [44] and in the enhanced and revised version of that paper [40].

Fig. 4.4 shows the non-zero-probability transitions for testing a RAM for the toggling fault $\uparrow i \Rightarrow \updownarrow j$ as presented in [40, 44]. Our aim was to understand the components of such a diagram and, given the basic input data including a fault model, to generate similar diagrams (including this one) algorithmically.

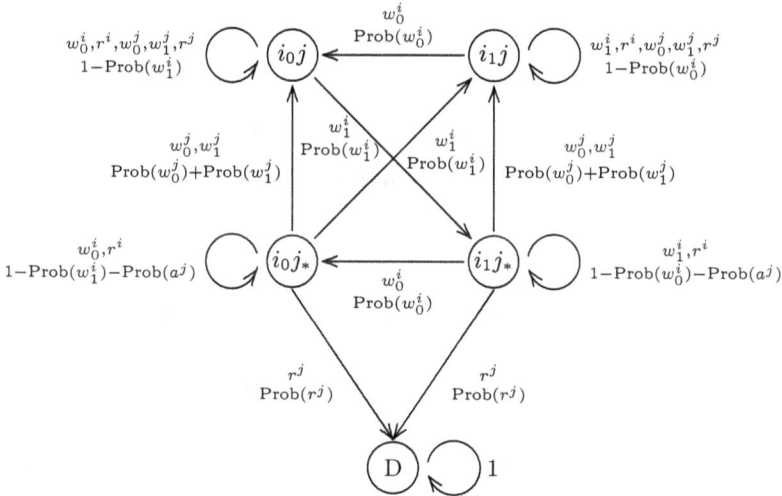

Fig. 4.4. Markov chain for the toggling fault $\uparrow i \Rightarrow \updownarrow j$, adapted from Fig. 3 of [40] to match the presentation in this paper.

The state names in Fig. 4.4 are to be read as follows: $i$ and $j$ refer to the two cells. A subscript of 0 or 1 indicates the actual state of the cell. A star as subscript means that the cell is faulty. The absence of a subscript means that the cell is considered fault-free (so far). The symbol $a_i$ indicates any operation on cell $i$. Thus $\text{Prob}(a_i) = \text{Prob}(r^i) + \text{Prob}(w_0^i) + \text{Prob}(w_1^i)$. The states in the top row are error-free; the states in the middle row indicate that an error is present, but has not yet been detected. In state D a fault has been detected. The probabilities are chosen to be as follows:

$$\mathrm{Prob}(r^i) = \mathrm{Prob}(r^j) = 1/(2n),$$
$$\mathrm{Prob}(w_0^i) = \mathrm{Prob}(w_1^i) = \mathrm{Prob}(w_0^j) = \mathrm{Prob}(w_1^j) = 1/(4n).$$

I show a few steps of this Markov chain. Initially, one can only assume that the state is $ij$, which is not shown; writing to $i$ initializes the state to either $i_0 j$ or $i_1 j$. From $i_1 j$ no operation can set up the fault for detection except $w_0^i$ leading to $i_0 j$. From there $w_1^i$ leads to $i_1 j_*$ where the error is present. The read operation $r^j$ detects the error. Writing anything to $j$ masks the error. Writing 0 to $i$ leads to $i_0 j_*$.

To define our first model of 1987, we started with a semiautomaton $A_0$ representing the fault-free circuit without outputs and with a finite set $\mathcal{F}_{A_0} = \{A_1, A_2, \ldots, A_n\}$ of semiautomata representing *faults of $A_0$*. This set is called a *fault model for $A_0$*. Let $A_i = (Q_i, X, \delta_i)$. From $A_0$ and $\mathcal{F}_{A_0}$ one builds the non-deterministic automaton $F(\mathcal{F}_{A_0})$ with $Q = \bigcup_{i=0}^{n} Q_i$ as the set of states and

$$\eta(p, x) = \{q \mid \exists i : 0 \leq i \leq n, q = \delta_i(p, x)\}$$

for $p \in Q$ and $x \in X$. This non-deterministic automaton is called the *fault schema*.

The key notion is that of a *fault observer*, just called *observer* in later versions of the model. It is defined as a non-deterministic automaton $\Omega(A_0, \mathcal{F}, \sigma) = (K, X, \omega, K_0, K_F)$, given the fault-free machine $A_0$, the fault model $\mathcal{F}(A_0) = \{A_1, A_2 \ldots, A_n\}$ and a *knowledge acquisition function* $\sigma$. The latter is explained further below. The five components of the observer are as follows.

- $K$ is the set of states of the form $k = (p, q_0, q_1, \ldots, q_n, S, T)$ with the following meanings: $p$ is the current state of the circuit under test, unknown to the experimenter. For $i = 0, 1, \ldots, n$, $q_i$ is the current state of $A_i$. $S$ is the subset of $\{0, 1, \ldots, n\}$ such that, for $l \in S$, the CUT has so far been consistent with $A_l$. $T$ is the subset of $\{0, 1, \ldots, n\}$ such that, for $l \in T$, the available information so far does not allow one to conclude that the CUT differs from $A_l$. Thus $S \subseteq T$.
- $X$ is the input alphabet.
- $\omega$ is the transition relation. Let $k = (p, q_0, q_1, \ldots, q_n, S, T) \in K$ with $S \subseteq T$, let $x \in X$, and let $k' = (p', q_0', q_1', \ldots, q_n', S', T') \in K$. Then $k' \in \omega(k, x)$ if and only if the following conditions are satisfied: $p' =$

$\delta_l(p, x)$ for some $l \in S$; $q'_l = \delta_l(q_l, x)$ for $l = 0, 1, 2 \ldots, n$; $S' = \{l \mid l \in S \text{ and } p' = \delta_l(p, x)\}$; $T' = \sigma(k, x)$. To guarantee that $S' \subseteq T'$, $\sigma$ should satisfy $S \subseteq \sigma(k, x) \subseteq T$ whenever $S \subseteq T$. Typically, the knowledge acquisition function uses the outputs of read operations.

- $K_0$ is the subset of $K$ that represents absolutely no knowledge about the CUT.

- $K_F$, called the *fault criterion,* is the subset of $K$ indicating that the CUT and $A_0$ differ (for fault detection) or, more generally, a subset of $K$ identifying the fault (for fault diagnosis).

A word $w$ *detects* (the presence of a fault) if $\emptyset \neq \omega(K_0, w) \subseteq K_F$. It *T-diagnoses* if $\omega(K_0, w) \neq \emptyset$ and the last components of the states in $\omega(K_0, w)$ are subsets of $T$.

In Fig. 4.5 the observer for the fault $\uparrow i \Rightarrow \updownarrow j$ as published in [7] is shown. $A_0$ and $A_1$ have the four states 00, 01, 10, 11; also, the CUT is assumed to have these states. States are numbered 0, 1, 2, 3 according to the binary representation. Commas separate the components of the CUT, of the machines $A_i$, of $S$ and of $T$. For example, $2, 32, 1, 01$ means $(10, 11, 10, \{1\}, \{0, 1\})$. In the diagram, the outgoing arrows indicate fault detection, and the ingoing ones indicate initial states. The initial choice of $S = \{1\}$ reflects the assumption that the fault is present, but undetected. $T = \{0, 1\}$ means that no machine has been ruled out. Details are explained in [7], but are not relevant for the present paper. In the observer the states labelled $a$, $b$, $c$, and $d$ are equivalent to the states $g$, $h$, $e$, and $f$, respectively. Reduction yields the automaton of [40, 44] shown above in Fig. 4.4.

In the next step, probabilities are added to construct the *probabilistic observer:* These are computed from a probability distribution $\pi$ on the set $\{0, 1, \ldots, n\}$ such that $\pi(i)$ is the probability of the CUT being machine $A_i$, and probability distributions $\alpha_i$ on the state sets $Q_i$ such that $\alpha_i(q)$ is the probability of $A_i$ being in state $q$ initially. This construct is a probabilistic automaton. Finally, the input process is modelled by a Markov chain. The resulting construct is called a *Markov test model.*

The paper [7] concludes with a brief indication of how the results of [40, 44] can be obtained algorithmically by our method.

Very shortly after the presentation in 1987 we discovered several shortcomings and even flaws in MODEL 1:

(1) The *identification of the states* of the various parts of a fault model and of a CUT to form a fault schema and the observer is only defined by state names. This causes problems when states are structured and

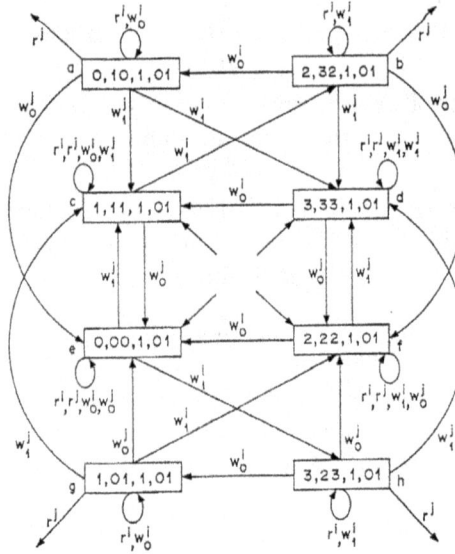

Fig. 4.5. The observer for the fault $\uparrow i \Rightarrow \updownarrow j$ according to MODEL 1 [7].

components of a state in one machine may be states in another machine.

(2) The model does not take into account that the *initial states* of the parts of a fault model and of a CUT are unknown and remain so even after deterministic initialization. Consequently, $K_0$ is defined ambiguously.

(3) Defining an appropriate *knowledge acquisition function* $\sigma$ is not as easy as we thought. We introduced this function so as to model more than the testing of RAMs. For the latter, the read operations suffice to define $\sigma$.

(4) For multiple faults our *probabilistic model* needs clarification on how the probability distributions $\pi$ and $\alpha_i$ are obtained.

We returned to the workbench. The immediate goals were to correct the initial-state problem and to simplify the model and with it the algorithm.

## 4.6. Salgótarján and Halifax 1988

Following 1987 we got involved in the Canadian Workshop for IC Testing. We organized the third and fifth workshops in the series, in Halifax in 1988 and in Ottawa in 1990.

Our revision of MODEL 1, referred to as MODEL 2 in the sequel, was completed in early 1988. We presented it at a conference on automata, languages, and programming systems in Salgótarján, Hungary, in May of 1988 as two invited papers: *Deterministic Diagnosis of Sequential Machines* [8]; *Probabilistic Diagnosis of Sequential Machines* [11]. After further revisions we presented this work again at the workshop in Halifax in October of 1988. With additional modifications, MODEL 2 was finally published as a journal paper [15]. As this publication is readily available, I sketch only the differences between the two models.

To define the fault model, we use Mealy automata instead of semiautomata. The *good machine type* is a Mealy automaton $A_0 = (Q_0, X, Y_0, \delta_0, \lambda_0)$. A fault type is a Mealy automaton $A = (Q, X, Y, \delta, \lambda)$. A *good machine* is a good machine type initialized to some state $q_0$, written as $(A_0, q_0)$. A *fault* is a fault type $A$ initialized to some state $q$, written as $(A, q)$. Let $I = \{0, 1, \ldots, n\}$ for some $n \geq 1$. Let $A_0$ be a good machine type and $A_i$ be fault types. Let $Q$ and $Y$ be finite sets such that $Q_i \subseteq Q$ and $Y_i \subseteq Y$ for all $i \in I$. For $i \in I$, let $P_i \subseteq Q_i$. Let $J = \{(i, q) \mid i \in I, q \in P_i\}$. A *fault model for $A_0$* is a family $\mathcal{F} = \mathcal{F}_{A_0} = \{(A_i, q) \mid (i, q) \in J\}$. With this setting we address the state identification and the initialization problems. If nothing is known about the initial states one chooses $P_i$ to be equal to $Q_i$.

There is nothing similar to the fault schema in MODEL 2. The *observer* is constructed directly from the fault model. It is a deterministic initialized semiautomaton $\Delta = \Delta(A_0, \mathcal{F}) = (D, X \times Y, \delta, d_0)$ that models the process by which one arrives at the conclusion that the CUT $(A, p)$ is a particular machine in $\mathcal{F}$. In the first step, every Mealy automaton $A' = (Q', X, Y', \delta', \lambda')$ in the model is transformed into a semiautomaton $\widetilde{A}' = (\widetilde{Q}', X \times Y', \widetilde{\delta}')$ as follows: (1) Let $\omega \notin Q$ and $\widetilde{Q}' = Q' \cup \{\omega\}$. (2) For $q \in \widetilde{Q}'$ and $(x, y) \in X \times Y'$ let $\widetilde{\delta}'(q, (x, y))$ be equal to $\delta'(q, x)$ if $q \in Q'$ and $\lambda'(q, x) = y$, and equal to $\omega$ in all other cases. The state $\omega$ is intended to denote an impossible situation. The set $D$ of states of the observer consists of all tuples $d$ with components $d_{i,q} \in \widetilde{Q}_i$, that is, $D = \{d \mid d_{i,q} \in \widetilde{Q}_i, (i, q) \in J\}$. The initial state $d_0$ of the observer is defined as $[d_0]_{i,q} = q$ expressing the fact that nothing is known. The transition function $\delta$ of the observer is given by $[\delta(d, (x, y))]_{i,q} = \widetilde{\delta}_i(d_{i,q}(x, y))$. This eliminates the ambiguities, in MODEL 1, concerning the choice of $K_0$, $\sigma$, and $K_F$; it subsumes the rôles of $S$, $T$, and $\sigma$ in the definition of $\delta$. A component $d_{i,q}$ of a state $d$ of the observer is equal to $\omega$ if and only if the observed behaviour of the CUT is known to be inconsistent with $(A_i, q)$. In Fig. 4.6 the observer, according to MODEL 2, for the fault $\uparrow i \Rightarrow \updownarrow j$ is shown. It happens to be isomorphic with the one according to MODEL 1 shown in Fig. 4.5, and hence its reduction is isomorphic with the transition graph of the Markov chain defined in [40] and shown in Fig. 4.4.

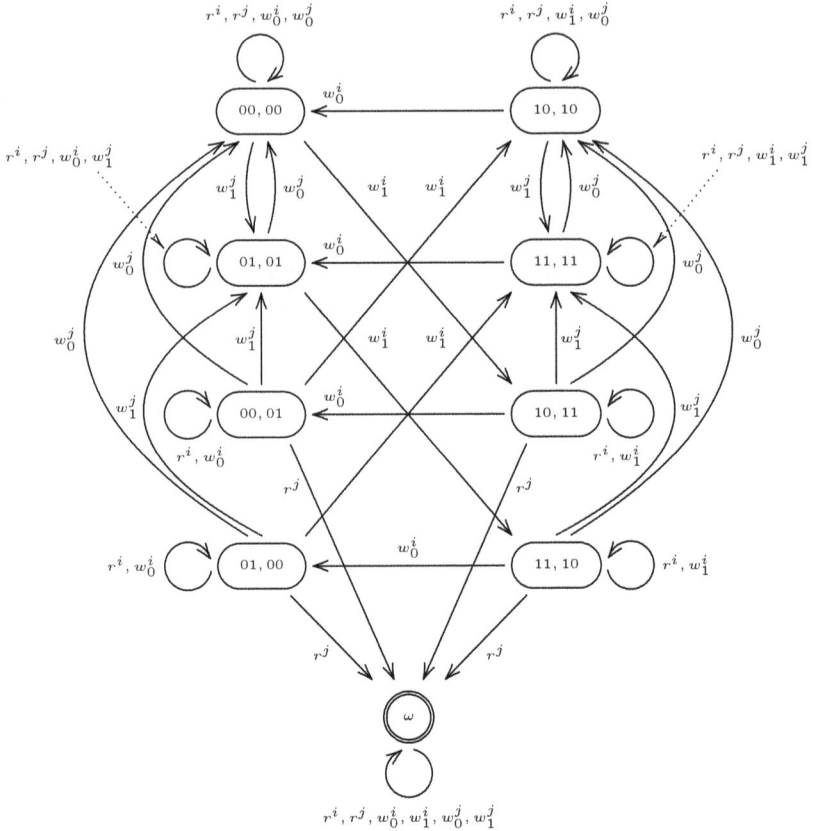

Fig. 4.6. The observer for the toggling fault $\uparrow i \Rightarrow \updownarrow j$, assuming the fault is present. The initial states are $(11, 11)$ and $(11, 10)$. Figure from our paper [39], adjusted to the present context.

The observer according to MODEL 2 applies even to some combinational circuits and, more importantly, allows for a clear definition of fault diagnosis. For this purpose, consider the set $K = \{(i, q, q') \mid (i, q) \in J, q' \in Q_i\}$. For $d \in D$ let $\|d\| = \{(i, q, q') \mid (i, q) \in J, q' = d_{i,q} \neq \omega\}$, called the *contents of* $d$. If the state of the observer is $d$, the contents of $d$ describes the machine type, initial state, and present state of those machines that have not been ruled out by the test so far. Now consider a partition $B$ of $K$ with blocks $B_1, B_2, \ldots, B_r$. A state $d$ of $\Delta$ is $B$-*decided* if $\|d\| \subseteq B_i$ for some block $B_i$. A word $w \in X^*$ $B$-*diagnoses* if $\delta(d_0, (w, v))$ is $B$-decided for every output $v \in Y^*$ having the same length as $w$. These definitions allow one to answer specific diagnostic questions depending on the choice of the partition $B$. In particular, notions such as *distinguishing sequence* or *homing sequence* introduced by Hennie [49, 50] can be expressed easily with these methods. Once a diagnosis goal has been specified by a partition $B$, the observer can be reduced by standard methods; it can also be transformed into an acceptor; the accepted language is regular, and the words in that language are $B$-diagnosing.

To model random testing, the probability distributions $\pi$ and $\alpha_i$ of MODEL 1 are replaced by a probability distribution $\pi$ on $J$. The probabilistic observer and, analogously, the probabilistic $B$-diagnoser are constructed as in MODEL 1. This allowed us to prove the following conjecture of [44]: *given any threshold $0 < \varepsilon < 1$, the random test length for stuck-at-0 faults in RAMs is bounded by a linear function of the number $n$ of memory cells, when the probability of an error remaining undetected does not exceed $\varepsilon$.* The deterministic test length for these faults is $4n$. That it is also linear for random tests is not obvious. This result is, however, far away from the general goal stated earlier: the random test length for many fault types is linear even if the deterministic test length is not.

The issue concerning the probability distributions and multiple faults, mentioned in the previous part of this paper was not resolved in the new model. In all other respects, it is far better: the initialization problem has been resolved; the construction is clear and concise; each part of the construction and of the model has a well-defined obvious meaning.

The experience with publishing the final paper of MODEL 2 in a journal was mixed. We intended to publish it for a readership beyond the testing community. After a rejection by a journal with a broader readership including researchers in automaton theory, we submitted it to the then young *Journal of Electronic Testing, Theory and Applications (JETTA)*. There it appeared.

MODEL 2 resulted in our final version of the deterministic observer. In 1992–1993 a program was developed for the observer construction, spearheaded by C.-J. Shi and involving a student, John, Michael Gössel, and me. Beyond a 2-page note, no material about this program seems to exist any more. In the years following 1992, John and I presented the general ideas in several survey-type papers [13, 16, 19, 21] emphasizing the rôle of automaton theory.

With MODEL 2, the general problem of random testing had not been solved. Nor had the problem of how to model multiple faults as compositions of single faults. Research on the former continued during a visit by René David in approximately 1992. On the latter we started to work sometime in 1991.

## 4.7. Random Testing of RAMs

We continued with the observer of MODEL 2. Two notions, used implicitly before, needed to be defined, that of a bounded fault and that of a non-evasive fault. A bounded fault involves a bounded number of memory cells regardless of the overall size of the memory. When only bounded faults are considered in the fault model, the size of the observer is independent of the size of the RAM. If a fault is evasive, there is an input sequence to the circuit after which the fault will not manifest itself under any subsequent input. For a non-evasive fault, the state $\omega$ can be reached from every reachable state of the observer, and $\omega$ is a sink state. For the Markov chain constructed from the observer to model random testing this means that the chain has only a single ergodic class, that consisting of $\omega$, and all other states are transient.

The probability distribution $\pi$ is no longer needed; neither are the probability distributions $\alpha_i$. Using the same input probabilities as before, the transition matrix of the Markov chain derived from the reduced observer for the toggling fault $\uparrow i \Rightarrow \updownarrow j$ is

$$\begin{pmatrix} 1 - 1/8n & 0 & 0 & 1/8n & 0 \\ 1/8n & 1 - 1/8n & 0 & 0 & 0 \\ 1/4n & 1/8n & 1 - 5/8n & 0 & 1/4n \\ 0 & 1/4n & 1/8n & 1 - 5/8n & 1/4n \\ 0 & 0 & 0 & 0 & 1 \end{pmatrix},$$

where $n$ is the size of the RAM.

Together with René David we proved, on the basis of these constructions, that the required random test length for any bounded, non-evasive fault of an $n$-bit RAM is bounded by $O(n/\varepsilon)$ where $0 < \varepsilon < 1$ is the error threshold. This result proves the conjecture of [40, 44] in far more general terms than we had dared to hope for.

There is one piece still missing, however: the bound is not tight at all. For the toggle fault and $\varepsilon = 10^{-3}$ the bound on the test length is about 14,000n [39] while simulations indicate a bound of 100n [40].

The publication of this fundamental result turned out not to be easy either. The paper was rejected by two journals, both more than suited to the subject, for different reasons. It finally appeared in the *Journal of Electronic Testing, Theory and Applications* [39].

## 4.8. Fault Algebra

A multiple fault is the presence of more than one single fault[13]. What is a single fault? While there does not seem to be a formal definition of the latter, the consensus seems to be that it is a fault resulting from a single physical defect. Various sets of single faults have been proposed in the literature as fault models. The one proposed by Thatte and Abraham [64], which comprises stuck-at, transition, and coupling faults, was used by us as the guiding example in the definition of fault composition.

The first formal definition of the composition of RAM faults was proposed by Brzozowski and Cockburn [33]. A $\delta$-*fault* is either the good RAM modelled by the Mealy automaton $M_0 = (Q, X, Y, \delta_0, \lambda)$ or a faulty RAM modelled by some Mealy automaton $M_k = (Q, X, Y, \delta_k, \lambda)$. Given two $\delta$-faults $M_k$ and $M_l$, their composition is the $\delta$-fault $M_{kol} = (Q, X, Y, \delta_{kol}, \lambda)$ with

$$\delta_{kol}(q, x) = \Big( \big( \delta_k(q, x) \oplus q \big) + \big( \delta_l(q, x) \oplus q \big) \Big) \oplus q,$$

for all $q \in Q$ and all $x \in X$, where $+$ and $\oplus$ denote the componentwise inclusive and exclusive or operations, respectively. While this construction works well for coupling faults, it fails, as noted by Cockburn [32], for transition and stuck-at faults.

Starting in about 1990, we attempted to find a formal definition of the composition of RAM faults that would be comprehensive, concise, and adequate. This came in three stages, refining the model of $\delta$-faults, simplifying the rules, correcting subtle, but important, inconsistencies with the physical situation, and exposing the fundamental concepts. As in [33], the states of the automata under consideration are tuples of bits[14]. A $\delta$-fault $M_k$ can differ from the good RAM $M_0$ in two ways: (1) the set of states $Q_k$ is a subproduct[15] of $Q_0$; (2) $\delta_0 \neq \delta_k$. Here $\lambda_k$ is just the restric-

---

[13]This common definition is too broad. A multiple fault consists of a set of several single faults each affecting at least one cell that is also affected by another fault in the set.

[14]The theory itself is initially not restricted to the binary case.

[15]Let $Q_0 = \overbrace{\{0, 1\} \times \{0, 1\} \times \cdots \times \{0, 1\}}^{k \text{ times}}$ for some $k \geq 1$. A *subproduct* of $Q_0$ is a set of the form $R_1 \times R_2 \times \cdots \times R_k$ with $R_i \subseteq \{0, 1\}$ for $i = 1, 2 \ldots, k$.

tion of $\lambda$ to $X \times Q_k$. The composition of $\delta$-faults $M_k$ and $M_l$ has state set $Q_k \cap Q_l$. When this set is empty, the composition of $M_k$ and $M_l$ is the *empty automaton* $\mathbf{0} = (\emptyset, X, Y, \emptyset, \emptyset)$. Otherwise, the transition function of the composite automaton is defined componentwise according to a fairly complicated distinction of cases. The composition is commutative, associative, and idempotent. Hence the $\delta$-faults form a semilattice with $\mathbf{0}$ as a zero element[16]. The partial order defined by the composition[17] describes the *masking of faults*, that is, $M_1 \leq M_2$ if the physical defects for $M_1$ and $M_2$ are present, but only the effects of the former are manifested. With $\mathfrak{S}$, $\mathfrak{T}$, and $\mathfrak{C}$ denoting stuck-at, transition, and coupling faults and $n$ being the size of the RAM, the sets $\mathfrak{S}_n$, $\mathfrak{T}_n$, $\mathfrak{C}_n$, $\mathfrak{ST}_n$, $\mathfrak{SC}_n$, $\mathfrak{TC}_n$, and $\mathfrak{STC}_n$ form semilattices with zero elements (not always the same). They can be defined abstractly by generators and relations. This first version of our attempt at defining a fault composition was published in 1992 in [14, 18]. Preceding manuscripts show our struggle with the details of the case distinction in the composition operation. In those papers we also noticed that one has to distinguish between two types of coupling faults: (1) the mere attempt to write into one cell affects the other cell; (2) the coupling occurs only if the write operation is successful. We proposed to model this by *two-step automata*, a rather awkward model to be replaced later by a far simpler and more natural one.

Our next text attempt [20] was to simplify and generalize the constructions. Thus we started with a set of hypotheses, which served as guidance and axioms at the same time; in this we were encouraged by discussions with Michael Gössel. The first three hypotheses are generic and apply to all fault types. They state that the set of faults within a given fault model together with a composition operation, say $\diamond$, form a semilattice, possibly with a zero element. The next five hypotheses concern the interaction between the physical defects leading to stuck-at, transition, and coupling faults. To deal with the two variants of coupling faults and further similar situations, we introduced the notions of *change-attempt-activated* and *change-success-activated* faults[18]. Let $\mathcal{A}_n$ and $\mathcal{S}_n$ be the corresponding sets

---

[16]The automaton $\mathbf{0}$ could result from the composition of incompatible faults, like a cell stuck at 0 and also at 1.

[17]$M_1 \leq M_2$ if and only if $M_1 = M_1 \circ M_2$.

[18]We simplified the notation: $M^{i=a}$, stuck-at fault, cell $i$ stuck at $a$; $M^{i\neg a}$, transition fault, cell $i$ does not change to $a$; $Mia \Rightarrow jb$, coupling fault, with $\bar{a}$ in $i$, writing $a$ to $i$ causes $j$ to contain $b$. Let $\odot$ denote a composition operation. The non-generic hypotheses for change-attempt-activated faults are: $M^{i=a} \odot M^{i=\bar{a}} = \mathbf{0}$, $M^{i=a} \odot M^{i\neg b} = M^{i=a}$, $M^{i=a} \odot M^{jb \Rightarrow ic} = M^{i=a}$. For change-success-activated faults one adds the following

of faults of an $n$-bit RAM. Clearly, $S_n \subsetneq A_n$. We defined a composition operation $\diamond$ similarly to the one of our earlier version, but without the complicated distinction of cases. The algebra $(S_n, \diamond)$ is a semilattice with $\mathbf{0}$ as zero, while $(A_n, \diamond)$ is not. The stuck-at, transition, and coupling faults are in $S_n$, and the non-generic five physical hypotheses hold for $\diamond$. In particular, the set $T_n^\diamond$ generated by the faults in the Thatte-Abraham model [64] with $\diamond$ as operation is a subsemilattice of $S_n$. For $A_n$ one defines another composition operation $\circ$ by the same expression as that for $\diamond$, but with modified conditions for its application. The operation satisfies the first three of the non-generic hypotheses. The set $A_n$ is closed under $\circ$, but $S_n$ is not. The set $T_n^\circ$ generated by the Thatte-Abraham model with $\circ$ as operation is a subsemilattice of $A_n$, and one has $S_n \cap T_n^\circ = T_n^\diamond$.

The main achievement of this second version of our model was that the definition of the composition operation is derived from the interaction of physical defects rather than by the properties of the abstract functional model. The modelling process has changed significantly: first formulate the physical phenomena in abstract terms as "hypotheses"; then define a composition operation and prove that it satisfies the hypotheses.

We published this second version in 1996 [20]. Later, we noticed an inconsistency between the definition of the state set of the composite automaton and the definition of the composition operations. These problems did not arise in the first version, as we only considered such faults for which the state sets are subproducts of the state set $Q$ of the fault-free RAM. In an erratum to [20] we solved this problem by adding the subproduct condition everywhere at the cost of excluding some fault types, like the stuck-equal fault; its state set $\{(0,0), (1,1)\}$ is not a subproduct.

We took the abstraction still one step further in [23]. Only $\delta$-faults are considered; hence it was sufficient and convenient to work with semiautomata instead of Mealy automata. Consider a set of physical defects of the CUT and the corresponding set $S$ of single faults represented as semiautomata. Thus, the notion of *single fault* is now tied to that of physical defect. Multiple defects lead to multiple faults. To model multiple faults, a composition operation $\odot$ for Mealy automata is needed. It must satisfy the generic hypotheses, that is, the algebra generated by $S$ with the operation $\odot$ must be a semilattice and, therefore, a homomorphic image of the free semilattice generated by $S$. The latter is isomorphic with the semilattice $(2^S, \cup)$ of subsets of $S$. Here $T \subseteq S$ denotes the simultaneous

---

two non-generic hypotheses: $M^{i \neg a} \odot M^{ia \Rightarrow jb} = M^{i \neg a}$, $M^{i=a} \odot M^{ib \Rightarrow jb} = M^{i=a}$. The last equation is a consequence of the previous ones and could be omitted.

presence of the faults in $T$. Thus, for $\odot$ to be defined, $T$ corresponds to the composition $\odot_{t \in T}\, t$. Here $\emptyset$ corresponds to the fault-free RAM. The non-generic hypotheses, to be derived from the physical defects, define a set $E$ of equations such that $(2^S, \cup)/E$ is the fault semilattice for the fault model $S$ under consideration[19]. These insights were then applied to the set $T$ of Thatte-Abraham faults as an example. There are three equations for change-attempt-activated faults and additional two equations for the change-success-activated faults, corresponding to the hypotheses above and leading to operations $\circ$ and $\diamond$ as before. The following statements are an extract from the main results of [23]:

(1) Let $\mathcal{P}$ be the set of subproduct faults (hence the set of $\delta$-faults of [18]). $\mathcal{P}^\circ = (\mathcal{P}, \circ)$ is a semilattice with $\mathbf{0}$ as zero element and the good RAM $M$ as identity element. $\mathcal{T}^\circ$ is a proper subsemilattice of $\mathcal{P}^\circ$.

(2) $\mathcal{P}^\diamond = (\mathcal{P}, \diamond)$ is an idempotent and commutative groupoid with $\mathbf{0}$ as zero and $M$ as identity, but not a semilattice.

(3) Let $\mathcal{A}$ and $\mathcal{S}$ be the set of change-attempt-activated and change-success-activated faults in $\mathcal{P}$, respectively. The algebra $\mathcal{S}^\diamond = (\mathcal{S}, \diamond)$ is a semilattice with $\mathbf{0}$ as zero and $M$ as identity. $\mathcal{T}^\diamond$ is a proper subsemilattice of $\mathcal{S}^\diamond$.

(4) A delta fault is change-attempt-activated, pattern-insensitive, and a subproduct fault if and only if it is equivalent to a fault in $\mathcal{T}^\circ$.

(5) A delta fault is change-success-activated, pattern-insensitive, and a subproduct fault if and only if it is equivalent to a fault in $\mathcal{T}^\diamond$.

(6) There is a homomorphism of $\mathcal{T}^\circ$ onto $\mathcal{T}^\diamond$. Its restriction to $\mathcal{T}^\diamond$ is the identity mapping.

Points (4) and (5) afford a complete characterization of pattern-insensitive subproduct faults as compositions of faults in the Thatte-Abraham model. Moreover, their proofs exhibit, for a given pattern-insensitive subproduct fault, how such a composition can be obtained.

## 4.9. Next?

Regarding the model for circuit testing, much can still be done.

- For the case of memory testing, the algebraic theory only applies to subproduct, change-activated[20] and pattern-insensitive faults. It is not clear how to include faults that violate these conditions. All three types

---

[19] I am omitting a few subtle points here.

[20] In the case of RAMs, a change-activated fault manifests itself only when a write operation is applied; a fault that results from a read operation is not change-activated.

are not uncommon. For example a stuck-equal fault is — in essence — just caused by a short; it is not a subproduct fault. Pattern-sensitive faults could be caused by leakage. A destructive-read fault, which could be the result of a failing refresh circuit, is not change-activated. Such faults are not covered by some of our algebraic results, but are covered by our results on random testing as they are non-evasive and bounded.

- Time-dependent faults — like a memory cell leaking — are not covered by either approach. We had some rudimentary ideas on how to model them, but they seemed to be far too complicated.

- An advantage of random testing has been claimed not only for memories, but also for arbitrary circuits, both combinational and sequential (see, for example, [35, 36, 41]). An adequate mathematical model does not seem to exist, let alone a proof of the properties of testing in these circumstances.

Solutions to the problems in this list will require many new ideas.

Rather than continue with testing related problems, we turned to another modelling problem in the context of software specification and verification. This happened around 2001. Again, John suggested the idea, having read a seminal paper on trace assertions [2]. The more we read the paper and the deeper we dug, the less we understood; the model seemed to be unnecessarily complicated. Our first attempt at clarifying the theory was published in a technical report [25] in 2003, soon to be followed by major improvements [26]. The complete model was published in 2005 and 2007 as *Representation of Semiautomata by Canonical Words and Equivalences* in two parts [28, 29]. In this setting the trace assertion method is modelled by abstract presentations of semiautomata using string rewriting for equivalence proofs. We dealt with the deterministic case and only very briefly discussed the non-deterministic setting. John later derived a similar representation for settable nondeterministic semiautomata [6]. A nondeterministic automaton is said to be *settable* if, for every state $q$, there is an input word $w_q$, such that the set of states reached from the initial states by input $w_q$ contains $q$ and no other state. Dropping the condition that the semiautomaton be settable seems to lead to a new kind of very difficult problems.

## 4.10. What Can Be Learnt?

I shall collect a few statements that I deem important for computer science in general or for modelling issues specifically. These may be personal and one may certainly disagree. The list is by no means complete. The principles and lessons are not new, but often neglected. The essential task of mathematical modelling is inherently difficult, and has many pitfalls and unsatisfactory, but tempting, sidetracks.

⇒ *In contrast to pure mathematics and even some branches of theoretical computer science, the laws of the application govern the modelling process. However, those laws are rarely expressed in unambiguous formal terms and may vary among publications.*

*Whatever mathematical model one proposes, it has to capture the essence of the problem at hand, no more, no less. The model must be proven to be consistent, that is, to cover the phenomena under consideration. The model must not use redundant or unexplained parameters (Occam's razor).*

Some mathematicians or theoretical computer scientists do not care whether their assumptions match any kind of physical reality. For others the area of application is of concern to a varying degree. We used the latter approach. One needs to keep the model simple: complicated constructs should not be needed if the technical process can be explained without them. Often one will have to prove "trivial" statements, frowned upon by pure theorists, as supporting evidence for the "correctness" of the model.

⇒ *One of the most important tasks is to gather detailed information about the problem at hand and to understand the terminology of the application field. Before one can set out to model a system, one has to get a precise understanding of the basic terms. This should allow one to identify the atomic building blocks as abstract entities and to express relationships between them.*

In our work on testing we realized quite early that faults could be modelled by Mealy automata, but did not take into account the connection between defects and their functional manifestation as faults. For this reason the notions of single and multiple faults remained vague initially. Similarly, in our first model the process of testing and diagnosis was not well understood, hence not quite correct and fraught with a complicated and completely unnecessary emulation of human knowledge-acquisition behaviour.

⇒ *Explanations by specialists in the field must be examined repeatedly. They usually "know" (or believe they know) what they mean by their explanations. In trying to model, one feels certain that one understands the explanations — but often the mental images of the specialist and the modeller differ.*

I had this kind of experience several times, for instance in a project to computerise a dentist's office in the late 1970s: after a large and tiring number of interviews with the dentist and his staff and many on-site observations the software was produced. In the evaluation phase I heard "this is not what I meant" more often than I liked.

In the context of testing, the important notions of "fault coverage" and "most difficult fault" remained unclear despite many explanations found in the engineering literature.

⇒ *One cannot prove that a model is correct. However, one must prove that the model is consistent with empirical knowledge.*

Initially, we did not take into account the difference between change-attempt and change-success. When only single faults were considered, as in the construction of the observer or of the Markov chain for random testing, this distinction was irrelevant. It turned out to be crucial for modelling multiple faults to prove that the respective composition models the actual multiple-fault behaviour.

⇒ *When considering a phenomenon, before trying to come up with a new model for it, one should consider existing models. In particular, one should attempt to re-formulate the parameters to fit an existing model.*

In computer science, various automaton or grammar models usually provide adequate and powerful tools to solve a problem. When defining new models instead, one often loses the connection to existing ones and the tools and knowledge provided by them for free. Re-inventing the basics, or even less, of automaton theory is quite common in both computer science and engineering[21].

⇒ *Theoretical Computer Science (Theoretical Informatics) has two distinct facets:*

*(1) There are purely mathematical areas of theoretical computer science with little immediate impact on the current evolution of software or hardware development, nor on the way people think about these issues.*

*(2) There are areas where theory can guide practice constructively.*

*It is not a good idea to ignore this distinction. The former may become relevant with a delay (as is common in mathematics, too); the latter, if accepted, can lead to significantly improved solutions right away, but also*

---

[21] For computer science education this would imply that a solid education in theoretical computer science spanning more than a single course and a concrete cross-relation between theoretical and non-theoretical courses. According to my experience, the latter seems to be very difficult to achieve. In retrospect, a label like 'Fundamentals of Computing' rather than 'Theoretical Computer Science' might have helped to avoid the problem altogether. While engineering students have to be fluent in mathematics at some level, many computer science students tend to avoid everything mathematical if at all possible.

*misdirect if applied prematurely.*

An eminent example of fundamental insights recognized only with a great delay is the work of Axel Thue of the early twentieth century on what is now called combinatorics on words [65, 66]. His seemingly, at the time, esoteric results now provide a mathematically sound foundation for problems like process analysis.

⇒   *The mere existence of an algorithmic solution to a given problem may be useless. One may have to exploit the special properties of the problem at hand. However, the given general solution is likely to provide guidance. Sometimes one has to sacrifice ideals to feasibility — this is a matter of expectations. The general solution usually helps one to identify the inevitable sacrifices*[22].

When a complete algorithmic solution is not feasible, it may still be possible to deal with all or most cases of practical interest. In the case of RAM testing, the restriction to the Thatte-Abraham model or to bounded faults affords mostly feasible solutions; the tests targeted to detect these kinds of faults also happen to detect many other faults outside the fault model. This collateral advantage is not usually captured by the theory.

⇒   *One needs to work through characteristic examples in every possible detail. A superficial sketch of an example is rarely enough.*

By avoiding hand-waving arguments, we often detected shortcomings of the original definitions, which would have remained unnoticed otherwise.

⇒   *Separate and group concepts according to their abstract rôles.*

In the case of our testing work, the separation of generic and physical conditions was crucial to our understanding of the distinction between properties that every fault composition must have and properties that result from specific physical defects.

⇒   *One needs to convince the practitioners in their language that the model is adequate, complete, and useful. One needs to convince the mathematicians (or the grant selection committee) that the work is worth anything at all.*

A profound paper may end up being rejected by both scientific communities, but for different reasons, as happened to two of our papers. Convincing requires exceptionally careful writing with both types of readership in mind. People in the field might not appreciate the usefulness of the work; theorists may consider it trivial.

We have seen referees' reports that state: (1) The authors proved ...

---

[22]It is not uncommon that people re-invent automaton theory, sometimes using new names for well-known concepts and they might even get huge grants for that.

results; a verification of these by simulation is missing and should be included using ... as benchmarks. (2) This is folklore in automaton theory ...

⇒ *Careful writing with attention to every detail is essential.*

John and I have a rather unusual way of co-operating: not only do we discuss and develop ideas together, we also write them down together in real time. Nearly every phrase, word, punctuation, illustration, choice of mathematic symbol gets discussed while we are writing. The text is cleaned up many times in such joint sessions. At the height of our co-operation we had weekly or biweekly meetings either in London or in Waterloo, often lasting more than five hours.

⇒ *Profound (modelling) research takes much time.*

This is a message not only to researchers who are eager to get their ideas published but also to those who adjudicate research. As our struggle with the testing scenario and, later, with trace assertions shows, to formulate a convincing, concise, and elegant model may require several iterations in which ideas get gradually clarified; blind alleys are sometimes part of the natural thinking process and may force one to backtrack. In both cases, circuit testing and trace assertions, we did not start from scratch: there were already rudimentary and accepted models that we could use as starting points. Without this advantage, our road would have been even more arduous.

The time required to conduct such foundational work as ours does not fit the research funding models of any funding agency I know. Typically, *projects* are funded for a small number of years, and too few get any really deep results unless one has them already in one's drawer. In some countries, such as Germany, research funding at universities has two or more sources: (1) base research funding from the university and (2) project funding from agencies. In such a setting, long-term work is feasible, as long as it is low-cost like the size of an average NSERC[23] grant in computer science. The former NSERC funding model was ideal for such work, funding a research programme rather than a project, based on the experience of the researcher. This model was changed several years ago: while NSERC still claims to fund research programmes, the new instability of the funding makes it work like project funding. Under the new NSERC rules, our joint work lasting nearly 20 years, would have been impossible to complete.

---

[23]Natural Sciences and Engineering Research Council (of Canada).

## 4.11. Chronology

Here is a brief chronology of our joint work on testing and on trace assertions. During this period both John and I separately also worked on related topics, which are not listed.

1985 • Approximate start of the co-operation.

1987 • First model using knowledge sets and a knowledge acquisition function, presented at the second Canadian Test Workshop in April in Winnipeg: *A Model for Sequential Machine Testing* [7].

• We attempt to get Canadian industry involved (e.g., NORTEL).

1988 • A corrected and simplified model was presented at the Second Conference on Automata, Languages and Programming Systems, the predecessor of AFL, in Salgótarján, Hungary, in May; further revised and presented at the third Canadian Test Workshop in October in Halifax: *Deterministic Diagnosis of Sequential Machines* [8, 9] and *Probabilistic Diagnosis of Sequential Machines* [11, 12].

• We organized the third Canadian Test Workshop in October in Halifax.

1990 • Bruce Cockburn's PhD on fault models and tests for RAMs [32]. Upper and lower bounds on test lengths. Certain coupling faults require more than linear test lengths (see also [33, 34]).

• I also started to work with Michael Gössel in Berlin, later Potsdam, on testing issues. We considered built-in self-tests.

• Founding of the MAVERIC research group [56].

1991 • We organized the fifth Canadian Test Workshop in October in Ottawa.

• Michael Gössel attended.

1992 • *A Model for Sequential Machine Testing and Diagnosis* published [15] (submitted in October of 1991).

• First model of fault composition (multiple faults) presented at the second Conference on Words, Languages and Combinatorics in August in Kyoto, Japan: *Component Automata and RAM Faults* [14, 18].

• Perry Wong and I defined the notions of *fault coverage* and *most difficult fault* in language theoretic terms: *How to Prove Fault Coverage — or: Testing for the Most Difficult Fault* [53], presented at the sixth Canadian Test Workshop in Montréal.

• General paper given at *2. Theorietag, Automaten und formale*

*Sprachen,* in Kiel, Germany, in October: *Automata Theoretic Considerations in Circuit Testing* [13].

- Work with René David: *Testing for Bounded Faults in RAMs* [37].

1993 • Invited paper given at the Seventh International Conference on Automata and Formal Languages (AFL) in Salgótarján, Hungary: *An Automaton Theoretic Approach to Circuit Testing* [16]. Fully published as *Applications of Automata and Languages to Testing* [17, 21] (1994 and 1996).

- *Random Test Length for Bounded Faults in RAMs* [38] presented at the Third European Test Conference (ETC93).

- *Observer: A Program for Fault Diagnosis of Sequential Circuits* by J. A. Brzozowski, H. Jürgensen, M. Gössel, C.-J. Shi.

1994 • Survey paper given at the 20th Summer School on Applications of Mathematics in Engineering in Varna, Bulgaria: *Theory of Circuit Testing* [19] (appeared 1995).

1995 • *Composition of Multiple Faults in RAMs* presented at the 1995 IEEE International Workshop on Memory Technology, Design and Testing in San Jose, California.

1996 • I started commuting between London and Potsdam. This lasted until 2010.

1997 • Notes on counting types of faults [22]. Paper on (random) testing for bounded faults in RAMs finally appears [39].

1999 • *Semilattices of Fault Semiautomata* [24, 23]. This concluded our joint work on circuit testing and, in particular, on multiple faults.

- Research focus shifted to software specification and verification.

2003 • First attempt, *Trace-Assertion Specifications of Deterministic Software Modules* [25].

2004 • An improved version presented as *Representation of Semiautomata by Canonical Words and Equivalences* at the Workshop on Descriptional Complexity of Formal Systems (DCFS) in London, Canada [26].

- *Theory of Deterministic Trace-Assertion Specifications* [27].

2005-07 • The complete model: *Representation of Semiautomata by Canonical Words and Equivalences* [28, 29].

**Thank You!**

Thank you, John, for our fruitful, intensive, and most enjoyable cooperation of almost twenty years!

# References

1. Z. ABAZI AND P. THÉVENOD-FOSSE, Markov models for the random testing analysis of cards, in *Digest of FTCS-16, the 16th International Symposium on Fault Tolerant Computing Systems, Vienna, July 1–3, 1986*, Los Alamitos, 1986, pp. 272–277, IEEE Computing Society Press.

2. W. BARTUSSEK AND D. PARNAS, Using assertions about traces to write abstract specifications for software modules, Tech. Rep. Number TR77-012, University of North Carolina at Chapel Hill, December 1977. Reprinted as [5]; also [3, 4].

3. W. BARTUSSEK AND D. PARNAS, Using assertions about traces to write abstract specifications for software modules, in *Information Systems Methodology, Proceedings ICS 65*, Berlin, 1978, pp. 211–236, *LNCS*, Springer Verlag. See also [2, 5, 4].

4. W. BARTUSSEK AND D. PARNAS, Using assertions about traces to write abstract specifications for software modules, in *Software Specification Techniques*, N. Gehani and A. D. McGettrick (eds.), pp. 111–130, AT&T Bell Telephone Laboratories, 1985. See also [2, 5, 3].

5. W. BARTUSSEK AND D. PARNAS, Using assertions about traces to write abstract specifications for software modules, in *Software Fundamentals: Collected Papers by David L. Parnas.*, M. Hoffman and D. M. Weiss (eds.), pp. 9–28, Addison-Wesley, Boston, 2001. Reprint of [2]; see also [3, 4].

6. J. A. BRZOZOWSKI, Representation of a class of nondeterministic semiautomata by canonical words, *Theoret. Comput. Sci.* **356**,1–2 (2006), 46–57.

7. J. A. BRZOZOWSKI AND H. JÜRGENSEN, A model for sequential machine testing, in *New Directions for IC Testing, Second Workshop, Winnipeg*, 1987. 17 pp.

8. J. A. BRZOZOWSKI AND H. JÜRGENSEN, Deterministic diagnosis of sequential machines, in *Second Conference on Automata, Languages and Programming Systems, Held in Salgótarján, Hungary, May 23–26, 1988*, F. Gécseg and I. Peàk (eds.), Department of Mathematics, Karl Marx University of Economics, Budapest, 1988, pp. 35–49, *Report 1988-4*.

9. J. A. BRZOZOWSKI AND H. JÜRGENSEN, Deterministic diagnosis of sequential machines, in [10], pp. 47–58.

10. J. A. Brzozowski and H. Jürgensen (eds.), *New Directions for IC Testing, Third Technical Workshop, Working Papers, Halifax*, 1988.

11. J. A. BRZOZOWSKI AND H. JÜRGENSEN, Probabilistic diagnosis of sequential machines, in *Second Conference on Automata, Languages and Programming Systems, Held in Salgótarján, Hungary, May 23–26, 1988*, F. Gécseg and I. Peàk (eds.), Department of Mathematics, Karl Marx University of Economics, Budapest, 1988, pp. 51–66, *Report 1988-4*.

12. J. A. BRZOZOWSKI AND H. JÜRGENSEN, Probabilistic diagnosis of sequential machines, in [10], pp. 59–71.

13. J. A. BRZOZOWSKI AND H. JÜRGENSEN, Automata theoretic considerations in circuit testing, in *2. Theorietag "Automaten und Formale Sprachen", Uni-*

*versität Kiel, 2./3. Oktober 1992*, W. Thomas (ed.), Institut für Informatik und praktische Mathematik, Universität Kiel, Kiel, 1992. 4 pp.

14. J. A. BRZOZOWSKI AND H. JÜRGENSEN, Component automata and RAM faults, in *Abstracts: The Second International Colloquium on Words, Languages, and Combinatorics, August 25–28, 1992; Workshop on Semigroups, Formal Languages and Combinatorics on Words, August 29–31, 1992*, M. Ito and H. Jürgensen (eds.), Kyoto, 1992, pp. 6–10.

15. J. A. BRZOZOWSKI AND H. JÜRGENSEN, A model for sequential machine testing and diagnosis, *J. of Electronic Testing: Theory and Applications* **3** (1992), 219–234.

16. J. A. BRZOZOWSKI AND H. JÜRGENSEN, An automaton theoretic approach to circuit testing, in *Abstracts, 7th International Conference on Automata and Formal Languages, Salgótarján*, 1993.

17. J. A. BRZOZOWSKI AND H. JÜRGENSEN, Applications of automata and languages to testing, Tech. Rep. Number 420, Department of Computer Science, The University of Western Ontario, 1994.

18. J. A. BRZOZOWSKI AND H. JÜRGENSEN, Component automata and RAM faults, in *Proceedings of the International Conference, Words, Languages, and Combinatorics II, Kyoto, Japan, 25–28 August 1992*, M. Ito and H. Jürgensen (eds.), Singapore, 1994, pp. 49–67, World Scientific.

19. J. A. BRZOZOWSKI AND H. JÜRGENSEN, Theory of circuit testing, in *Proceedings, 20th Summer School on Applications of Mathematics in Engineering, Varna, 1994*, M. Marinov and D. Ivanchev (eds.), Technical University of Sofia, Institute of Applied Mathematics and Informatics, Sofia, 1995, pp. 51–52.

20. J. A. BRZOZOWSKI AND H. JÜRGENSEN, An algebra of multiple faults in RAMs, *J. of Electronic Testing: Theory and Applications* **8** (1996), 129–142. Errata **9** (1996), 217 and **14** (1999), 305–306.

21. J. A. BRZOZOWSKI AND H. JÜRGENSEN, Applications of automata and languages to testing, *Publ. Math. (Debrecen)* **48** (1996), 201–215.

22. J. A. BRZOZOWSKI AND H. JÜRGENSEN, Counting of fault types. unpublished manuscript, 1997.

23. J. A. BRZOZOWSKI AND H. JÜRGENSEN, Semilattices of fault semiautomata, in *Jewels Are Forever; Contributions on Theoretical Computer Science in Honor of Arto Salomaa*, J. Karhumäki, H. Maurer, G. Păun and G. Rozenberg (eds.), Berlin, 1999, pp. 3–15, Springer-Verlag.

24. J. A. BRZOZOWSKI AND H. JÜRGENSEN, Semilattices of fault semiautomata, Tech. Rep. Number 535, Department of Computer Science, University of Western Ontario, 1999.

25. J. A. BRZOZOWSKI AND H. JÜRGENSEN, Trace-assertion specifications of deterministic software modules, Maveric Research Report Number 03-1, School of Computer Science, University of Waterloo, 2003.

26. J. A. BRZOZOWSKI AND H. JÜRGENSEN, Representation of semiautomata by canonical words and equivalences, in *Descriptional Complexity of Formal Systems (DCFS), Pre-Proceedings of a Workshop, London, Canada, 26–28 July, 2004*, L. Ilie and D. Wotschke (eds.), Department of Computer Science,

The University of Western Ontario, London, Canada, 2004, pp. 13–27, *Report No. 619*.

27. J. A. BRZOZOWSKI AND H. JÜRGENSEN, Theory of deterministic trace-assertion specifications, Tech. Rep. Number CS-2004-30, School of Computer Science, University of Waterloo, 2004.

28. J. A. BRZOZOWSKI AND H. JÜRGENSEN, Representation of semiautomata by canonical words and equivalences, *Int. J. Found. Comput. Sci.* **16** (2005), 831–850. Erratum **17** (2006), 1231–1232.

29. J. A. BRZOZOWSKI AND H. JÜRGENSEN, Representation of semiautomata by canonical words and equivalences, part II: Specification of software modules, *Int. J. Found. Comput. Sci.* **18** (2007), 1065–1087.

30. J. ČERNÝ, Poznámka k homogénnym experimentom s konečnými automatmi, *Mat. fyz. čas. SAV* **14**,3 (1964), 208–215.

31. J. ČERNÝ, A. PIRICKA AND B. ROSENAUEROVA, On directable automata, *Kybernetika* **7** (1971), 289–298.

32. B. F. COCKBURN, *Fault Models and Tests for Coupling Faults in Random-Access Memories*, PhD thesis, University of Waterloo, Los Alamitos, California, 1990.

33. B. F. COCKBURN AND J. A. BRZOZOWSKI, Detection of coupling faults in RAMs, *J. of Electronic Testing: Theory and Applications* **1**,2 (1990), 151–162.

34. B. F. COCKBURN AND J. A. BRZOZOWSKI, Near-optimal tests for classes of write-triggered coupling faults in RAMs, *J. of Electronic Testing: Theory and Applications* **3**,3 (1992), 251–264.

35. R. DAVID, *Random Testing of Digital Circuits, Theory and Applications*, Marcel Dekker, Inc., New York, 1998.

36. R. DAVID AND G. BLANCHET, About random fault detection of combinational networks, *IEEE Trans. Comput.* **25**,5 (1989), 637–650.

37. R. DAVID, J. A. BRZOZOWSKI AND H. JÜRGENSEN, Testing for bounded faults in RAMs, Tech. Rep. Number CS-92-30, Computer Science Department, University of Waterloo, 1992.

38. R. DAVID, J. A. BRZOZOWSKI AND H. JÜRGENSEN, Random test length for bounded faults in RAMs, in *ETC 93, Third European Test Conference, Rotterdam, The Netherlands, April 19–22, 1993, Proceedings*, Los Alamitos, California, 1993, pp. 149–158, IEEE Computer Society Press.

39. R. DAVID, J. A. BRZOZOWSKI AND H. JÜRGENSEN, Testing for bounded faults in RAMs, *J. of Electronic Testing: Theory and Applications* **10** (1997), 197–214.

40. R. DAVID, A. FUENTES AND B. COURTOIS, Random pattern testing versus deterministic testing of RAMs, *IEEE Trans. Comput.* **38**,5 (1989), 637–650.

41. R. DAVID AND P. THÉVENOD-FOSSE, Random testing of integrated circuits, *IEEE Trans. Instrumentation and Measurement* **30**,2 (1981), 20–25.

42. S. EILENBERG, *Automata, Languages, and Machines, Volumes A, B*, Academic Press, 1974, 1976.

43. P. FOSSE AND R. DAVID, Random testing of memories, in *GI – 7. Jahrestagung Informatik-Fachberichte*, H. J. Schneider (ed.), Berlin, 1977, vol. 10,

pp. 139–153, Springer-Verlag.

44. A. FUENTES, R. DAVID AND B. COURTOIS, Random pattern testing versus deterministic testing of RAMs, in *Digest of FTCS-16, the 16th International Symposium on Fault Tolerant Computing Systems, Vienna, July 1–3, 1986*, Los Alamitos, California, 1986, pp. 266–271, IEEE Computing Society Press. A revised version of this paper was published as [40].

45. M. GÖSSEL AND S. GRAF, *Error Detection Circuits*, McGraw-Hill, London, 1993.

46. S. GRAF AND M. GÖSSEL, *Fehlererkennungsschaltungen*, Akademie-Verlag, Berlin, 1987. English translation: [45].

47. J. GRUSKA AND H. JÜRGENSEN, Maturing of informatics, in *Images of Programming, Dedicated to the Memory of A. P. Ershov*, D. Bjørner and V. Kotov (eds.), pp. I-55–69, North-Holland, Amsterdam, 1991.

48. J. P. HAYES, Detection of pattern-sensitive faults in random-access memories, *IEEE Trans. Comput.* **24**,2 (1975), 150–157.

49. F. C. HENNIE, Fault-detecting experiments for sequential circuits, in *Switching Circuit Theory and Logical Design, Proceedings of the Fifth Annual Symposium, Princeton University, Princeton, N. J., November 11–13, 1964*, New York, 1964, pp. 95–110, IEEE.

50. F. C. HENNIE, *Finite-State Models for Logical Machines*, John Wiley & Sons, New York, 1968.

51. A. A. ISMAEEL AND M. A. BREUER, The probability of error detection in sequential random test vectors, *J. of Electronic Testing: Theory and Applications* **1** (1991), 245–256.

52. H. JÜRGENSEN, Towards computer science, in *People & Ideas in Theoretical Computer Science*, C. S. Calude (ed.), pp. 130–145, Springer-Verlag, Singapore, 1998.

53. H. JÜRGENSEN AND P. WONG, How to prove fault coverage – or: Testing for the most difficult fault, in *Proceedings of the 6th Workshop on New Directions for Testing*, Montréal, 1992, pp. 285–294.

54. Z. Kohavi and A. Paz (eds.), *Theory of Machines and Computations. Proceedings of an International Symposium on the Theory of Machines and Computations Held at Technion in Haifa, Israel on August 16–19, 1971*, New York, 1971, Academic Press.

55. A. KUMAR, *Biased random testing*, MSc Thesis, The University of Western Ontario, 2002.

56. MAVERIC RESEARCH GROUP, University of Waterloo. http://maveric. uwaterloo.ca/home.html.

57. E. F. MOORE, Gedanken-experiments on sequential machines, in *Automata Studies*, C. E. Shannon and J. McCarthy (eds.), pp. 129–153, *Annals of Mathematics Studies* Number 34, Princeton University Press, Princeton, New Jersey, ed. fifth printing, 1972, 1956.

58. L. NACHMAN, K. K. SALUJA, S. J. UPADHAYA AND R. REUSE, A novel approach to random pattern testing of sequential circuits, *IEEE Trans. Comput.* **47**,1 (1998), 129–134.

59. T. Nagell, A. Selberg, S. Selberg and K. Thalberd (eds.), *Selected Mathemat-*

*ical Papers of Axel Thue*, Universitetsforlaget, Oslo, 1977.

60.  J.-E. PIN, Sur les mots synchronisants dans un automate fini, *Elektron. Informationsverarbeit. Kybernetik* **14** (1978), 297–303.

61.  J. F. POAGE AND J. E. MCCLUSKEY, Derivation of optimum test sequences for sequential machines, in *Switching Circuit Theory and Logical Design, Proceedings of the Fifth Annual Symposium, Princeton University, Princeton, N. J., November 11–13, 1964*, New York, 1964, pp. 121–132, IEEE.

62.  J. SAKAROVITCH, *Elements of Automata Theory*, Cambridge University Press, Cambridge, 2009. English translation of *Éléments de théorie des automates*, Vuibert Informatique, Paris, 2003.

63.  P. H. STARKE, *Abstrakte Automaten*, VEB Deutscher Verlag der Wissenschaften, Berlin, 1969. English translation by I. Shepherd, *Abstract Automata*, North-Holland, Amsterdam, 1972.

64.  S. M. THATTE AND J. A. ABRAHAM, Testing of semiconductor random access memories, in *Digest of Papers, 7th Int. Conf. on Fault-Tolerant Computing, Los Angeles*, pp. 81–87, 1977.

65.  A. THUE, Über unendliche Zeichenreihen, *Skrifter udgivne af Videnskabs-Selskabet i Christiania (Norske Vid. Selsk. Skr.), I. Mathematisk-naturvidenskabelig klasse* **part 1**,7 (1906). 22 pp. Available from www.biodiversitylibrary.org/item/52020. Reprinted in [59], 139–158.

66.  A. THUE:, Über die gegenseitige Lage gleicher Teile gewisser Zeichenreihen, *Skrifter utgit av Videnskapsselskapet i Kristiania (Norske Vid. Selsk. Skr.), I. Mathematisk-naturvidenskabelig klasse* **part 1**,1 (1912). 67 pp. Available from www.biodiversitylibrary.org/item/52278. Reprinted in [59], 413–477.

67.  A. J. VAN DE GOOR, *Testing Semiconductor Memories: Theory and Practice*, John Wiley & Sons, Chichester, 1991.

68.  M. VOLKOV, Synchronizing automata and the Černý conjecture, in *2nd LATA 2008*, C. Martín-Vide, F. Otto and H. Fernau (eds.), Berlin, 2008, *LNCS* vol. 5196, Springer.

69.  B. W. WATSON, *Taxonomies and Toolkits of Regular Language Algorithms*, Proefschrift (doctoral thesis), Technische Universiteit Eindhoven, 1995.

70.  H.-J. WUNDERLICH, Multiple distributions for biased random test patterns, *IEEE Trans. Computer-Aided Design* **9**,6 (1990), 584–593.

# Chapter 5

# Is Complementation Evil?

Ernst L. Leiss

*Department of Computer Science*
*University of Houston*
*Houston Texas 77204-3010*
*USA*

Complementation has acquired a bad reputation over the years. This is strongly manifested in Meyer and Stockmeyer's result that adding this operator into the mix of operations of regular expressions defines regular languages for which the membership problem has non-elementary complexity (exceeds any fixed-sized stack of exponentiations). It is further driven home by a deceptively simple language equation over a single-letter alphabet with complementation and concatenation as the only operators whose solution is not regular (and therefore not context-free). Further afield, there is a result by Schlörer on general trackers in the area of inference control in statistical databases, where the presence of complementation defeats seemingly strong security defenses. Reexamining these and other examples tempers the bad reputation of complementation somewhat: complementation cannot achieve its misdeeds alone — it needs accomplices (in the form of other operators).

## Contents

## 5.1. Introduction

Complementation is one of the fundamental operations in mathematics and computer science. For example, in set theory, in logic, and in formal language theory it plays an important role, but it is also of vital importance in hardware implementations of instructions and in database theory, to give a few other areas. Nevertheless and in spite of its ubiquity, it is considered a "difficult" operation, certainly when comparing it to other well-known operations such as union or concatenation, to name two language-theoretically motivated ones.

Here, the notion of "difficult" depends on the context. Within the theory of formal languages, it is easily defined formally: we simply use complexity theory to measure difficulty. More specifically, when it comes to regular languages, we use the size of the smallest deterministic finite automaton (DFA) that accepts the language obtained by applying the operations, in terms of the complexity of the languages to which the operations are applied. Alternatively, it is also sometimes useful to consider the size of a smallest non-deterministic finite automaton (NFA). Clearly, the two measures are related, since the deterministic complexity is never more than 2 to the power of the non-deterministic complexity.

One relationship that will be useful for this paper is that between NFAs and regular expressions. Specifically, the length $|\alpha|$ of a regular expression $\alpha$ over the alphabet $A$ is precisely the number of letters of $A$ in $\alpha$. Thus, the length of the regular expression $aa \cup ab^\star$ over the alphabet $A = \{a, b\}$ is 4. As usual, we use the symbol $\cup$ to denote union, $\star$ to denote Kleene closure, and concatenation is ordinarily denoted by juxtaposition. There is a very useful relationship between the length of a regular expression and the number of states of a non-deterministic automaton, due to a construction by B. G. Mirkin [13]: for a given regular expression $\alpha$, his construction yields a non-returning NFA with exactly $|\alpha| + 1$ states. Moreover, this construction does not employ $\lambda$–transitions. A non-returning automaton is one where no transition from any state leads to the initial state. It follows now that the DFA for a non-returning NFA with $n$ states cannot have more than $2^{n-1} + 1$ states, since the initial state of the NFA cannot occur together with any other states in the resulting DFA. (In [4] we gave a slight refinement of the very elegant algorithm of Mirkin.)

If one looks at the union or concatenation of two regular languages represented by two non-returning NFAs with non-initial states $s_1$ and $s_2$, respectively, their union and the concatenation can be accepted by NFAs with $s_1 + s_2$ non-initial states, that is, the problem (in terms of non-initial states) is additive. However, if one takes the complement of a language presented by an NFA of size $s$, things become more difficult: effectively, we have to convert the NFA first to a DFA, which may result in an exponential explosion of the number of states, and only then can we flip accepting and rejecting states to obtain a DFA for the complement.

In other contexts, "difficulty" must be defined differently. While language equations appear to be very similar to formal languages (and indeed their solutions are formal languages), the application of operations may result in a somewhat surprising expansion of what the resulting language classes are. We will comment on several classes of language equations below. In the context of statistical databases, another topic we will consider below, "difficult" means that certain objectives (as we will outline them) in the realm of inference control may simply not be attainable.

In the remainder of this paper, we will first give three examples that indicate unequivocally that the introduction of complementation radically changes the outcome. These are extended regular expressions, which denote regular languages but are potentially of unimaginably large complexity; certain types of explicit language equations over a one-letter alphabet involving as operations only concatenation and complementation applied to single letters of the alphabet, which do not have any regular solutions (but do have non-context free ones); and finally, an example from inference control in statistical databases, where the availability of complementation implies that the responses to queries that are supposedly not permitted can be obtained with embarrassing ease. We then reexamine the language equation field, using two examples, one where concatenation is restricted to be left-concatenation, in which case the presence of complementation results in a complexity that is no more than doubly exponential in terms of the complexities of the constituent languages (in sharp contrast to the case induced by extended regular expressions, where the height of the stack of exponentiations is unbounded), and the case of implicit language equations involving only union and complementation, where the solutions have a rather low complexity. This leads to our conclusion that complementation alone is never particularly "difficult"; it is "difficult" only when it occurs in conjunction with other operations, and the extent of the "difficulty" depends on those operators.

## 5.2. Extended Regular Expressions

It is well known [12] that the equivalence problem for extended regular expressions has non-elementary complexity. In other words, if we add the complementation operator to the operators of ordinary (or restricted) regular expressions, namely union, concatenation, and star, the resulting expressions are known as extended regular expressions. Every extended regular expression over an alphabet $A$ denotes a regular language over $A$. However, the number of states of the smallest DFA that accepts the regular language denoted by an extended regular expression $\alpha$ of length $n$ (defined in the usual way, namely as the number of letters from the alphabet $A$ in $\alpha$) can be unimaginably large. Specifically, let $S(s, n)$ denote the following function of $n \geq 1$:

$$S(0, n) = n \quad \text{and,} \quad \text{for all } s \geq 1, \ S(s, n) = 2^{S(s-1,n)}.$$

In other words, $S(s, n)$ is a stack of height $s$ of powers of 2, the last of which is taken to the power of $n$. (It is not an exaggeration that $S(s, n)$ for larger values of $s$ is unimaginably large; to wit, $S(4, 2) = 2^{65536}$ which is much larger than $10^{21000}$. To put this number into perspective, it is generally accepted that the observable universe contains far fewer than $10^{100}$ atoms [15].) Then we can say that for any given $s \geq 1$, there exists an extended regular expression $\alpha$ of some length $n$ such that the smallest DFA accepting the language denoted by $\alpha$ has strictly more than $S(s, n)$ states.

The upshot of this is that adding complementation to the permitted operators in regular expressions radically changes the complexity of the languages denoted by the expressions from singly exponential (from a regular expression $\alpha$, to an NFA with $|\alpha| + 1$ states, to a DFA with no more than $2^{|\alpha|} + 1$ states) to one exceeding any fixed-size stack of powers of 2. Nevertheless, given an extended regular expression, the language it denotes is regular. In our next example of the power of exponentiation, we will see that we might end up with a language that is no longer even regular.

## 5.3. An Explicit Language Equation with a Unique, non-Regular Solution

Language equations are a simple extension of expressions. We form expressions in the usual way, using operators from a given list and applying them to operands that may be letters of the alphabet or variables; then we equate these expressions by setting them equal to either a variable (explicit equations) or a constant (implicit equations) (for more details, see [11]).

Any finite automaton can be trivially transformed into a set of explicit equations. For example, the following non-deterministic finite automaton $N = (\{a,b\}, \{q_0, q_1, q_2, q_3\}, \tau, q_0, \{q_0, q_2\})$ with the transition function $\tau$ given by

|       | $a$        | $b$        |
|-------|------------|------------|
| $q_0$ | $q_1, q_2$ | $q_0$      |
| $q_1$ | $q_3$      | $q_2$      |
| $q_2$ | $q_0$      | $q_1, q_3$ |
| $q_3$ | /          | $q_3$      |

results in the following system of language equations using as operators union and left-concatenation with a constant (this means that in any concatenation, the left operand must be a constant while the right operand may be anything), over the variables $X_1, X_2, X_3$, and $X_4$:

$$\star \quad X_0 = a(X_1 \cup X_2) \cup bX_0 \cup \lambda$$
$$X_1 = aX_3 \cup bX_2$$
$$X_2 = aX_0 \cup b(X_1 \cup X_3) \cup \lambda$$
$$X_3 = bX_2.$$

Here, the star with $X_0$ indicates that we want to solve for this variable since it corresponds to the initial state $q_0$, the empty word $\lambda$ occurs exactly with those variables that correspond to accepting states, and the overall objective is to solve the system of equations in the following sense: find four languages $L_1, L_2, L_3$, and $L_4$ such that substituting $L_i$ for the variable $X_i$ for $i = 1, 2, 3, 4$ yields four simultaneous language identities. It should be clear that each of the four variables uniquely represents the language that is accepted by the automaton if the initial state were the state corresponding to that variable.

Clearly, language equations are a more general concept than expressions, since any regular expression $\alpha$ (restricted or extended) can be converted into an equivalent equation (equivalent in the sense that the solution denotes the same language) by setting $\alpha$ equal to some variable $X$:

$$X = \alpha.$$

Language equations can be based on any alphabet. In particular, an alphabet containing only one letter is particularly simple. Obviously, any system of language equations over a one-letter alphabet must have a solution over that alphabet if it has any solution. This must be stated since complementation is dependent on the underlying alphabet, in contrast to the other operations union, concatenation, and star. To illustrate, the equation

$$X = aX \cup \lambda,$$

has the unique solution $X = a^\star$ regardless of the underlying alphabet $A$ (which must of course contain the letter $a$), but the equation

$$X = a\overline{X} \cup \lambda,$$

has infinitely many different solutions depending on the underlying alphabet $A$, as follows:

$$X = (aa)^\star \cup (aa)^\star a(A - \{a\})A^\star.$$

This now permits us to state our next example of the complications that the introduction of complementation generates [10, 11]. There exists a simple explicit language equation over the one-letter alphabet $A = \{a\}$ and over a single variable $X$, using as operators only concatenation and complementation, which has a unique solution, and this solution is not regular (and therefore not context-free, since any context-free language over a one-letter alphabet is also regular). This is a result that for the first time demonstrated that using regularity-preserving operations may result in non-regular solutions in the context of language equations. Here is the equation:

Let $\alpha^2$ denote the expression $\alpha\alpha$. In particular therefore

$$\overline{\alpha}^2 = \overline{\alpha}\,\overline{\alpha}.$$

Then the equation is

$$X = a\overline{\overline{X}^2}^2 .$$

One can verify [10] that this equation has the following unique solution:

$$\bigcup_{i \geq 0} a^{2^{3i} .. 2^{3i+2} - 1},$$

where $a^{m..n}$ denotes the set of words $a^i$ with $m \leq i \leq n$. This language is not regular and therefore not context-free.

## 5.4. General Trackers in Statistical Database Security

Databases are essentially organized repositories of information. Typically, access is direct; given a key, one may obtain the information that is associated with this key. However, there is another way of using this information; namely, by using statistical queries. In many such databases, there are legal or ethical or policy restrictions about who may or may not obtain access to information directly. If statistical queries are used, these restrictions translate into the desire to be able to ensure that one may not infer, from the responses to legitimate statistical queries, information associated with individual entries which is generally prohibited for this type of user. This is known as inference control.

To illustrate these concepts, consider a database containing, among other content, medical information about patients. In most jurisdictions, this type of information is protected: access to information associated with specific individuals may occur only on a need-to-know basis (implying appropriate authorization), which in turn translates into the requirement for the database administrator to be able to guarantee that people without this authorization may not obtain access to the information. It should be obvious why this is of importance — simply consider that the database contains information about the HIV status of each patient: most patients would not want this information to be publicly obtainable. At the same time, there may be legitimate public-health reasons that suggest statistical studies to improve treatment or prevention which would involve gathering statistics about the patients based on their HIV status. For example, one might want to design a campaign that aims at the prevention of HIV infections; it should be obvious that aspects such as educational achievement or socio-economic status of population groups likely to become infected would be of relevance in the design of this propaganda campaign. Thus, a statistician working with this database might formulate statistical queries designed to capture this information. The problem of inference control is then very simply stated: how can we guarantee that the statistician cannot combine the responses to different legitimate statistical queries to obtain direct information about a specific patient's HIV status?

Clearly, this is a very wide field of research, and we will select only a rather small aspect of it. Nevertheless, it should be clear that there are two important issues: what types of queries can be used, and how do we define what would be a query that provides unacceptable access (for the statistician)?

To address the second question first, generally one views queries as dangerous if they define a group of people too specifically; in the extreme case, this is when the query identifies exactly one individual. This depends, of course, on the context; for example, the set of primary keys. Thus, if a query effectively permits the user to identify a unique individual, it is obviously a query that must not be permitted within the context of statistical access. Taking this a step further, we might therefore stipulate that any query that identifies a set of individuals with fewer than $h$ members cannot be permitted. Here, $h$ is a parameter that presumably depends on the size of the database and the paranoia of the database administrator.

In keeping with the theme of this article, we will focus on the set operations that can be used in the formulation of the queries. So, we may look at queries that involve union of sets (Type 1) or we may look at queries that involve union and complement of sets (Type 2). Essentially, we are looking at SQL-like queries, except we impose the security restriction that all queries must involve at least $h$ elements, and we permit either only unions (or; Type 1) or unions and complementations (or and not; Type 2) of sets of primary keys. It should be clear that for the Type 2 context, we must now also impose a restriction about queries that are too large (identify too many entries in the database), since obviously by applying complementation, we can convert a query that is too large to one that is too small. Thus, for Type 2 queries, we impose the security restriction that the set of elements $NU(q)$ involved in a query $q$ must contain at least $h$ elements and must not contain more than $N - h$ elements where $N$ is the total number of entries in the database:

$$h \leq NU(q) \leq N - h.$$

Inference control then means that it is impossible to combine the responses to legitimate statistical queries (in our example, those that meet the above restriction on the size of the sets of keys involved) to obtain responses to queries that are not legitimate (do not obey the above restriction on set size).

While in the case of Type 1 queries, it requires a good deal of work to violate the objective (see for example [6]), it turns out to be embarrassingly easy to breach confidentiality requirements with Type 2 queries. Consider the notion of general tracker which was introduced by Schlörer [14]; this is any query $GT$ with the following property:

$$2h \leq NU(GT) \leq N - 2h.$$

In other words, it is obviously a legitimate statistical query, and it goes a bit beyond the requirements, in that it must define a larger set (at least of size $2h$) but not as large a set (no more than $N - 2h$) as an ordinary legitimate statistical query. General trackers can be constructed by trial-and error and exist in virtually all cases, unless the value of $h$ is unrealistically large [2].

Here is how we can use a general tracker for Type 2 queries to obtain the response to a query $q_{bad}$ that should not be obtainable (i.e., $q_{bad}$ violates the restriction above, namely $h \leq NU(q_{bad}) \leq N - h$). In this example, we assume that the response to any query is the sum of the confidential values associated with the keys defined by the query. We begin by computing the sum $x$ of all the database elements; then we see that exactly one of the two subsequent lines consists of legitimate queries (note that we do not know initially whether the set defined by the query $q_{bad}$ is too small or too large):

$$x := \mathrm{SUM}(GT) + \mathrm{SUM}(\underline{\mathrm{not}}\ GT),$$

$$\mathrm{SUM}(q_{bad}) = SUM(q_{bad}\ \underline{\mathrm{or}}\ GT) + \mathrm{SUM}(q_{bad}\ \underline{\mathrm{or}\ \mathrm{not}}\ GT) - x,$$

$$q_{bad}\ \textbf{is too small}$$

$$\mathrm{SUM}(q_{bad}) = 2x - [SUM(\underline{\mathrm{not}}\ q_{bad}\ \underline{\mathrm{or}}\ GT) + \mathrm{SUM}(\underline{\mathrm{not}}\ q_{bad}\ \underline{\mathrm{or}\ \mathrm{not}}\ GT)],$$

$$q_{bad}\ \textbf{is too large}$$

In this way, the inference control is obviously breached; here, it is impossible to maintain the confidentiality of the data as required.

There are very few methods that work reasonably well to achieve inference control; virtually all require the introduction of noise which falsifies the responses (see, for example, [7, 6]) which may not be acceptable to the users.

### 5.5. Boolean Expressions and Boolean Automata

After enumerating a catalog of instances where the introduction of complementation caused things to become difficult, if not impossible, we now pass on to examples that attenuate this negative image. Specifically, we show in this section how restricting concatenation to left-concatenation makes complementation behave much more reasonably. In the next section we show that eliminating concatenation altogether and retaining only union and complementation yields in the context of implicit equations very easily determined solutions. These two examples strongly suggest that complementation alone is not the villain; it needs to be abetted by other accomplices to do real damage.

A boolean automaton is essentially an NFA except that the transition function is defined in such a way that the result of applying it to a state and a letter yields not a set (or union) of states as in the NFA case, but a boolean function of the states. There exists an analog of the subset construction [1] proving that boolean automata accept precisely regular languages; moreover, since the set of all boolean functions in $n$ variables is precisely $S(2,n)$, the deterministic complexity of boolean automata is doubly exponential in the number of states of the given boolean automaton. Moreover there exist boolean automata with $n$ states for which the smallest DFA have exactly $2^{2^n}$ states [5, 9].

As we have observed in the case of NFAs, we can obtain in a completely trivial way a set of $n$ equations from a boolean automaton with $n$ states where the right-hand side of the equation for variable $X_i$ is derived from the transition function of the state $q_i$. More specifically, if the boolean automaton is $B = (A, q, \tau, q_0, F)$ where the alphabet $A = \{a_1, \ldots, a_k\}$ and the set of states $Q = \{q_1, \ldots, q_n\}$, then the equation for $X_i$ corresponding to state $q_i$ is exactly

$$X_i = a_1\tau(X_i, a_1) \cup a_2\tau(X_i, a_2) \cup \cdots \cup a_k\tau(X_i, a_k) \cup \delta(X_i),$$

where $\delta(X_i) = \lambda$ if $X_i \in F$ and $\delta(X_i) = \emptyset$ otherwise. Moreover, it follows that the boolean expressions on the right-hand side of these equations, which involve letters of the alphabet and variables combined by boolean operators, give rise to general boolean expressions in which no variables appear but the boolean operators are applied to constant languages which in this case would be all regular languages. Again, it can be seen that these boolean expressions denote regular languages and correspond to reduced DFAs of complexity no larger than $S(2,n)$ if $n$ is the number of letters over the alphabet in the boolean expression and the regular languages that occur in the expression are represented by regular expressions.

Here are two examples. First consider the explicit equation

$$X = ab\overline{\overline{X}} \quad \text{over the alphabet } A = \{a, b\}.$$

It has the unique solution $X = a(ba)^\star[\lambda \cup a(a \cup b)^\star]$.

Then consider the system of two explicit equations in the two variables $X$ and $Y$

$$X = a^\star \overline{bb^\star(\overline{Y} \cap X)}, \qquad Y = b\,\overline{(X \cap \overline{aY})}.$$

It has the unique solution $X = \lambda \cup a(a \cup b)^\star$ and $Y = (ba)^\star bb(a \cup b)^\star$.

Similarly, boolean expressions always denote regular languages and can be solved (that is, one can always find the language denoted by the boolean expression). As an example, consider the boolean expression

$$\alpha = \overline{a^\star b^\star \cup a(\overline{ab^\star} \cap \overline{ba^\star})}.$$

One can verify, either through direct construction of a DFA or through a generalized derivative method (see [11]), that this expression denotes the regular language

$$\lambda \cup a \cup [a(a \cup b) \cup b]b^\star.$$

The DFA is constructed by starting with the NFAs for the regular expressions $a^\star b^\star$, $a$, $a$, $b^\star$, and $ba^\star$, and then combining them using the complementation construction (convert to a DFA and then flip accepting and rejecting states), followed by applying the subsequent union, concatenation, and complementation constructions. The generalized derivative construction looks at the given boolean expression and takes derivative with respect to all words over the alphabet A, until the process terminates (see [8]).

## 5.6. Implicit Language Equations

Our second class of equations whose complexity is tractable in the presence of complementation are implicit equations involving regular languages as constant languages and having only union and complementation as operations. Clearly, this implies that all set operations are present. What is absent is the concatenation operation. An example of such a system of two implicit language equations in two unknowns over the alphabet $A = \{a, b\}$ is given by

$$a^\star = X \cap Y,$$
$$b^\star a^\star b^\star = X \cup Y.$$

It turns out that without additional complications, we can also deal with relations instead of equations, that is, we may stipulate that the constant language on the left-hand side either be contained in the right-hand side or contains the right-hand side. An example of such a system of implicit language relations over the alphabet $A = \{a, b\}$ is given by

$$a^\star = X \cap \overline{Y} \cup Z,$$
$$a^\star \supseteq X \cup Y \cup \overline{Z},$$
$$aa^\star \cup bb^\star \subseteq X \cup \overline{Y} \cap Z.$$

We note that the number of equations or relations and the number of variables need not be equal.

The theory of these implicit language relations was developed in [3]; one can characterize rather directly whether such a system has a solution, and if so, how to construct regular solutions. The paper also resolves the question of whether there exist finitely or infinitely many solutions. The complexity of the method depends only on the number of unions and intersections of the variables and their complements, implying immediately a complexity at most singly exponential in the number of variables.

In the first example above, it is clear that there exists a solution, for example $X = a^\star$ and $Y = b^\star a^\star b^\star$. Moreover, there are obviously infinitely many solutions; more interesting is that there are also infinitely many minimal solutions, minimal in the sense that any solution contains (at least) one minimal solution. The class of all minimal solutions is given by

$$X = a^\star \cup T,$$
$$Y = a^\star \cup (b^\star a^\star b^\star - T),$$

where $T$ is any subset of (the language denoted by) $b^\star a^\star b^\star$.

The second example above does not have a solution (see [8]).

For the third example, consider the following system of implicit relations over the alphabet $A = \{a, b\}$

$$a^\star = X \cup \overline{Y} \cap Z,$$
$$a^\star \supseteq X \cap Z \cup Y \cap \overline{Z},$$
$$aa^\star \cup bb^\star \subset X \cap \overline{Y} \cup Y \cap Z.$$

This system has infinitely many solutions including the unique maximal solution

$$(X, Y, Z) = (a^\star, (a \cup b)^\star, (a \cup b)^\star)$$

and the two minimal solutions

$$(X, Y, Z) = (aa^\star, bb^\star, b^\star) \quad \text{and} \quad (X, Y, Z) = (a^\star, bb^\star, bb^\star).$$

Finally, consider the following single implicit equation in two variables over the alphabet $A = \{a, b\}$,

$$\{b, bb, bbb\} = X \cup Y.$$

This equation has finitely many maximal solutions, namely precisely the following eight:

Let $S$ be the language denoted by

$$\overline{b \cup bb \cup bbb}.$$

Then the eight maximal solutions are

$$
\begin{aligned}
(X, Y) = {} & (S, A^\star), \\
& (A^\star, S), \\
& (S \cup \{b\}, A^\star - \{b\}), \\
& (S \cup \{bb\}, A^\star - \{bb\}), \\
& (S \cup \{bbb\}, A^\star - \{bbb\}), \\
& (S \cup \{b, bb\}, A^\star - \{b, bb\}), \\
& (S \cup \{b, bbb\}, A^\star - \{b, bbb\}), \\
& (S \cup \{bb, bbb\}, A^\star - \{bb, bbb\}).
\end{aligned}
$$

## 5.7. Conclusion

We started by giving illustrations from different areas of computer science where the presence of complementation significantly complicated things. In particular, we focused on formal language theory where the addition of complementation to the usual operations (union, concatenation, and star) either resulted in languages of non-elementary complexity (extended regular expressions, with an enormous quantitative change) or caused the languages to be non-regular altogether (constituting a qualitative change). We also pointed out that the use of general trackers in statistical databases which depends on complementation makes it embarrassingly easy to compromise such databases.

Having established that complementation in these cases resulted in significant changes in the outcomes, we then focused on the underlying reason why this is the case. We concluded that it is not so much complementation on its own that causes these changes as the interplay between complementation and other operators, in particular concatenation. Specifically, restricting concatenation to left-concatenation in the context of expressions resulted in complexities that were only doubly exponential and eliminating concatenation altogether yielded a singly exponential complexity for implicit language relations. This leads us to conclude that complementation can only be evil if it is abetted by other operations.

## Acknowledgment

The contents of this paper were presented at the conference "The Role of Theory in Computer Science" at the University of Waterloo, Canada, on June 24, 2015, honoring the life and work of Professor Janusz Brzozowski. This conference was supported by a grant from the Fields Institute, which is hereby gratefully acknowledged.

## References

1. J. A. BRZOZOWSKI AND E. L. LEISS, On equations for regular languages, finite automata, and sequential networks, *Theoret. Comput. Sci.* **10**,1 (1980).
2. D. E. DENNING AND J. SCHLÖRER, A fast procedure of finding a tracker in a statistical database, *ACM Trans. Database Syst.* **5**,1 (Mar. 1980), 88–102.
3. A. IONESCU AND E. L. LEISS, On the role of complementation in implicit language equations and relations, *J. Comput. System Sci.* **20**,2 (2014), 457–467.
4. E. L. LEISS, The complexity of restricted regular expressions and the synthesis problem for finite automata, *J. Comput. System Sci.* **23**,3 (1981).
5. E. L. LEISS, Succinct representation of regular languages by Boolean automata, *Theoret. Comput. Sci.* **13** (1981), 323–330.
6. E. L. LEISS, *Principles of Data Security*, Plenum Publishing Corporation, New York, NY, 1982. ISBN 0-306-41098-2.
7. E. L. LEISS, Randomizing, a practical method for protecting statistical databases against compromise, in *Proceedings, 8th International Conference on Very Large Data Bases*, Mexico City, September 1982, pp. 189–196.
8. E. L. LEISS, On classes of tractable unrestricted regular expressions, *Theoret. Comput. Sci.* **35** (February 1985), 313–327.
9. E. L. LEISS, Succinct representation of regular languages by Boolean automata ii, *Theoret. Comput. Sci.* **38**,133–136 (1985).
10. E. L. LEISS, Unrestricted complementation in language equations over a one-letter alphabet, *Theoret. Comput. Sci.* **132** (1994), 71–84.
11. E. L. LEISS, *Language Equations, Monographs in Computer Science*, Springer-Verlag, New York, 1999. ISBN 0-387-98626-X.
12. A. R. MEYER AND L. STOCKMEYER, Nonelementary Word Problems in Automata and Logic. Presented at the AMS Symposium on Complexity of Computation, April 1973.
13. B. G. MIRKIN, An algorithm for constructing a base in a language of regular expressions, *Iz. Akad. Nauk SSSR, Techn. Kibernet*, 1966, 113–119. (in Russian). Engl. Transl. Engineering Cybernetics 5, 110-116 (1966).
14. J. SCHLÖRER, Confidentiality of statistical records: A threat monitoring scheme for on-line dialog, *Methods Inf. Med* **15**,1 (Jan. 1976), 36–42.
15. WIKIPEDIA, Observable universe. https://en.wikipedia.org/w/index.php?title=Observable_universe&oldid=725501736, Acessed May 2015.

# Chapter 6

# Quasi-Distances and Weighted Finite Automata

Timothy Ng, David Rappaport and Kai Salomaa*

*School of Computing, Queen's University*
*Kingston, Ontario K7L 3N6, Canada*
{ng, daver, ksalomaa}@cs.queensu.ca

A neighbourhood of a language $L$ consists of all words that are within a given distance from a word of $L$. We show that the neighbourhood of a regular language $L$ with respect to an additive quasi-distance can be recognized by an additive weighted finite automaton (WFA). The size of the WFA is the same as the size of an NFA (nondeterministic finite automaton) for $L$, and the construction gives an upper bound for the state complexity of a neighbourhood of a regular language with respect to a quasi-distance. We give a tight lower bound construction for the determinization of an additive WFA using an alphabet of size five. The previously known lower bound construction needed an alphabet that is linear in the number of states of the WFA.

## Contents

*A preliminary version of this paper appeared in the Proceedings of the 17th International Workshop Descriptional Complexity of Formal Systems, Waterloo, Ontario, June 25–27, 2015.

## 6.1. Introduction

In many applications it is crucial to measure the similarity between data. How we define the distance between objects depends on what the objects we want to compare are, and why we want to compare them [7]. By the distance between languages $L_1$ and $L_2$ we mean the smallest distance between a word of $L_1$ and of $L_2$, respectively. This definition is natural for error correction applications; however, other definitions such as the relative distance or Hausdorff distance have also been considered [5, 7].

One of the most commonly used similarity measures for words is the Levenshtein distance [16], also called the edit distance [6, 14, 15, 18]. The edit distance between two words is the smallest number of substitution, insertion and deletion operations required to transform one word into another. The problem of computing the edit distance arises in many areas, such as computational biology, text processing and speech recognition. Pighizzini [18] has shown that the edit distance between a word and a language recognized by a one-way nondeterministic auxiliary pushdown automaton is computable in polynomial time. Konstantinidis [15] showed that the edit distance of a regular language, that is, the smallest edit distance between two distinct words in the language, can be computed in polynomial time. Han et al. [11] gave a polynomial time algorithm to compute the edit distance between a regular language and a context-free language. Error/edit systems for error correction have been studied by Kari and Konstantinidis [13], and the error correction capabilities of regular languages with respect to edit operations were recently investigated by Benedikt et al. [1, 2].

Edit distance is additive with respect to concatenation of words in the sense defined by Calude et al. [4]. A quasi-distance is a generalization of the notion of distance, in that it allows the possibility of distinct elements having distance zero. Calude et al. [4] showed that the neighbourhood of a regular language with respect to an additive distance or quasi-distance is regular. The neighbourhood of radius $r$ of a language $L$ consists of all words that have distance at most $r$ from some word of $L$.

In an additive weighted finite automaton (WFA) [21] the weight of a path is the sum of the weights of the individual transitions that make up the path and the weight of an accepted word $w$ is the minimum weight of a path from the start state to a final state that spells out $w$. Note that this differs significantly from weighted automata used, for example, in image processing applications [8, 9].

For a given nondeterministic finite automaton (NFA) $A$, an additive distance $d$ and radius $r$, Salomaa and Schofield [21] gave a construction for an additive weighted finite automaton which recognizes the neighbourhood of radius $r$ of the language recognized by $A$. The construction relies essentially on the fact that additive distances are finite, that is, the neighbourhood of any word is always finite. This makes the construction not suitable for quasi-distances, since neighbourhoods of additive quasi-distances are not guaranteed to be finite [4].

Here we show that neighbourhoods of a regular language with respect to an additive quasi-distance can be recognized by a WFA. Given an NFA $A$, the WFA recognizing a constant radius neighbourhood of $L(A)$ can be constructed in polynomial time. The construction relies on the property that the neighbourhoods with respect to a quasi-distance are regular and a finite automaton for the neighbourhood can be constructed effectively. The construction also yields an upper bound for the size of a deterministic finite automaton (DFA) needed to recognize the neighbourhood of radius $r$ of a regular language (given by an NFA) with respect to a quasi-distance. The upper bound is significantly better than the bound obtained by constructing an NFA for the neighbourhood [4] and then determinizing the NFA.

We also study the state complexity of additive WFAs. A WFA $A$ within a given weight bound $R$ recognizes a regular language, and Salomaa and Schofield [21] gave an upper bound for the size of a DFA for this language. They also gave a matching lower bound construction; however, the WFAs used for the lower bound construction needed an alphabet of size linear in the number of states of the WFA. As our main result we give a tight lower bound construction for the determinization of WFAs using a five-letter alphabet.

The paper concludes with a discussion of open problems on the state complexity of neighbourhoods of a regular language with respect to an additive distance or quasi-distance.

## 6.2. Definitions

We assume that the reader is familiar with the basics of finite automata and regular languages [23, 25]. More information on their descriptional complexity can be found in the surveys [12, 10]. A general reference for weighted finite automata is [8].

In the following, $\Sigma$ is always a finite alphabet, $\Sigma^*$ is the set of words over

$\Sigma$, $\Sigma^+$ is the set of non-empty words and $\varepsilon$ is the empty word. The length of a word $w$ is $|w|$. When there is no danger of confusion, a singleton set $\{w\}$ is denoted simply as $w$. The set of non-negative integers (respectively, rationals) is $\mathbb{N}_0$ (respectively, $\mathbb{Q}_0$).

### 6.2.1. *Finite Automata and Regular Languages*

A *nondeterministic finite automaton* (NFA) is a tuple $A = (Q, \Sigma, \delta, q_0, F)$ where $Q$ is a finite set of states, $\Sigma$ is an alphabet, $\delta$ is a multi-valued transition function $\delta : Q \times \Sigma \to 2^Q$, $q_0 \in Q$ is the initial state, and $F \subseteq Q$ is a set of final states. We extend the transition function $\delta$ to $Q \times \Sigma^* \to 2^Q$ in the usual way. A word $w \in \Sigma^*$ is *accepted* by $A$ if $\delta(q_0, w) \cap F \neq \emptyset$ and the language recognized by $A$ consists of all strings accepted by $A$.

The automaton $A$ is a *deterministic finite automaton* (DFA) if, for all $q \in Q$ and $a \in \Sigma^*$, $\delta(q, a)$ either consists of one state or is undefined. A DFA $A$ is *complete* if $\delta$ is defined for all $q \in Q$ and $a \in \Sigma$. Two states $p$ and $q$ of a DFA $A$ are equivalent if $\delta(p, w) \in F$ if and only if $\delta(q, w) \in F$ for every string $w \in \Sigma^*$. A DFA $A$ is *minimal* if each state of $Q$ is reachable from the initial state and no two states are equivalent.

The (right) Kleene congruence of a language $L \subseteq \Sigma^*$ is the relation $\equiv_L \subseteq \Sigma^* \times \Sigma^*$ defined by setting, for $x, y \in \Sigma^*$,

$$x \equiv_L y \text{ iff } [(\forall z \in \Sigma^*) \, xz \in L \Leftrightarrow yz \in L].$$

A language $L$ is regular if and only if the index of $\equiv_L$ is finite and, in this case, the index of $\equiv_L$ is equal to the size of the minimal complete DFA for $L$ [23, 25]. The minimal DFA for a regular language $L$ is unique. The *state complexity* of $L$, $\mathrm{sc}(L)$, is the size of the minimal complete DFA recognizing $L$.

We extend the definition of additive weighted finite automata [21] by also allowing $\varepsilon$-transitions.

**Definition 6.1.** An *additive weighted finite automaton* (WFA) is a 6-tuple $A = (Q, \Sigma, \gamma, \omega, q_0, F)$ where $Q$ is a finite set of states, $\Sigma$ is an alphabet, $\gamma : Q \times (\Sigma \cup \{\varepsilon\}) \to 2^Q$ is the transition function, $\omega : Q \times (\Sigma \cup \{\varepsilon\}) \times Q \to \mathbb{Q}_0$ is a partial weight function where $\omega(q_1, a, q_2)$ is defined if and only if $q_2 \in \gamma(q_1, a)$, $(a \in \Sigma \cup \{\varepsilon\})$ $q_0 \in Q$ is the initial state, and $F \subseteq Q$ is the set of accepting states.

Strictly speaking, the transitions of $\gamma$ are also determined by the domain of the partial function $\omega$. In the following by a WFA we always mean an additive weighted finite automaton as in Definition 6.1. By a transition of $A$ on symbol $a \in \Sigma$ we mean a triple $(q_1, a, q_2)$ such that $q_2 \in \gamma(q_1, a)$, $q_1, q_2 \in Q$. A computation path $\alpha$ of a WFA $A$ along a word $w = a_1 a_2 \cdots a_m$, $a_i \in \Sigma$, $i = 1, \ldots, m$, from state $p_1$ to $p_2$ is a sequence of transitions that spell out the word $w$,

$$\alpha = (q_0, a_1, q_1)(q_1, a_2, q_2) \cdots (q_{m-1}, a_m, q_m),$$

where $p_1 = q_0$, $p_2 = q_m$, and $q_i \in \gamma(q_{i-1}, a_i)$, $1 \leq i \leq m$. The weight of a computation path is

$$\omega(\alpha) = \sum_{i=1}^{m} \omega(q_{i-1}, a_i, q_i).$$

We let $\Theta(p_1, w, p_2)$ denote the set of all computation paths along a word $w$ from $p_1$ to $p_2$. The *language recognized by $A$ within the weight bound* $r \geq 0$ is the set of words for which there exists a computation path that is accepted by $A$ and has weight at most $r$, defined as

$$L(A, r) = \{w \in \Sigma^* : (\exists f \in F)(\exists \alpha \in \Theta(q_0, w, f)) \ \omega(\alpha) \leq r\}.$$

### 6.2.2. *Distance Measures and Neighbourhoods*

Intuitively, a distance is a numerical description of how far apart the objects are, and we view a distance on words as a function from $\Sigma^* \times \Sigma^*$ to the nonnegative rationals that takes the value zero only for two identical words, is symmetric, and satisfies the triangle inequality. More formally, a function $d : \Sigma^* \times \Sigma^* \to \mathbb{Q}_0$ is a *distance* if it satisfies, for all $x, y, z \in \Sigma^*$,

(1) $d(x, y) = 0$ if and only if $x = y$,
(2) $d(x, y) = d(y, x)$,
(3) $d(x, z) \leq d(x, y) + d(y, z)$.

The function $d$ is a *quasi-distance* [4] if it satisfies conditions (2) and (3) and $d(x, y) = 0$ always when $x = y$, that is, a quasi-distance allows the possibility that distinct words may have distance zero. If $d$ is a quasi-distance on $\Sigma$, we can define an equivalence relation $\sim_d$ on $\Sigma$ by setting $x \sim_d y$ if and only if $d(x, y) = 0$. Then the mapping $d'([x]_{\sim_d}, [y]_{\sim_d}) = d(x, y)$ is a distance over $\Sigma^* / \sim_d$ [4].

A quasi-distance $d$ is *integral* if for all strings $x$ and $y$, $d(x, y) \in \mathbb{N}$. Note that a distance is a special case of a quasi-distance and all properties that hold for quasi-distances apply also to distances.

The *neighbourhood* of radius $r$ of a language $L$ is the set

$$E(L, d, r) = \{x \in \Sigma^* : (\exists y \in L)\, d(x, y) \leq r\}.$$

A (quasi-)distance $d$ is said to be *finite* if the neighbourhood of any given radius of an individual word with respect to $d$ is finite. A (quasi-)distance $d$ is *additive* if for every factorization $w = w_1 w_2$ and radius $r \geq 0$,

$$E(w, d, r) = \bigcup_{r_1 + r_2 = r} E(w_1, d, r_1) \cdot E(w_2, d, r_2).$$

## 6.3. WFA Construction for a Quasi-Distance Neighbourhood

It is known that the neighbourhood of a regular language with respect to an additive quasi-distance is regular [4]. The next lemma constructs, based on an NFA $N$, a WFA for an additive quasi-distance neighbourhood of $L(N)$. Then by converting the WFA to a DFA, the construction yields an upper bound for the state complexity of quasi-distance neighbourhoods that is much improved compared to the original construction from [4].

Our construction is inspired by related constructions for distance measures in [22], but the significant difference is that, as opposed to additive distances, an additive quasi-distance need not be finite, i.e., a finite radius neighbourhood of a single word is, in general, infinite. The construction used for the proof of Lemma 6.1 uses WFAs with $\varepsilon$-transitions.

An additive (quasi-)distance $d$ is determined by the finite number of values $d(a, b)$, $d(a, \varepsilon)$, where $a, b \in \Sigma$. For the complexity estimate of the lemma we assume that $d$ is a fixed additive quasi-distance that is given by listing the values $d(a, b)$, $d(a, \varepsilon)$, $a, b \in \Sigma$.

**Lemma 6.1.** *Let $N = (Q, \Sigma, \delta, q_0, F)$ be an NFA with $n$ states, $d$ an additive quasi-distance, and $R \geq 0$ be a constant. There exists an additive WFA $A$ with $n$ states such that for any $0 \leq r \leq R$,*

$$L(A, r) = E(L(N), d, r).$$

*Furthermore, the WFA $A$ can be constructed in time $O(n^3)$.*

**Proof.** We define an additive WFA $A = (Q, \Sigma, \gamma, \omega, q_0, F)$ as follows. The transition function $\gamma$ is defined by setting, for $p \in Q$, $a \in \Sigma \cup \{\varepsilon\}$,

$$\gamma(p, a) = \{q : (\exists x \in \Sigma^*)\, q \in \delta(p, x) \text{ and } d(a, x) \leq R\}.$$

That is, for each pair of states $p, q$, we add a transition from $p$ to $q$ on $a \in \Sigma \cup \{\varepsilon\}$ in the WFA $A$ if there is a word $x \in \Sigma^*$ with $d(a, x) \leq R$ that takes $p$ to $q$ in the NFA $N$. The transition $(p, a, q)$ in $A$ has weight

$$\omega((p, a, q)) = \min_{x \in \Sigma^*} \{d(a, x) : q \in \delta(p, x)\}. \tag{6.1}$$

We claim that a word $w \in \Sigma^*$ spells out a path in $A$ with weight $r$ $(\leq R)$ from the start state $q_0$ to a state $q_1$ if and only if some word $u$ with $d(w, u) \leq r$ takes the state $q_0$ to $q_1$ in the NFA $N$.

We prove the "only if" direction of the claim using induction on the length of $w$. If $w = \varepsilon$, then either $q_0 = q_1$ or $A$ has an $\varepsilon$-transition from $q_0$ to $q_1$. Now the claim follows by the definition of the transition function $\gamma$ and the weight function $\omega$ of $A$. For the inductive step consider $w = ub$, $u \in \Sigma^*$, $b \in \Sigma$, where the claim holds for $u$. Since $w$ takes state $q_0$ to $q_1$ by a path with weight $r$ in the WFA $A$, the word $u$ takes $q_0$ to a state $p$ by a path of weight $r_1$, where $r_1 + \omega(p, b, q_1) = r$.

By the inductive assumption, there exists $u_p \in \Sigma^*$, $d(u, u_p) \leq r_1$ such that $u_p$ in the NFA $N$ takes $q_0$ to the state $p$. By the definition of the transition weights of $A$ in (6.1), there exists a word $v_{p,b}$, with $d(b, v_{p,b}) = \omega(p, b, q_1)$ such that in the NFA $N$ the word $v_{p,b}$ takes state $p$ to state $q_1$.

Since $d$ is additive and $r_1 + \omega(p, b, q_1) = r$, we have

$$E(u, d, r_1) \cdot E(b, d, \omega(p, b, q_1)) \subseteq E(w, d, r).$$

Thus, $d(w, u_p v_{p,b}) \leq r$ and in the NFA $N$ the word $u_p v_{p,b}$ takes the start state $q_0$ to $q_1$. This concludes the proof of the "only if" direction of the claim.

Next we establish the "if" direction of the claim. Assuming there exists a word $u$ with $d(w, u) \leq r$ that takes $q_0$ to $q_1$ in the NFA $N$, we have to verify that $w \in E(u, d, r)$. Again, by induction on the length of $w$, we first see that if $w = \varepsilon$, then, by the definition of the transition function $\gamma$, $A$ has an $\varepsilon$-transition from $q_0$ to $q_1$ having weight at most $d(\varepsilon, u)$. Now, for the inductive step, consider $w = w_1 b$, $w_1 \in \Sigma^*$, $b \in \Sigma$. Since $d$ is additive, we have $u = u_1 u_2$ such that

$$w_1 \in E(u_1, d, r_1) \text{ and } b \in E(u_2, d, r_2)$$

where $r_1 + r_2 = r$. Then by the inductive assumption, since there is a path in $N$ from $q_0$ to some state $p$ on the word $u_1$, there is a path in $A$ from $q_0$ to the state $p$ on the word $w_1$ with weight at most $r_1$. Now the NFA $N$ has a transition on symbol $b$ from $p$ to $q_1$, and according to the definition of the transition relation $\gamma$, $A$ has a transition from $p$ to $q_1$ with weight at most

$d(b, u_2) \leq r_2$. We conclude that $A$ has a path from $q_0$ to $q_1$ with weight at most $r_1 + r_2 = r$.

Since the start states of $A$ and $N$ coincide and $A$ and $N$ have the same set of final states, the claim implies that, for any $r \leq R$, $L(A, r) = E(L(N), d, r)$.

It remains to give an upper bound for the time complexity of finding the weights (6.1) in order to verify the claim concerning the time bound for constructing $A$. Since $d$ is additive, for given $p, q \in Q$ and $a \in \Sigma \cup \{\varepsilon\}$, the set of words $x$ such that $d(a, x) \leq R$ and $x$ takes $p$ to $q$ in the NFA $N$ is regular. This means that, for $p \in Q$ and $a \in \Sigma \cup \{\varepsilon\}$, the set $\gamma(p, a)$ can be efficiently constructed and the weights of the transitions of $N$ are computed as follows.

A word $x = b_1 b_2 \cdots b_m, b_i \in \Sigma$ is in the neighbourhood of $a$ of radius $R$ if and only if there exists an index $i \in \{1, \ldots, m\}$ such that

$$d(a, b_i) + \sum_{j \in \{1, \ldots, m\}, j \neq i} d(\epsilon, b_j) \leq R.$$

For the radius $R$ neighbourhood of $a$, $a \in \Sigma \cup \{\varepsilon\}$, we define the two-state WFA $B_a = (\{I_0, I_1\}, \Sigma, \eta, \rho, I_0, \{I_1\})$, shown in Figure 6.1. The states of $B_a$ are $\{I_0, I_1\}$. For each symbol $\sigma \in \Sigma$, we define self-loop transitions $\eta(q, \sigma) = q$ with weight $d(\sigma, \epsilon)$ for both states and the transition $\eta(I_0, \sigma) = I_1$ with weight $d(\sigma, a)$ for the transition which consumes the symbol $a$.

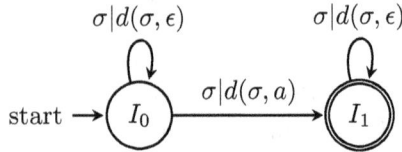

Fig. 6.1.   The WFA $B_a$ recognizing the language $\{x \in \Sigma : d(a, x) \leq R\}$.

Let $M_a = (\{I_0, I_1\} \times Q, \Sigma, \delta_a, \omega_a, (I_0, q_0), I_1 \times F)$ be the WFA obtained as a cross product of the WFA $B_a$ and the NFA $N$. The states of $M_a$ are of the form $(P, q)$, where $P \in \{I_0, I_1\}$ and $q \in Q$. The transitions of $M_a$ are defined by setting, for $q \in Q$, $\sigma \in \Sigma$,

$$\begin{aligned} \delta_a((I_0, q), \sigma) &= \{(I_0, \delta(q, \sigma)), (I_1, \delta(q, \sigma))\}, \\ \delta_a((I_1, q), \sigma) &= \{(I_1, \delta(q, \sigma))\}. \end{aligned}$$

The weights of transitions $((P_1, q_1), \sigma, (P_2, q_2))$ defined in $\delta_{M_a}$ are defined

$$\omega_a((P_1, q_1), \sigma, (P_2, q_2)) = \begin{cases} d(\sigma, \epsilon), & \text{if } P_1 = P_2; \\ d(\sigma, a), & \text{if } P_1 \neq P_2. \end{cases}$$

For states $p, q \in Q$, paths from states $(I_0, p)$ to $(I_1, q)$ are labelled by words $x$ with weight $d(a, x)$.

We compute the paths with the least weight for every pair of states of $M_a$. There are $2n$ states in the product machine, and minimal weight paths for every pair of states can be computed in time $O(n^3)$ via the Floyd-Warshall algorithm [6]. A transition from $p$ to $q$ on $a$ is added if there is a path from $(I_0, p)$ to $(I_1, q)$ with weight at most $R$. □

Lemma 6.1 gives the following result.

**Theorem 6.1.** *Suppose that $L$ has an NFA with $n$ states and $d$ is a quasi-distance. The neighbourhood of $L$ of radius $R$ can be recognized by an additive WFA having $n$ states within weight bound $R$. Given an NFA for $L$ the WFA can be constructed in polynomial time.*

The next proposition gives an upper bound for the size of a DFA recognizing the language of a WFA within a given weight bound. An analogous result is known [21] for an additive WFA model that does not allow $\varepsilon$-transitions.

**Proposition 6.1.** *If $A$ is a WFA with $n$ states where all transition weights are integers and $r \in \mathbb{N}_0$, then $L(A, r)$ can be recognized by a DFA with at most $(r + 2)^n$ states.*

**Proof.** The construction is modified from the proof of Theorem 5 of [21] to allow the possibility that the WFA has $\varepsilon$-transitions.

Let $A = (Q, \Sigma, \gamma, \omega, q_0, F_A)$, where $Q = \{q_0, q_1, \ldots, q_{n-1}\}$. Write $X_r = \{0, 1, 2, \ldots, r + 1\}$ and define a DFA

$$D = (X_r^n, \Sigma, \delta, p_0, F_D),$$

as follows. The set of final states is

$$F_D = \{(i_0, \ldots, i_{n-1}) \mid (\exists\, 0 \leq j \leq n - 1)\, i_j \leq r \text{ and } q_j \in F_A\}.$$

The initial state is $p_0 = (0, s_1, \ldots, s_{n-1})$ where, for $1 \leq j \leq n - 1$,

$$s_j = \min(\{r + 1\} \cup \{\omega(\alpha) \mid \alpha \in \Theta(q_0, \varepsilon, q_j)\}).$$

The transition relation $\delta$ is defined by setting for $(i_0, \ldots, i_{n-1}) \in X_r^n$ and $a \in \Sigma$,

$$\delta((i_0, \ldots, i_{n-1}), a) = (j_0, \ldots, j_{n-1}),$$

where, for $0 \leq x \leq n - 1$,

$$j_x = \min(\{r+1\} \cup \{k \mid k = i_z + \omega((q_z, a, q_x)), \ q_x \in \gamma(q_z, a), \ 0 \leq z \leq n-1\}.$$

A state $(i_0, \ldots, i_{n-1})$ of the DFA $D$ keeps track in the component $i_j$, $0 \leq j \leq n - 1$, the weight of the smallest weight path in $A$ that, on the input processed thus far, takes the initial state $q_0$ to the state $q_j$. A value $i_j = r+1$ is used to indicate that the weight of the smallest weight path from $q_0$ to $q_j$ is at least $r + 1$.

The initial state $p_0 = (0, s_1, \ldots, s_{n-1})$ satisfies the above property because $s_j$, $1 \leq j \leq n - 1$, is the smallest weight of a computation path along $\varepsilon$ from $q_0$ to $q_j$. Then, assuming that a state $(i_0, \ldots, i_{n-1}) \in X_r^n$ satisfies the claimed property after processing input string $u$, the transition function $\delta$ on input $a \in \Sigma$ is defined in a way that correctly updates the components to give the smallest weight from $q_0$ to each state of $A$ on an input spelling out $u \cdot a$. The choice of the set of final states $F_D$ guarantees that $L(D) = L(A, r)$.      $\square$

As a consequence of Theorem 6.1 and Proposition 6.1 we get in Corollary 6.1 an upper bound for the state complexity of the neighbourhood of a regular language with respect to an additive quasi-distance $d$ where all values $d(u, v)$, $u, v \in \Sigma^*$ are integers.

We note that if a quasi-distance $d$ associates a non-negative integer value with any pair of words, then the weights of the WFA $A$ constructed in the proof of Lemma 6.1 are integral. Furthermore, a neighbourhood with respect to a quasi-distance $d$ with rational values can be converted to a neighbourhood with respect to a quasi-distance with integral values by multiplying the radius and the values of $d$ by a suitably chosen constant. This can be done since the distance between any two words is determined by distances between two alphabet symbols and between alphabet symbols and the empty word.

**Corollary 6.1.** *Let $N$ be an NFA with $n$ states, $R \in \mathbb{N}_0$, and $d$ an integral quasi-distance. Then the neighbourhood $E(L(N), d, R)$ can be recognized by a DFA with $(R + 2)^n$ states.*

The upper bound $(R+2)^n$ is significantly better than what is obtained by first constructing an NFA for $E(L(N), d, R)$ as in [4] and then determinizing the NFA. If the set of states of $N$ is $Q$, Theorem 8 of [4] [1] constructs an NFA for $E(L(N), d, R)$ with set of states $Q \times D$ where $D \subseteq \mathbb{N}$, roughly speaking, consists of all integers at most $R$ that can be represented as a sum of distances between an element of $\Sigma$ and an element of $\Sigma^*$.

In the next section we will give a lower bound construction for the size of a DFA needed to simulate an additive WFA that matches the upper bound of Proposition 6.1.

## 6.4. State Complexity of Weighted Finite Automata

Salomaa and Schofield [21] gave a matching lower bound construction for Proposition 6.1 using a family of WFAs over an alphabet of size $2n-1$, where $n$ is the number of states of the WFA. Here we define a family of WFAs over a five-letter alphabet that reaches the upper bound $(r+2)^n$. Note that while our WFA definition allows the use of $\varepsilon$-transitions, the WFAs used below for the lower bound construction do not have $\varepsilon$-transitions.

Let $A_n = (Q_n, \Sigma, \gamma, \omega, 1, n)$ be an additive WFA with $Q_n = \{1, 2, \ldots, n\}$ and $\Sigma = \{a, b, c, d, e\}$. The transition function $\gamma$ with $q \in Q$ and $\sigma \in \Sigma$ is defined next.

$$\gamma(q, \sigma) = \begin{cases} \{1, 2\}, & \text{if } q = 1, \sigma = a \text{ or } q = 2, \sigma = b; \\ \{3\}, & \text{if } q = 1, \sigma = b \text{ or } q = 2, \sigma = a; \\ \{q + 1\}, & \text{if } q = 3, \ldots, n - 1 \text{ and } \sigma = a, b; \\ \{q\}, & \text{if } q = 1, \ldots, n \text{ and } \sigma = c, d, e. \end{cases}$$

The weight function $\omega$ for a transition $\alpha \in Q_n \times \Sigma \times Q_n$ is defined next.

$$\omega(\alpha) = \begin{cases} 1, & \text{if } \alpha = (1, c, 1); \\ 1, & \text{if } \alpha = (2, d, 2); \\ 1, & \text{if } \alpha = (q, e, q) \text{ for all } q \in Q; \\ 0, & \text{for all other transitions defined by } \gamma. \end{cases}$$

The transition diagram for $A_n$ is shown in Figure 6.2, with the non-zero weights of each transition marked after the alphabet symbols labeling the transition. For example, state 1 has self-loops on $a$ and $d$ with weight zero and self-loops on $c$ and $e$ with weight one.

---

[1] Theorem 8 of [4] assumes that $N$ is deterministic. However, the construction used in the proof works also for an NFA.

We will use the WFAs $A_n$ to give a lower bound for the size of DFAs for a language recognized by a WFA within a given weight bound. First, in Lemma 6.2, we establish a technical property of the weights of computations of $A_n$ reaching a particular state and for this purpose we introduce the following notation.

For $0 \leq k_i \leq r + 1$ and $1 \leq i \leq n$, we define the words

$$w(k_1, \ldots, k_n) = \begin{cases} ac^{k_n} bd^{k_{n-1}} ac^{k_{n-2}} \cdots ac^{k_3} bd^{k_2} c^{k_1}, & \text{if } n \text{ is odd;} \\ abd^{k_n} ac^{k_{n-1}} bd^{k_{n-2}} \cdots ac^{k_3} bd^{k_2} c^{k_1}, & \text{if } n \text{ is even.} \end{cases}$$

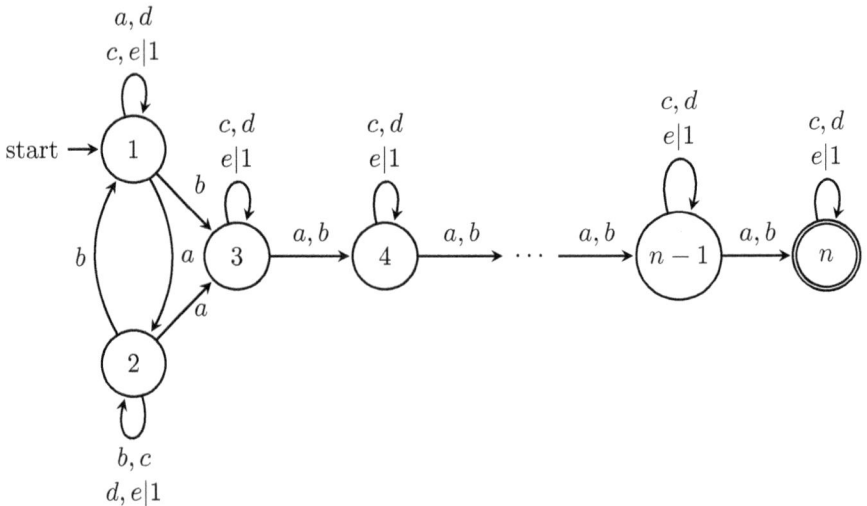

Fig. 6.2.  The weighted finite automaton $A_n$ used in the proof of Lemma 6.2.

**Lemma 6.2.** *Let $n \in \mathbb{N}$.  The WFA $A_n$ after processing the input $w(k_1, \ldots, k_n)$ can reach the state $s$, $1 \leq s \leq n$, on a path with weight $k_s$. Furthermore, any computation of $A_n$ on input $w(k_1, \ldots, k_n)$ that reaches state $s$, $1 \leq s \leq n$, has weight $k_s$.*

**Proof.** In the string $w(k_1, \ldots, k_n)$, occurrences of the symbols $a$ and $b$ alternate. Thus the computation of $A$ can exit states 1 and 2 after making a self-loop on $a$ in state 1 or a self-loop on $b$ in state 2 and, furthermore, this is the only way for the computation to get out of the "binary cycle" of states 1 and 2.

Below, using a case analysis, we verify that, for $1 \leq s \leq n$, $A_n$ has a computation with weight $k_s$ that ends in state $s$ and, furthermore, any computation ending in $s$ has weight $k_s$.

(i) First consider the case where $n$ is even. Consider a computation of $A_n$ that reaches a state $s$ where $s \geq 2$ is even. Note that after exiting the cycle of states 1 and 2, only the symbols $a$ or $b$ move the computation to the next state. Thus, the only way to reach $s$ is that the computation makes a self-loop on $b$ in state 2 directly before reading the substring $d^{k_s}$. After that, the following $k_s$ symbols $d$ are read via the weight-one transitions. This also applies for the case $s = 2$.

If $s \geq 3$ is odd, in order to reach state $s$, directly before reading the substring $c^{k_s}$ the computation must on input $a$ make a self-loop in state 1 and then the following $k_s$ symbols $c$ are read with transitions of weight one in state 1.

Finally consider the case $s = 1$. In order to end in state 1, the computation must not have made any self-loops on $a$ in state 1 or $b$ in state 2. If this is done, the computation ends in a state $z$ with $z \geq 2$. Thus, reading the final $b$ takes the computation from state 2 to state 1, where the transition on $d$ is taken $k_2$ times. The computation remains in state 1 and reads the rest of the word $c^{k_1}$ on the transition of weight 1 exactly $k_1$ times.

(ii) Next consider the case where $n$ is odd. The above argument remains the same, almost word for word. The only minor difference is in the case $s = n$. In order to reach state $n$, the computation must read the first symbol $a$ using a self-loop and then the following $k_n$ symbols $c$ using transitions of weight 1. (Note that when $n$ is odd, in $w(k_1, \ldots, k_n)$ the first symbol $a$ is followed by $k_n$ symbols $c$.)

$\square$

**Lemma 6.3.** *Let $A_n$ be the WFA defined above and $r \in \mathbb{N}$. Then the minimal DFA for $L(A_n, r)$ needs $(r + 2)^n$ states.*

**Proof.** It is sufficient to show that all words $w(k_1, \ldots, k_n)$, $0 \leq k_i \leq r + 1$, $i = 1, \ldots, n$, belong to distinct classes of $\equiv_{L(A_n, r)}$.

Consider two distinct words $w(k_1, \ldots, k_n)$ and $w(k'_1, \ldots, k'_n)$ with $0 \leq k_i, k'_i \leq r + 1, i = 1, \ldots, n$. There exists an index $j$ such that $k_j \neq k'_j$. Without loss of generality, we assume that $k_j < k'_j$. Choose

$$z = e^{r - k_j} a^{n-j}.$$

Since $k_j < k'_j \leq r + 1$, it follows that $r - k_j \geq 0$ and $z$ is a well-defined word. We claim that

$$w(k_1, \ldots, k_n) \cdot z \in L(A, r), \quad w(k'_1, \ldots, k'_n) \cdot z \notin L(A, r).$$

By Lemma 6.2, $A$ has a computation on input $w(k_1, \ldots, k_n)$ that ends in state $j$ with weight $k_j$. In state $j$, $A$ reads the first $r - k_j$ symbols $e$ of $z$, after which the total weight is $k_j + (r - k_j) = r$. The zero weight transitions on the suffix $a^{n-j}$ take the automaton from state $j$ to the final state $n$.

Now consider from which states $q$ the WFA $A$ can reach the accepting state $n$ on input $z$. On any state of $A$, the symbols $c, d, e$ define self-loops. On states $3 \leq q \leq n - 1$, transitions to state $q + 1$ only occur on $a, b$. For states $q = 1, 2$, a transition to state $q + 1$ occurs only on $a$. Thus, $A$ can reach the accepting state $n$ from a state $q$ on input $z$ only if $q = j$.

Thus, the only possibility for $A$ to accept $w(k'_1, \ldots, k'_n) \cdot z$ would be that the computation has to reach state $j$ on the prefix $w(k'_1, \ldots, k'_n)$. By Lemma 6.2, the weight of this computation can only be $k'_j$. But when continuing the computation on $z$ from state $j$, $A$ has to read the first $r - k_j$ symbols $e$, each with a self-loop transition having weight one. After this, the weight of the computation will be $k'_j + r - k_j > r$. Thus, $w(k'_1, \ldots, k'_n) \cdot z \notin L(A, r)$.

Thus, the equivalence relation $\equiv_{L(A,r)}$ has index at least $(r + 2)^n$. $\quad\square$

As a consequence of Lemma 6.3 and Proposition 6.1 we have

**Theorem 6.2.** *If $A$ is an $n$-state WFA with integer weights for transitions and $r \in \mathbb{N}$, then*

$$\mathrm{sc}(L(A, r)) \leq (r + 2)^n.$$

*For $n, r \in \mathbb{N}$, there exists an $n$-state WFA $A$ with integral weights, and having no $\varepsilon$-transitions, defined over a five-letter alphabet such that $\mathrm{sc}(L(A, r)) = (r + 2)^n$.*

## 6.5. Conclusion

For the state complexity of a language recognized by an additive WFA with a given weight we have established a tight lower bound using a constant size alphabet. The earlier known lower bound construction [21] used a variable alphabet that has size linear in the number of states of the WFA.

We have also constructed a WFA recognizing the neighbourhood of a regular language with respect to an additive quasi-distance. This yields an upper bound $(r + 2)^n$ for the state complexity of a neighbourhood of radius

$r$ of an $n$-state NFA language with respect to an additive quasi-distance. The upper bound is significantly better than a bound obtained by directly constructing an NFA for the neighbourhood [4] and then determinizing the NFA. The same upper bound $(r+2)^n$ has been known previously for neighbourhoods with respect to an additive distance. This then suggests the question, what is the state complexity of neighbourhoods with respect to additive (quasi-)distances? The lower bound for WFA determinization (in Lemma 6.3) uses a WFA that does not recognize a neighbourhood.

The authors have given a lower bound $(r+2)^n$ for the radius-$r$ neighbourhood of an $n$-state NFA language with respect to an additive distance [17]. Furthermore, the lower bound construction for additive neighbourhoods was extended to give a tight bound $(r+2)^{n-2}+1$ for the state complexity of pattern matching with $r$ errors in a $n$-state DFA language [17]. The latter result yields, in the special case of no errors, the worst-case state complexity bound for two-sided ideals obtained by Brzozowski et al. [3].

A limitation of the state complexity lower bound results for neighbourhoods of regular languages [17] is that the construction uses an alphabet that depends linearly on the number of states of the original NFA and the underlying distance is defined based on the radius $r$. The precise state complexity of neighbourhoods with respect to specific distances or quasi-distances remains open. Povarov [19, 20] has given a lower bound for the radius-one Hamming neighbourhood of a regular language that is tight within an order of magnitude. Shamkin [24] has also provided constructions for finite languages $L_n$ with $n \geq 4$ over a ternary alphabet, such that $L_n$ is recognized by an incomplete DFA with $n$ states. For radius $r \leq \frac{n}{2} - 1$, the lower bound for the radius $r$ Hamming neighbourhood has a state complexity of at least $2^{\lfloor \frac{n}{2} - r \rfloor}$ states.

# References

1. M. Benedikt, G. Puppis and C. Riveros, Bounded repairability of word languages, *J. Comput. System. Sci.* **79** (2013), 1302–1321.
2. M. Benedikt, G. Puppis and C. Riveros, The per-character cost of repairing word languages, *Theoret. Compt. Sci.* **539** (2014), 38–67.
3. J. Brzozowski and G. Jirásková, Quotient complexity of ideal languages, in *Latin American Theoretical Informatics Symposium*, A. López-Ortiz (ed.), pp. 208–221, *LNCS* vol. 6034, Springer, 2010.
4. C. Calude, K. Salomaa and S. Yu, Distances and quasi-distances between words, *J. Univ. Comput. Sci.* **8**,2 (2002), 141–152.

5. C. CHOFFRUT AND G. PIGHIZZINI, Distances between languages and reflexivity of relations, *Theoret. Compt. Sci.* **286** (2002), 117–138.

6. T. CORMEN, C. LEISERSON, R. RIVEST AND C. STEIN, *Introduction to Algorithms*, MIT Press, Cambridge, Massachuchetts, ed. 2nd ed., 2001.

7. M. DEZA AND E. DEZA, *Encyclopedia of Distances*, Springer-Verlag, Berlin-Heidelberg, 2009.

8. M. Droste, W. Kuich and H. Vogler (eds.), *Handbook of Weighted Automata, EATCS Monographs in Theoretical Computer Science*, Springer, 2009.

9. M. ERAMIAN, Efficient simulation of nondeterministic weighted finite automata, *J. Autom. Lang. Combin.* **9** (2004), 257–267.

10. Y. GAO, N. MOREIRA, R. REIS AND S. YU, A survey on operational state complexity, *CoRR* **abs/1509.03254v1** (Sept 2015). To appear in *Computer Science Review*.

11. Y.-S. HAN, S.-K. KO AND K. SALOMAA, The edit distance between a regular language and a context-free language, *Int. J. Found. Comput. Sci.* **24** (2013), 1067–1082.

12. M. HOLZER AND M. KUTRIB, Descriptional and computational complexity of finite automata — a survey, *Inform. Comput.* **209** (2011), 456–470.

13. L. KARI AND S. KONSTANTINIDIS, Descriptional complexity of error/edit systems., *J. Autom. Lang. Combin.* **9** (2004), 293–309.

14. S. KONSTANTINIDIS, Transducers and the properties of error detection, error-correction, and finite-delay decodability, *J. Univ. Comput. Sci.* **8** (2002), 278–291.

15. S. KONSTANTINIDIS, Computing the edit distance of a regular language, *Inform. Comput.* **205** (2007), 1307–1316.

16. V. LEVENSHTEIN, Binary codes capable of correcting deletions, insertions, and reversals., *Soviet Physics Doklady* **10**,8 (1966), 707–710.

17. T. NG, D. RAPPAPORT AND K. SALOMAA, State complexity of neighbourhoods and approximate pattern matching, in *19th DLT 2015*, I. Potapov (ed.), Liverpool, UK, July 27–30 2015, pp. 389–400, *LNCS* vol. 9168, Springer.

18. G. PIGHIZZINI, How hard is computing the edit distance?, *Inform. Comput.* **165** (2001), 1–13.

19. G. POVAROV, Descriptive complexity of the hamming neighborhood of a regular language, in *1st LATA 2007*, R. Loos, S. Z. Fazekas and C. Martín-Vide (eds.), pp. 509–520, 2007.

20. G. POVAROV, Finite transducers and nondeterministic state complexity of regular languages, *Russian mathematics (Iz. VUZ)* **54**,6 (2010), 19–25.

21. K. SALOMAA AND P. SCHOFIELD, State complexity of additive weighted finite automata, *Int. J. Found. Comput. Sci.* **18**,6 (2007), 1407–1416.

22. P. SCHOFIELD, Error quantification and recognition using weighted finite automata, Master's thesis, Queen's University, Kingston, Canada, 2006.

23. J. SHALLIT, *A Second Course in Formal Languages and Automata Theory*, Cambridge University Press, 2009.

24. S. SHAMKIN, Descriptional complexity of hamming neighbourhoods of finite languages, Master's thesis, Ural Federal University, Ekaterinburg, Russia,

2011. In Russian.

25. S. YU, Regular languages, in *Handbook of Formal Languages*, G. Rozenberg and A. Salomaa (eds.), vol. Vol. I, pp. 41–110, Springer, 1997.

# Chapter 7

# Open Problems About Regular Languages, 35 Years Later

Jean-Éric Pin

*IRIF, CNRS and Université Paris-Diderot,*
*Case 7014, 75205 Paris Cedex 13, France.*
Jean-Eric.Pin@liafa.univ-paris-diderot.fr

In 1980, Janusz A. Brzozowski presented a selection of six open problems about regular languages and mentioned two other problems in the conclusion of his article. These problems have been the source of some of the greatest breakthroughs in automata theory over the past 35 years. This survey article summarizes the state of the art on these questions and the hopes for the next 35 years.

## Contents

Thirty-five years ago, at the IFIP Congress in 1980, Janusz A. Brzozowski [8] presented a selection of six open problems about regular languages and mentioned two other topics in the conclusion of his article. These six open problems were, in order, *star height, restricted star height, group complexity, star removal, regularity of non-counting classes* and *optimality of prefix codes*. The two other topics were the *limitedness problem* and the *dot-depth hierarchy*.

These problems proved to be very influential in the development of automata theory and were the source of critical breakthroughs. The aim of this paper is to survey these results, to describe their impact on current research and to outline some hopes for the next thirty-five years. Due to the lack of space, the dot-depth hierarchy is treated in a separate article [61].

## 7.1. Terminology, Notation and Background

This goal of this section is to fix notation and terminology. We define in particular the notions of syntactic monoid, class of languages, variety, profinite word, profinite identity, semiring and weighted automaton.

In the sequel, $A$ denotes a finite alphabet and 1 denotes the empty word. A semigroup $S$ *divides* a semigroup $T$ if $S$ is a quotient of a subsemigroup of $T$.

### 7.1.1. *Quotients and Syntactic Monoid*

Given a language $L$ of $A^*$ and two words $x$ and $y$, the *left quotient* of $L$ by $x$ is the language

$$x^{-1}L = \{u \in A^* \mid xu \in L\}.$$

Similarly, the *right quotient* of $L$ by $y$ is the language

$$Ly^{-1} = \{u \in A^* \mid uy \in L\}.$$

Finally, we set

$$x^{-1}Ly^{-1} = \{u \in A^* \mid xuy \in L\}.$$

Observe that $(x^{-1}L)y^{-1} = x^{-1}Ly^{-1} = x^{-1}(Ly^{-1})$.

The *syntactic congruence* of a language $L$ of $A^*$ is the equivalence relation $\sim_L$ defined by $u \sim_L v$ if and only if, for every $x, y \in A^*$,

$$xuy \in L \iff xvy \in L,$$

or, equivalently, if

$$u \in x^{-1}Ly^{-1} \iff v \in x^{-1}Ly^{-1}.$$

The *syntactic monoid* of $L$ is the quotient $M(L)$ of $A^*$ by $\sim_L$ and the natural morphism $\eta : A^* \to A^*/\sim_L$ is called the *syntactic morphism* of $L$.

For instance, the syntactic monoid of the language $(ab)^*$ is the monoid $M = \{1, a, b, ab, ba, 0\}$ presented by the relations $a^2 = b^2 = 0$, $aba = a$, $bab = b$ and $0a = 0b = 0 = a0 = b0$.

### 7.1.2. Classes of Languages

Many properties of languages, such as being regular, finite, commutative, star-free, etc., are defined without any explicit reference to an alphabet. However, these properties do not define a set of languages, unless the alphabet is specified. The notion of class of languages is a convenient way to avoid this problem.

A *class of languages* $\mathcal{C}$ associates with each finite alphabet $A$ a set $\mathcal{C}(A)$ of regular languages[1] of $A^*$. A class $\mathcal{C}$ of languages is said to be closed under some operation, such as union, intersection, complement, quotients, product, star, etc., if, for each alphabet $A$, the set of languages $\mathcal{C}(A)$ is closed under this operation. Similarly, $\mathcal{C}$ is said to be *closed under Boolean operations* if, for each $A$, $\mathcal{C}(A)$ is a Boolean algebra of languages.

A monoid morphism $\varphi : A^* \to B^*$ is said to be

(1) *length-preserving* if $|\varphi(u)| = |u|$ for all $u \in A^*$, or equivalently, if $\varphi(A) \subseteq B$;

(2) *length-increasing* if $|\varphi(u)| \geqslant |u|$ for all $u \in A^*$, or equivalently, if $\varphi(A) \subseteq B^+$;

(3) *length-decreasing* if $|\varphi(u)| \leqslant |u|$ for all $u \in A^*$, or, equivalently, if $\varphi(A) \subseteq B \cup \{1\}$.

A class of languages $\mathcal{C}$ is *closed under inverses of morphisms* if for each morphism $\varphi : A^* \to B^*$, the condition $L \in \mathcal{C}(B)$ implies $\varphi^{-1}(L) \in \mathcal{C}(A)$. Closure under inverses of length-increasing, length-decreasing or length-preserving morphisms is defined in the same way.

### 7.1.3. Varieties of Languages and Varieties of Finite Monoids

Varieties constitute important examples of classes of languages. A *variety of languages* is a class of languages closed under Boolean operations, left and right quotients and inverses of morphisms. Star-free languages, which

---

[1]This definition can be extended to nonregular languages, but we are only interested in regular languages in this paper.

are defined in Section 7.2, form the most emblematic example of a variety of languages.

Closure under inverses of morphisms can be relaxed by requiring only closure under inverses of length-preserving, length-increasing or length-decreasing morphisms, leading to the notions of *lp-variety*, *li-variety* and *ld-variety*, respectively. These notions were introduced independently by Esik [27] and Straubing [85].

A *variety of finite monoids* is a class of finite monoids closed under taking submonoids, quotients and finite products. We refer the reader to the books [1, 26, 63] for more details on varieties of monoids.

Eilenberg's variety theorem [26] states that there is a bijective correspondence between varieties of languages and varieties of finite monoids.

**Theorem 7.1.1** *Let* **V** *be a variety of finite monoids. For each alphabet A, let* $\mathcal{V}(A)$ *be the set of all languages of* $A^*$ *whose syntactic monoid is in* **V**. *Then* $\mathcal{V}$ *is a variety of languages. Moreover, the correspondence* **V** $\to \mathcal{V}$ *is a bijection between varieties of finite monoids and varieties of languages.*

Let us just mention for the record that a generalization of Eilenberg's variety theorem also holds for *lp*-varieties, *li*-varieties and *ld*-varieties. See [27, 10, 49, 65, 66, 85] for more details.

### 7.1.4. *Profinite Words*

A finite monoid $M$ *separates* two words $u$ and $v$ of $A^*$ if there is a monoid morphism $\varphi : A^* \to M$ such that $\varphi(u) \neq \varphi(v)$. We set

$$r(u,v) = \min\{\operatorname{Card}(M) \mid M \text{ is a finite monoid that separates } u \text{ and } v \}$$

and $d(u,v) = 2^{-r(u,v)}$, with the usual conventions $\min \emptyset = +\infty$ and $2^{-\infty} = 0$. Then $d$ is a *metric* on $A^*$ and the completion of $A^*$ for this metric is denoted by $\widehat{A^*}$. The (concatenation) product on $A^*$ can be extended by continuity to $\widehat{A^*}$, making $\widehat{A^*}$ a compact topological monoid, called the *free profinite monoid*. Its elements are called *profinite words*.

This abstract definition does not make it easy to really understand what a profinite word is. Actually, although $\widehat{A^*}$ is known to be uncountable if $A$ is nonempty, it is difficult to exhibit "concrete" examples of profinite words, other than words of $A^*$. One such example can be obtained as a consequence of a standard result of semigroup theory:

> Given an element $s$ of a compact semigroup $S$, the closed subsemigroup of $S$ generated by $s$ contains a unique idempotent, usually denoted by $s^\omega$.

In particular, if $u$ is a profinite word, then $u^\omega$ is also a profinite word. For instance, if $A = \{x, y\}$, then $(xy)^\omega$ and $((xy)^\omega yx(yxy)^\omega)^\omega$ are examples of profinite words.

### 7.1.5. *Profinite Identities*

Let $M$ be a finite monoid. Let us equip $M$ with the discrete metric $d$, defined by $d(x, x) = 0$ and $d(x, y) = 1$ if $x \neq y$. Then every morphism $\varphi : A^* \to M$ is uniformly continuous since $d(x, y) < 2^{-|M|}$ implies $\varphi(x) = \varphi(y)$. Thus $\varphi$ admits a unique continuous extension $\widehat{\varphi} : \widehat{A^*} \to M$.

Let $u, v$ be two profinite words on some alphabet $B$. We say that a finite monoid $M$ *satisfies the profinite identity* $u = v$ if the equality $\widehat{\varphi}(u) = \widehat{\varphi}(v)$ holds for all morphisms $\varphi : B^* \to M$. For instance, a monoid is commutative if and only if it satisfies the identity $xy = yx$. It is *aperiodic* if and only if it satisfies the identity $x^\omega x = x^\omega$.

Reiterman's theorem [72] states that a class of finite monoids is a variety if and only if it can be defined by a set of profinite identities. Since varieties of languages are in bijection with varieties of finite monoids, one can also define varieties of languages by profinite identities. This was made precise by Gehrke, Grigorieff and the author [28] as follows.

Let $L$ be a regular language of $A^*$ and let $\eta : A^* \to M$ be its syntactic morphism. Then $\eta$ admits a unique continuous extension $\widehat{\eta} : \widehat{A^*} \to M$. In the same way, every monoid morphism from $B^*$ to $A^*$ admits a unique continuous extension $\widehat{\varphi} : \widehat{B^*} \to \widehat{A^*}$. Given two profinite words $u$ and $v$ on the alphabet $B$, we say that $L$ *satisfies the profinite identity* $u = v$ if the equality $\widehat{\eta}(\widehat{\varphi}(u)) = \widehat{\eta}(\widehat{\varphi}(v))$ holds for all morphisms $\varphi : B^* \to A^*$. Reiterman's theorem can now be transposed to varieties of languages:

> *A class of languages is a variety of languages if and only if it can be defined by a set of profinite identities.*

A similar characterization was also proved [28] for *lp*-varieties, *li*-varieties and *ld*-varieties. We just state this result for *ld*-varieties, the other cases being similar. Let us say that a regular language *satisfies the profinite ld-identity* $u = v$ if the equality $\widehat{\eta}(\widehat{\varphi}(u)) = \widehat{\eta}(\widehat{\varphi}(v))$ holds for all length-decreasing morphisms $\varphi : B^* \to A^*$. Then one can state

> *A class of languages is a ld-variety of languages if and only if it can be defined by a set of profinite ld-identities.*

We refer the reader to [2] for a detailed study of profinite identities defining varieties of finite monoids and to the survey [65] for profinite equations on languages.

### 7.1.6. Semirings

A *semiring* is a set $K$ equipped with two binary operations, written additively and multiplicatively, and two elements 0 and 1, satisfying the following conditions:

(1) $K$ is a commutative monoid for the addition with identity 0,

(2) $K$ is a monoid for the multiplication with identity 1,

(3) Multiplication is distributive over addition: for all $s, t_1, t_2 \in K$, $s(t_1 + t_2) = st_1 + st_2$ and $(t_1 + t_2)s = t_1 s + t_2 s$,

(4) for all $s \in K$, $0s = s0 = 0$.

Examples of semirings include $(\mathbb{N}, +, \times)$, $(\mathbb{Z}, +, \times)$ and the *tropical semirings* $(\mathbb{N} \cup \{+\infty\}, \min, +)$ and $(\mathbb{N} \cup \{-\infty\}, \max, +)$. The set of languages over $A^*$ also forms a semiring with union as addition and concatenation product as multiplication. Consequently, we adopt the algebraic notation which consists of writing $+$ for union, 0 for the empty language and $u$ for the language $\{u\}$, when $u$ is a word. Thus, for instance, $1 + ab + baa + bb$ denotes the language $\{1, ab, baa, bb\}$.

Let $K$ be a semiring. We let $K\langle\!\langle A \rangle\!\rangle$ (respectively $K[\![A]\!]$) denote the semiring of *formal power series* in noncommutative (respectively commutative) variables in $A$ with coefficients in $K$. We let also $K\langle A \rangle$ (respectively $K[A]$) denote the semiring of *polynomials* in noncommutative (respectively commutative) variables in $A$ with coefficients in $K$.

### 7.1.7. Weighted Automata

Let $K$ be a semiring. A *$K$-weighted automaton* (or *$K$-transducer*) is a quintuple $\mathcal{A} = (Q, A, E, I, F)$, where $Q$ (resp., $I$, $F$) is the *set of states* (resp., *initial* and *final* states) and $A$ is the *input alphabet*. The set of *transitions* $E$ is a subset of $Q \times A \times K \times Q$. A transition $(q, a, x, q')$ is also written as $q \xrightarrow{a|x} q'$. A path

$$q_0 \xrightarrow{a_1|x_1} q_1 \xrightarrow{a_2|x_2} q_2 \quad \cdots \quad q_{n-1} \xrightarrow{a_n|x_n} q_n$$

is successful if $q_0 \in I$ and $q_n \in F$. The *output* of this path is the product $x_1 x_2 \cdots x_n$.

The function $\tau : A^* \to K$ realized by $\mathcal{A}$ is defined as follows. Given a word $u \in A^*$, $\tau(u)$ is the sum of the outputs of all successful paths of label $u$. If there is no successful path of label $u$ the output is 0. Note that addition and product refer to the operations of the semiring $K$. Thus, if $K$ is the tropical semiring $(\mathbb{N} \cup \{+\infty\}, \min, +)$, the output of a path is the *sum* $x_1 + x_2 + \cdots + x_n$ and $\tau(u)$ is the *minimum* of the outputs of all successful paths of label $u$.

Automata with outputs in the tropical semiring are sometimes called *automata with distance* [32, 34, 35, 36] or *distance automata* [44, 43, 45].

## 7.2. Star Height

*Extended regular expressions* on the alphabet $A$ are defined recursively as follows:

(1) 0, 1 and $a$, for each $a \in A$, are regular expressions.
(2) If $E$ and $F$ are extended regular expressions, then $(E+F)$, $(EF)$ and $(E)^c$ and $(E)^*$ are regular expressions.

The *value* of an extended regular expression $E$ is the language of $A^*$ obtained from $E$ by interpreting $(E)^c$ as the complement of $E$ and the other operators as union, concatenation and star.

The *star height* of an extended regular expression is the maximum nested depth of stars in the expression. For instance

$$\left( \left( a(ba)^* b^c \right)^* + \left( b(aa)^* b + a \right)^* + \left( b(a+b)^* bb \right)^c \right)^*$$

is an extended regular expression of star height 3. More formally, the *star height* $h(E)$ of an extended regular expression $E$ is defined recursively by

(1) $h(0) = 0$, $h(1) = 0$ and, for each $a \in A$, $h(a) = 0$.
(2) If $E$ and $F$ are regular expressions, then $h((E)^c) = h(E)$, $h((E + F)) = h((EF)) = \max(h(E), h(F))$ and $h((E)^*) = h(E) + 1$.

The *star height* $h(L)$ of a regular language $L$ is the minimum of the star heights of the extended regular expressions representing $L$. In other words

$$h(L) = \min\{h(E) \mid E \text{ is an extended regular expression of value } L\}.$$

Note that allowing intersection would not change the star height of a language since $K \cap L = (K^c + L^c)^c$. The *star height problem* is the following question:

**Problem 1** *Is there an algorithm which computes the star height of a given regular language?*

A language of star height 0 is said to be *star-free*. For instance, the language $A^* = \emptyset^c$ is star-free and so is the language $(ab)^*$ on the alphabet $A = \{a, b\}$ since

$$(ab)^* = \left(bA^* \cup A^*a \cup A^*aaA^* \cup A^*bbA^*\right)^c = \left(b\emptyset^c \cup \emptyset^c a \cup \emptyset^c aa\emptyset^c \cup \emptyset^c bb\emptyset^c\right)^c.$$

Star-free languages were characterized by Schützenberger [77] in 1965.

**Theorem 7.2.1** *A language is star-free if and only if its syntactic monoid is aperiodic.*

Theorem 7.2.1 gives an algorithm to decide whether a language is star-free. For instance, the language $(aa)^*$ is not star-free, and hence has star height 1, since its syntactic monoid is the cyclic group of order 2, a non-aperiodic monoid.

Theorem 7.2.1 also suggests that languages of star height $\leqslant n$ form a variety of languages, and can therefore be characterized by a property of their syntactic monoid. This hypothesis, explicitly mentioned in Henneman's thesis [37] in 1971, has never been invalidated. However, the author [62] proved in 1978 that, for any finite monoid $M$, there is a finite language $F$ such that $M$ divides the syntactic monoid of $F^*$, with the following consequence:

**Proposition 7.2.1** *If the languages of star-height $\leqslant 1$ form a variety of languages, then all regular languages have star-height $\leqslant 1$.*

Proposition 7.2.1 appears to kill the algebraic approach, unless every language has star height 0 or 1. However, Straubing, Thérien and the author [67] proved in 1992 a weaker property: the languages of star-height $\leqslant n$ form a *ld-variety*.

**Theorem 7.2.2** *For each $n$, the class of all languages of star-height $\leqslant n$ is closed under Boolean operations, quotients and inverse of length-decreasing morphisms.*

As we have seen, *ld*-varieties of languages can be defined by profinite *ld-identities*. Therefore, it would suffice to find a single nontrivial *ld*-identity satisfied by all languages of star-height $\leqslant 1$ to prove the existence of a language of star-height $> 1$. Unfortunately, no such identity is known and we still have no example of a language of star height 2. Several past candidates have been turned down [67, 87, 75], but languages of the form $\pi^{-1}(1)$, where $\pi$ is a surjective morphism from $A^*$ onto a sufficiently complicated group (say the symmetric group $S_5$) might be reasonable candidates.

On the other hand, if you believe that all languages have star-height $\leqslant 1$, it "just" remains to prove that the languages of star-height $\leqslant 1$ are closed under inverses of morphisms. One difficulty is that even languages of the form $\varphi^{-1}(F^*)$, where $\varphi$ is a morphism and $F$ is finite, can be extremely complicated. In particular, we do not know whether the $ld$-variety generated by the languages of the form $F^*$, where $F$ is finite, is the variety of all regular languages. A very partial result has been obtained in this direction. Daviaud and Paperman [18] gave profinite equations characterizing the closure under Boolean operations and quotients of the set of languages of the form $u^*$, where $u$ is a word. However, finding a characterization of the $ld$-variety generated by these languages is still an open problem and moreover, there is still a giant step to pass from $u^*$ to $F^*$.

An interesting logical approach was proposed by Lippert and Thomas [53]. The idea was to consider star-free expressions with an additional constant $L$, where $L$ is a fixed language. However, Lippert and Thomas proved that the equivalence between star-free expressions and first-order logic [59] fails to extend to this setting: the relativized star-free expressions are strictly weaker than the corresponding first-order formulas.

## 7.3. Limitedness Problem and Restricted Star Height

This section treats two problems: the limitedness problem and the restricted star height problem. As we will see, the former one can be viewed as a warmup problem for the latter one.

### 7.3.1. *Limitedness Problem*

The limitedness problem is not only interesting on its own, but the tools introduced to solve it ultimately led to an elegant solution to the restricted star-height problem. They proved to be very influential in automata theory and they are still the topic of very active research.

The *Kleene star* of a language $L$ is defined as the infinite union

$$L^* = 1 + L + L^2 + \cdots = \sum_{n \geqslant 0} L^n.$$

The question arises whether this infinite sum can be truncated. A language is said to be *k-limited* if

$$L^* = 1 + L + \cdots + L^k = (1 + L)^k.$$

It is easy to see that $L$ is $k$-limited if and only if $1+L$ is $k$-limited. Moreover, if $L$ contains the empty word, then $L$ is $k$-limited if and only if $L^* = L^k$.

A language is *limited* (or has the *finite power property*) if it is $k$-limited for some $k > 0$. According to Simon [80], the *limitedness problem* was first proposed by Brzozowski in 1966 during the seventh SWAT (now FOCS) Conference. It can be stated as follows:

**Problem 2** *Decide whether a given regular language is limited or not.*

After some preliminary work by Linna [52] in 1973, the problem was solved independently by Hashiguchi [31] and Simon [79] in the late seventies, and an elegant semigroup solution was proposed by Kirsten [41] in 2002. Hashiguchi's solution worked directly on the minimal deterministic automaton recognizing $L$. Simon went in another direction and came up with a very simple reduction to a problem on weighted automata. Given the considerable influence of this method on subsequent research, it is worth explaining his idea. Given a regular language $L$, consider the function $f_L : A^* \to \mathbb{N} \cup \{+\infty\}$ defined by

$$f_L(u) = \begin{cases} \min\{n \mid u \in L^n\}, & \text{if } u \in L^*; \\ +\infty, & \text{otherwise.} \end{cases}$$

It is clear that $L$ is $k$-limited if and only if the range of $f_L$ is contained in $\{0, \cdots, k\} \cup \{+\infty\}$. Consequently, $L$ is limited if and only if $f_L$ has a finite range. Now, $f_L$ can be computed by a weighted automaton with output in the tropical semiring $(\mathbb{N} \cup \{+\infty\}, \min, +)$. Let us describe this construction on the example proposed by Simon [80] in his 1988 survey.

Let $A = \{a, b\}$ and $L = (a + b)(b^2 + (a + ba)b^*a)^*$. We start with a standard automaton $\mathcal{A}$ for $L$, represented on the left-hand side of Figure 7.1. Next we build an automaton $\mathcal{B}$ accepting $L^*$ by the standard construction and convert it to a weighted automaton by adding a 0-output to each transition of $\mathcal{A}$ and a 1-output to each new transition in $\mathcal{B}$ (the dashed transitions in Figure 7.1). Intuitively, there is a fee of 1 each time a path reaches state 1, and hence this weighted automaton realizes $f_L$. Thus, the limitedness problem can be reduced to the *finite range problem* for weighted automata.

**Problem 3** *Decide whether or not the behaviour of a given weighted automaton has a finite range.*

For the limitedness problem, it suffices to solve the finite range problem for weighted automata over the tropical semiring. But historically,

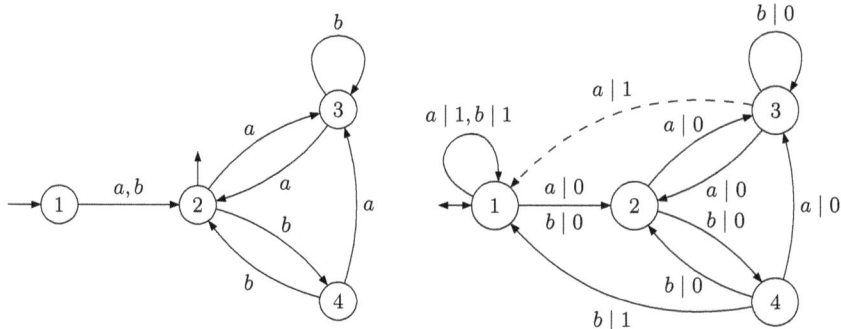

The minimal automaton $\mathcal{A}$ of $L$.     An automaton $\mathcal{B}$ for $L^*$, with weights added.

Fig. 7.1.   A 4-limited language: $L^* = (1 + L)^4$.

the finite range problem was first studied for the semiring $(\mathbb{N}, +, \times)$ by Mandel and Simon [56] in 1977 and for fields by Jacob [39] in 1978. The first solution for the tropical semiring was given by Simon [79] in 1978. Successive improvements were proposed by Hashiguchi [32, 35] (1982 and 1990), Leung [50] (1987) and Simon [80, 81] (1988 and 1994). See the survey [64] for more details.

**Theorem 7.3.1** *The finite range problem for the tropical semiring* $(\mathbb{N} \cup \{+\infty\}, \min, +)$ *is decidable.*

The complexity of the problem was also analyzed. Hashiguchi [36] showed in 2000 that every $n$-state distance automaton is either unlimited or limited by $2^{C(n)}$, where $C(n) = 4n^3 + n\ln(n+2) + n \leqslant 4n^3 + n^2 + 2n$. In 2004, Leung and Podolskiy [51] improved this bound to $C(n) = 3n^3 + n\ln n + n - 1$ and proved that limitedness of distance automata is decidable in PSPACE. The problem is in fact PSPACE-complete, as shown by Kirsten [44].

The limitedness problem is undecidable for context-free languages; see Hughues and Selkow [38]. Kirsten and Richomme [42, 46] also investigated the limitedness problem in trace monoids.

### 7.3.2. *Restricted Star Height*

Regular expressions on the alphabet $A$ are defined recursively as follows:

(1)  0, 1 and $a$, for each $a \in A$ are regular expressions.

(2)  if $E$ and $F$ are regular expressions, then $E + F$, $(E)(F)$ and $(E)^*$ are

regular expressions.

The notion of *restricted star height* of a regular expression is the maximum nested depth of stars in the expression. For instance

$$\left( \left( a(ba)^*b \right)^* + \left( b(aa)^*b + c \right)^* \right)^*$$

is a regular expression of height 3. More formally, the *restricted star height* $h(E)$ of a regular expression $E$ is defined recursively by

(1) $h(0) = 0$, $h(1) = 0$ and, for each $a \in A$, $h(a) = 0$.

(2) If $E$ and $F$ are regular expressions, then $h(E + F) = h(EF) = \max(h(E), h(F))$ and $h((E)^*) = h(E) + 1$.

The *value* $v(E)$ of a regular expression $E$ is the language of $A^*$ represented by $E$. Formally, $v$ is a function from the set of regular expressions to the set of regular languages of $A^*$ defined by

(1) $v(0) = 0$, $v(1) = 1$ and $v(a) = a$ for each $a \in A$,

(2) if $E$ and $F$ are two regular expressions, $v(E \cup F) = v(E) \cup v(F)$, $v(EF) = v(E)(F)$ and $v(E^*) = v(E)^*$.

The *restricted star height* $h(L)$ of a regular language $L$ is the minimum of the restricted star heights of the regular expressions which represent it. In other words

$$h(L) = \min\{h(E) \mid E \text{ is a regular expression such that } v(E) = L\}.$$

The star height problem was raised by L.C. Eggan [25] in 1963:

**Problem 4** *Is there an algorithm which computes the restricted star height of a given regular language?*

Dejean and Schützenberger [20] first proved in 1966 that for each $n \geqslant 0$, there exists a language of restricted star height $n$. Only a few partial results [11, 12, 13, 14, 37] were known until Hashiguchi [33] proved in 1982 that restricted star height one is decidable. A few years later, in 1988, Hashiguchi [34] succeeded to prove the general case: restricted star height is decidable. However, Hashiguchi's proof is hard to read and yields an algorithm of non-elementary complexity (cf. Lombardy's thesis [54], Annexe B and examples by Lombardy and Sakarovitch [55]). It took 25 years to obtain Hashiguchi's first solution to Eggan's problem but it took another 23 years until Kirsten [45] found a simplified proof in 2005. Just like for the limitedness problem, the idea of this proof is to reduce the restricted star-height problem to finding upper bounds for the function computed by a new kind of automata, the nested-distance desert automata. The resulting algorithm has a complexity in double exponential space.

Nested-distance desert automata are a particular case of *hierarchical cost automata*. A hierarchical cost automaton is a nondeterministic finite automaton equipped with a totally ordered finite set of counters, initially set to zero. Transitions can increment or reset a given counter, but then all counters of smaller rank have to be reset. A cost automaton is defined in a similar way, but the counters are not ordered and thus transitions can only increment or reset a given counter. These notions have been widely studied in the recent years, notably by Kirsten [44, 43], Bojanczyk and Colcombet [5, 6, 16, 17]. Very recently, Bojanczyk [5] proved that the limitedness problem for cost automata reduces to solving Gale-Stewart games with $\omega$-regular winning conditions, which leads to an entirely new proof of the decidability of the restricted star-height problem.

Even with the progress realised in the recent years, the complexity of the algorithms seemed to exclude the possibility of any practical computation. However, Fijalkow, Gimbert, Kelmendi and Kuperberg addressed the challenge by writing a C++-programme computing the star-height of regular languages accepted by (small) automata, as part of their package ACME++ (*Automata with Counters, Monoids and Equivalence*), freely available at http://www.liafa.univ-paris-diderot.fr/~nath/?page=acmepp.

Let me conclude these two sections on star-height by suggesting another problem. Let us define an *intermediate regular expression* as an extended regular expression allowing union and intersection but not complement. Intermediate regular expressions are clearly more general than regular expressions but less general than extended regular expressions. The *intermediate star-height* of a language is the minimum of the star heights of the intermediate regular expressions representing the language. The intermediate version of Problems 1 and 4 can now be stated as follows:

**Problem 5** *Are there languages of arbitrary intermediate star-height? Is there an algorithm which computes the intermediate star height of a given regular language?*

## 7.4. Group Complexity

In this section, all semigroups and groups are supposed to be finite.

The Krohn-Rhodes theorem states that every semigroup S divides a finite alternating wreath product of groups and aperiodic semigroups.

**Theorem 7.4.1 (Krohn-Rhodes 1966)** *Every semigroup $S$ divides a wreath product of the form*

$$A_0 \circ G_1 \circ A_1 \cdots A_{n-1} \circ G_n \circ A_n, \qquad (*)$$

*where $A_0, A_1, \ldots, A_n$ are aperiodic semigroups and $G_1, \ldots, G_n$ are groups.*

The *group complexity* of $S$ is the smallest possible integer $n$ over all decompositions of type $(*)$. Thus aperiodic semigroups have group complexity 0 and nontrivial groups have group complexity 1. However, the following problem is still open:

**Problem 6** *Is there an algorithm to compute the group complexity of a semigroup, given its multiplication table?*

This question generated intense research and several important tools of semigroup theory, like the *Rhodes expansion* and *pointlike sets* were introduced in connection with this problem. As a result, the group complexity of many semigroups has been computed. However, as of today, there is no known algorithm to decide whether a semigroup has group complexity 1 and the only known results regarding decidability, due to Karnofsky and Rhodes [40], date back to 1982.

**Theorem 7.4.2** *One can decide whether a semigroup divides a wreath product of the form $G \circ A$. One can decide whether a semigroup divides a wreath product of the form $A \circ G$.*

The book by J. Rhodes and B. Steinberg [74] is by far the most important reference on these questions. It contains a thorough presentation of the numerous tools introduced to attack Problem 6 as well as a detailed survey of the existing partial results up to 2009. Several authors, including Almeida, Auinger, Henckell, Margolis, Rhodes, Steinberg and Volkov enriched the literature since then and the reader is invited to look at the articles of these authors to follow recent progress.

Problem 6 is of course deeply related to the study of the wreath product and have strong connection with language theory. A key reason is that the syntactic semigroup of the composition of two sequential functions divides the wreath product of the syntactic semigroups of the two functions. Cohen and Brzozowski [15] and Meyer [60] used a refinement of the Krohn-Rhodes theorem for aperiodic semigroups to obtain an alternative proof of Schützenberger's characterization of star-free languages. Straubing

[82] took further advantage of wreath product decompositions to characterize various classes of regular languages and to state its influential wreath product principle [84], which was later generalized in several ways [68, 10].

It is interesting to see that in the opposite direction, major progress on wreath product decompositions came from language theory. For instance, the characterization of locally testable languages by Brzozowski-Simon [9] and McNaughton [58], Knast's description of dot-depth one languages [47, 48, 86] and Straubing's study of concatenation hierarchies [83] opened the way to Tilson's delay theorem [88].

## 7.5. Star Removal

Star removal is the only problem of the list that remained untouched, although it is certainly a fascinating question. The absence of references makes it hazardous to evaluate its difficulty, but I hope it will attract more attention in the future. Here is the problem.

Let $K$ be a regular language. Then the equation $K = XK$ has a maximal solution $L^*$. Then $K = L^*K$ and one can show that the equation in $R$:

$$K = L^*R$$

has a minimal solution $R = K - (L^* - 1)K$.

Iterating this process on $R$, we get a decomposition

$$K = L_1^* L_2^* \cdots L_k^* R_k,$$

where $R_k$ is the minimal solution of $K = L_1^* L_2^* \cdots L_k^* R$.

**Problem 7** *Does this process terminate (i.e., $L_k^* = 1$ at some point)?*

## 7.6. Regularity of Non-Counting Classes

A language $L$ of $A^*$ is said to be *noncounting of order $n$* if for all $x, y, u \in A^*$,

$$xu^n y \in L \iff xu^{n+1}y \in L.$$

Let $\sim_n$ be the smallest congruence on $A^*$ satisfying $x^n \sim_n x^{n+1}$ for all $x \in A^*$ and let $\mu : A^* \to A^*/\sim_n$ be the natural morphism. The problem of the regularity of non-counting classes can be stated formally as follows:

**Problem 8** *Is $\mu^{-1}(m)$ a regular language for every $m \in A^*/\sim_n$?*

An extended version of the problem was studied by McCammond [57].

**Problem 9** *Let $\sim_{n,m}$ be the smallest congruence on $A^*$ satisfying $x^n \sim x^{n+m}$ for all $x \in A^*$. Are the congruence classes regular?*

The problem is not yet entirely solved but generated intense research. The results by de Luca and Varricchio [19] (1990), McCammond [57] (1991), Guba [29, 30] (1993), Do Lago [21, 22, 23, 24] (1996, 1998, 2001, 2002) can be summarized in the following theorems:

**Theorem 7.6.1** *Problem 9 has a positive answer for $n \geqslant 3$ and $m > 0$.*

**Theorem 7.6.2** *Problem 9 has a negative answer for $n = 2$ and $m > 1$.*

For $n = 2$, $m = 1$ ($x^3 = x^2$), the problem is still open, but a partial result is known. Let us say that a word is *overlap-free* if it contains no factor of the form $xyxyx$ for any $x \in A^+$ and $y \in A^*$. If it contains no proper factor of the form above, then the word is said to be *almost overlap-free*.

**Theorem 7.6.3 (Plyushchenko and Shur 2011 [69, 71, 70])** *For $n = 2$ and $m = 1$, the congruence class of a word containing an overlap-free or an almost overlap-free word is a regular language.*

The regularity of noncounting classes is also reminiscent of Burnside's celebrated problem, posed by Burnside in 1902. Burnside asked whether a $k$-generated group satisfying the identity $x^n = 1$ is necessarily finite. In 1968, Novikov and Adian disproved the conjecture for every odd $n$ larger than 4381, a bound that was later reduced to 665 by Adian. Ivanov also disproved the conjecture for each even $n$ divisible by $2^9$ and larger or equal to $2^{48}$. The problem has been solved positively for $k = 1$ and for $k > 1$ and $n = 2, 3, 4$ and 6, but is still open for $n = 5$ and $k > 1$.

### 7.7. Optimality of Prefix Codes

Recall that a language $X$ of $A^+$ is a *code* if the condition

$$x_1 \cdots x_n = x_1' \cdots x_m' \quad \text{(where } x_i, x_i' \in X\text{)}$$

implies $n = m$ and $x_i = x_i'$ for $i = 1, \ldots, n$. It is a prefix code if any two distinct words in $X$ are incomparable for the prefix order.

A language of $A^*$ can be identified with an element of $\mathbb{Z}\langle\!\langle A \rangle\!\rangle$, the set of formal series in noncommutative variables in $A$ and coefficients in $\mathbb{Z}$.

Let $\alpha : \mathbb{Z}\langle\langle A \rangle\rangle \to \mathbb{Z}\langle A \rangle$ be the natural morphism mapping a series in noncommutative variables onto its commutative version. For instance, if $X = ba + abab + baab + bbab$, then $\alpha(X) = ab + 2a^2b^2 + ab^3$.

A language $X$ is *commutatively prefix* if $\alpha(X) = \alpha(P)$ for some prefix code $P$. In other words, $X$ is commutatively prefix if there exists a bijection from $X$ to some prefix code mapping every word of $X$ to one of its anagrams.

A nontrivial result, Theorem 14.6.4 in the book of Berstel, Perrin and Reutenauer [4], states that a language $X$ is commutatively prefix if and only if the series $(1 - \alpha(X))/(1 - \alpha(A))$ has nonnegative coefficients. Schützenberger [76] proposed in 1965 the following conjecture:

**Conjecture 1** *Every code is commutatively prefix.*

This conjecture generated intense research and was proved in some particular cases, but a counterexample was ultimately found by Peter Shor [78] in 1983. The code

$$X = \{ba, ba^7, ba^{13}, ba^{14}, a^3b, a^3ba^2, a^3ba^4, a^3ba^6, a^8b,$$
$$a^8ba^2, a^8ba^4, a^8ba^6, a^{11}b, a^{11}ba^2, a^{11}ba^4\}$$

is not commutatively prefix. Following the discovery of this counterexample, Perrin suggested a weaker version of Schützenberger's conjecture. A code is said to be *maximal* if it is not properly contained in any other code.

**Problem 10** *Is every finite maximal code commutatively prefix?*

This problem is closely related to a question on optimal encodings [3]. A monoid morphism $\gamma : B^* \to A^*$ is a (prefix) *encoding* if $\gamma(B)$ is a (prefix) code. Let $p$ be a probability on $B$, representing for instance the frequency of the letters of $B$. For instance, if $B$ is the usual latin alphabet, $p(a)$ could be the frequency of each letter in written English. Suppose also that each letter $a$ of $A$ has a cost $c(a)$, which, in practice, is often interpreted as the time to send the symbol $a$. The cost of a word $a_1a_2 \cdots a_n$ is then defined as the sum $c(a_1) + \cdots + c(a_n)$. The *average weighted cost* of $\gamma$ is the quantity

$$W(\gamma) = \sum_{b \in B} p(b)c(b)$$

and the *optimal encoding problem* is to find, given $A$, $B$, $p$ and $c$, an encoding $\gamma$ such that $W(\gamma)$ is minimal. Thus a positive solution to Problem 10 would imply that an optimal encoding can always chosen to be prefix.

Interestingly, Problem 10 is also strongly related to a problem on formal power series. Let $X \subseteq A^+$. A pair $(P, S)$ of subsets of $A^*$ is called a *positive* *factorization* for $X$ if each word $w$ factorizes uniquely into $w = sxp$ with $p \in P$, $s \in S$, $x \in X$. In terms of formal power series in $\mathbb{N}\langle A \rangle$, this means that

$$A^* = SX^*P \quad \text{or equivalently} \quad 1 - X = P(1 - A)S.$$

This condition implies that $X$ is commutatively prefix. Moreover, if $P$ and $S$ are finite, then $X$ is a finite maximal code. These results motivated the following conjecture, known as the factorization conjecture.

**Conjecture 2** *For any finite maximal code $X$ over $A$, there exist two polynomials $P, S \in \mathbb{N}\langle A \rangle$ such that $1 - X = P(1 - A)S$.*

A positive answer to the factorization conjecture would also solve positively Problem 10. Both questions are still open, but in 1985, Reutenauer [73] proved the following weaker version of the factorization conjecture.

**Theorem 7.7.1** *For any finite maximal code $X$ over $A$, there exist two polynomials $P, S \in \mathbb{Z}\langle A \rangle$ such that $1 - X = P(1 - A)S$.*

Reutenauer's theorem gives strong evidence that the factorization conjecture might be true. For a complete discussion, the reader is referred to the book of Berstel, Perrin and Reutenauer [4] and to the survey papers of Bruyère and Latteux [7] and of Béal, Berstel, Marcus, Perrin, Reutenauer and Siegel [3].

## 7.8. Conclusion

Janusz A. Brzozowski really has excellent taste! The challenging problems he selected 35 years ago fostered intense studies and are still at the heart of current research. Only two of them, the limitedness problem and the restricted star height problem, have been completely solved. One of them, the regularity of non-counting classes, is almost solved. Significant progress has been done on group complexity and on optimality of prefix codes. Only little progress is to be reported on star height and the star removal problem remained untouched.

The amount of new ideas created or expanded to solve these questions, mixing algebra, logic and automata theory are cause for optimism and one can hope for a complete solution of some of Brzozowski's open problems within the next 35 years.

## Dedication and Acknowledgments

This paper is dedicated to Janusz A. Brzozowski for his 80th birthday. I would like to thank Jeffrey Shallit for his kind invitation to the Brzozowski conference and for his useful comments on this paper. The author was funded from the European Research Council (ERC) under the European Union's Horizon 2020 research and innovation programme (grant agreement No 670624).

## References

1. J. ALMEIDA, *Finite semigroups and universal algebra. Series in Algebra*, vol. 3, World Scientific, Singapore, 1994.
2. J. ALMEIDA AND P. WEIL, Relatively free profinite monoids: an introduction and examples, in *NATO Advanced Study Institute Semigroups, Formal Languages and Groups*, J. Fountain (ed.), vol. 466, pp. 73–117, Kluwer Academic Publishers, 1995.
3. M.-P. BÉAL, J. BERSTEL, B. H. MARCUS, D. PERRIN, C. REUTENAUER AND P. H. SIEGEL, Variable-length codes and finite automata, in *Selected topics in information and coding theory*, I. Woungang (ed.), pp. 505–584, *Ser. Coding Theory Cryptol.* vol. 7, World Sci. Publ., Hackensack, NJ, 2010.
4. J. BERSTEL, D. PERRIN AND C. REUTENAUER, *Codes and Automata, Encyclopedia of Mathematics and its Applications* vol. 129, Cambridge University Press, 2009. 634 pages.
5. M. BOJAŃCZYK, Star height via games, in *30th LICS 2015*, pp. 214–219, IEEE Computer Society, 2015.
6. M. BOJAŃCZYK AND T. COLCOMBET, Bounds in w-regularity, in *21th LICS 2006*, pp. 285–296, IEEE Computer Society, 2006.
7. V. BRUYÈRE AND M. LATTEUX, Variable-length maximal codes, in *Automata, languages and programming (Paderborn, 1996)*, pp. 24–47, *LNCS* vol. 1099, Springer, Berlin, 1996.
8. J. A. BRZOZOWSKI, Developments in the theory of regular languages, in *IFIP Congress*, pp. 29–40, 1980.
9. J. A. BRZOZOWSKI AND I. SIMON, Characterizations of locally testable events, *Discrete Math.* **4** (1973), 243–271.
10. L. CHAUBARD, J.-É. PIN AND H. STRAUBING, Actions, wreath products of C-varieties and concatenation product, *Theoret. Comput. Sci.* **356** (2006), 73–89.
11. R. S. COHEN, *Cycle rank of transition graphs and the star height of regular events*, PhD thesis, University of Ottawa, Ottawa, 1968.
12. R. S. COHEN, Star height of certain families of regular events, *J. Comput. System Sci.* **4** (1970), 281–297.
13. R. S. COHEN, Techniques for establishing star height of regular sets, *Math. Systems Theory* **5** (1971), 97–114.

14. R. S. COHEN AND J. A. BRZOZOWSKI, General properties of star height of regular events, *J. Comput. System Sci.* **4** (1970), 260–280.

15. R. S. COHEN AND J. A. BRZOZOWSKI, Dot-depth of star-free events, *J. Comput. Syst. Sci.* **5**,1 (1971), 1–16.

16. T. COLCOMBET, The theory of stabilisation monoids and regular cost functions, in *Automata, languages and programming. Part II*, Berlin, 2009, pp. 139–150, *Lecture Notes in Comput. Sci.* vol. 5556, Springer.

17. T. COLCOMBET, Regular cost functions, Part I: Logic and algebra over words, *Log. Methods Comput. Sci.* **9**,3 (2013), 3:3, 47.

18. L. DAVIAUD AND C. PAPERMAN, Classes of languages generated by the kleene star of a word, in *40th MFCS 2015 Part I*, G. F. Italiano, G. Pighizzini and D. Sannella (eds.), pp. 167–178, *LNCS* vol. 9234, Springer, 2015.

19. A. DE LUCA AND S. VARRICCHIO, On noncounting regular classes, in *Automata, languages and programming (Coventry, 1990)*, pp. 74–87, *LNCS* vol. 443, Springer, New York, 1990.

20. F. DEJEAN AND M. P. SCHÜTZENBERGER, On a question of Eggan, *Inform. Control* **9** (1966), 23–25.

21. A. P. DO LAGO, On the Burnside semigroups $x^n - x^{n+m}$, *Internat. J. Algebra Comput.* **6**,2 (1996), 179–227.

22. A. P. DO LAGO, Maximal groups in free Burnside semigroups, in *LATIN'98*, C. L. Lucchesi and A. V. Moura (eds.), pp. 65–75, *LNCS* vol. 1380, Springer, Berlin, 1998.

23. A. P. DO LAGO, Local groups in free groupoids satisfying certain monoid identities, *Internat. J. Algebra Comput.* **1–2** (2002), 357–369. International Conference on Geometric and Combinatorial Methods in Group Theory and Semigroup Theory (Lincoln, NE, 2000).

24. A. P. DO LAGO AND I. SIMON, Free Burnside semigroups, *Theor. Inform. Appl.* **35**,6 (2001), 579–595 (2002). A tribute to Aldo de Luca.

25. L. C. EGGAN, Transition graphs and the star height of regular events, *Michigan Math. J.* **10** (1963), 385–397.

26. S. EILENBERG, *Automata, languages, and machines. Vol. B*, Academic Press [Harcourt Brace Jovanovich Publishers], New York, 1976. With two chapters ("Depth decomposition theorem" and "Complexity of semigroups and morphisms") by Bret Tilson, Pure and Applied Mathematics, Vol. 59.

27. Z. ÉSIK, Extended temporal logic on finite words and wreath products of monoids with distinguished generators, in *6th DLT 2002*, M. E. A. Ito (ed.), Berlin, 2002, pp. 43–58, *LNCS* vol. 2450, Springer.

28. M. GEHRKE, S. GRIGORIEFF AND J.-É. PIN, Duality and equational theory of regular languages, in *ICALP 2008, Part II*, L. Aceto and al. (eds.), Berlin, 2008, pp. 246–257, *LNCS* vol. 5126, Springer.

29. V. S. GUBA, The word problem for the relatively free semigroup satisfying $T^m = T^{m+n}$ with $m \geqslant 4$ or $m = 3$, $n = 1$, *Internat. J. Algebra Comput.* **3**,2 (1993), 125–140.

30. V. S. GUBA, The word problem for the relatively free semigroup satisfying $T^m = T^{m+n}$ with $m \geqslant 3$, *Internat. J. Algebra Comput.* **3**,3 (1993), 335–347.

31. K. HASHIGUCHI, A decision procedure for the order of regular events, *Theoret.*

*Comput. Sci.* **8** (1979), 69–72.

32. K. HASHIGUCHI, Limitedness theorem on finite automata with distance functions, *J. Comput. System Sci.* **24** (1982), 233–244.

33. K. HASHIGUCHI, Regular languages of star height one, *Inform. Control* **53** (1982), 199–210.

34. K. HASHIGUCHI, Algorithms for determining relative star height and star height, *Inform. Comput.* **78**,2 (1988), 124–169.

35. K. HASHIGUCHI, Improved limitedness theorems on finite automata with distance functions, *Theoret. Comput. Sci.* **72**,1 (1990), 27–38.

36. K. HASHIGUCHI, New upper bounds to the limitedness of distance automata, *Theoret. Comput. Sci.* **233**,1-2 (2000), 19–32.

37. W. HENNEMAN, *Algebraic theory of automata*, PhD thesis, Massachusetts Institute of Technology, 1971.

38. C. E. HUGHES AND S. M. SELKOW, The finite power property for context-free languages, *Theoret. Comput. Sci.* **15**,1 (1981), 111–114.

39. G. JACOB, La finitude des représentations linéaires de semi-groupes est décidable, *J. Algebra* **52** (1978), 437–459.

40. J. KARNOFSKY AND J. RHODES, Decidability of complexity one-half for finite semigroups, *Semigroup Forum* **24**,1 (1982), 55–66.

41. D. KIRSTEN, The finite power problem revisited, *Inf. Process. Lett.* **84**,6 (2002), 291–294.

42. D. KIRSTEN, The star problem and the finite power property in trace monoids: reductions beyond C4, *Inform. Comput.* **176**,1 (2002), 22–36.

43. D. KIRSTEN, Desert automata and the finite substitution problem (extended abstract), in *STACS 2004*, V. Diekert and M. Habib (eds.), pp. 305–316, *LNCS* vol. 2996, Springer, Berlin, 2004.

44. D. KIRSTEN, Distance desert automata and the star height one problem (extended abstract), in *1st Foundations of Software Science and Computation Structures*, M. Nivat (ed.), pp. 257–272, *LNCS* vol. 2987, Springer, Berlin, 2004.

45. D. KIRSTEN, Distance desert automata and the star height problem, *Theoret. Informatics Appl.* **39**,3 (2005), 455–509.

46. D. KIRSTEN AND G. RICHOMME, Decidability equivalence between the star problem and the finite power problem in trace monoids, *Theory Comput. Syst.* **34**,3 (2001), 193–227.

47. R. KNAST, A semigroup characterization of dot-depth one languages, *RAIRO Inform. Théor.* **17**,4 (1983), 321–330.

48. R. KNAST, Some theorems on graph congruences, *RAIRO Inform. Théor.* **17**,4 (1983), 331–342.

49. M. KUNC, Equational description of pseudovarieties of homomorphisms, *Theoret. Informatics Appl.* **37** (2003), 243–254.

50. H. LEUNG, *An algebraic method for solving decision problems in finite automata theory*, PhD thesis, Department of Computer Science, The Pennsylvania State University, 1987.

51. H. LEUNG AND V. PODOLSKIY, The limitedness problem on distance automata: Hashiguchi's method revisited, *Theoret. Comput. Sci.* **310**,1-3

(2004), 147–158.

52. M. LINNA, Finite power property of regular languages, in *Automata, languages and programming (Proc. Sympos., Rocquencourt, 1972)*, Nivat (ed.), pp. 87–98, North Holland, Amsterdam, 1973.

53. D. LIPPERT AND W. THOMAS, Relativized star-free expressions, first-order logic, and a concatenation game, in *Semigroups, theory and applications (Oberwolfach, 1986)*, pp. 194–204, *Lecture Notes in Math.* vol. 1320, Springer, Berlin, 1988.

54. S. LOMBARDY, *Approche structurelle de quelques problèmes de la théorie des automates*, PhD thesis, École nationale supérieure des télécommunications, Paris, 2001.

55. S. LOMBARDY AND J. SAKAROVITCH, Star height of reversible languages and universal automata, in *LATIN 2002*, S. Rajsbaum (ed.), pp. 76–90, *LNCS* vol. 2286, Springer, Berlin, 2002.

56. A. MANDEL AND I. SIMON, On finite semigroups of matrices, *Theoret. Comput. Sci.* **5** (1977), 101–111.

57. J. McCAMMOND, The solution to the word problem for the relatively free semigroups satisfying $T^a = T^{a+b}$ with $a \geqslant 6$, *Internat. J. Algebra Comput.* **1**,1 (1991), 1–32.

58. R. McNAUGHTON, Algebraic decision procedures for local testability, *Math. Systems Theory* **8**,1 (1974), 60–76.

59. R. McNAUGHTON AND S. PAPERT, *Counter-free automata*, *M.I.T. Research Monograph* Number 65, The M.I.T. Press, Cambridge, Mass.-London, 1971. With an appendix by William Henneman.

60. A. R. MEYER, A note on star-free events, *J. Assoc. Comput. Mach.* **16** (1969), 220–225.

61. J.-É. PIN, The Brzozowski hierarchy, 45 years later. This volume, Chapter 8.

62. J.-É. PIN, Sur le monoïde de $L^*$ lorsque $L$ est un langage fini, *Theoret. Comput. Sci.* **7** (1978), 211–215.

63. J.-É. PIN, *Varieties of formal languages*, North Oxford, LondonandPlenum, New-York, 1986. (Traduction de Variétés de langages formels).

64. J.-É. PIN, Tropical semirings, in *Idempotency*, J. Gunawardena (ed.), pp. 50–69, Cambridge University Press, 1998.

65. J.-É. PIN, Equational descriptions of languages, *Int. J. Found. Comput. S.* **23** (2012), 1227–1240.

66. J.-E. PIN AND H. STRAUBING, Some results on ⌋-varieties, *Theoret. Informatics Appl.* **39** (2005), 239–262.

67. J.-É. PIN, H. STRAUBING AND D. THÉRIEN, Some results on the generalized star-height problem, *Inform. Comput.* **101** (1992), 219–250.

68. J.-É. PIN AND P. WEIL, The wreath product principle for ordered semigroups, *Communications in Algebra* **30** (2002), 5677–5713.

69. A. N. PLYUSHCHENKO, On the word problem in free Burnside semigroups with the identity $x^2 = x^3$, *Izv. Vyssh. Uchebn. Zaved. Mat.* **11** (2011), 89–93.

70. A. N. PLYUSHCHENKO AND A. M. SHUR, Almost overlap-free words and the word problem for the free Burnside semigroup satisfying $x^2 = x^3$, *Internat. J. Algebra Comput.* **21**,6 (2011), 973–1006.

71. A. N. PLYUSHCHENKO AND A. M. SHUR, On Brzozowski's conjecture for the free Burnside semigroup satisfying $x^2 = x^3$, in *15th DLT 2011*, G. Mauri and A. Leporati (eds.), pp. 362–373, *LNCS* vol. 6795, Springer, Heidelberg, 2011.

72. J. REITERMAN, The Birkhoff theorem for finite algebras, *Algebra Universalis* **14**,1 (1982), 1–10.

73. C. REUTENAUER, Noncommutative factorization of variable-length codes, *J. Pure Appl. Algebra* **36**,2 (1985), 167–186.

74. J. RHODES AND B. STEINBERG, *The q-theory of finite semigroups*, *Springer Monographs in Mathematics*, Springer, New York, 2009.

75. J. M. ROBSON, More languages of generalised star height 1, *Theoret. Comput. Sci.* **106**,2 (1992), 327–335.

76. M.-P. SCHÜTZENBERGER, Codes à longueur variable. Lecture held in 1965, at a seminar in Royan (also published in École de printemps "Théorie des codes", 1979, p. 247—271), 1965.

77. M.-P. SCHÜTZENBERGER, On finite monoids having only trivial subgroups, *Inform. Control* **8** (1965), 190–194.

78. P. W. SHOR, A counterexample to the triangle conjecture, *J. Combin. Theory Ser. A* **38**,1 (1985), 110–112.

79. I. SIMON, Limited subsets of a free monoid, in *Proc. 19th Annual Symposium on Foundations of Computer Science*, pp. 143–150, IEEE, Piscataway, N.J., 1978.

80. I. SIMON, Recognizable sets with multiplicities in the tropical semiring, in *Mathematical foundations of computer science, 1988 (Carlsbad, 1988)*, M. Chytil, L. Janiga and V. Koubek (eds.), pp. 107–120, *LNCS* vol. 324, Springer, Berlin, 1988.

81. I. SIMON, On semigroups of matrices over the tropical semiring, *RAIRO Inform. Théor. Appl.* **28**,3-4 (1994), 277–294.

82. H. STRAUBING, Families of recognizable sets corresponding to certain varieties of finite monoids, *J. Pure Appl. Algebra* **15**,3 (1979), 305–318.

83. H. STRAUBING, Finite semigroup varieties of the form $V * D$, *J. Pure Appl. Algebra* **36**,1 (1985), 53–94.

84. H. STRAUBING, The wreath product and its applications, in *Formal properties of finite automata and applications (Ramatuelle, 1988)*, pp. 15–24, *LNCS* vol. 386, Springer, Berlin, 1989.

85. H. STRAUBING, On logical descriptions of regular languages, in *LATIN 2002*, S. Rajsbaum (ed.), Berlin, 2002, pp. 528–538, *LNCS* vol. 2286, Springer.

86. D. THÉRIEN, Catégories et langages de dot-depth un, *RAIRO Inform. Théor. Appl.* **22**,4 (1988), 437–445.

87. W. THOMAS, Remark on the star-height-problem, *Theoret. Comput. Sci.* **13**,2 (1981), 231–237.

88. B. TILSON, Categories as algebra: an essential ingredient in the theory of monoids, *J. Pure Appl. Algebra* **48**,1-2 (1987), 83–198.

# Chapter 8

# The Dot-Depth Hierarchy, 45 Years Later

Jean-Éric Pin

*IRIF, CNRS and Université Paris-Diderot,*
*Case 7014, 75205 Paris Cedex 13, France.*
Jean-Eric.Pin@liafa.univ-paris-diderot.fr

In 1970, R. S. Cohen and Janusz A. Brzozowski introduced a hierarchy of star-free languages called the dot-depth hierarchy. This hierarchy and its generalisations, together with the problems attached to them, had a long-lasting influence on the development of automata theory. This survey article reports on the numerous results and conjectures attached to this hierarchy.

## Contents

This paper is a follow-up of the survey article *Open problems about regular languages, 35 years later* [57]. The *dot-depth hierarchy*, also known as the *Brzozowski hierarchy*, is a hierarchy of star-free languages first in-

troduced by Cohen and Brzozowski [25] in 1971. It immediately gave rise
to many interesting questions, and an account of the early results can be
found in Brzozowski's survey [20] from 1976.

## 8.1. Terminology, Notation and Background

Most of the terminology used in this paper was introduced in [57]. Here we
just complete these definitions by giving the ordered versions of the notions
of syntactic monoid and variety of finite monoids.

### 8.1.1. *Syntactic Order and Positive Varieties*

An *ordered monoid* is a monoid equipped with an order $\leqslant$ compatible with
the multiplication: $x \leqslant y$ implies $zx \leqslant zy$ and $xz \leqslant yz$.

The *syntactic preorder*[1] of a language $L$ of $A^*$ is the relation $\leqslant_L$ defined
on $A^*$ by $u \leqslant_L v$ if and only if, for every $x, y \in A^*$,

$$xuy \in L \Rightarrow xvy \in L.$$

The *syntactic congruence* of $L$ is the associated equivalence relation $\sim_L$,
defined by $u \sim_L v$ if and only if $u \leqslant_L v$ and $v \leqslant_L u$.

The *syntactic monoid* of $L$ is the quotient $M(L)$ of $A^*$ by $\sim_L$ and the
natural morphism $\eta : A^* \to A^*/\sim_L$ is called the *syntactic morphism* of $L$.
The syntactic preorder $\leqslant_L$ induces an order on the quotient monoid $M(L)$.
The resulting ordered monoid is called the *syntactic ordered monoid* of $L$.

For instance, the syntactic monoid of the language $\{a, aba\}$ is the
monoid $M = \{1, a, b, ab, ba, aba, 0\}$ presented by the relations $a^2 = b^2 =
bab = 0$. Its syntactic order is given by the relations $0 < ab < 1$, $0 < ba < 1$,
$0 < aba < a$, $0 < b$.

The syntactic ordered monoid of a language was first introduced by
Schützenberger [86] in 1956, but thereafter, he apparently only used the
syntactic monoid.

A *positive variety of languages* is a class of languages closed under finite unions, finite intersections, left and right quotients and inverses of
morphisms. A *variety of languages* is a positive variety closed under complementation.

Similarly, a *variety of finite ordered monoids* is a class of finite ordered
monoids closed under taking ordered submonoids, quotients and finite products. Varieties of finite (ordered) *semigroups* are defined analogously. If **V**

---

[1]Unfortunately, the author used the opposite order in earlier papers (from 1995 to 2011).

is a variety of ordered monoids, let $\mathbf{V}^d$ denote the dual variety, consisting of all ordered monoids $(M, \leqslant)$ such that $(M, \geqslant) \in \mathbf{V}$. We refer the reader to the books [2, 28, 62] for more details.

Eilenberg's variety theorem [28] admits the following ordered version [63]. Let $\mathbf{V}$ be a variety of finite ordered monoids. For each alphabet $A$, let $\mathcal{V}(A)$ be the set of all languages of $A^*$ whose syntactic ordered monoid is in $\mathbf{V}$. Then $\mathcal{V}$ is a positive variety of languages. Furthermore, the correspondence $\mathbf{V} \to \mathcal{V}$ is a bijection between varieties of finite ordered monoids and positive varieties of languages.

By Reiterman's theorem [83], varieties of finite monoids can be defined by a set of profinite identities of the form $u = v$, where $u$ and $v$ are profinite words. Similarly, varieties of finite ordered monoids can be defined by a set of profinite identities of the form $u \leqslant v$ (see [73]).

### 8.1.2. *li-Varieties Versus +-Varieties*

Let us first recall that a monoid morphism $\varphi : A^* \to B^*$ is *length-increasing* if for all $u \in A^*$, $|\varphi(u)| \geqslant |u|$ or equivalently, if $\varphi(A) \subseteq B^+$. A class of languages closed under finite unions, finite intersections, left and right quotients and inverses of length-increasing morphisms is a *positive li-variety of languages*. A positive $li$-variety of languages closed under complementation is a *li-variety of languages*.

In fact, $li$-varieties are almost the same thing as $+$-varieties, a notion due to Eilenberg [28]. A *+-class of languages* $\mathcal{C}$ associates with each finite alphabet $A$ a set $\mathcal{C}(A)$ of regular languages of $A^+$, that is, not containing the empty word. A *positive +-variety of languages* is a $+$-class of languages closed under finite unions, finite intersections, left and right quotients and inverses of semigroup morphisms. A *+-variety of languages* is a positive $+$-variety closed under complementation.

The precise correspondence between $li$-varieties and $+$-varieties is discussed in [105] and [69], pp. 260–261, but we will only need the following result. Let us say that a (positive) $li$-variety of languages $\mathcal{V}$ is *well suited* if, for each alphabet $A$, $\mathcal{V}(A)$ contains the languages $\{1\}$ and $A^+$. If $\mathcal{V}$ is a (positive) well-suited $li$-variety, then the languages of the form $L \cap A^+$, where $L \in \mathcal{V}(A)$, form a (positive) $+$-variety $\mathcal{V}^+$. If $\mathcal{W}$ is a (positive) $+$-variety of languages, then the languages of the form $L$ or $L \cup \{1\}$, where $L$ is in $\mathcal{W}$, form a (positive) well-suited $li$-variety $\mathcal{W}'$. Moreover the correspondences $\mathcal{V} \to \mathcal{V}^+$ and $\mathcal{W} \to \mathcal{W}'$ are inverse bijective correspondences between well-suited $li$-varieties and $+$-varieties.

The reader may wonder why two such closely related notions are needed. On the one hand, the notion of $li$-variety fits perfectly with the more general theory developed in [105] and is also more flexible. For instance, the notion of polynomial closure defined in Section 8.3 is easier to define (see [69], pp. 260–261 for a discussion). On the other hand, Eilenberg's variety theorem can be extended to both +-varieties and $li$-varieties, but it is easier to state for +-varieties: there is a bijective correspondence between +-varieties and varieties of finite semigroups. In other words, languages of a +-variety can be characterized by a property of their syntactic semigroup. By comparison, $li$-varieties require the use of the syntactic morphism instead of the syntactic semigroup[105]. But since all $li$-varieties considered in this paper are well-suited, they are also in bijection with varieties of finite semigroups.

## 8.2. The Dot-Depth Hierarchy

Let us first come back to the original definition from [25]. Given an alphabet $A$, the languages $\emptyset$, $\{1\}$ and $\{a\}$, where $a \in A$, are called *basic languages*. Let $\mathcal{E}$ be the class of basic languages.

Given a class $\mathcal{C}$ of languages, let $\mathcal{BC}$ be its Boolean closure and let $\mathcal{MC}$ be its monoid closure, that is, the smallest class of languages containing $\mathcal{C}$ and the language $\{1\}$ and closed under concatenation product. Star-free languages can be constructed by alternately applying the operators $\mathcal{B}$ and $\mathcal{M}$ to the class $\mathcal{E}$. This leads to a hierarchy of star-free languages, called the dot-depth hierarchy. The question arises to know whether one should start with the operator $\mathcal{B}$ or $\mathcal{M}$, but the equality $\mathcal{BMBE} = \mathcal{BMBME}$ shows that it just makes a difference for the lower levels.

In his 1976 survey, Brzozowski suggested to start the hierarchy at $\mathcal{B}_0 = \mathcal{BME}$, the class of finite or cofinite[2] languages. The *dot-depth hierarchy* is the sequence obtained from $\mathcal{B}_0$ by setting $\mathcal{B}_{n+1} = \mathcal{BMB}_n$ for all $n \geqslant 0$.

It is interesting to quote Brzozowski's original motivations as reported in [20].

> The following motivation led to these concepts. Feedback-free networks of gates, i.e., combinational circuits, constitute the simplest and degenerate forms of sequential circuits. Combinational networks are, of course, characterized by Boolean functions. This suggested that (a) all Boolean operations should be considered together when studying the formation of aperiodic

---

[2]A language is cofinite if its complement is finite.

> *languages from the letters of the alphabet, and (b) since con-catenation (or "dot" operator) is linked to the sequential rather than the combinational nature of a language, the number of con-catenation levels required to express a given aperiodic language should provide a useful measure of complexity.*

The term *aperiodic languages* refers to the characterization of star-free languages obtained by Schützenberger [87] in 1965.

**Theorem 8.2.1** *A language is star-free if and only if its syntactic monoid is aperiodic.*

## 8.3. Concatenation Hierarchies

Further developments lead to a slight change in the definition, motivated by the connection with finite model theory presented in Section 8.4 and by the algebraic approach discussed in Section 8.5. The main change consisted in replacing products by marked products. A language $L$ of $A^*$ is a *marked product* of the languages $L_0, L_1, \ldots, L_n$ if

$$L = L_0 a_1 L_1 \cdots a_n L_n$$

for some letters $a_1, \ldots, a_n$ of $A$.

Given a set $\mathcal{L}$ of languages, the *polynomial closure* of $\mathcal{L}$ is the set of languages that are finite unions of marked products of languages of $\mathcal{L}$. The polynomial closure of $\mathcal{L}$ is denoted by Pol $\mathcal{L}$ and the Boolean closure of Pol $\mathcal{L}$ is denoted by $\mathscr{B}$Pol $\mathcal{L}$. Finally, let co-Pol $\mathcal{L}$ denote the set of complements of languages in Pol $\mathcal{L}$.

Concatenation hierarchies are now defined by alternating Boolean operations and polynomial operations. For historical reasons, they are indexed by half-integers. More precisely, the *concatenation hierarchy* based on $\mathcal{L}$ is the sequence defined inductively as follows: $\mathcal{L}_0 = \mathcal{L}$ and, for each $n \geqslant 0$,

(1) $\mathcal{L}_{n+1/2} = \text{Pol } \mathcal{L}_n$ is the polynomial closure of the level $n$,

(2) $\mathcal{L}_{n+1} = \mathscr{B}\mathcal{L}_{n+1/2} = \mathscr{B}\text{Pol } \mathcal{L}_n$ is the Boolean closure of the level $n + 1/2$.

The classes of the form $\mathcal{L}_n$ are called the *full levels* and the classes of the form $\mathcal{L}_{n+1/2}$ are called the half levels of the hierarchy.

The dot-depth hierarchy corresponds to the full levels of the concatenation hierarchy based on the class $\mathcal{B}_0$ of finite or cofinite languages. It should be noted that, except for level 0, this hierarchy coincides with the concatenation hierarchy starting with the class of languages $\mathcal{L}_0$ defined by $\mathcal{L}_0(A) = \{\emptyset, \{1\}, A^+, A^*\}$.

Another natural concatenation hierarchy is the *Straubing-Thérien hierarchy*, based on the class of languages $\mathcal{V}_0$ defined by $\mathcal{V}_0(A) = \{\emptyset, A^*\}$. Other initial classes of languages have been considered in the literature, but here we will stick to these two examples.

It is not clear at first sight whether these hierarchies do not collapse, but this question was solved in 1978 by Brzozowski and Knast [21]. Thomas [114, 115] gave a different proof based on game theory.

**Theorem 8.3.1** *The dot-depth hierarchy is infinite.*

Let $D_n$ be the sequence of languages of $\{a, b\}^*$ defined by $D_0 = \{1\}$ and $D_{n+1} = (aD_nb)^*$. Then one can show that $D_0 \in \mathcal{B}_0$ and for all $n > 0$, $D_n \in \mathcal{B}_n - \mathcal{B}_{n-1}$.

The Straubing-Thérien hierarchy is also infinite and the following diagram, in which all inclusions are proper, summarizes the relations between the two hierarchies.

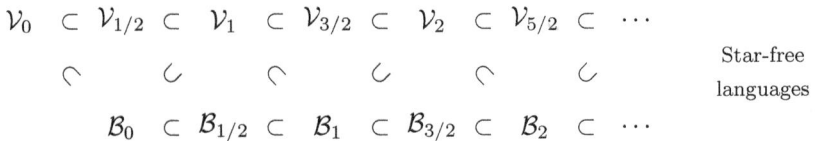

$$\mathcal{V}_0 \quad \subset \quad \mathcal{V}_{1/2} \quad \subset \quad \mathcal{V}_1 \quad \subset \quad \mathcal{V}_{3/2} \quad \subset \quad \mathcal{V}_2 \quad \subset \quad \mathcal{V}_{5/2} \quad \subset \quad \cdots$$

Star-free languages

$$\mathcal{B}_0 \quad \subset \quad \mathcal{B}_{1/2} \quad \subset \quad \mathcal{B}_1 \quad \subset \quad \mathcal{B}_{3/2} \quad \subset \quad \mathcal{B}_2 \quad \subset \quad \cdots$$

The *dot-depth problem* asks whether the dot-depth hierarchy is decidable.

**Problem 1** *Given a half integer $n$ and a regular language $L$, decide whether $L$ belongs $\mathcal{B}_n$.*

The corresponding problem for the hierarchy $\mathcal{V}_n$ is also open and the two problems are intimately connected. A particularly appealing aspect of this problem is its close connection with finite model theory.

## 8.4. Connection with Finite Model Theory

Let us associate with each word $u = a_0 a_1 \ldots a_{n-1}$ over the alphabet $A$ a relational structure

$$\mathfrak{M}_u = \big\{ \{0, 1, \ldots, n-1\}, <, (\mathbf{a})_{a \in A} \big\},$$

where $<$ is the usual order on the domain and $\mathbf{a}$ is a predicate giving the positions $i$ such that $a_i = a$. For instance, if $u = abaab$, then $\mathbf{a} = \{0, 2, 3\}$ and $\mathbf{b} = \{1, 4\}$. Given a sentence $\varphi$, the language defined by $\varphi$ is

$$L(\varphi) = \{u \in A^+ \mid \mathfrak{M}_u \text{ satisfies } \varphi\}.$$

The structure associated to the empty word has an empty domain, which leads to potential problems in logic, since some inference rules are not sound when empty structures are allowed. There are two possible solutions to this problem. The first one consists in ignoring the empty word. In this case, one makes the convention that a language $L$ of $A^*$ is defined by $\varphi$ if $L(\varphi) = L \cap A^+$. The second possibility is to adopt the convention that sentences beginning with a universal quantifier are true and sentences beginning with an existential quantifier are false in the empty model.

For the study of the dot-depth hierarchy, one needs to slightly expand the signature by adding three relational symbols min, max and $S$, interpreted respectively as the minimal element (0 in our example), the maximal element (4 in our example) and the successor relation $S$, defined by $S(x, y)$ if and only if $y = x + 1$.

First order formulas are now built in the usual way by using these symbols, the equality symbol, (first-order) variables, Boolean connectives and quantifiers. For instance, the sentence

$$\exists x \; \exists y \; \big((x < y) \wedge (\mathbf{a}x) \wedge (\mathbf{b}y)\big),$$

intuitively interpreted as *there exist two positions $x < y$ in the word such that the letter in position $x$ is an $a$ and the letter in position $y$ is a $b$*, defines the language $A^* a A^* b A^*$.

McNaughton and Papert [55] showed that a language is first-order definable if and only if it is star-free. Thomas [113] (see also [56]) refined this result by showing that the dot-depth hierarchy corresponds, level by level, to the quantifier alternation hierarchy of first-order formulas, defined as follows.

A formula is said to be a $\Sigma_n$-formula if it is equivalent to a formula of the form $Q(x_1, \ldots, x_k)\varphi$ where $\varphi$ is quantifier free and $Q(x_1, \ldots, x_k)$ is a sequence of $n$ blocks of quantifiers such that the first block contains only existential quantifiers (note that this first block may be empty), the second block universal quantifiers, etc. For instance, $\exists x_1 \exists x_2 \forall x_3 \forall x_4 \forall x_5 \exists x_6 \; \varphi$, where $\varphi$ is quantifier free, is in $\Sigma_3$. Similarly, if $Q(x_1, \ldots, x_k)$ is formed of $n$ alternating blocks of quantifiers beginning with a block of universal quantifiers (which again might be empty), we say that $\varphi$ is a $\Pi_n$-formula.

Let $\Sigma_n$ (resp., $\Pi_n$) denote the class of languages which can be defined by a $\Sigma_n$-formula (resp., a $\Pi_n$-formula) and by $\mathscr{B}\Sigma_n$ the Boolean closure $\Sigma_n$-formulas. Finally, set, for every $n \geqslant 0$, $\Delta_n = \Sigma_n \cap \Pi_n$. If needed, we use the notation $\Sigma_n[<]$, $\Sigma_n[<, S]$ or $\Sigma_n[<, S, \min, \max]$, depending on the signature. Note that the distinction between the signatures $\{<, S\}$ and

$\{<, S, \min, \max\}$ is only useful for the levels $\Sigma_1$, $\Pi_1$ and $\mathscr{B}\Sigma_1$. Indeed, for $n \geqslant 2$, the following equalities hold:

$$\Sigma_n[<, S, \min, \max] = \Sigma_n[<, S], \qquad \Pi_n[<, S, \min, \max] = \Pi_n[<, S],$$
$$\Delta_n[<, S, \min, \max] = \Delta_n[<, S], \qquad \mathscr{B}\Sigma_n[<, S, \min, \max] = \mathscr{B}\Sigma_n[<, S].$$

The resulting hierarchy is depicted in the following diagram:

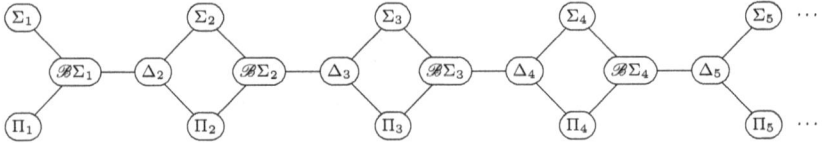

The next theorem summarizes the results of [55, 113, 56].

**Theorem 8.4.1**

(1) *A language is first-order definable if and only if it is star-free.*

(2) *A language is in $\Pi_n[<]$ if and only if its complement is in $\Sigma_n[<]$.*

(3) *A language is in $\Sigma_n[<]$ if and only if it is in $\mathcal{V}_{n-1/2}$.*

(4) *A language is in $\Sigma_n[<, S, \min, \max]$ if and only if it is in $\mathcal{B}_{n-1/2}$.*

(5) *A language is in $\mathscr{B}\Sigma_n[<]$ if and only if it is in $\mathcal{V}_n$.*

(6) *A language is in $\mathscr{B}\Sigma_n[<, S, \min, \max]$ if and only if it is in $\mathcal{B}_n$.*

In particular, deciding whether a language has dot-depth $n$ is equivalent to a very natural problem in finite model theory.

The classes $\Delta_n$ also have a natural description in terms of unambiguous products. A marked product $L = L_0 a_1 L_1 \cdots a_n L_n$ of $n$ languages $L_0, L_1, \ldots, L_n$ is *unambiguous* if every word $u$ of $L$ admits a unique factorization of the form $u_0 a_1 u_1 \cdots a_n u_n$ with $u_0 \in L_0$, $u_1 \in L_1$, $\ldots$, $u_n \in L_n$.

The *unambiguous polynomial closure* UPol $\mathcal{L}$ of a class of languages $\mathcal{L}$ is the class of languages that are finite disjoint unions of unambiguous products of the form $L_0 a_1 L_1 \cdots a_n L_n$, where the $a_i$'s are letters and the $L_i$'s are elements of $\mathcal{L}$.

The following result was proved by Weil and the author [71] in 1995.

**Theorem 8.4.2**

(1) *A language is in $\Delta_{n+1}[<]$ if and only if it is in UPol $\mathcal{V}_n$.*

(2) *A language is in $\Delta_{n+1}[<, S, \min, \max]$ if and only if it is in UPol $\mathcal{B}_n$.*

The Straubing-Thérien hierarchy is pictured in the diagram below. A similar diagram for the Brzozowski hierarchy could be obtained by replacing each occurrence of $\mathcal{V}$ by $\mathcal{B}$.

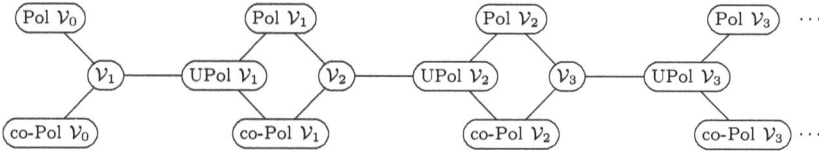

## 8.5. Algebraic Approach

The algebraic approach to the study of concatenation hierarchies arises from the following two results [28].

**Theorem 8.5.1** *Each full level $\mathcal{V}_n$ is a variety of languages and every half-level $\mathcal{V}_{n+1/2}$ is a positive variety of languages.*

A similar result holds for the Brzozowski hierarchy.

**Theorem 8.5.2** *Each full level $\mathcal{B}_n$ is a li-variety of languages and every half-level $\mathcal{B}_{n+1/2}$ is a positive li-variety of languages.*

We let $\mathbf{V}_n$ denote the variety of finite monoids corresponding to $\mathcal{V}_n$ and $\mathbf{V}_{n+1/2}$ the variety of ordered monoids corresponding to $\mathcal{V}_{n+1/2}$. Similarly, let $\mathbf{B}_n$ denote the variety of finite semigroups corresponding to $\mathcal{B}_n$ and $\mathbf{B}_{n+1/2}$ the variety of ordered semigroups corresponding to $\mathcal{B}_{n+1/2}$.

The next results involve three operations on varieties: the *semidirect product*, the *Mal'cev product* and the *Schützenberger product*. The semidirect product, denoted by $\mathbf{V} * \mathbf{W}$, and the Mal'cev product, denoted by $\mathbf{V} \circledM \mathbf{W}$, are binary operations. The Schützenberger product, denoted by $\Diamond\mathbf{V}$, is a unary operation. Giving the precise definitions of these operations would lead us too far afield, but they can be found in [2, 24, 28, 66, 64, 76, 85, 98, 104, 118] for the semidirect product, in [24, 66, 64, 72, 74, 98] for the Mal'cev product and in [100, 59, 61, 65, 66] for the Schützenberger product.

The author, generalizing an early result of Reutenauer [84], used the Schützenberger product to prove the following result [61, 66].

**Theorem 8.5.3** *For every $n > 0$, $\mathbf{V}_{n+1} = \Diamond\mathbf{V}_n$.*

A nice connection between the hierarchies $\mathbf{V}_n$ and $\mathbf{B}_n$ was discovered by Straubing [101] (see also Pin-Weil [76] for the half levels). A semigroup $S$ is said to be *locally trivial* if, for every idempotent $e \in S$ and every $s \in S$, $ese = e$. Let $\mathbf{LI} = [\![ese = e]\!]$ be the variety of locally trivial semigroups. We let $[\![e \leqslant ese]\!]$ denote the variety of ordered semigroups, such that, for every idempotent $e \in S$ and every $s \in S$, $e \leqslant ese$. The dual variety $[\![e \geqslant ese]\!]$ is defined in the same way.

**Theorem 8.5.4** *For every* $n > 0$, $\mathbf{B}_n = \mathbf{V}_n * \mathbf{LI}$ *and* $\mathbf{B}_{n+1/2} = \mathbf{V}_{n+1/2} * \mathbf{LI}$.

It is very likely that this result extends to the intermediate classes $\Delta_n$, giving $\Delta_n[<, S, \min, \max] = \Delta_n[<] * \mathbf{LI}$, but to the author's knowledge, this has only been proved[112] for $n \leqslant 2$.

Weil and the author [71, 74] established another useful relation.

**Theorem 8.5.5** *The variety* $\mathbf{V}_{n+1/2}$ *is equal to the Mal'cev product* $[\![e \leqslant ese]\!] \,\circledM\, \mathbf{V}_n$.

A similar result holds for the varieties $\Delta_n$, as a consequence of a more general result on the unambiguous product [58, 70].

**Theorem 8.5.6** *A language belongs to* $\Delta_{n+1}[<]$ *if and only if its syntactic monoid belongs to* $\mathbf{LI} \,\circledM\, \mathbf{V}_n$.

The algebraic counterpart of the Straubing-Thérien hierarchy is summarized in Figure 8.1, in which the symbol $\leftrightarrow$ indicates the equivalence between the algebraic characterizations and the logical descriptions. Again, one gets a similar diagram for the Brzozowski hierarchy by replacing each occurrence of $\mathbf{V}$ by $\mathbf{B}$ and by considering the signature $\{<, S, \min, \max\}$ instead of $\{<\}$. The algebraic approach gives algebraic characterizations of the concatenation hierarchies, but do not necessarily lead to decidability results. Let us now examine the decidability questions in more details.

## 8.6. Known Decidability Results

A language belongs to $\mathcal{V}_0$ if and only if its syntactic monoid is trivial.

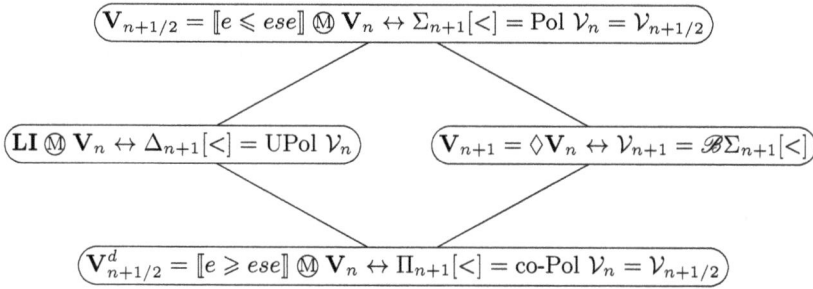

$$\boxed{\mathbf{V}_{n+1/2} = [\![e \leqslant ese]\!] \textcircled{M} \, \mathbf{V}_n \leftrightarrow \Sigma_{n+1}[<] = \mathrm{Pol}\,\mathcal{V}_n = \mathcal{V}_{n+1/2}}$$

$$\boxed{\mathbf{LI} \textcircled{M} \, \mathbf{V}_n \leftrightarrow \Delta_{n+1}[<] = \mathrm{UPol}\,\mathcal{V}_n} \qquad \boxed{\mathbf{V}_{n+1} = \Diamond \mathbf{V}_n \leftrightarrow \mathcal{V}_{n+1} = \mathscr{B}\Sigma_{n+1}[<]}$$

$$\boxed{\mathbf{V}^d_{n+1/2} = [\![e \geqslant ese]\!] \textcircled{M} \, \mathbf{V}_n \leftrightarrow \Pi_{n+1}[<] = \text{co-Pol}\,\mathcal{V}_n = \mathcal{V}_{n+1/2}}$$

Fig. 8.1.

### 8.6.1. Levels 1/2 and 1

The level $1/2$ is also easy to study [71]. The variety $\mathcal{V}_{1/2}$ consists of the languages that are finite union of languages of the form $A^* a_1 A^* \cdots a_k A^*$, where $a_1, \ldots, a_k$ are letters and the variety $\mathcal{B}_{1/2}$ consists of the languages that are finite union of languages of the form $u_0 A^* u_1 A^* \cdots u_{k-1} A^* u_k$, where $u_0, \ldots, u_k$ are words.

**Theorem 8.6.1**

(1) *A regular language belongs to* $\mathcal{V}_{1/2}$ *if and only if its ordered syntactic monoid satisfies the identity* $1 \leqslant x$.

(2) *A language belongs to* $\mathcal{B}_{1/2}$ *if and only if its ordered syntactic semigroup belongs to the variety* $[\![e \leqslant ese]\!]$.

The variety $\mathcal{V}_1$ consists of the languages that are Boolean combinations of languages of the form $A^* a_1 A^* \cdots a_k A^*$, where $a_1, \ldots, a_k$ are letters. The decidability of $\mathcal{V}_1$ was obtained by Imre Simon [95] in 1975. Recall that a monoid is $\mathcal{J}$-trivial if two elements generating the same ideal are equal.

**Theorem 8.6.2** *A language belongs to* $\mathcal{V}_1$ *if and only if its syntactic monoid is* $\mathcal{J}$-trivial.

It follows that $\mathbf{V}_1$ is the variety $\mathbf{J}$ of $\mathcal{J}$-trivial monoids. This variety of $\mathcal{J}$-trivial monoids is characterized by the identities $(x^{\omega+1} = x^\omega$ and $(xy)^\omega = (yx)^\omega$, or, alternatively, by the identities $y(xy)^\omega = (xy)^\omega = (xy)^\omega x$. Simon's original proof is based on a very nice argument of combinatorics on words. Simon's theorem inspired much subsequent research, and a number of alternative proofs have been proposed [97, 107, 1, 2, 40, 42, 43,

44]. Let me just mention two important consequences in semigroup theory. Recall that a monoid $M$ *divides* a monoid $N$ if $M$ is a quotient of a submonoid of $N$. The first result is due to Straubing [99] and the second one to Straubing and Thérien [107].

**Theorem 8.6.3** *A monoid is $\mathcal{J}$-trivial if and only if it divides a monoid of upper unitriangular Boolean matrices.*

**Theorem 8.6.4** *A monoid is $\mathcal{J}$-trivial if and only if it is a quotient of an ordered monoid satisfying the identity $1 \leqslant x$.*

The languages of dot-depth one are the Boolean combinations of languages of the form $u_0 A^* u_1 A^* \cdots u_{k-1} A^* u_k$, where $k \geqslant 0$ and $u_0, u_1, \cdots u_k \in A^+$. The decidability of $\mathcal{B}_1$ was obtained by Knast [45, 46] and the proof was improved by Thérien [111]. This result also had a strong influence on subsequent developments, notably in finite semigroup theory.

**Theorem 8.6.5** *A regular language belongs to $\mathcal{B}_1$ if and only if its syntactic semigroup satisfies Knast identity:*

$$(x^\omega p y^\omega q x^\omega)^\omega p y^\omega s (x^\omega r y^\omega s x^\omega)^\omega = (x^\omega p y^\omega q x^\omega)^\omega (x^\omega r y^\omega s x^\omega)^\omega.$$

### 8.6.2. The Classes $\Delta_2$

The variety $\mathbf{UPol}\,\mathcal{V}_1$ is equal to $\Delta_2[<]$. According to a result of Schützenberger [88], it consists of the finite disjoint unions of the unambiguous products of the form $A_0^* a_1 A_1^* a_2 \cdots a_k A_k^*$, where $a_1, \ldots, a_k \in A$ and $A_0, A_1, \ldots, A_k$ are subsets of $A$. It corresponds to the variety $\mathbf{DA}$ of all monoids in which each regular $\mathcal{D}$-class is an idempotent subsemigroup [88]. This variety can be defined by the profinite identity $(xy)^\omega y (xy)^\omega = (xy)^\omega$. Therefore we have

**Theorem 8.6.6** *A language belongs to $\Delta_2[<]$ if and only if its syntactic monoid belongs to $\mathbf{DA}$.*

The variety $\mathbf{DA}$ has numerous applications, nicely summarized by Tesson and Thérien in their survey *Diamonds are forever: the variety $\mathbf{DA}$* [109].

The first application relates $\mathbf{DA}$ to another fragment of first-order logic. Let $\mathbf{FO}^k[<]$ be the class of languages that can be defined by a first-order sentence using at most $k$ variables and let $\mathbf{FO}[<] = \bigcup_{k \geqslant 0} \mathbf{FO}^k[<]$. We have already seen that $\mathbf{FO}[<]$ is the variety of star-free languages. One can show that $\mathbf{FO}[<] = \mathbf{FO}^3[<]$ and it is not difficult to see that a language is in $\mathbf{FO}^1[<]$ if and only if its syntactic monoid is idempotent and commutative. The following result is due to Thérien and Wilke [112].

**Theorem 8.6.7** *A language belongs to $\mathbf{FO}^2[<]$ if and only if its syntactic monoid belongs to* **DA**.

Etessami, Vardi and Wilke proved in [29] that $\mathbf{FO}^2[<]$ is also the class of languages captured by a fragment of temporal logic called unary temporal logic. Finally, Schwentick, Thérien and Vollmer [89] proved that a language is accepted by a partially ordered two-way automaton if and only if its syntactic monoid belongs to **DA**. See also the article of Diekert, Gastin and Kufleitner [27] for alternative proofs of these results.

Let us now consider the signature $\{<, S\}$. We already mentioned that the variety corresponding to $\Delta_2[<, S]$ is $\mathbf{DA} * \mathbf{LI}$. Moreover, Almeida [3] proved that $\mathbf{DA} * \mathbf{LI} = \mathbf{LDA}$, the variety of all finite semigroups $S$ such that, for all $e \in S$, the inclusion $eSe \in \mathbf{DA}$ holds. It follows that $\Delta_2[<, S]$ is also decidable.

### 8.6.3. Level 3/2

Two general decidability results are consequences of the results of Section 8.5. The first one is due to Straubing [101] (see also [76] for the half levels) and is a consequence of Theorem 8.5.4, except for the case $n = 1$, which follows from Theorems 8.6.2 and 8.6.5.

**Theorem 8.6.8** *For each $n \geqslant 1$, the variety $\mathbf{B}_n$ is decidable if and only if the variety $\mathbf{V}_n$ is decidable. Similarly, the variety $\mathbf{B}_{n+1/2}$ is decidable if and only if the variety $\mathbf{V}_{n+1/2}$ is decidable.*

Given a set of profinite identities defining a variety of finite monoids **V**, Weil and the author[72] gave a set of identities defining the varieties $[\![e \leqslant ese]\!] \; \textcircled{m} \; \mathbf{V}$ and $\mathbf{LI} \; \textcircled{m} \; \mathbf{V}$. This leads in particular to a set of profinite identities for $\mathbf{V}_{3/2}$ [72].

**Theorem 8.6.9** *A language belongs to $\mathcal{V}_{3/2}$ if and only if its ordered syntactic monoid satisfies the profinite identities $u^\omega \leqslant u^\omega v u^\omega$, where $u$ and $v$ are idempotent profinite words on the same alphabet. This condition is decidable.*

The decidability of $\mathcal{V}_{3/2}$ was also proved by Arfi [8, 9] as a consequence of Hashiguchi's results [38]. See also the model theoretic approach of Selivanov [91] for alternative proofs.

The decidability of $\mathcal{B}_{3/2}$ now follows from Theorem 8.6.8. A direct characterization of $\mathcal{V}_{3/2}$ and $\mathcal{B}_{3/2}$ using forbidden patterns was given Glaßer and Schmitz [32, 34]. It leads to an **NL**-algorithm for the membership problem for $\mathcal{B}_{3/2}$.

Very recently, Almeida, Bartonova, Klíma and Kunc [5] improved the result of Weil and the author [72] to get the following decidability result.

**Theorem 8.6.10** *If $\Sigma_n[<]$ is decidable, then $\Delta_{n+1}[<]$ is decidable.*

This result can be translated in two ways. In terms of varieties of languages:

$$\text{if } Pol\, \mathcal{V}_{n-1} \text{ is decidable, then } UPol\, \mathcal{V}_n \text{ is decidable,}$$

or in terms of varieties of monoids:

$$\text{if } \mathbf{V}_{n-1/2} \text{ is decidable, then } \mathbf{LI} \textcircled{m} \mathbf{V}_n \text{ is decidable.}$$

### 8.6.4. *Level 2 and Beyond*

Let us return to the level 2 of the Straubing-Thérien hierarchy. A simple description of the languages of $\mathcal{V}_2$ was obtained by Straubing and the author [68] in 1981:

**Theorem 8.6.11** *A language belongs to $\mathcal{V}_2(A)$ if and only if it is a Boolean combination of languages of the form $A_0^* a_1 A_1^* a_2 \cdots a_k A_k^*$, where $a_1, \ldots, a_k \in A$ and $A_0, A_1, \ldots, A_k$ are subsets of $A$.*

In the same article, Straubing and the author gave an algebraic characterisation of $\mathbf{V}_2$ similar to Theorem 8.6.3.

**Theorem 8.6.12** *A monoid belongs to $\mathbf{V}_2$ if and only if it divides a monoid of upper triangular Boolean matrices.*

However, it is not clear whether Theorem 8.6.12 leads to an effective characterization and despite numerous partial results [6, 7, 26, 75, 102, 103, 108, 117, 118], the decidability of $\mathcal{V}_2$ remained a major open problem for 20 years. It was finally settled by Place and Zeitoun in 2014 [78].

**Theorem 8.6.13** *The variety of languages $\mathcal{V}_2 = \mathscr{B}\Sigma_2[<]$ is decidable.*

In the same paper [78], Place and Zeitoun also obtained three other decidability results.

**Theorem 8.6.14** *The positive varieties of languages $\Sigma_3[<]$, $\Pi_3[<]$ and $\Delta_3[<]$ are decidable.*

On a two-letter alphabet, this result was first established in [33]. The algebraic translation of Theorem 8.6.14 states that the varieties of ordered monoids $\mathcal{V}_{5/2}$ and $\mathcal{V}_{5/2}^d$ are decidable. In view of Theorem 8.6.10, this also gives the decidability of $\Delta_4[<]$.

To obtain these results, Place and Zeitoun considered a more general question than membership, the separation problem. Let us say that a language $S$ *separates* two languages $K$ and $L$ if $K \subseteq S$ and $L \cap S = \emptyset$. The *separation problem* can be formulated for any class $\mathcal{C}$ of languages.

**Problem 2** *Is the following problem decidable: given two disjoint regular languages $K$ and $L$, is there a language $S \in \mathcal{C}$ separating $K$ and $L$.*

Note that if the separation problem is decidable for $\mathcal{C}$, then $\mathcal{C}$ is decidable. Indeed, since $L$ is the unique language separating $L$ and $L^c$, $L$ belongs to $\mathcal{C}$ if and only if $L$ and $L^c$ are separable.

As shown by Almeida [4], the separation problem is related to a problem on finite semigroups (finding the 2-pointlike sets relative to a variety of semigroups). The separation problem for star-free languages was first solved by Henckell [39] in its semigroup form. Successive improvements can be found in [41, 79, 82].

A major result of Place and Zeitoun [78] is the following much stronger result.

**Theorem 8.6.15** *If the separation problem for $\Sigma_n[<]$ is decidable, then $\Sigma_{n+1}[<]$ is decidable.*

The latest result, due to Place [77] states that the separation problem is decidable for $\Sigma_3[<]$ and $\Pi_3[<]$. New decidability results follow, as a corollary of Theorem 8.6.15 and 8.6.10.

**Theorem 8.6.16** *The positive varieties of languages $\Sigma_4[<]$, $\Pi_4[<]$ and the varieties of languages $\Delta_4[<]$ and $\Delta_5[<]$ are decidable.*

The decidability of the other levels is still open, and the following diagram summarizes the known results on the quantifier alternation hierarchy. Due to the lack of space, the signature is omitted. Thus $\Sigma_n$ stands for $\Sigma_n[<]$.

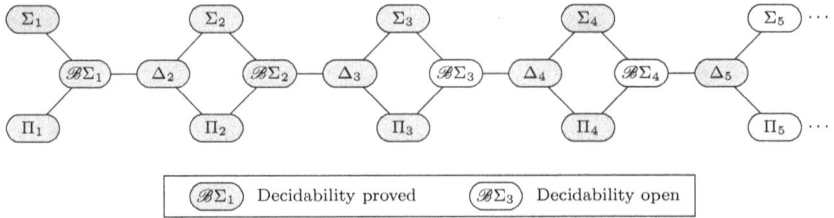

For the signature $\{<, S, \min, \max\}$, the decidability of $\Sigma_n$ and $\Pi_n$, for $n \leqslant 4$ and that of $\mathscr{B}\Sigma_n$, for $n \leqslant 2$, follows from Theorem 8.6.8. The decidability of $\Delta_n$, for $n \leqslant 4$, follows from the decidability of $\Sigma_n$ and $\Pi_n$. Finally $\Delta_5$ seems to be the only fragment known to be decidable in the signature $\{<\}$, but still pending for the signature $\{<, S\}$.

We have seen the importance of the operation $\mathbf{V} \to \mathbf{V} * \mathbf{LI}$, where $\mathbf{V}$ is a variety of monoids. However, Auinger proved that decidability is not always preserved by this operation [10]. In other words, there exists a decidable variety $\mathbf{V}$ such that $\mathbf{V} * \mathbf{LI}$ is not decidable. Surprisingly, as shown by Steinberg [96], the same operation preserves the decidability of pointlikes. This implies the following result, which was recently reproved by Place and Zeitoun [80] in a simpler way.

**Theorem 8.6.17** *Let $\mathbf{V}$ be a variety of finite monoids. If separability is decidable in the variety of languages corresponding to $\mathbf{V}$, then it is also decidable in the variety corresponding to $\mathbf{V} * \mathbf{LI}$.*

In the same paper, Place and Zeitoun [80] proved the following result.

**Theorem 8.6.18** *Let $\mathcal{F}$ be one of the fragments $\Sigma_n$, $\Pi_n$ or $\mathscr{B}\Sigma_n$. If separation is decidable in $\mathcal{F}[<]$, then it is decidable in $\mathcal{F}[<, S, \min, \max]$.*

It follows that separation is decidable for $\Delta_2[<, S]$ and for $\Sigma_n[<, S, \min, \max]$ and $\Pi_n[<, S, \min, \max]$ for $n \leqslant 3$.

To the knowledge of the author, the decidability of the other levels is still open. We recommend the recent survey of Place and Zeitoun [81] for a presentation of the new ideas and new results on the expressiveness of fragments of first-order logic.

## 8.7. Other Developments

In this section, we list several research topics related to concatenation hierarchies. We apologize for not giving much detail, but presenting any of these topics would require an independent article. However, we tried to give some relevant bibliography for the interested reader.

### 8.7.1. *Other Hierarchies*

Several subhierarchies of star-free languages were presented in Brzozowski's survey [20]. An interesting subhierarchy of $\mathcal{V}_1$ is obtained by limiting the number of marked products [94]. In particular, if only one product is allowed, one gets the variety of languages $\mathcal{J}_1$ consisting of the Boolean closure of the languages of the form $A^*aA^*$. As was already mentioned, this variety is equal to $\mathbf{FO}^1[<]$ and the corresponding variety of monoids is the variety $\mathbf{J}_1$ of idempotent and commutative monoids.

A subhierarchy of $\mathcal{B}_1$ can be defined in a similar way. The first level of this subhierarchy is the *li*-variety of *locally testable languages*, which consists of the Boolean closure of the languages of the form $uA^*$, $A^*v$ and $A^*wA^*$, where $u$, $v$ and $w$ are words of $A^*$. An algebraic characterization of this class was obtained independently by McNaughton [54] and by Brzozowski and Simon [22]. Let us say that a semigroup $S$ is locally idempotent and commutative if, for each idempotent $e \in S$, the semigroup $eSe$ is idempotent and commutative. We let $\mathbf{LJ}_1$ denote the variety of all locally idempotent and commutative semigroups.

**Theorem 8.7.1** *A language is locally testable if its syntactic semigroup is locally idempotent and commutative.*

In fact, it is relatively easy to prove that a language is locally testable if its syntactic semigroup belongs to the variety $\mathbf{J}_1 * \mathbf{LI}$, but the really difficult part of the proof is the equality $\mathbf{LJ}_1 = \mathbf{J}_1 * \mathbf{LI}$. Historically, this result was the first decidability for a variety of the form $\mathbf{V} * \mathbf{LI}$ and it became very influential for this reason. Locally testable languages give another parameter to play with: one can assume in the definition that $|u|, |v| < k$ and $|w| \leqslant k$, which leads to the notion of *k-testable language*.

By limiting iteratively the number of marked products, one can also define tree-like hierarchies [12, 13, 14, 59, 61], which also admit an algebraic counterpart in terms of Schützenberger product.

Another interesting way to obtain subhierarchies is to limit the number of Boolean operations. Such Boolean hierarchies were extensively studied by Selivanov and his coauthors [35, 47, 91, 90, 93].

Finally, several subhierarchies of $\Delta_2 = \mathbf{FO}^2$ were considered in the recent years [30, 48, 49, 50, 51, 53, 52, 106, 119].

### 8.7.2. *Connection with Complexity Classes*

Bearing comparison with Brzozowski's original motivation, a result of Barrington and Thérien [11] gives evidence that the dot-depth provides a useful measure of complexity for Boolean circuits. More precisely, these authors found a remarkable correspondence between languages of dot-depth $n$ and Boolean $\mathbf{AC}^0$-circuits of depth $n$.

Another surprising connection between language hierarchies and the structure of complexity classes is offered by the theory of leaf languages [16, 17, 18, 19, 23, 36, 37, 92, 93, 116].

### 8.8. Conclusion

Several surveys related to concatenation hierarchies can be found in the literature [20, 31, 60, 64, 67, 81, 110]. Moreover, the study of concatenation hierarchies is not limited to words and similar hierarchies were considered for infinite words, for traces, for data words [15] and even for tree languages.

Since its introduction in 1971, the dot-depth hierarchy has been the topic of numerous investigations. The reason for this success is to be found in the variety of approaches successively proposed to solve the difficult problems raised by this hierarchy. Automata theory, combinatorics on words, semigroup theory, finite model theory, all these areas joined forces to produce increasingly sophisticated tools, leading to substantial progress, notably on decidability questions. Let us hope that the next 45 years will see even more progress and that the decidability of the dot-depth hierarchy will finally be established.

### Acknowledgments

This paper is dedicated to Janusz A. Brzozowski for his 80th birthday. I would like to thank Jeffrey Shallit for his kind invitation to the Brzozowski conference and for his useful comments on this paper. The author was funded from the European Research Council (ERC) under the European Union's Horizon 2020 research and innovation programme (grant agreement No. 670624).

# References

1. J. ALMEIDA, Implicit operations on finite $\mathcal{J}$-trivial semigroups and a conjecture of I. Simon, *J. Pure Appl. Algebra* **69**,3 (1991), 205–218.

2. J. ALMEIDA, *Finite semigroups and universal algebra. Series in Algebra*, vol. 3, World Scientific, Singapore, 1994.

3. J. ALMEIDA, A syntactical proof of locality of DA, *Internat. J. Algebra Comput.* **6**,2 (1996), 165–177.

4. J. ALMEIDA, Some algorithmic problems for pseudovarieties, *Publ. Math. Debrecen* **54**,suppl. (1999), 531–552. Automata and formal languages, VIII (Salgótarján, 1996).

5. J. ALMEIDA, J. BARTONOVÁ, O. KLÍMA AND M. KUNC, On decidability of intermediate levels of concatenation hierarchies, in *19th DLT 2015*, I. Potapov (ed.), pp. 58–70, *LNCS* vol. 9168, Springer, 2015.

6. J. ALMEIDA AND O. KLÍMA, A counterexample to a conjecture concerning concatenation hierarchies, *Inform. Process. Lett.* **110**,1 (2009), 4–7.

7. J. ALMEIDA AND O. KLÍMA, New decidable upper bound of the second level in the Straubing-Thérien concatenation hierarchy of star-free languages, *Discrete Math. Theor. Comput. Sci.* **12**,4 (2010), 41–58.

8. M. ARFI, Polynomial operations on rational languages, in *STACS 87*, F. J. Brandenburg, G. Vidal-Naquet and M. Wirsing (eds.), pp. 198–206, *LNCS* vol. 247, Springer, Berlin, 1987.

9. M. ARFI, Opérations polynomiales et hiérarchies de concaténation, *Theoret. Comput. Sci.* **91**,1 (1991), 71–84.

10. K. AUINGER, On the decidability of membership in the global of a monoid pseudovariety, *Internat. J. Algebra Comput.* **20**,2 (2010), 181–188.

11. D. A. M. BARRINGTON AND D. THÉRIEN, Finite monoids and the fine structure of NC$^1$, *J. Assoc. Comput. Mach.* **35**,4 (1988), 941–952.

12. F. BLANCHET-SADRI, Games, equations and the dot-depth hierarchy, *Comput. Math. Appl.* **18**,9 (1989), 809–822.

13. F. BLANCHET-SADRI, Some logical characterizations of the dot-depth hierarchy and applications, *J. Comput. System Sci.* **51**,2 (1995), 324–337.

14. F. BLANCHET-SADRI, Inclusion relations between some congruences related to the dot-depth hierarchy, *Discrete Appl. Math.* **68**,1-2 (1996), 33–71.

15. M. BOJAŃCZYK, C. DAVID, A. MUSCHOLL, T. SCHWENTICK AND L. SEGOUFIN, Two-variable logic on data words, *ACM Trans. Comput. Log.* **12**,4 (2011), Art. 27, 26.

16. B. BORCHERT, D. KUSKE AND F. STEPHAN, On existentially first-order definable languages and their relation to NP, in *25th ICALP*, K. G. Larsen, S. Skyum and G. Winskel (eds.), pp. 17–28, *LNCS* vol. 1443, Springer, Berlin, 1998.

17. B. BORCHERT, D. KUSKE AND F. STEPHAN, On existentially first-order definable languages and their relation to NP, *Theor. Inform. Appl.* **33**,3 (1999), 259–269.

18. B. Borchert, K.-J. Lange, F. Stephan, P. Tesson and D. Thérien, The dot-depth and the polynomial hierarchy correspond on the delta levels, in *8th DLT 2004*, pp. 89–101, *LNCS* vol. 3340, Springer, Berlin, 2004.

19. B. Borchert, K.-J. Lange, F. Stephan, P. Tesson and D. Thérien, The dot-depth and the polynomial hierarchies correspond on the delta levels, *Int. J. Found. Comput. Sci.* **16**,4 (2005), 625–644.

20. J. A. Brzozowski, Hierarchies of aperiodic languages, *Theoret. Informatics Appl.* **10**,2 (1976), 33–49.

21. J. A. Brzozowski and R. Knast, The dot-depth hierarchy of star-free languages is infinite, *J. Comput. System Sci.* **16**,1 (1978), 37–55.

22. J. A. Brzozowski and I. Simon, Characterizations of locally testable events, *Discrete Math.* **4** (1973), 243–271.

23. H.-J. Burtschick and H. Vollmer, Lindström quantifiers and leaf language definability, *Int. J. Found. Comput. Sci.* **9** (1998), 277–294.

24. L. Chaubard, J.-É. Pin and H. Straubing, Actions, wreath products of $\mathcal{C}$-varieties and concatenation product, *Theoret. Comput. Sci.* **356** (2006), 73–89.

25. R. S. Cohen and J. A. Brzozowski, Dot-depth of star-free events, *J. Comput. Syst. Sci.* **5**,1 (1971), 1–16.

26. D. Cowan, A result on the dot-depth hierarchy for inverse monoids, in *Semigroups, automata and languages (Porto, 1994)*, pp. 41–57, World Sci. Publ., River Edge, NJ, 1996.

27. V. Diekert, P. Gastin and M. Kufleitner, A survey on small fragments of first-order logic over finite words, *Int. J. Found. Comput. Sci.* **19**,3 (2008), 513–548.

28. S. Eilenberg, *Automata, languages, and machines. Vol. B*, Academic Press [Harcourt Brace Jovanovich Publishers], New York, 1976. With two chapters ("Depth decomposition theorem" and "Complexity of semigroups and morphisms") by Bret Tilson, Pure and Applied Mathematics, Vol. 59.

29. K. Etessami, M. Y. Vardi and T. Wilke, First-order logic with two variables and unary temporal logic, *Inform. Comput.* **179**,2 (2002), 279–295. LICS'97 (Warsaw).

30. L. Fleischer, M. Kufleitner and A. Lauser, Block products and nesting negations in $\mathrm{FO}^2$, in *9th CSR 2014*, E. A. Hirsch, S. O. Kuznetsov, J.-É. Pin and N. K. Vereshchagin (eds.), pp. 176–189, *LNCS* vol. 8476, Springer, 2014.

31. C. Glasser and H. Schmitz, Decidable hierarchies of starfree languages, in *FST TCS 2000: Foundations of software technology and theoretical computer science (New Delhi)*, pp. 503–515, *LNCS* vol. 1974, Springer, Berlin, 2000.

32. C. Glasser and H. Schmitz, Languages of dot-depth 3/2, in *STACS 2000*, pp. 555–566, *LNCS* vol. 1770, Berlin, 2000.

33. C. Glasser and H. Schmitz, Level 5/2 of the Straubing-Thérien hierarchy for two-letter alphabets, in *5th DLT 2001*, W. Kuich, G. Rozenberg and A. Salomaa (eds.), pp. 251–261, *LNCS* vol. 2295, Berlin, 2002.

34. C. GLASSER AND H. SCHMITZ, Languages of dot-depth 3/2, *Theory Comput. Syst.* **42**,2 (2008), 256–286.

35. C. GLASSER, H. SCHMITZ AND V. SELIVANOV, Efficient algorithms for membership in Boolean hierarchies of regular languages, in *STACS 2008*, S. Albers and P. Weil (eds.), pp. 337–348, *LIPIcs. Leibniz Int. Proc. Inform.* vol. 1, Schloss Dagstuhl. Leibniz-Zent. Inform., Wadern, 2008.

36. C. GLASSER, S. TRAVERS AND K. W. WAGNER, Perfect correspondences between dot-depth and polynomial-time hierarchy, in *10th DLT 2006*, pp. 408–419, *LNCS* vol. 4036, Springer, Berlin, 2006.

37. C. GLASSER, S. TRAVERS AND K. W. WAGNER, Perfect correspondences between dot-depth and polynomial-time hierarchies, *J. Comput. System Sci.* **80**,7 (2014), 1359–1373.

38. K. HASHIGUCHI, Representation theorems on regular languages, *J. Comput. System Sci.* **27** (1983), 101–115.

39. K. HENCKELL, Pointlike sets: the finest aperiodic cover of a finite semigroup, *J. Pure Appl. Algebra* **55**,1-2 (1988), 85–126.

40. K. HENCKELL AND J.-É. PIN, Ordered monoids and $j$-trivial monoids, in *Algorithmic problems in Groups and Semigroups*, B. J.-C., S. Margolis, J. Meakin and M. Sapir (eds.), Boston, 2000, pp. 121–137, *Trends in Mathematics*, Birkhäuser.

41. K. HENCKELL, J. RHODES AND B. STEINBERG, Aperiodic pointlikes and beyond, *Internat. J. Algebra Comput.* **20**,2 (2010), 287–305.

42. P. M. HIGGINS, A proof of Simon's theorem on piecewise testable languages, *Theoret. Comput. Sci.* **178**,1-2 (1997), 257–264.

43. O. KLÍMA, Piecewise testable languages via combinatorics on words, *Discrete Math.* **311**,20 (2011), 2124–2127.

44. O. KLÍMA AND L. POLÁK, Alternative automata characterization of piecewise testable languages, in *17th DLT 2013*, pp. 289–300, *LNCS* vol. 7907, Springer, Heidelberg, 2013.

45. R. KNAST, A semigroup characterization of dot-depth one languages, *RAIRO Inform. Théor.* **17**,4 (1983), 321–330.

46. R. KNAST, Some theorems on graph congruences, *RAIRO Inform. Théor.* **17**,4 (1983), 331–342.

47. A. S. KONOVALOV AND V. L. SELIVANOV, Boolean algebras of regular languages, *Algebra Logika* **52**,6 (2013), 676–711, 779, 781.

48. A. KREBS AND H. STRAUBING, An effective characterization of the alternation hierarchy in two-variable logic, in *32nd International Conference on Foundations of Software Technology and Theoretical Computer Science*, pp. 86–98, *LIPIcs. Leibniz Int. Proc. Inform.* vol. 18, Schloss Dagstuhl. Leibniz-Zent. Inform., Wadern, 2012.

49. M. KUFLEITNER AND A. LAUSER, The join levels of the Trotter-Weil hierarchy are decidable, in *37th MFCS 2012*, pp. 603–614, *LNCS* vol. 7464, Springer, Heidelberg, 2012.

50. M. KUFLEITNER AND A. LAUSER, Quantifier alternation in two-variable first-order logic with successor is decidable, in *STACS 2013*, pp. 305–316, *LIPIcs. Leibniz Int. Proc. Inform.* vol. 20, Schloss Dagstuhl. Leibniz-Zent.

Inform., Wadern, 2013.

51. M. KUFLEITNER AND P. WEIL, On FO$^2$ quantifier alternation over words, in *34th MFCS 2009*, pp. 513–524, *LNCS* vol. 5734, Springer, Berlin, 2009.

52. M. KUFLEITNER AND P. WEIL, On logical hierarchies within FO$^2$-definable languages, *Log. Methods Comput. Sci.* **8**,3 (2012), 3:11, 30.

53. M. KUFLEITNER AND P. WEIL, The FO$^2$ alternation hierarchy is decidable, in *Computer science logic 2012*, pp. 426–439, *LIPIcs. Leibniz Int. Proc. Inform.* vol. 16, Schloss Dagstuhl. Leibniz-Zent. Inform., Wadern, 2012.

54. R. MCNAUGHTON, Algebraic decision procedures for local testability, *Math. Systems Theory* **8**,1 (1974), 60–76.

55. R. MCNAUGHTON AND S. PAPERT, *Counter-free automata*, The M.I.T. Press, Cambridge, Mass.-London, 1971. With an appendix by William Henneman, M.I.T. Research Monograph, No. 65.

56. D. PERRIN AND J.-É. PIN, First-order logic and star-free sets, *J. Comput. System Sci.* **32**,3 (1986), 393–406.

57. J.-É. PIN, Open problems about regular languages, 35 years later. This volume, Chapter 7.

58. J.-É. PIN, Propriétés syntactiques du produit non ambigu, in *7th ICALP*, J. W. de Bakker and J. van Leeuwen (eds.), Berlin, 1980, pp. 483–499, *LNCS* vol. 85, Springer.

59. J.-É. PIN, Arbres et hiérarchies de concaténation, in *10th ICALP*, Berlin, 1983, pp. 617–628, *LNCS* vol. 154, Springer.

60. J.-É. PIN, Concatenation hierarchies, decidability results and problems, in *Combinatorics on words, progress and perspectives*, L. Cummings (ed.), Berlin, 1983, pp. 195–228, Academic Press.

61. J.-É. PIN, Hiérarchies de concaténation, *RAIRO Inform. Théor.* **18** (1984), 23–46.

62. J.-É. PIN, *Varieties of formal languages*, North Oxford, London, 1986. (Traduction de Variétés de langages formels).

63. J.-É. PIN, A variety theorem without complementation, *Russian Mathematics (Izvestija vuzov.Matematika)* **39** (1995), 80–90.

64. J.-É. PIN, Syntactic semigroups, in *Handbook of formal languages*, G. Rozenberg and A. Salomaa (eds.), vol. 1, ch. 10, pp. 679–746, Springer Verlag, 1997.

65. J.-É. PIN, Bridges for concatenation hierarchies, in *25th ICALP*, K. G. Larsen, S. Skyum and G. Winskel (eds.), Berlin, 1998, pp. 431–442, *LNCS* vol. 1443, Springer.

66. J.-É. PIN, Algebraic tools for the concatenation product, *Theoret. Comput. Sci.* **292** (2003), 317–342.

67. J.-É. PIN, Theme and variations on the concatenation product, in *4th CAI 2011*, F. Winkler (ed.), Berlin, 2011, pp. 44–64, *LNCS* vol. 6742, Springer.

68. J.-É. PIN AND H. STRAUBING, Monoids of upper triangular matrices, in *Semigroups (Szeged, 1981)*, pp. 259–272, *Colloq. Math. Soc. János Bolyai* vol. 39, North-Holland, Amsterdam, 1985.

69. J.-É. PIN AND H. STRAUBING, Some results on C-varieties, *Theoret. Informatics Appl.* **39** (2005), 239–262.

70. J.-E. PIN, H. STRAUBING AND D. THÉRIEN, Locally trivial categories and unambiguous concatenation, *J. of Pure and Applied Algebra* **52** (1988), 297–311.

71. J.-E. PIN AND P. WEIL, Polynomial closure and unambiguous product, in *22th ICALP*, Z. Fülöp and F. Gécseg (eds.), Berlin, 1995, pp. 348–359, *LNCS* vol. 944, Springer.

72. J.-E. PIN AND P. WEIL, Profinite semigroups, Mal'cev products and identities, *J. of Algebra* **182** (1996), 604–626.

73. J.-E. PIN AND P. WEIL, A reiterman theorem for pseudovarieties of finite first-order structures, *Algebra Universalis* **35** (1996), 577–595.

74. J.-E. PIN AND P. WEIL, Polynomial closure and unambiguous product, *Theory Comput. Systems* **30** (1997), 1–39.

75. J.-E. PIN AND P. WEIL, A conjecture on the concatenation product, *ITA* **35** (2001), 597–618.

76. J.-E. PIN AND P. WEIL, The wreath product principle for ordered semigroups, *Communications in Algebra* **30** (2002), 5677–5713.

77. T. PLACE, Separating regular languages with two quantifier alternations, in *30th LICS 2015*, pp. 202–213, IEEE, 2015.

78. T. PLACE AND M. ZEITOUN, Going higher in the first-order quantifier alternation hierarchy on words, in *41st ICALP 2014 Part II*, J. Esparza, P. Fraigniaud, T. Husfeldt and E. Koutsoupias (eds.), pp. 342–353, *LNCS* vol. 8573, Springer, Heidelberg, 2014. Full version on `arXiv:1404.6832 [cs.FL]`.

79. T. PLACE AND M. ZEITOUN, Separating regular languages with first-order logic, in *Joint Meeting of the Twenty-Third EACSL Annual Conference on Computer Science Logic (CSL) and the Twenty-Ninth Annual ACM/IEEE Symposium on Logic in Computer Science (LICS), CSL-LICS '14, Vienna, Austria, July 14 - 18, 2014*, T. A. Henzinger and D. Miller (eds.), pp. 75:1–75:10, ACM, 2014.

80. T. PLACE AND M. ZEITOUN, Separation and the successor relation, in *STACS 2015*, E. W. Mayr and N. Ollinger (eds.), pp. 662–675, *LIPIcs* vol. 30, Schloss Dagstuhl - Leibniz-Zentrum Fuer Informatik, 2015.

81. T. PLACE AND M. ZEITOUN, The tale of the quantifier alternation hierarchy of first-order logic over words, *ACM SIGLOG News* **2**,3 (Aug. 2015), 4–17.

82. T. PLACE AND M. ZEITOUN, Separating regular languages with first-order logic, *Logical Methods in Computer Science* **12**,5 (2016), 1–30.

83. J. REITERMAN, The Birkhoff theorem for finite algebras, *Algebra Universalis* **14**,1 (1982), 1–10.

84. C. REUTENAUER, Sur les variétés de langages et de monoïdes, in *Theoretical computer science (Fourth GI Conf., Aachen, 1979)*, pp. 260–265, *LNCS* vol. 67, Springer, Berlin-New York, 1979.

85. J. RHODES AND B. STEINBERG, *The q-theory of finite semigroups, Springer Monographs in Mathematics*, Springer, New York, 2009.

86. M.-P. SCHÜTZENBERGER, Une théorie algébrique du codage, *Séminaire Dubreil. Algèbre et théorie des nombres* **9** (1955-1956), 1–24. `http://eudml.org/doc/111094`.

87. M.-P. SCHÜTZENBERGER, On finite monoids having only trivial subgroups,

*Inform. Control* **8** (1965), 190–194.

88. M.-P. SCHÜTZENBERGER, Sur le produit de concaténation non ambigu, *Semigroup Forum* **13**,1 (1976/77), 47–75.

89. T. SCHWENTICK, D. THÉRIEN AND H. VOLLMER, Partially-ordered two-way automata: a new characterization of DA, in *5th DLT 2001*, W. Kuich, G. Rozenberg and A. Salomaa (eds.), pp. 239–250, *LNCS* vol. 2295, Springer, Berlin, 2002.

90. V. SELIVANOV AND A. KONOVALOV, Boolean algebras of regular languages, in *15th DLT 2011*, pp. 386–396, *LNCS* vol. 6795, Springer, Heidelberg, 2011.

91. V. L. SELIVANOV, A logical approach to decidability of hierarchies of regular star-free languages, in *STACS 2001 (Dresden)*, A. Ferreira and H. Reichel (eds.), pp. 539–550, *LNCS* vol. 2010, Springer, Berlin, 2001.

92. V. L. SELIVANOV, Relating automata-theoretic hierarchies to complexity-theoretic hierarchies, in *Fundamentals of computation theory (Riga, 2001)*, pp. 323–334, *LNCS* vol. 2138, Springer, Berlin, 2001.

93. V. L. SELIVANOV AND K. W. WAGNER, A reducibility for the dot-depth hierarchy, *Theoret. Comput. Sci.* **345**,2-3 (2005), 448–472.

94. I. SIMON, *Hierarchies of Events with Dot-Depth One*, PhD thesis, University of Waterloo, Waterloo, Ontario, Canada, 1972.

95. I. SIMON, Piecewise testable events, in *Proc. 2nd GI Conf.*, H. Brackage (ed.), pp. 214–222, *LNCS* vol. 33, Springer Verlag, Berlin, Heidelberg, New York, 1975.

96. B. STEINBERG, A delay theorem for pointlikes, *Semigroup Forum* **63**,3 (2001), 281–304.

97. J. STERN, Characterizations of some classes of regular events, *Theoret. Comput. Sci.* **35**,1 (1985), 17–42.

98. H. STRAUBING, Aperiodic homomorphisms and the concatenation product of recognizable sets, *J. Pure Appl. Algebra* **15**,3 (1979), 319–327.

99. H. STRAUBING, On finite $\mathcal{J}$-trivial monoids, *Semigroup Forum* **19**,2 (1980), 107–110.

100. H. STRAUBING, A generalization of the Schützenberger product of finite monoids, *Theoret. Comput. Sci.* **13**,2 (1981), 137–150.

101. H. STRAUBING, Finite semigroup varieties of the form $V * D$, *J. Pure Appl. Algebra* **36**,1 (1985), 53–94.

102. H. STRAUBING, Semigroups and languages of dot-depth 2, in *Automata, languages and programming (Rennes, 1986)*, pp. 416–423, *LNCS* vol. 226, Springer, Berlin, 1986.

103. H. STRAUBING, Semigroups and languages of dot-depth two, *Theoret. Comput. Sci.* **58**,1-3 (1988), 361–378. Thirteenth International Colloquium on Automata, Languages and Programming (Rennes, 1986).

104. H. STRAUBING, The wreath product and its applications, in *Formal properties of finite automata and applications (Ramatuelle, 1988)*, pp. 15–24, *LNCS* vol. 386, Springer, Berlin, 1989.

105. H. STRAUBING, On logical descriptions of regular languages, in *LATIN 2002*, S. Rajsbaum (ed.), Berlin, 2002, pp. 528–538, *LNCS* vol. 2286, Springer.

106. H. STRAUBING, Algebraic characterization of the alternation hierarchy in

$FO^2[<]$ on finite words, in *Computer science logic 2011*, pp. 525–537, *LIPIcs. Leibniz Int. Proc. Inform.* vol. 12, Schloss Dagstuhl. Leibniz-Zent. Inform., Wadern, 2011.

107. H. STRAUBING AND D. THÉRIEN, Partially ordered finite monoids and a theorem of I. Simon, *J. Algebra* **119**,2 (1988), 393–399.

108. H. STRAUBING AND P. WEIL, On a conjecture concerning dot-depth two languages, *Theoret. Comput. Sci.* **104**,2 (1992), 161–183.

109. P. TESSON AND D. THÉRIEN, Diamonds are forever: the variety DA, in *Semigroups, algorithms, automata and languages (Coimbra, 2001)*, pp. 475–499, World Sci. Publ., River Edge, NJ, 2002.

110. P. TESSON AND D. THÉRIEN, Logic meets algebra: the case of regular languages, *Log. Methods Comput. Sci.* **3**,1 (2007), 1:4, 37.

111. D. THÉRIEN, Catégories et langages de dot-depth un, *RAIRO Inform. Théor. Appl.* **22**,4 (1988), 437–445.

112. D. THÉRIEN AND T. WILKE, Over words, two variables are as powerful as one quantifier alternation, in *STOC'98*, J. S. Vitter (ed.), pp. 234–240, ACM, New York, 1999.

113. W. THOMAS, Classifying regular events in symbolic logic, *J. Comput. System Sci.* **25**,3 (1982), 360–376.

114. W. THOMAS, An application of the Ehrenfeucht-Fraïssé game in formal language theory, *Mém. Soc. Math. France (N.S.)* ,16 (1984), 11–21. Logic (Paris, 1983).

115. W. THOMAS, A concatenation game and the dot-depth hierarchy, in *Computation theory and logic*, pp. 415–426, *LNCS* vol. 270, Springer, Berlin, 1987.

116. K. W. WAGNER, Leaf language classes: a survey, in *Machines, computations, and universality*, pp. 60–81, *LNCS* vol. 3354, Springer, Berlin, 2005.

117. P. WEIL, Inverse monoids of dot-depth two, *Theoret. Comput. Sci.* **66**,3 (1989), 233–245.

118. P. WEIL, Some results on the dot-depth hierarchy, *Semigroup Forum* **46**,3 (1993), 352–370.

119. P. WEIS AND N. IMMERMAN, Structure theorem and strict alternation hierarchy for $FO^2$ on words, *Log. Methods Comput. Sci.* **5**,3 (2009), 3:4, 23.

# Chapter 9

# Depth of Closed Classes of Truth Functions in Many-Valued Logic

Arto Salomaa

*Turku Centre for Computer Science*
*Turku University, 392 Quantum Building*
*20014 Turun yliopisto, Finland*
asalomaa@utu.fi

Functions of several variables ranging over a finite set $S$ and with values in $S$ can be viewed as truth functions in many-valued logic. A class $\mathcal{F}_S$ of such functions is *closed* if no composition of functions leads outside $\mathcal{F}_S$. The *depth* of a closed class indicates how "far" the class is from the class of all functions. This paper investigates interconnections between depth and finding finite generator sets, as well as the cardinality of all closed classes. *Independent classes* constitute a central auxiliary notion. Some results carry over to a more general set-up, where the set $S$ is not necessarily finite, or a general closure operation is considered.

## Contents

## 9.1. Set-Up and Basic Problems

In this paper we consider functions $f(x_1, \ldots, x_k)$ of finitely many variables whose domain is a fixed finite set $S$ with $n \geq 2$ elements, and whose range is included in $S$. The class of such functions is denoted by $\mathcal{P}_S$, $\mathcal{P}_n$, or simply $\mathcal{P}$ if $n$ is understood.

This set-up occurs in many diverse situations. Depending on the interpretation, different questions will be important.

The interpretation we have in mind in this paper is *many-valued logic*. The set $S$ consists of $n$ *truth values*, and the functions are *truth functions*. However, our considerations will be independent of any interpretation.

We make the following **convention**, valid throughout this paper: $n$ always stands for the number of elements in the basic set $S$, and as truth-values we take the first $n$ natural numbers, or sometimes the first $n$ non-negative integers. Arithmetical operations are carried out modulo $n$. Clearly, there are altogether $n^n$ functions of one variable in the set $S^S$, whereas the total number of functions of $k$ variables is $n^{n^k}$. Although these numbers are finite, in the classes considered below the number $k$ of variables is unbounded.

Before we continue, we want to mention another research area, apart from many-valued logic, applying the same set-up of functions. Biochemically motivated *reaction systems* have been vigorously investigated in recent years [1, 2, 14, 15]. Although the setup is the same, problems different from those investigated in many-valued logic are central.

When we speak of "functions", without further specifications, we always mean functions, over a finite set $S$, in the set-up defined above. A specific function can always be defined by listing the function values for different combinations of the argument values. For instance, the truth function of the *Łukasiewicz implication* $c(x,y)$ in 6-valued logic is defined either by $c(x,y) = \max(1, 1 - x + y)$, or else by its truth-table

$$
\begin{array}{|llllll}
1 & 2 & 3 & 4 & 5 & 6 \\
1 & 1 & 2 & 3 & 4 & 5 \\
1 & 1 & 1 & 2 & 3 & 4 \\
1 & 1 & 1 & 1 & 2 & 3 \\
1 & 1 & 1 & 1 & 1 & 2 \\
1 & 1 & 1 & 1 & 1 & 1
\end{array}
$$

Here we have omitted the indices $1, \ldots, 6$ from the rows and columns. In the interpretation of this implication the value 1 is considered to be the "greatest" truth value. However, in this paper semantic considerations concerning the "meaning" of the truth values are irrelevant. Axiomatization of many-valued logics [7, 16] lies outside the scope of the paper.

As agreed above, we let $\mathcal{P}_S$ (or, more briefly, $\mathcal{P}$) denote the class of all functions (of an arbitrary finite number of variables). The class is denumerably infinite. Given a subclass $\mathcal{F}$, we form *compositions* of functions in

$\mathcal{F}$. For instance, starting with a binary function $f(x, y)$, we obtain among others the following functions:

$$f_1(x) = f(f(x, x), x), \quad f_2(x, y, z) = f(x, f(y, z)), \quad f_3(x, y) = f(y, f(x, y)).$$

Starting with a binary function $f(x, y)$ and a ternary function $g(x, y, z)$ we obtain, for instance, the composition

$$f_4(x, y, z, u, v) = f(g(x, y, x), g(u, g(y, u, v), f(v, g(x, y, z)))).$$

Whenever a function is expressed as a composition of some functions, we say that the latter functions *generate* the former function. Thus, each of the functions $f_1, f_2, f_3$ is generated by $f$, whereas $f_4$ is generated by $f$ and $g$.

The *closure* $\mathrm{CL}(\mathcal{F})$ of a class $\mathcal{F}$ of functions consists of all functions generated by functions in $\mathcal{F}$. A class of functions $\mathcal{F}$ is *closed* if $\mathrm{CL}(\mathcal{F}) = \mathcal{F}$.

A subclass $\mathcal{F}_1$ of a class $\mathcal{F}$ of functions is said to be *complete in $\mathcal{F}$* if

$$\mathrm{CL}(\mathcal{F}_1) = \mathcal{F}.$$

Classes complete in $\mathcal{P}_n$ are termed, briefly, *complete*. A complete finite subclass of $\mathcal{F}$ is a *basis* of $\mathcal{F}$ if no proper subclass of it is complete in $\mathcal{F}$. Thus, a class having a basis always implies that the class is finitely generated.

It is well-known that, for any $n$, there are singleton complete classes. Functions in such singleton classes are called *Sheffer functions* [7, 9–11, 17].

If a class has a finite complete subclass, it always has a basis. One of the central problems concerns the existence of a basis for a given class of functions. To get a feeling of the problem, we consider an example.

Let $S = \{0, 1, 2, 3\}$ and $\mathcal{F}$ consists of the linear functions

$$f_0 = 0, \quad f_k(x_1, \ldots, x_k) = 2x_1 + \cdots + 2x_k \pmod{4},$$

for $k = 1, 2, \ldots$. This class $\mathcal{F}$ has no basis because the class of functions $\{f_i \mid i \le k\}$ is closed, for any $k$. Indeed, identifying two variables in $f_k$ results in the function $f_{k-2}$. In general, any proper composition of functions in this set gives a function $f_i$ with $i < k$.

In this paper we deal with problems concerning the notions introduced above. We also give proofs of some results originally presented in sources not easily available. Interpretations of the results to many-valued logic lie outside the scope of the paper.

## 9.2. Precomplete Classes

A subclass $\mathcal{F}'$ of class $\mathcal{F}$ is termed *precomplete* in $\mathcal{F}$ if it is not complete in $\mathcal{F}$ but

$$\mathrm{CL}(\mathcal{F}' \cup \{g\}) = \mathcal{F}, \text{ for every } g \in (\mathcal{F} - \mathcal{F}').$$

Classes precomplete in $\mathcal{P}_n$ are termed, briefly, *precomplete*.

Precomplete classes constitute a central auxiliary notion in the study of completeness. In 2- and 3-valued logic (that is, in $\mathcal{P}_2$ and $\mathcal{P}_3$) there are 5 and 18 precomplete classes, respectively [6, 18]. In this section we prove that the number of precomplete classes is finite, for any $n$. The result is originally due to A.V. Kuznetsov [18].

We begin with the following result.

**Theorem 9.1.** *A closed class $\mathcal{F}$ of functions has a basis if and only if the conditions*

$$\mathcal{F}_1 \subseteq \mathcal{F}_2 \subseteq \cdots, \quad and \quad \bigcup_{i=1}^{\infty} \mathcal{F}_i = \mathcal{F}$$

*where $\mathcal{F}_i$ are closed classes, imply the existence of an index $k$ such that*

$$\mathcal{F}_k = \mathcal{F}.$$

**Proof.** If $\mathcal{F}$ has a basis, all elements of it have to belong to some class $\mathcal{F}_k$ in the above sequence of classes. Consider the converse, and choose $\mathcal{F}_i$ be the closed subclass of $\mathcal{F}$ generated by functions with at most $i$ variables. Hence, $\mathcal{F}$ is generated by the functions in it with at most $k$ variables, which is a finite set. This implies the existence of a basis for $\mathcal{F}$.  □

**Theorem 9.2.** *If $\mathcal{F}$ is a closed class with a basis, then an arbitrary closed class $\mathcal{F}' \neq \mathcal{F}$ can be extended to a precomplete class in $\mathcal{F}$.*

**Proof.** If $\mathcal{F}'$ is precomplete, there is nothing to prove. Otherwise, there is a function $f_1 \in \mathcal{F} - \mathcal{F}'$ such that $\mathcal{F}' \cup \{f_1\} = \mathcal{F}_1$ is not complete in $\mathcal{F}$. If $\mathcal{F}_1$ is precomplete, we are through. Otherwise, we treat $\mathcal{F}_1$ as our originally given class, and choose a function $f_2 \in \mathcal{F} - \mathcal{F}_1$ such that $\mathcal{F}_1 \cup \{f_2\} = \mathcal{F}_2$ is not complete in $\mathcal{F}$. Continuing in this way, we obtain a (possibly infinite) chain of proper inclusions

$$\mathcal{F}' \subsetneq \mathcal{F}_1 \subsetneq \mathcal{F}_2 \cdots.$$

The class

$$\mathcal{F}' \cup \bigcup_{i=1}^{\infty} \mathcal{F}_i$$

is, by the construction, either precomplete, or else equals $\mathcal{F}$. The latter possibility is excluded because it would imply, by Theorem 9.1, that $\mathcal{F} = \mathcal{F}_k$, for some $k$. This would contradict the construction of the classes $\mathcal{F}_i$. $\square$

**Corollary 9.1.** *Every closed class contained in $\mathcal{P}_n$, $n \geq 2$, and different from $\mathcal{P}_n$ can be extended to a precomplete class.*

We are now ready for the main result in this section.

**Theorem 9.3.** *The number of classes precomplete in a closed class $\mathcal{F}$ having a basis is finite.*

**Proof.** Denote by $\mathcal{F}_i$ the (closed) subclass of $\mathcal{F}$, generated by functions in $\mathcal{F}$ with at most $i$ variables. It is a consequence of Theorem 9.1 that $\mathcal{F} = \mathcal{F}_k$, for some $k$. Let now $\mathcal{H}$ be an arbitrary class precomplete in $\mathcal{F}$. Further, let $\mathcal{H}_k$ be the subclass of $\mathcal{H}$, consisting of all functions in $\mathcal{H}$ with at most $k$ variables. We claim that $\mathcal{H}$ is uniquely determined (but not necessarily generated) by the class $\mathcal{H}_k$. Since the number of such classes $\mathcal{H}_k$ is finite (a very rough upper bound being $2^{n^{n^k}}$), Theorem 9.3 follows from our claim.

To establish the claim, note first that $\mathcal{H}_k$ is a proper subclass of $\mathcal{F}_k$ because, otherwise, $\mathcal{H}$ would be complete in $\mathcal{F}$. On the other hand, it is a direct consequence of precompleteness that a class $\mathcal{H}'$ precomplete in $\mathcal{F}$ but different from $\mathcal{H}$ yields a different class $\mathcal{H}'_k$. $\square$

**Corollary 9.2.** *For any $n \geq 2$, the number of classes precomplete in $\mathcal{P}_n$ is finite.*

It is not known whether or not every class precomplete in $\mathcal{P}_n$ has a basis. This is known to be the case for the values $n = 2, 3$; see [3, 6].

## 9.3. Strong Precompleteness

In view of the importance of precomplete classes, we introduce now a strengthening of the notion. We require that precompleteness extends to certain natural subclasses of the classes considered. We restrict the attention to closed subclasses of $\mathcal{P}_n$.

By the *k-restriction* $\mathrm{RE}_k(\mathcal{F})$, where $k = 1, 2, \ldots$, of a class $\mathcal{F}$ we mean the class of all functions in $\mathcal{F}$ having at most $k$ variables. A subclass $\mathcal{F}$ of

$\mathcal{P}_n$ is *strongly precomplete* if $CL(RE_k(\mathcal{F}))$ is precomplete in $RE_k(CL(\mathcal{P}_n))$, for all $k \geq 1$.

Clearly, every strongly precomplete class is precomplete. Moreover, it is generated by functions in it with 2 variables. We now determine all strongly precomplete classes. It turns out that there are not many of them. First we need some auxiliary notation.

Permutations in the symmetric group $\sigma_n$ can be viewed as functions in $\mathcal{P}_n$. Let $\beta$ be precomplete in $\sigma_n$. (Thus, $\beta$ is a maximal subgroup of $\sigma_n$. It is not unique.) Denote by $\mathcal{H}_n^\beta$ the subclass of $RE_1(\mathcal{P}_n)$, consisting of elements of $\beta$ and all non-permutations, that is, all functions assuming at most $n-1$ values. Further, let $\mathcal{H}_n'$ denote the subclass of $RE_1(\mathcal{P}_n)$, consisting of all permutations and all functions assuming at most $n-2$ values.

**Lemma 9.1.** *For any $n \geq 2$, the classes $\mathcal{H}_n^\beta$ and $\mathcal{H}_n'$ are the only classes precomplete in $RE_1(\mathcal{P}_n)$.*

**Proof.** The precompleteness of each the first classes follows by the definition of $\beta$. That $\mathcal{H}_n'$ is precomplete follows because any function $f \in (RE_1(\mathcal{P}_n) - \mathcal{H}_n')$ assumes exactly $n-1$ values. The function $f$ and $\sigma_n$ generate all functions assuming exactly $n-1$ values.

Consider any class $\mathcal{H}$ precomplete in $RE_1(\mathcal{P}_n)$. If it misses a permutation $p$ and a function $g$ assuming at most $n-1$ values, then we have $p \notin (\mathcal{H} \cup \{g\})$. Hence, $\mathcal{H}$ is not precomplete in $\mathcal{P}_n$. If $\mathcal{H}$ contains all permutations but misses all functions assuming exactly $n-1$ values and an additional function $g_1$, then the addition of $g_1$ to $\mathcal{H}$ does not yield a set complete in $RE_1(\mathcal{P}_n)$. Hence, the classes of Lemma 9.1 are the only classes precomplete in $RE_1(\mathcal{P}_n)$                                    □

We are now in the position to determine all strongly precomplete classes. Out of the 5 precomplete subclasses of $\mathcal{P}_2$, only 1-restrictions of the classes of monotone and self-dual functions are precomplete in $RE_1(\mathcal{P}_2)$. Only the former of these classes is generated by the 2-variable functions in it.

Now let $n \geq 3$ and $\mathcal{H}$ be strongly precomplete in $\mathcal{P}_n$, where $n \geq 3$. Hence, $RE_1(\mathcal{H})$ is one of the classes of Lemma 9.1. Clearly, $\mathcal{H}$ contains a function $f$ depending essentially on at least 2 variables and assuming all $n$ values. (These two conditions are often referred to as the *Slupecki conditions*.) It is easy to see that $\mathcal{H}_n^\beta \cup \{f\}$ is complete. The same conclusion holds for $\mathcal{H}_n' \cup \{f\}$ if $n \geq 5$. (See, for instance, [8–10, 18].) Consequently, $\mathcal{H}$ is not precomplete.

This leaves the cases $n = 4$ and $n = 3$. If $n = 4$ and $\text{RE}_1(\mathcal{H}) = \mathcal{H}_4'$, the class $\mathcal{H}$ is complete, since it contains a function satisfying the Slupecki conditions, as well as all one-variable functions assuming exactly 2 values. Finally, assume that

$$n = 3 \text{ and } \text{RE}_1(\mathcal{H}) = \mathcal{H}_3'.$$

Here we have to check through the 18 precomplete classes [3]. Only the class of linear functions is generated by the 2-variable functions in it, and qualifies as a strongly precomplete class.

Hence, we have established the following result.

**Theorem 9.4.** *There are no strongly precomplete classes in* $\mathcal{P}_n$ *if* $n \geq 4$. *In* $\mathcal{P}_3$ *(resp.,* $\mathcal{P}_2$*) linear (resp., monotone) functions constitute the only strongly precomplete class.*

## 9.4. Depth

The *depth* of a closed class indicates how "far" the class is from $\mathcal{P}_n$. The notion of depth can be defined with respect to an arbitrary closed class. For simplicity, we define the notion only for $\mathcal{P}_n$.

The *depth* of a closed class $\mathcal{F}$ is defined inductively as follows. The depth of $\mathcal{P}_n$ equals 0. The depth of $\mathcal{F} \neq \mathcal{P}_n$ equals $d > 0$ if, for all elements $f \in \mathcal{P}_n - \mathcal{F}$, the depth of $\text{CL}(\mathcal{F} \cup \{f\})$ is less than or equal to $d - 1$ and, for some $f_0 \in \mathcal{P}_n - \mathcal{F}$, the depth of $\text{CL}(\mathcal{F} \cup \{f\})$ equals $d - 1$. Thus, the depth of a precomplete class equals 1.

A closed class $\mathcal{F}$ is of *infinite depth* if, for all natural numbers $t$, there are functions $f_1, \ldots, f_t$ such that

$$f_1 \notin \mathcal{F}, \ f_i \notin \text{CL}(\mathcal{F} \cup \{f_1, \ldots, f_{i-1}\}),$$

for all $i$, $2 \leq i \leq t$. A closed class $\mathcal{F}$ is of *strongly infinite depth* if there is an infinite sequence of functions $f_1, f_2, \ldots$ such that the above conditions hold for all values of $i$.

Clearly, every class of strongly infinite depth is of infinite depth. We establish below that the converse does not hold true. Indeed, this is one of the cases, where the existence of an arbitrary long sequence of elements satisfying a certain condition does not imply the existence of an infinite sequence satisfying the same condition.

The following result (also see [13]) gives an appropriate tool for the comparison between infinite depth and strongly infinite depth.

**Theorem 9.5.** *For each $n \geq 2$, the class $\mathcal{P}_n$ contains a class without basis exactly when $\mathcal{P}_n$ contains a class of strongly infinite depth. More specifically, if a class $\mathcal{F}$ with a basis is included in a class without basis, then $\mathcal{F}$ is of strongly infinite depth. Conversely, every class of strongly infinite depth is a subclass of some class without basis.*

**Proof.** Assume that $\mathcal{F} \subsetneq \mathcal{F}_1$, where $\mathcal{F}$ has a basis and $\mathcal{F}_1$ doesn't have one. Consequently, $\mathcal{F}$ has a finite subclass $\mathcal{H}$ such that $\mathcal{H}' = \mathrm{CL}(\mathcal{H}) \subseteq \mathcal{F}$. Since $\mathcal{F}_1$ has no basis, there is a function $f_1 \in \mathcal{F}_1 - \mathcal{H}'$. We proceed inductively and denote

$$\mathcal{H}_k = \mathrm{CL}(\mathcal{H}' \cup \{f_1, \ldots, f_k\}), \ k \geq 1.$$

Since $\mathcal{F}_1$ has no basis there is, for any $k$, a function $f_{k+1} \in \mathcal{F}_1 - \mathcal{H}_k$. The infinite sequence $f_1, f_2, \ldots$ thus constructed shows that $\mathcal{F}$ (as well as $\mathcal{H}'$) is of strongly infinite depth.

Conversely, assume that $\mathcal{F}$ is of strongly infinite depth, and let $f_1, f_2, \ldots$ be the sequence involved. We claim that the class

$$\mathcal{F}_1 = \mathcal{F} \cup \bigcup_{i=1}^{\infty} \{f_i\}$$

has no basis. Assume the contrary: a finite subclass $\mathcal{H}$ of $\mathcal{F}_1$ satisfies $\mathcal{F}_1 \subseteq \mathrm{CL}(\mathcal{H})$. Since $\mathcal{H}$ is finite, we have

$$\mathcal{H} \subseteq \mathcal{F} \cup \{f_1, \ldots, f_t\},$$

for some $t$. Consequently,

$$f_{t+1} \in \mathcal{F}_1 \subseteq \mathrm{CL}(\mathcal{H}) \subseteq \mathrm{CL}(\mathcal{F} \cup \{f_1, \ldots, f_t\}),$$

which contradicts the definition of the sequence $f_i$, $i = 1, 2, \ldots$ Hence, $\mathcal{F}_1$ has no basis. $\square$

Observe that the converse part of the above proof does not work if $\mathcal{F}$ is of infinite depth because then the infinite sequence of functions is not available.

It was shown by Post [6] that every subclass of $\mathcal{P}_2$ has a basis. On the other hand, it can be seen from *Post's lattice* (presented in [6]; also see [5]) that, for instance, the truth-functions corresponding to conjunction, disjunction and implication generate each a singleton class of infinite depth. Combining these results with Theorem 9.5 and the well-known fact [19] that there are subclasses without basis of $\mathcal{P}_n$, for all $n \geq 3$, we obtain the following result.

**Corollary 9.3.** *Some classes of infinite depth are not of strongly infinite depth. The class* $\mathcal{P}_n$, $n \geq 3$, *contains subclasses of strongly infinite depth, whereas no such subclasses are contained in* $\mathcal{P}_2$.

We conclude this section with some related notions also discussed in [13]. A sequence of $t + 1$, $t \geq 1$, of closed classes

$$\mathcal{F} = \mathcal{F}_1, \mathcal{F}_2, \ldots, \mathcal{F}_{t+1} = \mathcal{P}_n$$

is termed a *composition sequence* of $\mathcal{F}$ if, for every $i$, $1 \leq i \leq t$, the class $\mathcal{F}_i$ is precomplete in the class $\mathcal{F}_{i+1}$. The number $t$ is referred to as its *length*.

Given a class $\mathcal{F}$, consider functions $f_1, \ldots, f_t$ such that

$$f_1 \notin \mathcal{F}, \ f_i \notin \mathrm{CL}(\mathcal{F} \cup \{f_1, \ldots, f_{i-1}\}),$$

for all $i$, $2 \leq i \leq t$. Such a sequence of functions is termed a *D-sequence of* $\mathcal{F}$. Again, the number $t$ is referred to as its *length*.

Neither composition sequences nor D-sequences are unique. Every proper closed subclass of $\mathcal{P}_n$ possesses a D-sequence but not necessarily a composition sequence. The following theorem contains some rather obvious consequences of the definitions and is given without a proof.

**Theorem 9.6.** *For any natural number $d$ and a closed class $\mathcal{F}_1$, the following conditions are equivalent:*

- *The depth of $\mathcal{F}_1$ is $d$.*
- *The length if the longest D-sequence of $\mathcal{F}_1$ is $d$.*
- $\mathcal{F}_1$ *possesses a composition sequence of length $d$ but no D-sequence of length $d + 1$.*

*If $\mathcal{F}_1$ possesses no subclasses of a finite depth then it possesses no subclasses which are of infinite depth but not of sequentially infinite depth.*

Clearly, if a closed class $\mathcal{F}_1$ of depth $d_1$ is properly included in a closed class $\mathcal{F}_2$ of depth $d_2$, then $d_1 \geq d_2 + 1$. If the equality holds, then $\mathcal{F}_1$ is precomplete in $\mathcal{F}_2$. However, it is possible that $\mathcal{F}_1$ is precomplete in $\mathcal{F}_2$ but still $d_1 > d_2 + 1$. For instance, the class $D_1$ in Post's lattice is precomplete in class $D_3$, but the depth of the latter equals 1 and the depth of the former equals 3.

## 9.5.  Independent Classes, Strongly Infinite Depth and Non-Denumerability

In this section we introduce the notion of an *independent class* of functions. It can be used to construct a continuum of closed classes, each of which is of strongly infinite depth and has no basis.

By definition, an infinite class of functions

$$\mathcal{G} = \{g_i | i \geq 1\}$$

is *independent* if

$$g_j \notin \mathrm{CL}(\{g_i | i \geq 1, \ i \neq j\}), \text{ for all } j \geq 1.$$

We present below, extending the result in [19], a general method of constructing independent subclasses of $\mathcal{P}_n$, $n \geq 3$. The next theorem discusses the use of infinite classes.

**Theorem 9.7.** *Let $\mathcal{G}$ be an independent class, and $\mathcal{G}_1$ its infinite subclass such that the difference $\mathcal{G} - \mathcal{G}_1$ is also infinite. Then $\mathcal{G}_1$ possesses no basis and is of strongly infinite depth. Consequently, each independent class $\mathcal{G}$ gives rise to a continuum of closed classes without basis and of strongly infinite depth.*

**Proof.** Clearly, the class $\mathcal{G}_1$ is also independent. The definition of an independent class guarantees that $\mathcal{G}_1$ has no basis. The elements of the difference $\mathcal{G} - \mathcal{G}_1$ constitute a sequence showing that $\mathcal{G}_1$ is of strongly infinite depth. The last sentence of the theorem follows because there are non-denumerably many different choices for $\mathcal{G}_1$. $\qquad\square$

Extending the result of [19], we now present a general method of constructing independent classes in $\mathcal{P}_n$.

Assume that $n \geq 3$ and $t, u, v$ are three distinct elements in the set $\{1, 2, \ldots, n\}$. For $k = 2, 3, \ldots$, define the function $f_k^{tuv}$ as follows:

- $f_k^{tuv}(v, v, \ldots, v) = u$;
- $f_k^{tuv}(x_1, x_2, \ldots, x_k) = u$ if one of the variables $x_i$ assumes the value $u$ and the other variables assume the value $v$; and
- $f_k^{tuv}(x_1, x_2, \ldots, x_k) = t$ in all other cases.

Let $\mathcal{F}^{tuv}$ denote the subclass of $\mathcal{P}_n$, consisting of functions $f_2^{tuv}, f_3^{tuv}, \ldots$

**Lemma 9.2.** *The class $\mathcal{F}^{tuv}$ is independent.*

**Proof.** Choose an arbitrary index $r \geq 2$, and consider the function $f_r^{tuv}$. We claim that

$$f_r^{tuv} \notin \mathrm{CL}(\mathcal{F}^{tuv} - \{f_r^{tuv}\}).$$

Assume the contrary. Then $f_r^{tuv}$ is obtained either as a composition sequence of the form $f_i^{tuv}(f_j^{tuv}(\ldots),\ldots)$, or by identifying variables in some $f_k^{tuv}$, $k > r$. In the former case we assign the value $u$ to one variable outside the inner function and the value $v$ to all other variables. Then $f_r^{tuv}$ assumes the value $u$ for this assignment. However, the composition assumes the value $t$.

In the latter case, where $f_r^{tuv}$ is obtained by identifying variables in some $f_k^{tuv}$, $k > r$, we assign the value $u$ to the variable resulting from the identification, and the value $v$ to all other variables. Again $f_r^{tuv}$ assumes the value $u$ for this assignment, whereas $f_k^{tuv}$ assumes the value $t$. Hence, a contradiction arisen in both cases, and our claim holds true. □

We can choose the values $t, u, v$ to comply with our eventual interpretation of the truth values and the meaning of the functions.

The following result, a striking contrast to the situation in $\mathcal{P}_2$, is a direct consequence of Theorem 9.7 and Lemma 9.2.

**Corollary 9.4.** *For each $n \geq 3$, the class $\mathcal{P}_n$ contains a continuum of subclasses, each of which is of strongly infinite depth and has no basis.*

### 9.6. Another Denumerable Collection of Classes

By Corollary 9.4, there is a one-to-one correspondence in $\mathcal{P}_n$, $n \geq 3$, between subclasses of strongly infinite depth and all subclasses (not necessarily closed ones). On the other hand, we have seen in Theorem 9.3 that any subclass with a basis has only a finite number of precomplete classes in it.

We now remove the assumption concerning the basis and prove that even then the collection of precomplete subclasses is at most denumerable. However, we do not know any example of a class having an infinite number of precomplete subclasses. Such a class has no basis.

**Theorem 9.8.** *All classes $\mathcal{F} \subseteq \mathcal{P}_n$ possesses at most denumerably many precomplete subclasses.*

**Proof.** Consider the $k$-restrictions

$$\mathcal{F}_k = \mathrm{RE}_k\,\mathcal{F}, \; k = 1, 2, \ldots$$

Let $\mathcal{F}'_k$ be an arbitrary proper subset of $\mathcal{F}_k$. We now claim that, for any $k$ and $\mathcal{F}'_k$, there is at most one class $\mathcal{H}$ precomplete in $\mathcal{F}$ such that

$$\mathcal{H} \cap \mathcal{F}_k = \mathcal{F}'_k.$$

To prove this claim, we let $\mathcal{H}$ be any closed class satisfying this condition. Let $T_k$ denote the subclass of $\mathcal{F}$, consisting of all functions $f$ such that

$$\mathrm{CL}(\mathcal{F}'_k \cup \{f\}) \cap \mathcal{F}_k = \mathcal{F}'_k.$$

Thus, $T_k$ consists of functions whose addition to $\mathcal{F}'_k$ still results in our chosen class $\mathcal{H}$. If $\mathcal{H}$ satisfies

$$\mathcal{H} \cap \mathcal{F}_k = \mathcal{F}'_k,$$

it also satisfies

$$\mathcal{H} \subseteq \mathcal{F}'_k \cup T_k.$$

This inclusion cannot be proper if $\mathcal{H}$ is precomplete in $\mathcal{F}$. (Recall that $\mathcal{F}'_k$ is properly included in $\mathcal{F}_k$.) Hence, the precomplete class, if any, is uniquely determined by $\mathcal{F}'_k$, and our claim follows.

For any class precomplete in $\mathcal{F}$, the items $k$ and $\mathcal{F}'_k$ can be found. Thus, precomplete classes correspond to elements in finite sets in a denumerable collection of sets, which proves Theorem 9.8.

$\square$

### 9.7. Remarks Concerning Generalizations

In the considerations above the basic set $S$ is finite, and closure is defined in terms of composition of functions. Most of the notions and many of the results carry over to this more general set-up. For the sake of completeness, we mention a few facts, without details, along these lines. See, for instance, [12, 13].

Let the basic set $S$ be arbitrary and CL a general closure operation for subsets of $S$, satisfying the following four conditions.

(1) $X \subseteq \mathrm{CL}(X)$, for all $X \subseteq S$.
(2) $\mathrm{CL}(\mathrm{CL}(X)) = \mathrm{CL}(X)$, for all $X \subseteq S$.
(3) $X \subseteq Y$ implies $\mathrm{CL}(X) \subseteq \mathrm{CL}(Y))$, for all $X, Y \subseteq S$.
(4) $\mathrm{CL}(\emptyset) = \emptyset$.

Clearly, closure with respect to composition of functions satisfies these conditions.

The notions of closed, complete and precomplete sets, as well as sets having a basis, carry over without changes. The same holds true with respect to notions involving depth, composition sequences and D-sequences.

Theorems 9.1,9.2,9.3,9.5,9.6 carry over almost without changes. Remarkable exceptions are the "only if" part of Theorem 9.1 and the converse part of Theorem 9.5. Consider the former.

Assume that the basic set $S$ is non-denumerable, and define $CL(X) = X$ if $card(X) < card(S)$, and $CL(X) = S$ if $card(X) = card(S)$. (Here $card(X)$ refers to the cardinality of $X$.) Clearly, the conditions 1–4 are satisfied. Now the implication given in Theorem 9.2 holds. But $S$ has no basis.

In our original set-up there are rich possibilities for functional constructions if the basic set $S$ is allowed to be the set of natural numbers. (Closure refers to closure under composition of functions.) Then one obtains independent classes of *one-variable* functions. Starting with an arbitrary subset $Y$ of natural numbers $\geq 3$, we define the function $f_Y(x)$ by

- $f_Y(x) = x$ if $x \in Y$.
- $f_Y(x) = x + 1$ if $x \notin Y$.

The class of such functions is independent because all functions satisfy the condition $f_Y(1) = 2$, whereas an arbitrary composition COMP of the functions satisfies $COMP(1) > 2$.

## 9.8. Conclusion

We have studied interrelations between completeness, precompleteness, depth and independent classes. Some of the results carry over to cases, where there are infinitely many truth-values, or a general closure operation is considered. A strengthening of the notion of precompleteness was introduced. We have also given methods of constructing closed classes without a basis. It is well known [6] that closed subclasses of $\mathcal{P}_2$ constitute a denumerable set, whereas this does not hold true for $\mathcal{P}_3$ [19]. Independent classes constitute a general method of obtaining such non-denumerable collections. An interesting contrast is that the set of closed subclasses of *linear* functions in $\mathcal{P}_n$ is denumerable [4]. We hope to return to linear functions in another context.

# References

[1] R. BRIJDER, A. EHRENFEUCHT, M. MAIN AND G. ROZENBERG, A tour of reaction systems, *Int. J. Found. Comput. Sci.* **22**,7 (2011), 1499–1517.

[2] A. EHRENFEUCHT AND G. ROZENBERG, Reaction systems, *Fund. Inform.* **75**,1–4 (2007), 263–280.

[3] V. GNIDENKO, On the orders of precomplete classes in three-valued logic, *Problemy Kibernetiki* **8** (1962), 341–346. (in Russian).

[4] D. LAU, Über die Anzahl von abgeschlossenen Mengen linearer Funktionen der $n$-wertigen Logik, *Elektr. Informationsverarb. Kybern.* **14** (1978), 561–563.

[5] D. LAU, *Function Algebras on Finite Sets. Basic Course on Many-Valued Logic and Clone Theory*, Springer-Verlag, 2006.

[6] E. POST, The two-valued iterative systems of mathematical logic, *Princeton Annals of Math. Studies* **5** (1941).

[7] J. B. ROSSER AND A. R. TURQUETTE, *Many-Valued Logics*, North-Holland, Amsterdam, 1952.

[8] A. SALOMAA, On many-valued systems of logic, *J. Philosophical Soc. Finland* **22**,115–159 (1959).

[9] A. SALOMAA, On the composition of functions of several variables ranging over a finite set, *Ann. Univ. Turkuensis* **41** (1960).

[10] A. SALOMAA, A theorem concerning the composition of functions of several variables ranging over a finite set, *J. Symb. Logic* **25** (1960), 203–208.

[11] A. SALOMAA, On basic groups for the set of functions over a finite domain, *Ann. Acad. Scient. Fennicae* **338** (1963).

[12] A. SALOMAA, On some algebraic notions in the theory of truth functions, *Acta Philos. Fennica* **18** (1965), 193–202.

[13] A. SALOMAA, On the heights of closed sets of operations in finite algebras, *Ann. Acad. Scient. Fennicae* **363** (1965).

[14] A. SALOMAA, Functional constructions between reaction systems and propositional logic, *Int. J. Found. Comput. Sci.* **24** (2013), 147–159.

[15] A. SALOMAA, Minimal reaction systems defining subset functions, in *Computing with new resources — Essays dedicated to Jozef Gruska on the occasion of his 80th birthday*, C. Calude, R. Freivalds and I. Kazuo (eds.), pp. 436–446, *LNCS* vol. 8808, Springer, 2014.

[16] A. SALOMAA, On axiomatizations of general many-valued propositional calculi, in *Discrete Mathematics and Computer Science*, G. Paun, G. Rozenberg and A. Salomaa (eds.), Editura Academiei Romane, Bucuresti, 2014.

[17] R. Stanković and J. Astola (eds.), *On the Contributions of Arto Salomaa to Multiple-Valued Logic*, *TICSP series* vol. 50, 2009. The papers [8–13] are printed in this volume.

[18] S. V. YABLONSKIJ, Functional constructions in $k$-valued logic, *Publ. Matem. Inst. V.A. Steklov* **51** (1958), 5–142. (in Russian).

[19] J. I. YANOV AND A. A. MUCHNIK, On the existence of $k$-valued closed classes not having a finite basis, *Doklady Akad. Nauk SSSR* **127** (1959), 44–46. (in Russian).

# Chapter 10

# CSP for Parallelising Brzozowski's DFA Construction Algorithm

Tinus Strauss

*FASTAR Research Group, University of Pretoria, South Africa*

Bruce W. Watson

Derrick G. Kourie

*FASTAR Research Group, Dept. of Information Science, Stellenbosch University, South Africa*
*CAIR Research Group, CSIR, South Africa*

Loek Cleophas

*FASTAR Research Group, Dept. of Information Science, Stellenbosch University, South Africa*
*Foundations of Language Processing Group, Umeå University, Sweden*
`{tinus,bruce,derrick,loek}@fastar.org`

CSP, a simple and elegant process algebra, is used to specify five successive parallel versions of Brzozowski's sequential algorithm for constructing deterministic finite automata from regular expressions. Early versions were not sufficiently mature to easily map to a programming language. However, each version exposed new possibilities for refinement so that later versions could subsequently be implemented (in Go). The exercise illustrates the value of the lightweight use of process algebras for supporting abstract thinking when attempting to solve computational problems in a parallel fashion. The emphasis here is on algorithm specification and not on the implementation.

## Contents

## 10.1. Introduction

Some years ago we launched a research project to investigate whether and how classical sequential algorithms could effectively be parallelised, and to explore the consequences of such parallelisation. The project was prompted by the perception that the shift to multicore hardware platforms has not been accompanied by a comparable migration to parallel application software for these platforms. On the contrary, for the most part these multicore machines continue to run standard sequential application software. The operating system generally treats each such sequential application as one single task to be run on a single core, despite the fact that other cores are idle. The net result is significantly under-utilised core capacity.

To carry out this work we needed a clear and concise notation for specifying parallel algorithms, and an effective parallel programming language for implementing the algorithms. Thus far, the use of CSP as a specification notation and Go as a programming language has served our purposes well. A selection of our results has been published. (See, for example, [7, 8, 9, 10].)

In this text we focus on the problem of developing parallel versions of Brzozowski's algorithm for constructing a deterministic finite automaton (DFA) from an arbitrary regular expression. The language of the resulting DFA is, of course, the same as that represented by the regular expression.

Note that Ziadi and Champarnaud [12] have also proposed a parallel version of a sequential algorithm that converts a regular expression into a finite automaton. However, in their case, the regular expression has to be in so-called star-normal form and the result is a so-called Glushkov automaton—a certain kind of *nondeterministic* finite automaton.

Section 10.2 introduces the notation and definition of topics relevant to the problem. This includes regular expressions, their languages and their derivatives. It also includes DFAs and their languages. Finally, it includes a brief introduction to the syntax and semantics of the CSP notation used in our specifications. As additional background, the well-known sequential version of Brzozowski's construction algorithm is recapitulated in Section 10.3.

Thereafter, we discuss CSP specifications of various parallel versions of the algorithm. These specifications are presented in the historical order in which they were proposed, each proposal stimulating new refinements of its predecessor. Although Go implementations of all recent specifications have been benchmarked, we do not dwell on the details of these benchmarking experiments in this text. Some of these experiments are discussed in [9], and it is hoped to publish additional results in the future.

## 10.2. Preliminaries

This section introduces concepts and notation that are relevant to the remainder of the text. More in depth explanations can be found in the cited source documents. The information relates to strings, finite automata and the CSP specification language.

### 10.2.1. *Strings and Languages*

In this section, we present definitions and properties related to strings and languages.

An alphabet is a finite nonempty set of *symbols*. Throughout this text, we assume a fixed finite alphabet denoted by $\Sigma$. In explicit form, it is written as $\{\alpha_1, \ldots, \alpha_n\}$.

A sequence $w$ of 0 or more symbols from $\Sigma$ is called a string. The length of string $w$ is denoted by $|w|$. The empty string is written as $\varepsilon$ and $|\varepsilon| = 0$. The concatenation of two strings $v$ and $w$ is also a string, and is written as $vw$. $\Sigma^*$ denotes the set of all strings over $\Sigma$ including $\varepsilon$. Furthermore, we define $\Sigma^+ = \Sigma^* - \{\varepsilon\}$. Any subset of $\Sigma^*$ is called a language over $\Sigma$. If $\mathcal{L}$

and $\mathcal{L}'$ are two languages over $\Sigma$, then $\mathcal{L} \cdot \mathcal{L}'$ is also a language over $\Sigma$ such that

$$w \in \mathcal{L} \cdot \mathcal{L}' \Leftrightarrow \exists x \in \mathcal{L} \wedge \exists y \in \mathcal{L}' : w = xy.$$

A regular expression (regex) is an expression that defines a language over an alphabet. Given an alphabet $\Sigma$, Table 10.1 recursively specifies all regexes, $r$, that are in the set, $R$, of regexes over $\Sigma$. In each case, the language associated with each of these regexes is also specified[1]. The final column of Table 10.1 provides the so-called derivative of the given regex with respect to a symbol $\alpha \in \Sigma$. This notion of the derivative of a regex was defined by Brzozowski [1].

Table 10.1. Regex $r \in R$, language $\mathcal{L}(r)$ and derivative $\alpha^{-1}r$ where $\alpha \in \Sigma$.

| Range | Regex $r$ | Language $\mathcal{L}(r)$ | Derivative $\alpha^{-1}r$ |
|---|---|---|---|
| | $\varepsilon \in R$ | $\mathcal{L}(\varepsilon) = \{\varepsilon\}$ | $\emptyset$ |
| | $\emptyset \in R$ | $\mathcal{L}(\emptyset) = \emptyset$ | $\emptyset$ |
| $\forall \beta : \Sigma$ | $\beta \in R$ | $\mathcal{L}(\beta) = \{\beta\}$ | $\varepsilon$ if $\beta = \alpha$ and $\emptyset$ if $\beta \neq \alpha$ |
| $\forall E \in R$ | $E^* \in R$ | $\mathcal{L}(E^*) = \mathcal{L}(E)^*$ | $\alpha^{-1}E \cdot E^*$ |
| $\forall E \in R$ | $E^+ \in R$ | $\mathcal{L}(E^+) = \mathcal{L}(E)^+$ | $\alpha^{-1}E \cdot E^*$ |
| $\forall E, F \in R$ | $E + F \in R$ | $\mathcal{L}(E + F) = \mathcal{L}(E) \cup \mathcal{L}(F)$ | $\alpha^{-1}E \cup \alpha^{-1}F$ |
| $\forall E, F \in R$ | $E \cdot F \in R$ | $\mathcal{L}(E \cdot F) = \mathcal{L}(E) \cdot \mathcal{L}(F)$ | $\alpha^{-1}E \cup \alpha^{-1}F$ if $\varepsilon \in \mathcal{L}(E)$ |
| | | | $\alpha^{-1}E$ if $\varepsilon \notin \mathcal{L}(E)$ |

Languages that can be represented by regular expressions are called regular languages. Note that there is a one-to-many mapping from a regular language to regular expressions. For example the elements of the set of regexes $\{E+F, F+E\}$ map to $\mathcal{L}(E) \cup \mathcal{L}(F)$ (which is, of course, the same set as $\mathcal{L}(F) \cup \mathcal{L}(E)$). Similarly, each element in the set of regexes $\{E^*, E+E^*\}$ has the regular language $\mathcal{L}(E)^*$. It is non-trivial to determine whether two arbitrary regexes have the same regular language.

The Brzozowski algorithm described here relies on set operations such as $\cup$ and $\in$ where the operands are regex sets. If equality tests on regexes are applied at the level of their corresponding languages, rather than at the syntactical level (so that, for example, $\{E^*, E^+\} \cup \{E.E, E+E^*\}$ evaluates to $\{E^*\}$ and the boolean expression $(E+F) \in \{(F+E), E^*, E.F\}$ evaluates to true), then the algorithm produces a so-called *minimal* DFA. If equality of regexes is sometimes or always interpreted strictly at a syntactical level, the algorithm still produces a valid, albeit non-minimal result. In practice,

---

[1]For notational convenience, we refrain from using more elaborate notation such as $R_\Sigma$ to explicitly reflect $R$'s dependence on $\Sigma$. Also note that some texts use $\cup$ instead of $+$ as a regex operator).

"similarity test" heuristics are applied to determine equality of regexes at the language level up to varying levels of accuracy [11]. Details of the similarity tests used in our implementations are beyond the scope of the present text [1, Def 5.2].

In our CSP specification, we rely on notation used in classical CSP texts to indicate a sequence of symbols. In that context $\langle\rangle$ indicates the empty sequence, $\langle x \rangle$ indicates the sequence consisting of the single symbol $x$, $\langle x \rangle^\frown s$ indicates the sequence resulting from appending symbol $x$ to the front of sequence $s$, and $s^\frown \langle y \rangle$ is the sequence resulting from adding symbol $y$ to the tail end of sequence $s$.

### 10.2.2. *Automata*

A deterministic finite automaton (DFA), $\mathcal{D}$, is conventionally represented by a quintuple, say $(D, \Sigma, \delta, S, F)$. Here $D$ is the set of $\mathcal{D}$'s states; $\Sigma$ is its alphabet; $\delta$ is a transition function (not necessarily total) that maps a state and an alphabet symbol to a state; $S \subseteq D$ a singleton set containing the start state; and $F \subseteq D$ is the set of final states[2]. A DFA $\mathcal{D}$ can be represented as a (transition) graph. Each node of the transition graph corresponds to a state in $D$. The graph has an arc labelled by symbol $a$ from state $p$ to state $q$ iff $\delta(a, p) = q$. The language of a DFA is defined in terms of its *extended transition function* $\delta^* : Q \times \Sigma^* \to Q$.

$$\delta^*(q, w) = \begin{cases} q, & \text{if } w = \varepsilon; \\ \delta^*(\delta(q, a), v), & \text{if } w = av \text{ where } a \in \Sigma \text{ and } v \in \Sigma^*. \end{cases}$$

The right language of a state $q \in D$ is defined as

$$\overrightarrow{\mathcal{L}}(\mathcal{D}, q) = \{w \mid \delta^*(q, w) \in F\}$$

The language of DFA $\mathcal{D}$, $\mathcal{L}(\mathcal{D})$, is then defined as the right language of the start state, $s \in S$, namely $\overrightarrow{\mathcal{L}}(\mathcal{D}, s)$.

The symbol $\mathcal{L}$ is thus used as an overloaded function, because $\mathcal{L}(\mathcal{D})$ denotes the language of DFA $\mathcal{D}$, whereas $\mathcal{L}(E)$ denotes the language of the regular expression $E$.

---

[2]For algorithmic elegance, we have slightly modified the conventional notation. It is more common to use the symbol $Q$ instead of $D$ to represent the set of states and to use $s$ to represent the start state explicitly rather than the singleton set $S$ to represent it implicitly.

### 10.2.3. *CSP*

CSP is concerned with specifying a system of communicating sequential processes (hence the CSP acronym) in terms of sequences of events, called traces. In the CSP paradigm one event occurs either before or after another, but never contemporaneously. Thus events are considered to be atomic. Processes are envisaged to engage with events in their environment. Because events are atomic, such engagement abstracts away from time entirely, so that the engagement may be considered to be instantaneous. In CSP, therefore, only the notions of "before" and "after" are relevant in discussing events and their sequencing (or traces). Various operators are available to describe the sequence in which events may occur, as well as to connect processes. Table 10.2.3 summarises the CSP operators used in this article.

Table 10.2.    Selected CSP operators and operands.

| | |
|---|---|
| $a \to P$ | event $a$ **then** process $P$ |
| $a \to P \mid b \to Q$ | $a$ then $P$ **choice** $b$ then $Q$ |
| $x : A \to P(x)$ | **set choice** of $x$ from set $A$ then $P(x)$ |
| $P \square Q$ | process $P$ **external choice** process $Q$ |
| $P \parallel Q$ | $P$ in **parallel** with $Q$ |
| | Synchronize on common events in the alphabet of $P$ and $Q$ |
| $P \mid\mid\mid Q$ | $P$ **interleaved** with $Q$ |
| | No synchronizing on any events; $P$ and $Q$ run independently |
| $P \,;Q$ | process $P$ **followed by** process $Q$ |

While full details of the operator semantics and laws for their manipulation are available in [5, 4] we provide a little more background information about these operators and their operands here.

The names of the operations illustrated in Table 10.2.3 are in bold. Generally, these are infix binary operators, having events, a set of events or processes as operands. Processes may be named without parameters (e.g., $P$) or with parameters (e.g., $P(x)$). Processes may also be anonymous. In this case, a specification is given between parentheses — for example as $(a \to P)$ — but the specified process has no name. Note that *SKIP* designates a special process that engages in no further event, but that simply terminates successfully.

The **then** operator, $\to$, takes an event as its left operand and a process as its right operand. It specifies a process that engages with the left operand event when that event occurs in the process's environment and subsequently behaves as the process in its right operand.

The **choice** operator has a special syntax in that its operands are neither events nor processes. Instead, it serves as an operator having two (or even a sequence of) disjoint then-specifications as operators. It is used to define a process that initially engages with the first event in one of the then-specification operands. Thereafter it behaves as the process indicated in the relevant then-specification's right hand side. Thus, the specification $a \rightarrow P \mid b \rightarrow Q$ specifies a process that either engages in $a$ and then behaves as $P$ or engages in $b$ and then behaves as $Q$, depending on whether $a$ or $b$ occur first in the environment[3].

The **set choice** operator is merely syntactic sugar for the choice operator—i.e., the following have identical semantics:

$$a \rightarrow P(a) \mid b \rightarrow P(b) \mid c \rightarrow P(c) \text{ and } x : \{a, b, c\} \rightarrow P(x)$$

The **external choice** operator is similar to the choice operator, but takes processes as operands. This frees the specifier from explicitly naming the first possible event to occur in the operand processes.

A process, say $R$, specified as a **parallel** synchronisation of other processes, for example $R = (x : A \rightarrow P(x)) \parallel (y : B \rightarrow Q(y))$, means the following. If the environment offers an event $z \in (A \cap B)$, then $R$ engages in that event and subsequently behaves as the process $P(z) \parallel Q(z)$. However, if the environment offers an event $z \notin (A \cap B)$ then $R$ results in deadlock.

In contrast, a process, say $R$, specified as the **interleaving** of other processes, for example $R = P \mid\mid\mid Q$, means processes $P$ and $Q$ engage with events in the environment entirely independently of one another. Suppose, for example, $R$ is specified as $(x : A \rightarrow P(x)) \mid\mid\mid (y : B \rightarrow Q(y))$. In this case, if an event $z \in (A \backslash B)$ is offered by the environment, then $R$'s subsequent behaviour is described by $P(z) \mid\mid\mid (y : B \rightarrow Q(y))$. Dually, if an event $z \in (B \backslash A)$ is offered by the environment, then $R$'s subsequent behaviour is described b $(x : A \rightarrow P(x)) \mid\mid\mid Q(z)$. Finally, if an event $z \in (A \cap B)$ is offered by the environment, then $R$'s subsequent behaviour is nondeterministic, either being described by $P(z) \mid\mid\mid (y : B \rightarrow Q(y))$ or by $(x : A \rightarrow P(x)) \mid\mid\mid Q(z)$.

In the process specification $R = P \, ; Q$, the **followed by** operator is used to specify process $R$ that behaves as process $P$ until $P$ terminates successfully. Thereafter, process $R$ behaves as process $Q$.

---

[3]Here and elsewhere, we ignore the complication that could arise if the environment offers an event in which more than one operand is ready to engage. This takes us into the realm of non-determinism. CSP has very precise semantics to deal with non-determinism, but it is beyond the scope of this text. See [5, 4] for further elaboration.

CSP allows for the notion of **channels** as part of a process's environment. Channels synchronously connect processes to one another. Each channel has a specific alphabet determining events (or messages) that are communicated across it. If $b$ designates a channel and $e$ is an element of its alphabet, then $e$ is an event that can occur on this channel. The notation $b!e$ indicates that event $e$ is to be output on channel $b$. Dually, the notation $b?x$ indicates that any one of the events in the alphabet of $b$ is to be input (received) on channel $b$ into variable $x$. This channel notation is used to specify a special case of parallel synchronisation as in the process $R = (b!e \rightarrow P) \parallel (b?x \rightarrow Q(x))$. Here, $R$ is a process that engages in the event $e$ and thereafter behaves as the process $P \parallel Q(e)$. This can also be interpreted as processes communicating the message $e$ over the channel $b$. The one process writes $e$ onto channel $b$ and the other process reads from channel $b$ into variable $x$.

The CSP syntax allows for the specification of new instance of a process $R$ using a label, say $\ell$. Thus $\ell! : R$ is a process defined by $R$, but with each channel named in $R$, say $c$, renamed to $\ell! : c$. Thus, for example, $\big\|\big\|_{i \in [0,N)} \ell_i : R$ represents the interleaving of $N$ processes defined according the template definition in $R$, but with channels labelled by $\ell_0, \ell_1, \ldots, \ell_{N-1}$ respectively.

The syntax **if** $C$ **then** $P$ **else** $Q$ **fi** specifies a process that behaves as process $P$ if the Boolean expression $C$ is true and behaves as process $Q$ otherwise.

In deploying CSP, we have made the following assumptions relating to atomic execution. Firstly, if an event maps to a function call, then that function is assumed to be a sequence of code in the original sequential algorithm that runs uninterruptedly to completion on some processor. Furthermore, in the interest of conciseness and without loss of generality, it will sometimes be convenient to subsume certain assignment operations of the sequential program into the actual parameter list of a process invocation. For example, instead of specifying some recursive parameterised process $P(D)$ as

$$P(D) = \cdots (D := D \cup \{q\}) \, ; P(D)$$

we regard the specification

$$P(D) = \cdots P(D \cup \{q\})$$

as equivalent. This means that operations that are needed to compute the actual parameters for a process invocation are regarded as taking place atomically, i.e., they cannot be interrupted by any other process's activity.

Similarly, where the CSP syntax for a conditional is used, as in

$$\textbf{if } C \textbf{ then } P \textbf{ else } Q \textbf{ fi}$$

it is assumed that the computation of the condition, $C$, takes place atomically and prior to the activation of any first event possible in the constituent processes, $P$ and $Q$. This is the case, for example, where similarity between regular expressions has to be computed as in a Boolean expression such as $d \notin (D \cup T)$ where $d$ is a regex and $D$ and $T$ are sets of regexes.

These instances of atomic activity are highlighted, not because they deviate from CSP syntax, but because they represent potential opportunities for a more fine-grained specification of the algorithm than is given in the various parallel specifications to follow.

## 10.3. Sequential Algorithm

Brzozowski's DFA construction algorithm [1] employs derivatives of regexes to construct a DFA. The algorithm takes a regex $E$ as input and constructs a DFA $\mathcal{D}$ such that $\mathcal{L}(\mathcal{D}) = \mathcal{L}(E)$.

The algorithm identifies each DFA state with a regex. Elements of $D$ may therefore interchangeably be referred to either as regexes or as states, depending on the context of the discussion. The start state corresponds to the input regex, $E$. Each remaining state is identified with a regex, say $d$, such that if $\delta(a, q) = d$ then $d$ corresponds with the derivative $a^{-1}q$. In fact, it can be shown that the language of each state's associated regex is also the right language of that state.

The well-known sequential version of the algorithm is given in Dijkstra's guarded command language [2] in Figure 10.1 and is called *SBRZ*. The notation assumes that the set operations carried out on regexes ensure 'uniqueness' of the elements at some unspecified level of *similarity*. (Refer to Subsection 10.2.1.)

*SBRZ* maintains two sets of regexes (or states): a set $T$ ('to do') containing the regexes for which derivatives need to be calculated; and another set $D$ ('done') containing the regexes for which derivatives have been found already. When the algorithm terminates, $T$ is empty and $D$ contains the states of the automaton which recognises $\mathcal{L}(E)$.

*SBRZ* iterates through all the elements $q \in T$, finding derivatives with respect to all the alphabet symbols and depositing these new states (regexes) into $T$ in those cases where no similar regex has already been deposited into $T \cup D$.

**func** $SBRZ(E, \Sigma) \rightarrow$
   $\delta, S, F := \varnothing, \{E\}, \varnothing;$
   $D, T := \varnothing, S;$
   **do** $(T \neq \varnothing) \rightarrow$
      **let** $q$ be some state such that $q \in T$;
      $D, T := D \cup \{q\}, T \setminus \{q\};$
      { *build out-transitions from $q$ on all alphabet symbols* }
      **for** $(\alpha : \Sigma) \rightarrow$
         { *find derivative of $q$ with respect to $\alpha$* }
         $d := \alpha^{-1}q;$
         **if** $d \notin (D \cup T) \rightarrow T := T \cup \{d\}$
         ▯   $d \in (D \cup T) \rightarrow$ **skip**
         **fi**;
         { *Update function $\delta$ to make a transition from $q$ to $d$ on $\alpha$* }
         $\delta := \delta \cup \{\langle\langle q, \alpha \rangle, d\rangle\};$
      **rof**;
      **if** $\varepsilon \in \mathcal{L}(q) \rightarrow F := F \cup \{q\}$
      ▯   $\varepsilon \notin \mathcal{L}(q) \rightarrow$ **skip**
      **fi**
   **od**;
   **return** $(D, \Sigma, \delta, S, F)$
**cnuf**

Fig. 10.1.   Brzozowski's DFA construction algorithm.

Each $q$, once processed in this fashion, is then removed from $T$ and added into $D$.

In each iteration of the inner **for** loop (i.e., for each alphabet symbol), the $\delta$ relation is updated to contain the mapping from state $q$ to its derivative $d$ with respect to the relevant alphabet symbol $\alpha$. Note that the function $\delta$ is treated here as a set of pairs, the first element of the pair being itself the pair $\langle q, \alpha \rangle$ and the second element being the $d$.

Finally, if state $q$ represents a regex whose language contains the empty string[4], $\varepsilon$, then that state is included in the set of final states $F$. Thus, states corresponding to regexes such as $\varepsilon$ or $r_1 + \varepsilon$ would be designated as final

---

[4]Such a regex is called "nullable".

states because $\varepsilon$ is in the languages of the respective regexes. (Table 10.1 indicates that $\mathcal{L}(\varepsilon) = \{\varepsilon\}$ and $\mathcal{L}(r_1 + \varepsilon) = \mathcal{L}(r_1) \cup \{\varepsilon\}$.)

In the forthcoming sections we present five different process-oriented specifications of *SBRZ*. These are referred to as *PBRZ0*, *PBRZ1*, ..., *PBRZ4*, respectively. In each case, the specification is structured as a number of communicating sequential processes that may be executed in parallel, communicating through specified synchronous channels.

## 10.4. *PBRZ0*

The original parallel specification of *SBRZ* is called *PBRZ0*. It is the parallel composition of top-level processes, each process itself being composed of several other concurrent processes. On first considering how to parallelise the original sequential algorithm, this particular overall architectural structure suggested itself as a natural mapping. The resulting specification was proposed in a 2006 presentation to the Prague Stringology Conference[7]. It is presented here with some small modifications.

The specification is based on considering the following actions in the outer loop of *SBRZ*:

(1) Select $q$, the next state from $T$ to be processed.
(2) Do the following for each such $q$:

    (a) Use similarity tests to update $D$ and $T$ based on $q$
    (b) For each $\alpha \in \Sigma$ find the derivative, $\alpha^{-1}q$, as per the inner loop
    (c) Check $\mathcal{L}(q)$ to update $F$ if $q$ is a final state.

Notice that once action 1 has been carried out, actions 2a, 2b and 2c can take place in parallel. Indeed, action 1 can immediately be repeated, even before these other actions have completed. These actions can be embedded within parallel synchronised processes, and channels can be used to communicate information from one process to another to synchronise activities as necessary.

Three top level processes running in parallel[5] synchronicity were thus postulated. They were called *OUTER0*, *DERIVERS0* and *UPDATERS0*. The *PBRZ0* parallel specification of the Brzozowski algorithm is thus

$$PBRZ0(D,T) = OUTER0(D,T) \parallel DERIVERS0 \parallel UPDATERS0.$$

---

[5]In this text we do not deem it necessary to distinguish between the terms concurrent and parallel.

Note that the sets $D$ and $T$ are required as parameters for the *OUTER0* process, because they will be explicitly altered within this process. However, we assumed that these sets are globally available for read-only purposes within the other two processes, *DERIVERS0* and *UPDATERS0*. It will be convenient to regard the alphabet $\Sigma$ as well as the set of final states, $F$, and the transition function, $\delta$, as being globally available to all sub-processes of *PBRZ0*.

Furthermore, we also assumed that the initialising statement of the sequential algorithm (namely $\delta, S, F := \varnothing, \{E\}, \varnothing;$) is executed before the concurrent algorithm starts off. Given a regex, $E$, $PBRZ0(\varnothing, \{E\})$ is therefore intended to deliver identical results to $SBRZ(\{E\}, \Sigma)$.

Figure 10.2 provides a graphical representation of the structure of *PBRZ0*. The various processes in this figure and their interaction will be described in greater detail in the forthcoming subsections.

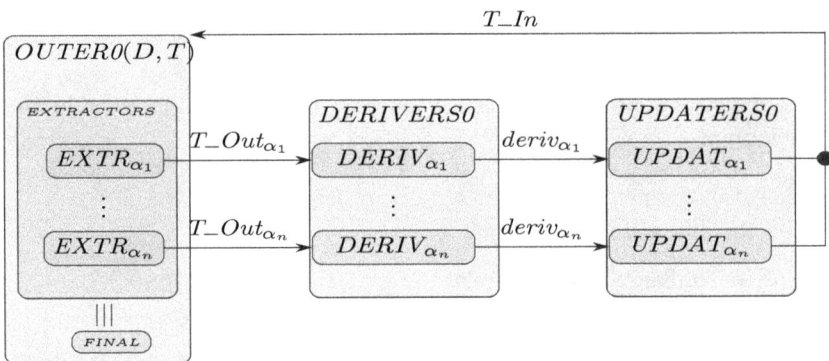

Fig. 10.2.   Graphical representation of the *PBRZ0* process.

### 10.4.1. *The OUTER0 Process*

The *OUTER0* process has these two sets as parameters, $D$ and $T$. As in the sequential case, $D$ contains all the regexes for which derivatives have been found to date and $T$ is the set of regexes for which derivatives are still to be found. The regexes in $D$ correspond to nodes in the DFA that is being constructed.

The *OUTER0* process is defined as follows in terms of a choice between two anonymous sub-processes.

$OUTER0(D, T) =$

$(\square_{q\in T}\,(\textit{T\_Out}!q \to$

$\qquad (\textit{EXTRACTORS}(q)\ |||\ \textit{FINAL}(q))\,;\,\textit{OUTER0}(D \cup \{q\}, T \setminus \{q\}))$

$\square$

$\qquad (\textit{T\_In}?d \to \textit{OUTER0}(D, T \cup \{d\}))$

The anonymous processes are operands of $\square$, the binary infix process choice operator. They appear as CSP process expressions enclosed between parenthesis before and after $\square$.

The first anonymous sub-process operand in the choice sends out on the *T\_Out* channel an arbitrary[6] regex, $q$ in $T$. Thereafter, the *OUTER0* process behaves as the parallel composition of two processes that take $q$ as a parameter: $\textit{EXTRACTORS}(q)$ and $\textit{FINAL}(q)$. This parallel composition has to run to completion before the *OUTER0* process repeats, now with $q$ added to $D$ and removed from $T$.

Before considering the details of the processes $\textit{EXTRACTORS}(q)$ and $\textit{FINAL}(q)$, consider the second anonymous sub-process operand of the $\square$ operator in *OUTER0*. This process monitors a channel called *T\_In*, inputting a regex $d$ from the channel whenever such an input becomes available. Thereafter *OUTER0* repeats with $d$ added to $T$. Again, we assume that this set union operation is atomic. This corresponds to the part in the sequential algorithm where the derivative $d$ is added to $T$ inside the inner loop.

Now consider the two sub-processes within the first anonymous process of *OUTER0*, namely *EXTRACTORS* and *FINAL*. These are specified as executing as a parallel composition.

We begin with *EXTRACTORS*. Its purpose is to express the fact that its parameter $q$ has to be broadcast to a set of processes, each of which will independently compute the derivative of $q$ with respect to a different symbol in $\Sigma$. To model this, *EXTRACTORS* is specified as the parallel interleaving of a set of processes $\textit{EXTR}_{\alpha_i}$, there being one such process for each $\alpha_i$ in $\Sigma$. Here we use the subscript $\alpha_i$ in the process's name, *EXTR*, to indicate a process that has the value of $\alpha_i$ available as a local constant:

$$\textit{EXTRACTORS}(q) =|||_{\alpha_i:\Sigma} \textit{EXTR}_{\alpha_i}(q)$$

Each $\textit{EXTR}_{\alpha_i}$ process outputs, entirely independently of its peer processes, its parameter, $q$, along its own channel, $\textit{T\_Out}_{\alpha_i}$, and then terminates

---

[6]This random choice is also expressed by using the external choice operator indexed over the set $T$, i.e., by $\square_{q\in T}$.

successfully. The CSP specification to express this is as follows:

$$EXTR_{\alpha_i}(q) = (T\_Out_{\alpha_i}!q \to SKIP)$$

As will be seen a little later, for each alphabet symbol $\alpha_i$ in $\Sigma$, the process $EXTR_{\alpha_i}(q)$ has a companion process, $DERIV_{\alpha_i}$. Each $DERIV_{\alpha_i}$ process will receive the outputted $q$ on the associated $T\_Out_{\alpha_i}$ channel.

The FINAL process checks whether or not $\epsilon \in \mathcal{L}(q)$. If this is indeed the case, then FINAL adds $q$ to the set of final states and terminates successfully; otherwise FINAL terminates successfully without engaging in any action:

$$FINAL(q) = \text{if} \, (\varepsilon \in \mathcal{L}(q)) \, \text{then} \, F := F \cup \{q\} \, \text{else} \, SKIP$$

Note that the set of events that take place in EXTRACTORS and FINAL are disjoint. The parallel composition of these two processes can therefore be described by the arbitrary interleaving of their respective event trace sets.

### 10.4.2. The DERIVERS0 Process

The DERIVERS0 process finds, in parallel, the derivatives of a regex with respect to each of the symbols $\alpha_i \in \Sigma$. The objective is to define DERIVERS0 in such a way that each of its sub-processes can resume computing yet another derivative for a given alphabet symbol as soon as its task is complete, independently of the progress of its peer sub-processes. Here, a first order definition of DERIVERS0 is given that does not fully meet this objective. This objective can be achieved by a simple refinement of the overall specification, as will be discussed later.

For present purposes, process DERIVERS0 is taken as the parallel interleaving over $\alpha_i \in \Sigma$ of the sub-processes denoted as $DERIV_{\alpha_i}$, i.e.,

$$DERIVERS0 = |||_{\alpha_i \Sigma} DERIV_{\alpha_i}$$

where each sub-process $DERIV_{\alpha_i}$ receives input on its associated channel $T\_Out_{\alpha_i}$ of the regex, $q$, whose derivative with respect to $\alpha_i$ is needed. It then emits on channel $deriv_{\alpha_i}$ the pair consisting of $q$ and the associated derivative of $q$ with respect to $\alpha_i$. Then it repeats itself.

$$DERIV_{\alpha_i} = T\_Out_{\alpha_i}?q \to deriv_{\alpha_i}!(q, \alpha_i^{-1}q) \to DERIV_{\alpha_i}$$

Recall that the regex data received on channel $T\_Out_{\alpha_i}$ is put there by process $EXTR_{\alpha_i}$. Thus, in theory, the sub-processes $DERIV_{\alpha_i}$ and $EXTR_{\alpha_i}$ can synchronise independently on events on channel $T\_Out_{\alpha_i}$ and run ahead of a pair of their peer sub-processes, say $DERIV_{\alpha_j}$ and $EXTR_{\alpha_j}$. However, a fresh regex, $q$, can only be offered to $DERIV_{\alpha_i}$ via $EXTR_{\alpha_i}$ once its parent process, $EXTRACTORS$, has completed, since only then can the recursive call to $OUTER0$ take place. Unfortunately, $EXTRACTORS$ can only complete once *all* its constituent sub-processes have completed. So in practice, the potential gains to be had from parallelism at this level cannot be realised under the current specification. This deficiency will be further addressed in subsection 10.5.1, where a buffer will be placed on each of these channels.

### 10.4.3. *The UPDATERS0 Process*

The $UPDATERS0$ process is designed to receive a regex and its derivative with respect to $\alpha_i$ as a pair $(q, d)$ from each $deriv_{\alpha_i}$ channel. This is to happen independently of the state of readiness to receive some other regex and derivative pair on an alternative channel, say $deriv_{\alpha_j}$. In each case, the pair is passed on for updating $\delta$ and the derivative is considered for possible updating of $T$.

The $UPDATERS0$ process is specified as the parallel interleaving of $UPDAT_{\alpha_i}$ processes for each $\alpha_i$ in $\Sigma$. This can be expressed as follows:

$$UPDATERS0 = |||_{\alpha_i : \Sigma} \; UPDAT_{\alpha_i}$$

After receiving the regex and derivative pair on the $deriv_{\alpha_i}$ channel, each $UPDAT_{\alpha_i}$ process behaves as the parallel interleaving of two sub-processes. One, called $UPT_{\alpha_i}$, corresponds to the action of conditionally adding the derivative to $T$. The other, called $UPD_{\alpha_i}$, corresponds to the action of unconditionally updating $\delta$.

$$UPDAT_{\alpha_i} = (deriv_{\alpha_i}?\langle q, d \rangle \rightarrow (UPT_{\alpha_i}(d) \;|||\; UPD_{\alpha_i}(\langle q, d \rangle)) \;) \;; UPDAT_{\alpha_i}$$

$UPT_{\alpha_i}(d)$ establishes whether or not $d$ is in $D \cup T$. If it is, then $UPT_{\alpha_i}$ simply terminates successfully. Otherwise, it outputs $d$ on the $T\_In$ channel, thus feeding $d$ back to $OUTER0$ where $d$ is added to $T$. After this, the sub-process terminates successfully.

$$UPT_{\alpha_i}(d) = \text{if } (d \notin (D \cup T)) \text{ then } T\_In!d \rightarrow SKIP \text{ else } SKIP$$

$UPD_{\alpha_i}$ unconditionally updates $\delta$ and then terminates. The relation is updated by adding an entry into $\delta$ that represents a transition from $q$ to $d$ as a result of symbol $\alpha_i$. This is depicted here:

$$UPD_{\alpha_i}(q, d) = \delta := \delta \cup \{\langle \langle q, \alpha_i \rangle, d \rangle\}$$

Note that $UPDAT_{\alpha_i}$ starts again after the two sub-processes terminate successfully. Only then will a given $UPDAT_{\alpha_i}$ sub-process be ready to input another $\langle q, d \rangle$ pair from its respective $deriv_{\alpha_i}$ channel. Once more, each of the $deriv_{\alpha_i}$ channels could be modelled as a buffer. This would ensure that any holdup in the execution of sub-processes $UPT_{\alpha_i}$ and $UPD_{\alpha_i}$ (in particular, the computation of the Boolean result of the condition in $UPT_{\alpha_i}$) will not delay $DERIV\alpha_i$ in providing more data to the buffer on channel $deriv_{\alpha_i}$. However, in the interests of simplicity, this will not be modelled here. Instead, we illustrate in the next section how the idea of buffering can be included between the $DERIV_{\alpha_i}$ and $EXTR_{\alpha_i}$ processes, as previously suggested.

### 10.5.  PBRZ1

In $PBRZ0$ channel $deriv_{\alpha_i}$ connects process $DERIV_{\alpha_i}$ and process $EXTR_{\alpha_i}$. CSP channels are synchronous, meaning when $EXTR_{\alpha_i}$ is ready to output a message (a regex) onto this channel, it cannot do so until the receiving process, $DERIV_{\alpha_i}$, is ready to input the message. This implies that $EXTRACTORS$ will only terminate once $q$ has been read by all the $DERIV_{\alpha_i}$ processes. Only once all the $EXTR_{\alpha_i}$ processes have terminated successfully does a new recursive instance of the $OUTER0$ process start up and only then will this new instance of $OUTER0$ produce another $q$. So if, for example, there is a very slow $DERIV_{\alpha_i}$ process, all the others will have to wait for it to complete before continuing. This is clearly not desirable. Work for any process should ideally be produced at least as fast as it can consume the work.

For this reason it was decided to connect each $DERIV_{\alpha_i}$ and $EXTR_{\alpha_i}$ process through a dedicated buffer. New $q$'s can then be placed into the buffers without having to wait for all the $DERIV_{\alpha_i}$ processes to complete.

### 10.5.1.  The BUFFERS Process

As suggested in [5], a buffer may be modelled using a process called $BUFF$. It behaves like a queue—messages enter at a left channel and exit on a right channel in the same order in which they arrived.

$$BUFF = P_{\langle\rangle} \quad \text{where}$$
$$P_{\langle\rangle} = left?x \rightarrow P_{\langle x \rangle}$$
$$P_{\langle x \rangle ^\frown s} = (left?y \rightarrow P_{\langle x \rangle ^\frown s ^\frown \langle y \rangle} \mid right!x \rightarrow P_s)$$

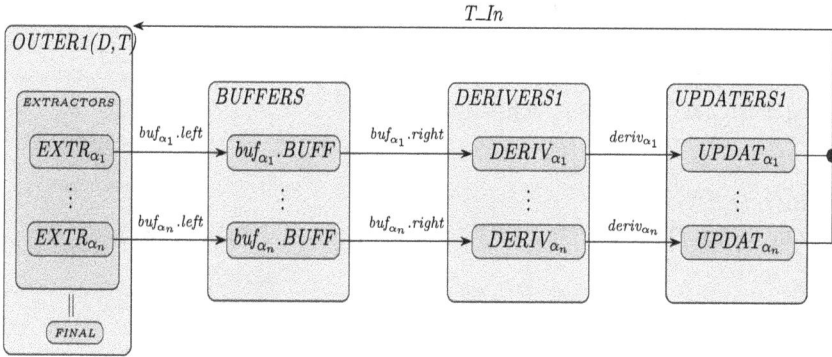

Fig. 10.3.   Graphical representation of the *PBRZ1* process.

Since each pair of processes, $EXTR_{\alpha_i}$ and $DERIV_{\alpha_i}$, is to be connected through a buffer, multiple labelled copies of the *BUFF* process are required. By CSP convention, the labelled process $buf_{\alpha_i}$:*BUFF* is defined exactly as *BUFF*, except that channel names in *BUFF* are prepended by the label used, in this case the symbol $buf_{\alpha_i}$.

As a matter of convenience we will define a process called *BUFFERS* as the interleaved composition of all these labelled *BUFF* processes:

$$BUFFERS \ = \ |||_{\alpha_i:\Sigma} \ (buf_{\alpha_i}:BUFF)$$

The remaining step is to modify the respective definitions of the $DERIV_{\alpha_i}$ and $EXTR_{\alpha_i}$ processes so that each pair interacts through its respective buffer. Each $EXTR_{\alpha_i}(q)$ sub-process is defined to repeatedly pass on data (the next $q$ it receives from its parent process) on the left channel of its associated buffer:

$$EXTR_{\alpha_i}(q) = (buf_{\alpha_i}.left!q \rightarrow SKIP)$$

Note that $q$ will be received on the same channel, $buf_{\alpha_i}.left$, that is referenced in the process $buf_{\alpha_i}$:*BUFF*. This is because, as just indicated above, $buf_{\alpha_i}$:*BUFF* is defined precisely as *BUFF*, except that all channel references in *BUFF*, including channel *left*, are to be prepended by the label, $buf_{\alpha_i}$.

Dually, each corresponding $DERIV_{\alpha_i}$ sub-process is defined to repeatedly input data (a regex, $q$) from the right channel of its associated buffer and deposit that data on channel $next_{\alpha_i}$:

$$DERIV_{\alpha_i} = buf_{\alpha_i}.right?q \rightarrow deriv_{\alpha_i}!(q, \alpha_i^{-1}q) \rightarrow DERIV_{\alpha_i}$$

### 10.5.2. Putting Everything Together

A complete system that can be built from the preceding processes is designated $PBRZ1(D,T)$. It is defined as follows:


$PBRZ1(D,T) =$
  $OUTER1(D,T) \parallel BUFFERS \parallel DERIVERS1 \parallel UPDATERS1$


Here the definition $UPDATERS1$ is precisely the same as that of $UPDATERS0$ given in the previous section. The definitions of $OUTER1$(D,T) and $DERIVERS1$ are structurally the same as those of $OUTER0$(D,T) and $DERIVERS0$ respectively. However, as will clearly be seen by comparing Figures 10.2 and 10.3, all references to channel $T\_Out_{\alpha_i}$ in $OUTER0$(D,T) should be replaced by $buff_{\alpha_i}.left$ in $OUTER1$(D,T). Similarly, all references to channel $T\_Out_{\alpha_i}$ in $DERIVERS0$ should be replaced by $buff_{\alpha_i}.right$ in $DERIVERS1$.

$PBRZ1(\varnothing, \{E\})$ is therefore also a concurrent specification of the sequential algorithm given in Figure 10.1. We would expect its implementation to be a more efficient alternative to $PBRZ0(\varnothing, \{E\})$. Figure 10.3 depicts the major constituent processes of $PBRZ1$. It should be clear from the diagram that each $EXTR_{\alpha_i}$, $DERIV_{\alpha_i}$ pair is now connected via a buffer.

Note that a set of buffer pairs can easily and analogously be defined to operate between the $DERIV_{\alpha_i}$ and $UPDAT_{\alpha_i}$ process pairs. We refrain from presenting those details here.

After proposing CSP specifications $PBRZ0$ and $PBRZ1$ for $SBRZ$, an investigation into a suitable implementation language was launched. For various reasons[7] it was decided to rely on Go. However, once mapping from specification to implementation started, it was realised that the gap between these two specifications and the implementation language was rather wide. In addition, various modifications to the overall structure of the specifications suggested themselves as likely to enhance the efficiency of the implemented versions. These are discussed in the forthcoming sections.

---

[7]Reasons for deciding on Go include the fact that it supports light-weight processes called go-routines, and that it contains typed channels as part of the language. Further reasons include the fact that Go allows one to easily create custom data structures and Go documentation is readily available.

## 10.6. *PBRZ2*

The next CSP parallel specification version of *SBRZ* resulted from inter-
actively adapting and evolving *PBRZ1* until a specification was obtained
that was more closely aligned with the Go implementation language. The
resulting specification is designated *PBRZ2*. Initial empirical results of the
Go version of this specification (as well as its successor to be discussed
below) were published in [9].

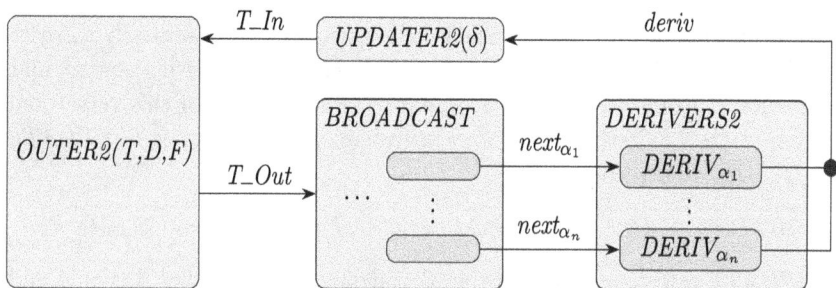

Fig. 10.4.   The communications network of the *PBRZ2* process.

*PBRZ2* is now composed of *four* concurrent processes. The *OUTER2*
process that corresponds to the outer loop of the algorithm in Figure 10.1
is retained, but in modified form as will be discussed. The second process, *DERIVERS2*, is also retained from the earlier versions and computes
the derivatives of regular expressions. A new process called *BROADCAST*
is now responsible for distributing a given regular expression from $T$ to
the components of *DERIVERS2*. The final process *UPDATER2* mod-
ifies the transition relation $\delta$ and is a simplified version of the earlier
*UPDATERS1* process. Figure 10.4 shows the communicating processes
of *PBRZ2*, along with their associated connecting channels. The process
definition for *PBRZ2* is given by:

$PBRZ2(T, D, F, \delta) =$
    $OUTER2(T, D, F) \parallel BROADCAST \parallel DERIVERS2 \parallel UPDATER(\delta)$

Notice that in addition to *PBRZ1*'s $T$ and $D$ parameters, *PBRZ2* has two
more parameters, $F$ and $\delta$. Also note that *PBRZ2* no longer relies on buffers
as did *PBRZ1*.

### 10.6.1. *The OUTER2 Process*

In the *OUTER2* process, an initial event, *init*, makes explicit the fact that certain initialising actions are needed in the Go program. Thereafter, the process repeatedly performs actions to modify $T$, $D$, and $F$.

$$OUTER2(T, D, F) = init \rightarrow OUTER2'(T,D,F)$$

This repetition is modelled by the process that is called *OUTER2'*. It is a refactored version of the previously defined *OUTER0* process. The *OUTER0* process had a choice between two behaviours. These were modelled as anonymous processes. The two behaviours were essentially to write $q \in T$ to a *T_Out* channel, update $F$ and repeat; or to receive a new regular expression $d$ from channel *T_In*, update $T$ and repeat. In this refactored version of *OUTER0* the anonymous processes are given names *F_UPDATE* and *T_UPDATE* respectively.

$$OUTER2'(T, D, F) = F\_UPDATE(T, D, F) \ \square \ T\_UPDATE(T, D, F)$$

*F_UPDATE* selects a regex $q$ from $T$, outputs it on channel *T_Out!q* and then behaves as process *FINAL*.

$$F\_UPDATE(T, D, F) = \square_{q \in T} (T\_Out!q \rightarrow FINAL(q, T, D, F))$$

As before, *FINAL* updates $F$. The description of the update actions marginally differs from the earlier one. Here, a recursive call to *OUTER2'* removes $q$ from $T$ and adds $q$ to $D$. As before, $q$ is also added into $F$ if $\varepsilon \in \mathcal{L}(q)$.

$$FINAL(q, T, D, F) = \text{if} \, \varepsilon \in \mathcal{L}(q) \, \text{then} \, OUTER2'(T \setminus \{q\}, D \cup \{q\}, F \cup \{q\})$$
$$\text{else} \, OUTER2'(T \setminus \{q\}, D \cup \{q\}, F))$$

*T_UPDATE* receives new regexes from the *T_In* channel and initiates a recursive call to *OUTER2'* conditionally updating $T$ if the regex is neither in $T$ or $D$:

$$T\_UPDATE(T, D, F) = T\_In?d \rightarrow$$
$$\text{if} \, d \notin T \cup D \, \text{then} \, OUTER2'(T \cup \{d\}, D, F)$$
$$\text{else} \, OUTER2'(T, D, F)$$

### 10.6.2. *The BROADCAST Process*

The *BROADCAST* process connects *OUTER2'* and *DERIVERS2*. It is responsible for communicating the regular expressions from *OUTER2'* to each $DERIV_{\alpha_i}$ process. It does this by repeatedly reading a regular expression, $q$, from its input channel $T\_Out$ and "broadcasting" it to the $|\Sigma|$ output channels $next_{\alpha_1}, next_{\alpha_1}, \ldots, next_{\alpha_{|\Sigma|}}$. Note that for each $\alpha_i \in \Sigma$, the channel $next_{\alpha_i}$ corresponds to the channel $buf_{\alpha_i}.right$ used in *PBRZ1*.

$$BROADCAST = (T\_Out?q \rightarrow |||_{\alpha_i:\Sigma} (next_{\alpha_i}!q \rightarrow SKIP)) ; BROADCAST$$

The semantics of the above specification is as follows. After $q$ has been received on channel $T\_Out$ it is copied onto *each* of the channels $next_{\alpha_1}, next_{\alpha_1}, \ldots, next_{\alpha_{|\Sigma|}}$. The interleaved operator expresses two facts.

(1) Each and every channel $next_{\alpha_i}$ receives a copy of $q$ to send out further.
(2) The order of arrival of these copies at the various $next_{\alpha_i}$ channels is not pre-specified. Each channel is served a copy of $q$ when it is ready to receive it. If more than one $next_{\alpha_i}$ channel is ready to receive a copy of $q$, then one of these is non-deterministically chosen to receive its copy first, and then the next is non-deterministically chosen, etc.

Once a $next_{\alpha_i}$ channel has received its copy of $q$ and passed it on to its partner $DERIV_{\alpha_i}$ process, the anonymous process $(next_{\alpha_i}!q \rightarrow SKIP)$ terminates successfully. When all of these anonymous processes have terminated successfully, the $BROADCAST$ process repeats itself, sending on the next regular expression $q$ on offer on the $T\_Out$ channel.

### 10.6.3.  *The DERIVERS2 Process*

As before, *DERIVERS2* is responsible for calculating the derivatives of a given regular expression with respect to each alphabet symbol. This corresponds to the inner **for** loop in Figure 10.1. Again *DERIVERS2* is modelled as the concurrent interleaving of $|\Sigma|$ processes, each responsible for calculating the derivative with respect to a given $\alpha_i \in \Sigma$.

$$DERIVERS2 = |||_{\alpha_i:\Sigma} DERIV_{\alpha_i}$$

Each $DERIV_{\alpha_i}$ repeatedly reads a regular expression $q$ from its input channel $next_{\alpha_i}$ and then sends out the triple $\langle q, \alpha_i, \alpha_i^{-1}q \rangle$ on a channel *deriv*.

$$DERIV_{\alpha_i} = next_{\alpha_i}?q \rightarrow deriv!\langle q, \alpha_i, \alpha_i^{-1}q \rangle \rightarrow DERIV_{\alpha_i}$$

Note that, unlike in the specifications of *DERIVERS0* and *DERIVERS1* where there was a $deriv_{\alpha_i}$ channel for each $\alpha_i \in \Sigma$, in the present specification we choose to use single output channel *deriv*. Thus *deriv* is a multiplexed channel in the sense that it carries the output produced by all $DERIV_{\alpha_i}$ processes. Even though the channel is a shared resource, it can be written to in any arbitrary interleaved sequence, and the $|||$ operator used in *DERIVERS2* expresses this fact.

### 10.6.4. *The UPDATER2 Process*

In order to complete the DFA, we need to record all the state transitions in $\delta$. This is the responsibility of *UPDATER2*. It is modelled as a repeating process that reads a triple $\langle q, \alpha, d \rangle$ from the *deriv* channel and sends one element of the triple, $d$, on channel $T\_In$ to the previously described $T\_UPDATE$ subprocess of *OUTER2'*. *UPDATER2* then recurses, with $\delta$ now updated to incorporate $\langle \langle q, \alpha \rangle, d \rangle$ as one of its mapping elements. This update is expressed in the specification by using the set union operator.

$$UPDATER2(\delta) = deriv?\langle q, \alpha, d \rangle \rightarrow T\_In!d \rightarrow UPDATER2(\delta \cup \{\langle \langle q, \alpha \rangle, d \rangle\})$$

When the *PBRZ2* was implemented in Go, certain opportunities for further optimisation suggested themselves. These are discussed in the next specification.

### 10.7. *PBRZ3*

The *BROADCAST* process of *PBRZ2* selects one regex, $q$, from $T$ at a time and then arranges for $|\Sigma|$ processes to concurrently compute and pass on a derivative of $q$, each process determining the derivative with respect to one specific symbol from $\Sigma$. Only when all of these $|\Sigma|$ processes have run to completion can *BROADCAST* send out the next regex. This seemed unnecessarily restrictive.

Instead, a fourth variant of the *PBRZ* process, *PBRZ3*, defines a process that computes the derivatives of a given regex with respect to all the symbols in $\Sigma$. The variant requires that $N$ such processes are instantiated, each dealing with a different regex. Its communications network is similar to that of *PBRZ2* and is shown in Figure 10.5.

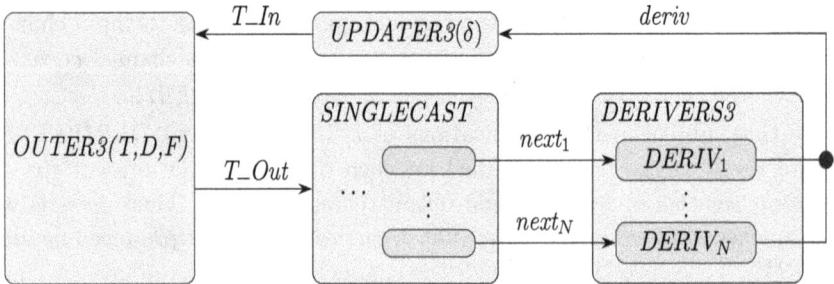

Fig. 10.5.   The communications network of the *PBRZ3* process.

The process definition for *PBRZ3* is therefore given by

$$PBRZ3(T, D, F, \delta) =$$
$$OUTER3(T, D, F) \parallel SINGLECAST \parallel DERIVERS3 \parallel UPDATER3(\delta)$$

Note that this specification differs from *PBRZ2* principally in that the *BROADCAST* process has been replaced with a process called *SINGLECAST*. It will be further described below. In this case *OUTER3*(T,D,F) is identical to *OUTER2*(T,D,F) as defined in Subsection 10.6.1 and *UPDATER3*($\delta$) is exactly as defined in Subsection 10.6.4 for *PBRZ2*.

### 10.7.1. *The SINGLECAST Process*

Figure 10.5 shows the *SINGLECAST* process and *DERIVERS3* process each having $N$ subprocesses and these subprocesses communicate through $N$ channels called $next_i$ where $i = 1, \ldots, N$. This is in contrast to the *BROADCAST* process and *DERIVERS3* process shown in Figure 10.3. In this latter case, the *BROADCAST* process and *DERIVERS3* process each have $|\Sigma|$ subprocesses and these communicate through $|\Sigma|$ channels called $next_{\alpha_i}$ where $\alpha_i \in \Sigma$.

The definition of *SINGLECAST* is as follows:

$$SINGLECAST =$$
$$(T\_Out?q \rightarrow (\underset{i:[0,N)}{\square} (next_i!q \rightarrow SKIP))) \,; SINGLECAST$$

Thus, unlike *BROADCAST*, when the *SINGLECAST* process receives a $q$ on the *T_Out* channel, it passes this $q$ to the first available $next_i$ channel[8]. Once the relevant anonymous process ($next_i!q \rightarrow SKIP$) has passed its received $q$ along its $next_i$ channel, it terminates successfully and *SINGLECAST* is immediately recursively called to retrieve the next available $q$. This activation of a single anonymous process at a time and immediately continuing to receive the next $q$ once it has completed, is expressed through the use of the external choice operator. Recall that the *BROADCAST* process relied on the use of the interleaving operator and this meant that all the relevant anonymous subprocesses had to run to completion before the next $q$ could be dealt with.

---

[8]If more than one $next_i$ channel is available, one is picked non-deterministically.

### 10.7.2.  The Revised DERIVERS3 Process

The definition of $DERIVERS3$ now requires slight modification in the indexing of processes—i.e., we now index over the integer set $[0, N)$ rather than over the alphabet $\Sigma$.

$$DERIVERS3 = |||_{i:[0,N)} \; DERIV_i$$

The $DERIV_i$ subprocesses could now be defined in one of several possible ways. Here is an example:

$$DERIV_i = (next_i?q \rightarrow |||_{\alpha_j:\Sigma} ADERIV_{\alpha_j}) \, ; DERIV_i$$

$$\text{where } ADERIV_{\alpha_j} = deriv!\langle q, \alpha_j, \alpha_j^{-1}q \rangle \rightarrow SKIP$$

This definition of $DERIV_i$ states that after inputting $q$, the derivatives of $q$ with respect to the various alphabet symbols should each be placed onto the $deriv$ channel in some interleaved fashion.

### 10.8.  PBRZ4

By pumping individually computed derivatives onto the $deriv$ channel under high load conditions, $PBRZ3$ is in danger of flooding the channel with short messages. An alternative approach is to collect the derivates of $q$ with respect to the various alphabet symbols into a set and then transmit the set on the $deriv$ channel. This is the fifth variant, $PBRZ4$, proposed here. Its high-level definition is analogous to what has gone before, namely:

$PBRZ4(T, D, F, \delta) =$
$\quad OUTER4(T, D, F) \parallel SINGLECAST \parallel DERIVERS4 \parallel UPDATER4(\delta)$

where the definition $SINGLECAST$ corresponds to its definition given in the previous section.

The high-level definition of $OUTER4$(T,D,F) corresponds identically to the high-level definition of s of $OUTER3$(T,D,F), which is, in turn, is identical to $OUTER2$(T,D,F) as defined in Subsection 10.6.1. However, a slight adaptation is required to one of the subprocesses, namely $T\_UPDATE$, as will be briefly explained below.

The definition of $DERIVERS4$, too, corresponds to the definition of $DERIVERS3$, namely

$$DERIVERS4 = |||_{i:[0,N)} \; DERIV_i$$

However, the definition of the $DERIV_i$ processes have to be slightly modified as follows:

$$DERIV_i = (next_i?q \rightarrow ADERIV_i(\Sigma, q, \emptyset, \emptyset)) \,;\, DERIV_i$$

$ADERIV_i(S, q, R, U) = $ if $S \neq \emptyset$

    then $\square_{\alpha \in S} ADERIV_i(S \setminus \{\alpha\}, q, R \cup \{\alpha^{-1}q\}, U \cup \{\langle\langle q, \alpha\rangle, \alpha^{-1}q\rangle\})$

    else $deriv!\langle R, U\rangle \rightarrow SKIP$

Thus, the new regexes to be conditionally added to $T$, namely $\{\alpha^{-1}q\}$, are collected in set $R$. Similarly, the transitions to be added to $\delta$, namely $\{\langle\langle q, \alpha\rangle, \alpha^{-1}q\rangle\}$, are collected in set $U$. These two sets are sent as a pair down channel *deriv*.

As before, this channel passes its data on to the *UPDATER4* process. However, because the data now arrives as a tuple of sets, $R$ and $U$, on the *deriv* channel, the definition of the *UPDATER4* process is slightly different from that of *UPDATER3* process, namely

$$UPDATER4(\delta) = deriv?\langle R, U\rangle \rightarrow T\_In!R \rightarrow UPDATER4(\delta \cup U)$$

Finally, the definition of one of the subprocesses of *OUTER4* has to be modified to receive a *set* of regexes, $R$, on the *T\_In* channel rather than an individual regex. This process is called *T\_UPDATE* and was previously defined in Subsection 10.6.1. The revised definition receives the regex set $R$ on the *T\_In* channel. Those regexes in $R$ that are not already in $D$ (i.e., $R\backslash D$) are then inserted into $T$ and *OUTER4* then recurses. The process may therefore be defined as:

$$T\_UPDATE(T, D, F) = T\_In?R \rightarrow OUTER4(T \cup (R\backslash D), D, F)$$

## 10.9. Conclusion

No doubt, we could offer several more parallel variants of *SBRZ*, incorporating buffers and alternative architectural arrangements. That would go beyond our present intention. This has been to highlight the use of CSP as an example of a relatively simple and expressive notation to support thinking about and inventing parallel algorithms.

We have therefore stuck to a fairly high-level, abstract specification of the task at hand. We have not used model checking tools such as FDR3 [3] to verify that our specifications are deadlock or livelock free. Neither have we used correctness checking features of CSP such as the hiding operator to verify formally that traces (or indeed failures or divergences) of refined specifications are compatible with those of the higher level abstractions from which they were derived.

Instead, the CSP and subsequent Go implementations (not described here) have iteratively evolved from one another. Our conclusion from this and other experiences is that the use of a process algebra such as CSP can significantly assist in developing the parallel implementations. However, we believe that this is precisely because we have eschewed an overly formal and rigorous enforcement of CSP. Our experience here is consistent with our experience in respect of using formal methods to evolve correct algorithms [6]: that formal methods can be of great practical value, provided that the formality is balanced with pragmatism.

In the present case, for example, had we insisted on putting each variant through a model checker and refining it until we were absolutely sure it was free from syntactic and semantic errors, we would significantly have delayed the actual implementation. Since the implementation of *PBRZ2* stimulated the features in *PBRZ3* and *PBRZ4*, we might never have arrived at these proposals. As a matter of fact, it is easy to see that if several processes were to be naïvely implemented, then they would never terminate. (*F_UPDATE*(T,D,F) in the various versions is one such example.) But the primary concern in the present specifications was to specify in CSP the principle architectural components of a parallel version of *SBRZ*. In the interests of simplicity, we therefore deliberately refrained from incorporating into the specifications features to model graceful termination.

Of course, in the actual Go implementations, termination could not be ignored. Go versions of *PBRZ2*, *PBRZ3* and *PBRZ4* have been tested and benchmarked. To date, only the results with respect to *PBRZ2* have been reported in the literature [9]. The results pertaining to *PBRZ3* and *PBRZ4* will be reported is due course. The broad picture to emerge is that modest speedups are usually attained by the various parallel versions. The speedup values are typically spread around the value of 2—sometimes more, sometimes less, depending on the data being processed. Furthermore, the speedup does not appear to depend significantly on the number of cores available nor on the various parallel versions. Deeper investigation of the reasons for this could lead to further revisions to the architectures used to date. However, we also note in passing that erratic exceptions in both directions have been found in the timing measurements — i.e., on some occasions the speedup factor is less than 1 and in other cases, it is greater than the number of processors. This points to potential deficiencies in the timing instruments and we conjecture that operating system influences are the root cause of the inaccuracies. Further investigations in this regard are under way.

# References

1. J. A. BRZOZOWSKI, Derivatives of regular expressions, *J. ACM* **11**,4 (1964), 481–494.
2. E. W. DIJKSTRA, *A Discipline of Programming*, Prentice Hall, 1976.
3. T. GIBSON-ROBINSON, P. ARMSTRONG, A. BOULGAKOV AND A. ROSCOE, FDR3 — a modern refinement checker for CSP, in *Tools and Algorithms for the Construction and Analysis of Systems*, pp. 187–201, *LNCS* vol. 8413, Springer, 2014.
4. C. A. R. HOARE, Communicating sequential processes, *Commun. ACM* **26**,1 (1983), 100–106.
5. C. A. R. HOARE, Communicating sequential processes (electronic version), 2004.
6. D. G. KOURIE AND B. W. WATSON, *The Correctness-by-Construction Approach to Programming*, Springer, 2012.
7. T. STRAUSS, D. G. KOURIE AND B. W. WATSON, A concurrent specification of Brzozowski's DFA construction algorithm, in *Proceedings of the Prague Stringology Conference, Prague, Czech Republic, August 28-30, 2006*, J. Holub and J. Zdárek (eds.), pp. 90–99, Department of Computer Science and Engineering, Faculty of Electrical Engineering, Czech Technical University, 2006.
8. T. STRAUSS, D. G. KOURIE AND B. W. WATSON, A concurrent specification of Brzozowski's DFA construction algorithm, *Int. J. Found. Comput. Sci.* **19**,1 (2008), 125–135.
9. T. STRAUSS, D. G. KOURIE, B. W. WATSON AND L. CLEOPHAS, A process-oriented implementation of Brzozowski's DFA construction algorithm, in *Proceedings of the Prague Stringology Conference 2014, Prague, Czech Republic, September 1-3, 2014*, J. Holub and J. Zdárek (eds.), pp. 17–29, Department of Theoretical Computer Science, Faculty of Information Technology, Czech Technical University in Prague, 2014.
10. T. STRAUSS, D. G. KOURIE, B. W. WATSON AND L. CLEOPHAS, Process-based Aho-Corasick failure function construction, in *Proceedings of Communicating Process Architectures (CPA) 2015, the 37th WoTUG conference on concurrent and parallel systems*, August 2015.
11. B. WATSON, M. FRISHERT AND L. CLEOPHAS, Combining regular expressions with near-optimal automata, in *Inquiries Into Words, Constraints And Contexts*, A. Arppe, L. Carlson, K. Lindén, J. Piitulainen, M. Suominen, M. Vainio, H. Westerlund and A. Yli-Jyrä (eds.), pp. 163–171, CSLI Studies in Computational Linguistics ONLINE, 2005.
12. D. ZIADI AND J.-M. CHAMPARNAUD, An optimal parallel algorithm to convert a regular expression into its Glushkov automaton, *Theoret. Comput. Sci.* **215**,1-2 (February 1999), 69–87.

# Chapter 11

# Programming Examples of Space-Filling Curves

Andrew L. Szilard

*Professor Emeritus*
*Dept. of Computer Science*
*Western University, London, Ont. Canada*
als@csd.uwo.ca

More than a hundred years ago, starting with G. Peano and followed by D. Hilbert, H. von Koch, and W. Sierpiński, mathematicians were forced to realize that curves of potentially infinite length could be constructed by iterating simple geometric transformation rules, that these curves could be approximated by fractured lines, and that some of these curves were space-filling, as they could be arbitrarily close to any point in a closed region of the plane, as if they were two-dimensional. These curves, while only mathematical curiosities at first, were termed monster curves for their peculiar properties, such as being nowhere differentiable. The study of these curves gave rise to some useful applications. L-systems and recursive turtle graphics made possible a concise definition, analysis and simple implementations of these curves, using only a few lines of code. Recursive tiling of planar regions is intimately related to these curves. A number of illustrated programming examples are given through graphical interpretation of L-systems.

## Contents

## 11.1. Introduction

The subject of space-filling curves is intriguing, not just for mathematicians and computer scientists, but also for artists, engineers and architects. Already during the period 1890–1920, the fascinating mathematical properties of these curves were studied intensely by G. Peano, D. Hilbert, W. Sierpiński and G. Pólya, among others. In 1967, B. Mandelbrot invented the word *fractal* to denote a recursively defined self-similar curve of potentially infinite length [9]. Following that, M. Gardner [5] reintroduced the subject for non-mathematicians in his articles in the journal *Scientific American* and popularized a space-filling curve, Flowsnake, newly discovered and named by W. Gosper. In 1968, A. Lindenmayer [8] introduced L-systems to study the growth structure of filamentous plants; later the system was adopted to model the development of complex higher plants and patterns in nature. In 1970's, A. Szilard, together with R. Quinton [18], used a graphical interpretation of L-systems to define a variety of space-filling curves. Their interpretations were based on using the primitives of the LOGO programming language popularized by S. Papert. P. Prusinkiewicz [12] used graphical interpretations of L-systems to model growth patterns of complex plants, space-filling curves and complex patterns in nature. In the late 1980's, M. Barnsley [3] used iterated systems of contracting functions to define fractals. Since the mid 1990's, books have been published detailing crucial defining mathematical properties of these curves. It is important to mention H. Sagan's book *Space-filling Curves* [13]. The 21st century brought a huge amount of digital image and animation content to the Internet. Space-filling curves have attracted a number of recent Peano disciples, who are proud to display their imaginative creations in their blog pages. In 2006, G. Allouche et al. [1] modelled a Sierpińskiesque Kolam design.

An attempt will be made here to give precise accounts of constructing some simple and some historically significant space-filling curves using the resources of the LOGO language. Furthermore, the concept of flow-tiles will be introduced, and concrete examples of this concept will also be implemented in LOGO. Flow-tiles are important in the construction of proofs of statements that describe certain properties of space-filling curves — properties such as self-avoidance — and proofs of the property that the fractured lines that approximate the space-filling curves can be arbitrary close to any point within a region of interest.

Tiles are used in decorative designs, such as that in the works of M. C. Escher, mosaics, Islamic art and architecture. Girih tiles are a remarkable set of tiles used in ancient Islamic decorative designs. The concept of mathematical tiling is an important subject in formal systems, combinatorics and logic. A formal tile-set is a set of polygons distinguished by their shapes, size and colour schemes, etc. Copies of these tiles are used to cover a region of the plane while obeying some tile-placement rules such as, in addition to having no overlap of tiles, adjacently-placed tiles might need matching edge colours, etc. Many posed decision problems were based on such formal systems, for example, the question of aperiodic tiling of the plane, due to H. Wang. Tiling is also useful in covering simple closed plane curves to find the 2D Jordan content (area) of the curve and showing mathematical properties of space-filling curves.

## 11.2. LOGO Primitives

To present the ideas and implementations of recursively defined space-filling curves and corresponding tiling procedures with graphical and tiling interpretation of L-systems, we will use only some basic primitives of the rich repertoire of the LOGO language [19, 17] whose details are referenced in a extended version of this paper[1].

## 11.3. L-Systems, Recursion

Formal systems by A. Lindenmayer, now called L-systems, were introduced in connection with a theory proposed to model the development of filamentous organisms. The stages of development are represented by strings of letters corresponding to filaments of cells, each letter represents a cell. The developmental instructions, which are presumed to generate the organisms, are modelled by rewriting rules or productions. These rules are applied simultaneously to all letters to reflect the simultaneity of growth in the organism. The simplest version of the theory assumes that the growth is deterministic, and it is free from the influence of other cells, i.e., a single context-free rule for each letter.

A *deterministic informationless L-system*, in short a D0L-system, is a triple $(\Sigma, h, v)$, where $\Sigma$ is a finite non-empty set, called the *alphabet,*

---

[1]www.dcc.fc.up.pt/~rvr/resources/Files/programmingspacefillingcurves.pdf

$v \in \Sigma^\star$, where $\Sigma^\star$ is the free monoid generated by $\Sigma$, and $\lambda$ is its identity, $v$ is called the *axiom* and $h$ is a mapping $h : \Sigma \to \Sigma^\star$. Furthermore $h$ is extended to $h : \Sigma^\star \to \Sigma^\star$ as follows:

$$h(ab) = h(a)h(b) \text{ for all } a, b \in \Sigma^\star, \text{ and } h(\lambda) = \lambda,$$

$h$ is called the *set of parallel rewriting rules*. We do not distinguish between $h$ and its homomorphic extension. The mapping $h$ is usually given as a finite set $\{a \to w \mid h(a) = w, a \in \Sigma, w \in \Sigma^\star\}$.

The *language*, $L$, of a D0L-system is defined as follows:

$$L(\Sigma, h, v) = \{v, h(v), h(h(v)), \ldots\} = \{h^n(v) \mid n \in \mathbb{N}\},$$

where $h^0(v) = v$, and $h^n(v) = h(h^{n-1}(v)) = h^{n-1}(h(v))$ for $n > 0$; $h^n(v)$ is called the $n$th *generation of the axiom* $v$.

The following is an example of a simple D0L-system, $F$, that generates the sequence of Fibonacci words, defined by the following concatenating recursion: $f_0 = a$, $f_1 = b$, and for $n > 1$, $f_n = f_{n-2}f_{n-1}$.

We define $F = (\{a, b\}, h, a)$, where $h = \{a \to b, b \to ab\}$; in other words $h(a) = b$ and $h(b) = ab$. And

$$L(F) = \{a, b, ab, bab, abbab, \ldots, h^n(a), \ldots\}.$$

We note that for $n > 1$,

$$h^n(a) = h^{n-1}(h(a)) = h^{n-1}(b) = h^{n-2}(h(b)) = h^{n-2}(ab) =$$
$$= h^{n-2}(a)h^{n-2}(b) = h^{n-2}(a)h^{n-2}(h(a)) = h^{n-2}(a)h^{n-1}(a),$$

which shows that for all $n$, we have $h^n(a) = f_n$.

The following LOGO program, **P1**, with its top-level procedure **fb :n**, is coded to print $h^n(a)$.

```
to a :n  ; calls the procedure b with a decremented value
         ; of n, types "a into the buffer
if n = 0
make "n :n−1 ifelse :n>0 [b :n][type "a]
end


to b :n  ; calls a then b recursively with a decremented
         ; value of n, types "b into the buffer if n = 0
make "n :n−1 ifelse :n>0 [a :n b :n][type "b]
end


to fb :n  ; calls a :n  if n > 0, prints the print−buffer,
          ; the nth Fibonacci word.
          ; The first word is generation 0.
if :n>0 [a :n] print "
end       ; End P1
```

The LOGO command line below tests the code fb :n for values 1 to 6.

make "i 1    repeat 6 [fb :i    make "i :i+1]

```
a
b
ab
bab
abbab
bababbab
```

The LOGO procedures **a** and **b** in **P1** are mutually recursive procedures that call each other with a successively decremented parameter **n**. When the recursion attains the parameter value 0 for **n**, the appropriate letter is typed into the print-buffer which is printed at the end.

Similarly for any D0L-system $S = (\Sigma, h, v)$, we code a set of mutually recursive procedures that implement the printing of the $n$th generation of the axiom of $S$.

One needs only to code a one-parameter letter-procedure for each letter $\sigma$ of $\Sigma$. Each such procedure decrements its parameter value and then recursively calls each procedure named by the letters of $h(\sigma)$ in the order of the spelling of the word $h(\sigma)$. When the continually decremented value of $n$ finally becomes 0, then each procedure $x$ is to type its letter, the letter "x, into the print-buffer.

A top-level, one-parameter procedure $S(n)$ is coded to call in sequence, with the same parameter $n$, each letter-procedure that is named by the letters of $v$, in the order given by the spelling of the axiom $v$.

For example, given

$$S = (\{a, b, c\}, h, aa),$$

where $h = \{a \rightarrow abc, b \rightarrow bc, c \rightarrow c\}$, then

$$L(S) = \{aa, abcabc, abcbccabcbcc, abcbccbcccabcbccbccc, \ldots\}.$$

The corresponding code, **P2**, to print the $n$th generation of $aa$, the axiom in $S$, is the following

```
to a :n ;  calls a,b,c with a decremented value of n,
           ; types a into the buffer if n = 0
make "n :n−1 ifelse   :n>0 [a :n b :n c :n][type "a]
end

to b :n ;  calls b then c recursively with a decremented
```

```
                          ;  n,  types  b  into  the  buffer  if  n = 0
make  "n  :n−1  ifelse    :n>0 [b  :n   c  :n] [type  "b]
end

to  c  :n  ;  calls  c  recursively  with  a  decremented  n,
                          ;  types  c  into  the  buffer  if  n = 0

make  "n  :n−1  ifelse  :n>0 [c  :n]  [type  "c]
end

to  s  :n  ;  if  n > 0,   s :n  calls  a :n  twice,
                          ;  it  prints  the  print−buffer  containing
                          ;  the  nth  word  in  L(S).
if  :n>0 [a  :n  a  :n]  print  "
end        ;  End P2
```

The LOGO command line below tests the code **s** :n for values $1 \cdots 6$.

```
make  "i  1   repeat  6 [s  :i   make  "i  :i+1]
```

```
aa
abcabc
abcbccabcbcc
abcbccbcccabcbccbccc
abcbccbcccbccccabcbccbcccbcccc
abcbccbcccbccccbcccccabcbccbcccbccccbccccc
```

## 11.4. Interpretation of L-Systems

Whereas A. Lindenmayer used L-systems with a strong biological interpretation, in this paper we interpret the letters of the alphabet of L-systems as formal procedures to create mathematical objects.

One of the simplest interpretations might be a numeric one, namely to compute the length of the word of the $n$th generation of the axiom. This is coded by transforming the LOGO program **P1** that prints a word of an L-system, to one to compute the length of the $n$th word by incrementing a global variable, "k, instead of typing each letter. The original value of "k is set to zero, then its final value is the word length. To accomplish this, a procedure **ink** is used to increment "k each time **ink** is called. The resulting code transformation of **P1** is the following:

```
to  a  :n  ;  calls  the  procedure  b  with  a  decremented  value
           ;  of  n,  increments  k  if  n = 0
```

```
make "n  :n−1 ifelse   :n>0 [b :n][ink]
end

to b :n ;  calls procedures a then b recursively with a
         ; decremented value of n, increments k if n = 0
make "n :n−1 ifelse :n>0 [a :n b :n][ink]
end

to f :n ; calls a :n  if n > 0, types the value of k,
        ; the nth fibonacci number, and a blank. the 1st
        ; such number is 0.
make "k 0 if :n>0 [a :n] type :k type "\
end

to g :m ; generates the first m fibonacci numbers and
        ; prints the results.
make "i 0 repeat :m [f :i make "i :i+1] print "
end

to ink   ; increments "k
make "k :k+1
end      ; End transformed P1
```

To test the code for **f**, we included the procedure **g** :m. The following shows a test and its result:

```
g 10
0 1 1 2 3 5 8 13 21 34
```

A similar code transformation for **P2** would produce the following result:

```
g 10
0 2 6 12 20 30 42 56 72 90
```

Obviously, these are grossly inefficient ways to calculate the $n$th Fibonacci number, or the values of the expression $(n + 1)n$ as in the second example.

## 11.5. Line-Graphic Interpretation, Grint, of L-Systems, von Koch Star

L-systems are used in specifying and constructing graphical images of recursively defined mathematical objects such as fractal curves, recursive tiling and space-filling curves.

Fig. 11.1.

The famous von Koch star snowflake construction serves as an example (Figure 11.1 (left)). The geometric construction starts with the three sides of an equilateral triangle. The middle third of each side becomes a base of an equilateral triangle on that side extending outside the original triangle and then the bases of these new small triangles are deleted. The result, in the first instance, is a six-pointed star. The construction proceeds on the 12 line-segments of the six-pointed star: again the middle third segment of each line-segment will be the base of an equilateral triangle extending outward from the star, and then these bases are deleted to make a more intricate polygon. This process goes on: at each round of the construction, the number of line-segments increase by a factor of 4. The process yields a fractal curve that is nowhere differentiable and approximating it by polygons of increasing complexity yields perimeters of unbounded length, but the enclosed area is finite. Figure 1 (left) shows a display of the first few rounds of such construction with an added feature of colour and expansion of the coloured polygons that approximate the fractal curve of the von Koch star snowflake. Figure 11.1 (right) is a similar display with the axiom changed to *aaaaaa*.

The L-system $vK$ that generates the nested polygons of Figure 11.1 is the following:

$$vK = (\{a, b\}, \{a \to abaa, b \to abab\}, bbb),$$

where the *line-graphic interpretation*, also called *grint*, $G$, of the letter $a$ is to draw a unit line-segment and rotate counter-clockwise 60°, while that of $b$ is to draw a unit line-segment and rotate clockwise 120°. When mapped into LOGO statements, we have

$$G(a) = [\textbf{fd } :k \textbf{ lt } 60], \quad G(b) = [\textbf{fd } :k \textbf{ rt } 120]$$

and the code for $vK$ include a mutual recursion:

```
to a :n
make "n :n−1 ifelse :n>0 [a :n b :n a :n a :n]
                        [fd :k lt 60]
end

to b :n
make "n :n−1 ifelse :n>0 [a :n b :n a :n b :n]
                        [fd :k rt 120]
end
```

To clear the screen, to set the start- (or root-) coordinates and the value of the scalable constant "k, and to decrease "k's value for each next generation by a factor 3, before calling b :n thrice, is the procedure vK :n, given as follows:

```
to vK :n ; creates the nth approximation to the von Koch
         ; star snowflake.
make "k 2400/power 3 :n cs pu setx −240 sety −360 pd
        repeat 3 [b :n]
end        ; End vK
```

The next L-system, $TM$, that generates the Thue-Morse words, is simpler both in its rules and in its grint; yet its generated fractal curve converges to the same limit as the von Koch star snowflake:

$$TM = (\{a, b\}, \{a \to ab, b \to ba\}, bbb), \ G(a) = [\textbf{fd } :k], \ G(b) = [\textbf{lt } 120].$$

The value of :k here, however, decreases only by a factor $\sqrt{3}$ at each subsequent generation.

The L-system $vK2 = (\{a, b\}, \{a \to ab, b \to aa\}, bbb)$, has the same grint, $G$, as that of $vK$ but it has simpler rules. Here, also, the value of :k decreases by a factor $\sqrt{3}$ at each new generation. It is an example of "less is more", as its generation $2n$ is the same as the $n$th generation of $vK$, and its generation $(2n+1)$ is the same as the $n$th generation of $vK$, when the axiom there is changed to $a^6$. Furthermore, all the tiling rules that are introduced in the next section, apply equally to $vK2$ as well. Figure 11.2 shows the objects created by the line-graph interpretation of the initial development of $vK2$.

Fig. 11.2.

## 11.6. Recursive Tiling, Flow-Tiles, Flints, Proper Tile-Words, Flow-Lines, Flow-Graphs

As stated earlier, L-systems can be used to define a sequence of tile placements. This is accomplished by assigning a tile value to each letter of the alphabet. The set of such tile values is called the *tile-set*. A tile is an arbitrarily 2D-translated and/or 2D-rotated copy of an element of the tile-set. A tile in this work is a simply-connected plane region defined by the interior of a Jordan curve given by a LOGO procedure. Usually we display a tile as a framed coloured polygon. A non-polygon or 3D generalization of this concept will not be explored here.

To specify the unique placement and orientation of tiles, each tile is given an *entry point* and an *exit point* on its perimeter and also an *entry direction* and an *exit direction* at these points.

These directions are relative to the perimeter of the tiles, so when the tile is rotated, these directions rotate consistently as well. Tiles so equipped are called *flow-tiles*. For each word over the alphabet, the corresponding sequence of flow-tiles is determined by the spelling of the word. The spatial placement and orientation of each flow-tile in the tile sequence is then determined by the following adjacency placement rule: a flow-tile $B$ can be adjacently placed to follow flow-tile $A$ iff

(1) the exit point of tile $A$ is coincident with the entry point of tile $B$, and

(2) tile $B$ is rotated so that its entry direction is the same as the exit direction of tile $A$.

A sequence of flow-tiles that follow this placement rule is called a *flow-tile-word* or *tile-word* in short. A tile-word is termed *rooted* when the position and the orientation of its first tile is specified, i.e., when the translated values of the $(x, y)$ coordinates of the entry point and the rotated value of the entry direction are given. The default value of the entry-direction of a rooted tile is the positive $y$-axis, i.e., 12 o'clock. A tile-word is termed *proper* if no two of its tiles overlap. Flow-tiles are usually features added to the grints of L-systems. For each letter of the alphabet there is exactly one flow-tile. It inherits the line graphics associated with the letter. The entry and exit points are, respectively, the starting and ending points of the grint and so are there the entry and exit directions. The inherited grint of a flow-tile is called its *flow-line*. The flow-tile associated with a letter of an L-system is called its *flint*. The flow-tile-interpreted L-system is called *flinted*, while a line-graphic interpreted one is called *grinted*.

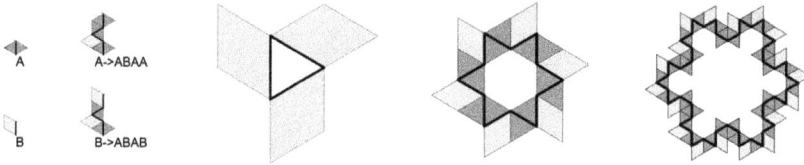

Fig. 11.3.

Figure 11.3 displays a flow-tile set, consisting of two flow-tiles, the parallel tile-rewriting rules to tile the Von Koch star snowflake and the resulting generations $0, 1$ and $2$ for the axiom *bbb*.

In Figure 11.3, the letter $a$, in addition to its previous grint, is now also associated with a flow-tile, a $60°$ rhombus, oriented as shown. The small diagonal is the unit line-segment specified in $G(a)$. This is the flow-tile $A$, whose entry point is at the bottom of the rhombus and its exit point is on the top. The entry direction is the direction that the tile inherits from drawing $G(a)$'s line-segment from bottom to top, it inherits its exit direction from $G(a)$ as it exits, i.e., the heading of the turtle after $G(a)$'s left turn by $60°$.

The LOGO procedure to draw the tile $A$ first, and then the line-segment and turn, as defined by $G(a)$, is coded as [ta **fd** :k **lt** 60], where the procedure ta is given as follows:

```
to ta  ; draws a 60 degrees rhombus of sides k, ta preserves
       ; the original turtle position and its heading into
       ; the small diameter.
lt 60 repeat 2 [fd :k rt 120 fd :k rt 60] rt 60
end
```

Similarly to the letter $a$, the letter $b$, as well, in addition to its previous grint, is now also associated with a flow-tile, the flow-tile $B$ in Figure 11.3, a $60°$ rhombus, oriented as shown. The 1st side of the rhombus is the unit line-segment specified in $G(b)$. The entry and exit points of flow-tile $B$ are, respectively, at the bottom and the top of the 1st side. The tile's entry direction is the direction that the tile inherits from drawing $G(b)$'s line-segment from bottom to top. Its exit direction is inherited from $G(b)$ as it exits there, i.e., the heading of the turtle after $G(b)$'s right rotation by 120°. After drawing the 1st side of the rhombus, the turtle turns counter-clockwise 60° to draw the 2nd side, etc.

The LOGO procedure to draw the tile $B$ with the line-segment and turn, as defined by $G(b)$, might be coded as [tb **fd** :k **rt** 120], where the procedure **tb** is given as follows:

```
to tb
; to the left , draws a 60 degrees rhombus of sides k,
      ; tb preserves the turtle 's position and its heading
      ;into the first side .
repeat 2 [fd :k lt 60 fd :k lt 120]
end
```

In the tiled version, the constants in vK were revised, and the value of k was reduced, as the tiled curve now needs more space, much more in the initial instances of the generations, and the initial position, the root, had to be more centred.

To distinguish the tiles in the tile-set, different members of the set are painted with different colours. To distinguish the flow-lines, the lines inherited from the the original grint, from the lines outlining the tiles, a larger line-width is used to draw the flow-lines. To code this, features are added to **ta** and **tb** and vK.

To establish the line-width of the flow-lines, a variable ps stands for pen-size. In vK we code [**make** "ps 11−2∗:n psw], where **psw** establishes the pen-size, the formula $11 - 2n$ assures that increasingly finer pens are used for large values of $n$. For $n > 5$, resolution-related problems arise.

```
to psw ; prepare to write with a wide pen as defined by :ps
setpensize :ps pd
end
```

To establish the line-width 0 for drawing the perimeter of the flow-tiles, the procedure ps0 is used

```
to ps0 ; prepare to write with a sharp pen
setpensize 0 pd
end
```

To accomplish these pen-size alternations in **ta** and **tb**, at the starts and the ends of their codes ps0 and psw are called, respectively. The procedure psw is called first in vK to set the initial pen-size.

To colour the tiles $A$ and $B$, colouring procedures **ca** and **cb**, respectively, are used.

```
to ca  ;  flies  to  the  centre  of  the  rhombus  to  flood
       ;  with  colour  9
pu fd  :k/2 setfc 9 fill bk :k/2 pd
end

to cb  ;  flies  close  to  the  centre  of  the  rhombus  to  flood
       ;  with  colour  2
pu lt  30 fd :k   setfc 2 fill bk :k rt 30 pd
end
```

Fig. 11.4.

The complete program vK for the flinted Von Koch snowflake is in the extended version of this article. It is interesting to note that the flint for the language of the L-system vK with other axioms may also result in an infinite language of proper tile-words, if the initial generations are proper. An example of this is displayed in Figure 11.4. The axiom is $a^6$ with generations 0, 1 and 2.

A *flow-graph* is the image of the homomorphically extended grint on the free monoid of the alphabet, mapping words in the language of an L-system into graph objects, and *flow-tiling* is that of the so-extended flint. Flow-graphs are a main source of the design of space-filling curves.

## 11.7. The Peano Curve

Historically, the first mathematical construction and presentation of a space-filling fractal curve was given by G. Peano. The specification of this curve is given below by the flinted L-system *Peano*. The tile-replacement rules and some initial generations are displayed in Figure 11.5 (left). The two middle squares display the 2nd and 3rd generation of the axiom *a*. The bottom three squares display generationa 0, 1, and 2 of the axiom *dddd*, whose flow-lines give an octagon and whose fast intricate polygon development is convincing of its space-filling quality. Figure 11.5 (right) shows its 3rd generation.

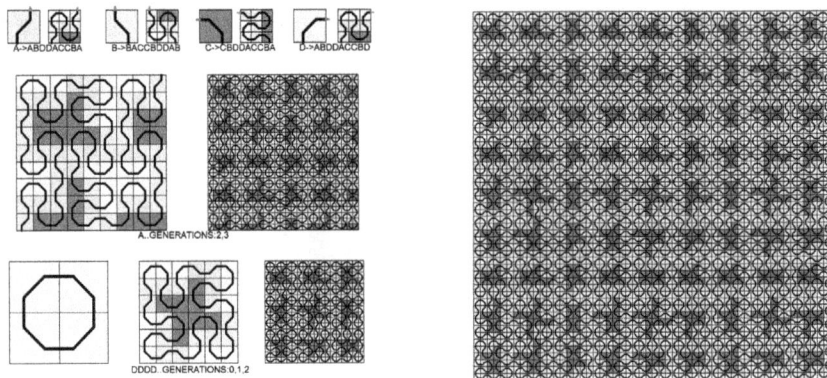

Fig. 11.5.

$Peano = (\{a, b, c, d\}, h, a)$, where $h$ is given by the following four rules:

$$a \rightarrow abddaccba, b \rightarrow baccbddab, c \rightarrow cbddaccba, d \rightarrow abddaccbd;$$

the flow-lines are given by the following line-graphics interpretation: $G(a) = $ [g j f h g], $G(b) = $ [g h f j g], $G(c) = $ [g h f h g], $G(d) = $ [g j f j g], where the four procedures mentioned here are coded as follows; the value of the scalable global constant :k must be established previously:

| to h | to j | to f | to g |
|------|------|------|------|
| lt 45 | rt 45 | fd :k | fd :k/2 |
| end | end | end | end |

To add coloured flow-tile creating procedures to these grints, procedures are needed first to draw and to colour fill squares suited to the flow-lines. The procedures dsl :fc and dsr :fc will do this.

```
to dsl : fc  ; Alters pensize to 0, turns left 90 degrees,
              ; moves to the corner, draws 3 sides, returns
              ; to the origin, hues with :fc
ps0 l fd :fs r repeat 3 [fd :sd r] fd :ls r hue :fc psw
end
```

```
to dsr :fc   ; Alters pensize to 0, turns right 90 degrees,
              ; moves to the corner, draws 3 sides, returns
              ; to the origin, hues with :fc
ps0 r fd :fs l repeat 3 [fd :sd l] fd :ls l hue :fc psw
end
```

```
to hue :fc   ; Flies to the middle of the square, floods it
              ; with the colour :fc, and returns to its start
pu fh setfc :fc fill bk :fs pd
end
```

The following additional self-explanatory procedures are used above.

```
to f            to l            to r
fd :k           lt 90           rt 90
end             end             end
```

The complete program for the flinted Peano L-system is given in the extended version of this paper. The top-level procedure Peano :n establishes the scalable constant :k and related other constants as well as the root position. The value of :k is scaled down by a factor of 3 for each next greater generation, and the screen is cleared before a :n is rooted and called.

## 11.8. The Hilbert Curve

D. Hilbert, the great Prussian-born mathematician and a contemporary of G. Peano, is the author of the next recursively defined space-filling curve that bears his name. A flinted L-system formulation is displayed by Figure 11.6 (left). It shows the flow-tile rewriting rules in its first two rows and the resulting tiling generated from the tile-axiom $A$ in its third row. The fourth row shows the initial development from the flow-tile axiom $AJBAJB$, where the flow-lines create a polygon, starting with a rectangle. The last row shows the same, but starting with the flow-tile axiom $ABAB$, where the generated polygon sequence of the flow-lines starts with a square. Figure 11.6 (right) is generation 4. The colour of the tiles reveal the recursive-subdivision idea of the inductive proof that the curve is

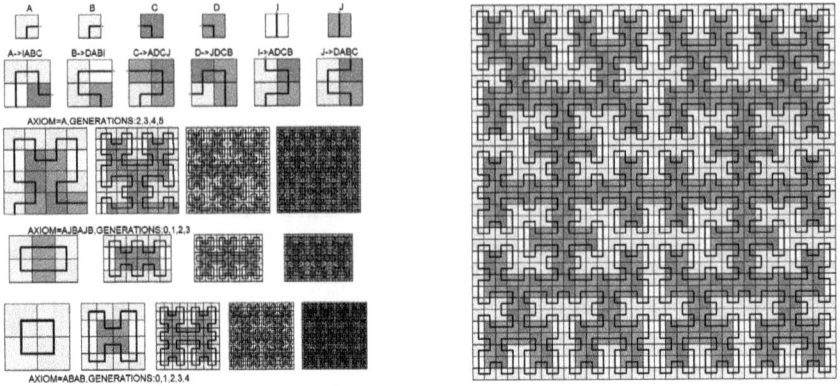

Fig. 11.6.

space-filling.

The L-system Hilbert is given as follows:

$Hilbert = (\{a, b, c, d, i, j\}, h, a)$, where $h$ is given by the following six rules:

$$h = (a \to iabc, b \to dabi, c \to adcj, d \to jdcb, i \to adcb, j \to dabc).$$

The line-graphic interpretation, $G$, of the letters are given by the following LOGO drawing procedures: $G(a) = [\text{frf}]$, $G(b) = [\text{frf}]$, $G(c) = [\text{flf}]$, $G(d) = [\text{flf}]$, $G(i) = [\text{ff}]$, $G(j) = [\text{ff}]$, where the corresponding codes for these procedures are as follows:

| to f | to ff | to flf | to frf | to l | to r |
|------|-------|--------|--------|------|------|
| fd :k | f f | f l f | f r f | lt 90 | rt 90 |
| end | end | end | end | end | end |

where :k is a global variable whose value is established in the top-level procedure **Hilbert :n**.

The flint code is a prefixing of each flow-line procedure with a call to a colour-filled-square-drawing procedure **s :fc**

```
to s :fc  ; Draws & fills a square starting at the midpoint
          ; of the base, its inner colour is given by :fc
l ps0 repeat 4 [frf] r pu f setfc :fc fill bk :k psw :ps pd
end
```

**Hilbert :n** is the top-level procedure to set initial values to global variables, including the $(x, y)$ coordinates for the root, before calling for the $n$th generation of the axiom $a$. The complete program **Hilbert :n** to generate the *n*th flow-tile word of `a` `:n` can be found in the extended version of this paper.

## 11.9. An Intriguing Flow-Tile Interpretation for the L-system Als

Figure 11.7 shows the rules and an initial development of a flinted L-system, *Als*, whose flow-lines are restricted to the hexagonal grid, and its tile-set, $\{A, B, C\}$, is made up of a rhombus, a trapezoid and an eight-sided concave polygon. $A, B$ and $C$ are tightly covered, respectively, by 2, 3 and 7 copies of an equilateral triangle. The L-system

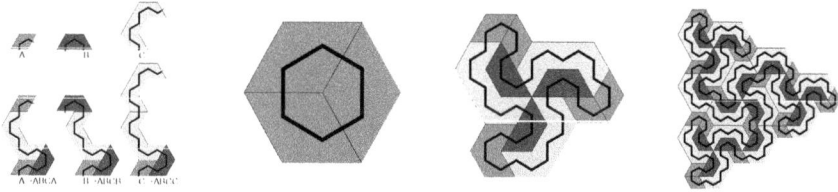

Fig. 11.7.

*Als* is defined as follows: $Als = (\{a, b, c\}, h, aaa)$, where $h = (a \rightarrow abca, b \rightarrow abcb, c \rightarrow abcc)$. Its grint, $G$, is coded as follows: $G(a) = [\text{ frffrf }]$, $G(b) = [\text{ flf } \quad \text{flf } \quad \text{flf }]$, and $G(c) = [\text{ flf } \quad \text{frffrf } \quad \text{flf } \quad \text{frffrf } \quad \text{flf }]$ with

| to frffrf | to flf | to f | to r | to l |
|-----------|--------|------|------|------|
| f r f f r f | f l f | fd :kh | rt 60 | lt 60 |
| end | end | end | end | end |

and where the value of `:kh` exists in a scalable global variable `"kh`. The program `Als` `:n` to draw the *n*th approximation to the space-filling polygon can be found in the extended version of this paper.

Fig. 11.8.

The first few initial members of the *Als* polygon sequence is given in

Figure 11.8. Clearly, this sequence of polygons will be space filling if it is properly scaled to a given equilateral triangle, but this L-system recursion, with different but carefully chosen initial axioms, would be space filling for other than just triangular regions. One only needs to make *ad-hoc* experiments with proper placement of flow-tiles, in an initial part of the sequence, and their flow-lines will present the answer.

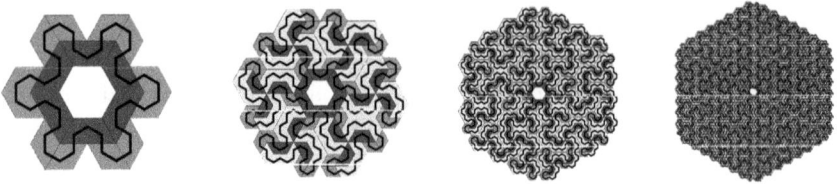

Fig. 11.9.

In Figure 11.9, the given initial members of a potentially infinite sequence already show that the tiling approaches a nearly hexagonal region. The tile-rewriting is based on the rules given by Figure 11.7; however, the axiom for the L-system is now an 18-letter tile-word, namely $(AAB)^6$. The 6-fold rotational symmetry of the displayed tile-words is obvious. The flow-lines, a fractal polygon sequence, inherit the space-filling property from the tile-sequence.

Figure 11.10 shows the first five members of a similar sequence; however, the "space-filled" region has now a fractal border, not unlike the the Von Koch star snow flake. The tile-rewriting is still based on the rules given by Figure 11.7; however, the axiom now is a 12-letter tile-word, $(AB)^6$. These figures also have a 6-fold symmetry. Many axioms, including $C^6$ and $B^2$, not shown, also give new developments. To increase the composition power of the letters of a flinted L-system, with an aim of creating new tiling sequences based on proper tile-words, one includes new letters with new flow-tile rules and use an axiom that includes some new letters.

Figure 11.11 shows such one: $Als2$. $Als2 = (\{a, b, c, d\}, h, abddba)$, where $h = (a \rightarrow abca, b \rightarrow abcb, c \rightarrow abcc, d \rightarrow abcd)$.

In Figure 11.11, the new flow-tile, $D$, a 6-sided polygon, appears twice in the axiom, and only twice in each generation as well, since $D$ is not involved in the other letter-rules. Furthermore, in the rule for $D$, $D$ appears only once on the right-hand side. The flow-graph of $Als2$ was introduced in an article as a puzzle by the author and his brilliant coauthor, R. Quinton.

A somewhat simpler shapes of tiles, namely a rhombus and a rhomboid,

Fig. 11.10.

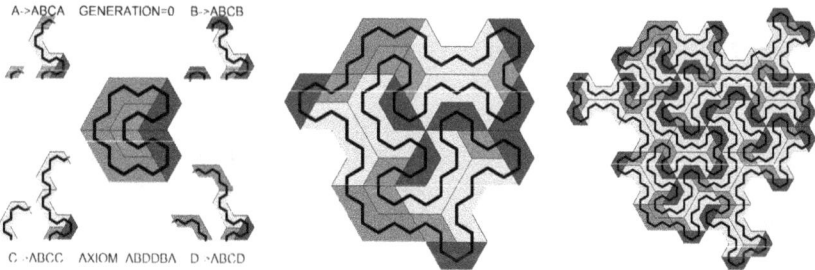

Fig. 11.11.

are used for the flints for the L-system $Als3$ with its eight rules displayed by Figure 11.12.

$Als3 = (a, b, c, d, e, g, i, j, h, ddd)$, where $h$ is given by the following set

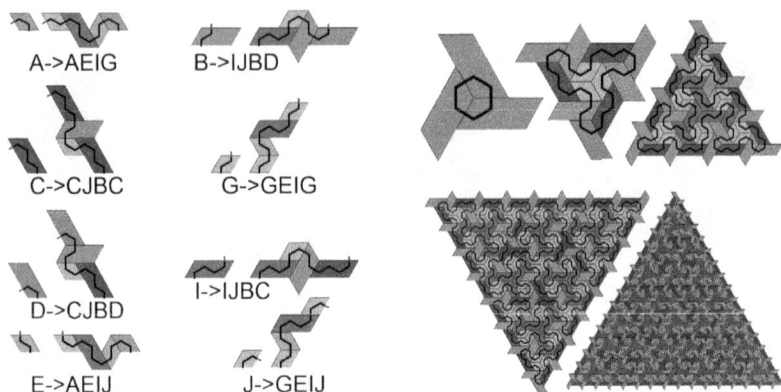

Fig. 11.12.

of productions:

$$h = \{a \rightarrow aeig, b \rightarrow ijbd, c \rightarrow cjbc, d \rightarrow cjbd, e \rightarrow aeij, g \rightarrow geig,$$
$$i \rightarrow ijbc, j \rightarrow geij\}.$$

For *Als*3 the grint code, $G$, is given in terms of LOGO procedures p and q:
$G(a) = G(d) = [\text{p p}]$, $G(b) = G(g) = [\text{q p}]$, $G(c) = [\text{p q p p}]$, $G(e) = [\text{p q}]$,
$G(i) = [\text{q q p p}]$, $G(j) = [\text{q q}]$.

```
to p                          to q
fd :k lt 60 fd :k             fd :k rt 60 fd :k
end                           end
```

Figure 11.12 shows also the initial development of the flow-tile word $DDD$, in generations 0 to 4.

The development has a three-fold rotational symmetry. The polygon sequence of the flow-lines, starting with a regular hexagon, when scaled to an equilateral triangle tend to space-fill the triangle. The code is omitted for drawing the flow-tiles as colour-filled rhombi and rhomboids.

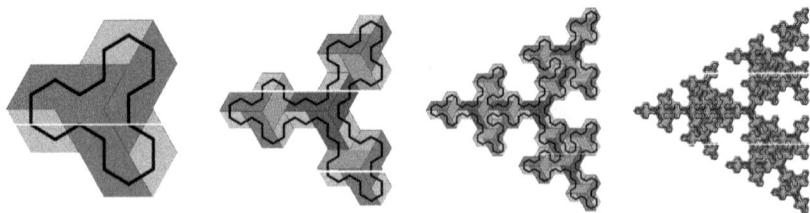

Fig. 11.13.

Figure 11.13 is one of the examples of a variant of *Als3*, it is using the same flow-tile rules as given in Figure 11.12 for *Als3*, but the axiom is now a six-letter tile-word *IJIJIJ*. Generations 0 to 3 are shown.

## 11.10. Tiling of the Gosper FLowSNake Curve and of the Gosper Polygons

Gosper's FLowSNake curve is another strangely mysterious space-filling curve designed on the tessellation of the plane covered by regular hexagons. The grinted L-system *Gosper*, given below, generates a variation of this curve. It has four rules, which allow a simple space-filling tiling enhancement of the curve.

Fig. 11.14.

*Gosper* = $(\{a, b, c, d\}, h, a)$, where $h = \{a \rightarrow accaabd, b \rightarrow bccaabd, c \rightarrow bcdcbad, d \rightarrow acdcbad\}$.

For Gosper, the grint, $G$, is also in terms of the above LOGO codes p and q: $G(a) = [\text{p p}], G(b) = [\text{q p}], G(c) = [\text{q q}], G(d) = [\text{p q}]$. Figure 11.14 shows the rewriting rules for the flow-tiles $A$, $B$, $C$ and $D$, as well as the result of two additional generations for the flow-tile axiom $A$. The codes for constructing the coloured rhombi are omitted. Based on *Gosper*, a class of L-systems, *Gosper*($\alpha$), is defined by replacing the axiom $a$ with a proper tile-word $\alpha$, which is formed from copies of the tiles $A$, $B$, $C$ and $D$. The following are some examples.

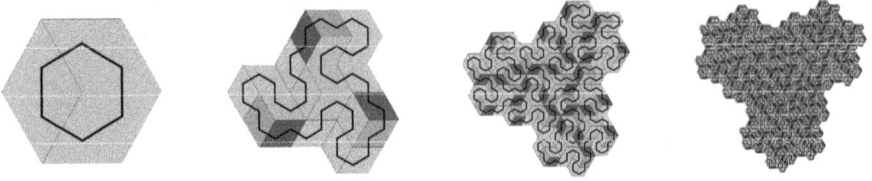

Fig. 11.15.

Figure 11.15 shows some generations of *Gosper*(*aaa*), initially a regular hexagon; the flow-lines quickly become a space-filling fractal polygon. Being adventurous, one chooses an axiom by laying down a properly formed tile-word over $A$, $B$, $C$ and $D$ and then applies the *Gosper* rules to see the surprise.

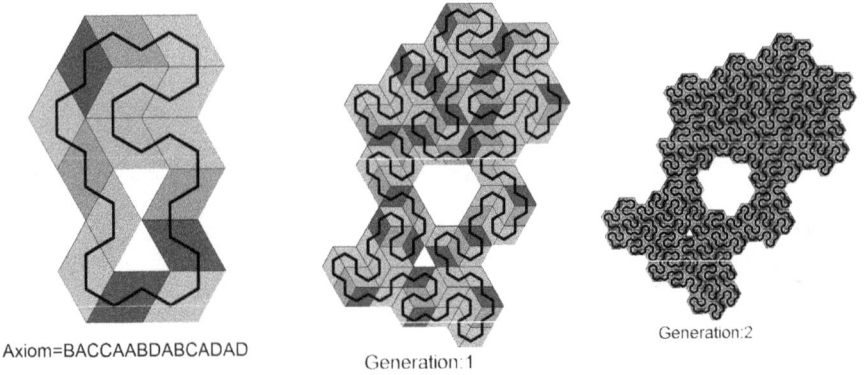

Axiom=BACCAABDABCADAD

Generation:1

Generation:2

Fig. 11.16.   This shows such a development of the tile-word $BACCAABDABCADAD$, whose flow lines, a polygon, develops to space-fill a region that is not simply connected, as the hole in the middle remains unfilled.

The *FLowSNake* curve, originally presented in another form, is reflected in the flow-lines of the following flinted L-system, *FLSN*, whose tile rewriting rules are shown in Figure 11.17. $FLSN = (\Sigma, h, a)$, where $\Sigma = \{a, b, c, d, e, g, i, j\}$ and

$$h = \{\ a \rightarrow jaibjde, b \rightarrow jaibjde, c \rightarrow cabcdge, d \rightarrow cabcdge, e \rightarrow caibjde,$$
$$g \rightarrow jabcdge, i \rightarrow caibjde, j \rightarrow jabcdge\}.$$

The flow-line graphics, $G$, for *FLSN* is given as follows: $G(a) = [\text{f r f}]$, $G(b) = [\text{f r r f}]$, $G(c) = [\text{f l f}]$, $G(d) = [\text{f l l f}]$, $G(e) = [\text{f l f}]$, $G(g) =$

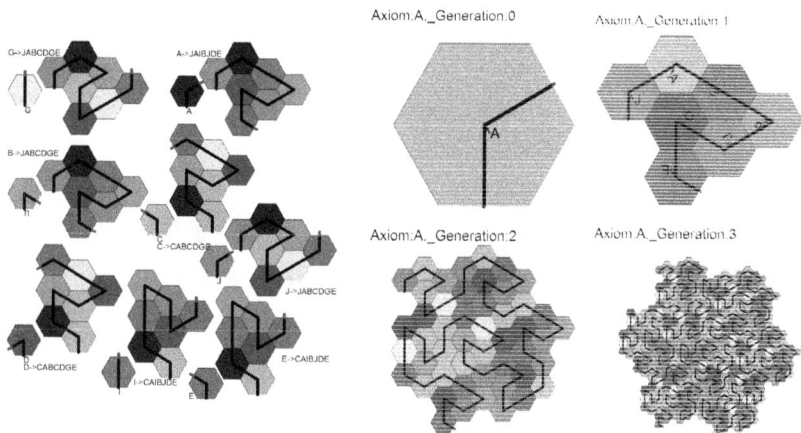

Fig. 11.17.

[f f], $G(i) = $ [f f], $G(j) = $ [f r f], where the LOGO procedures f, r and l are coded as follows:

```
to f            to r            to l
   fd :k           rt 60           lt 60
end             end             end
```

where "k is a scalable global variable whose value, :k, is assigned in a top-level procedure. The code for the simple procedure to render the colour-filled regular hexagonal tiles, a procedure which is called before calling the flow-line procedure for each letter in $\Sigma$, is contained in the program *FLSN* in the extended version of this paper.

As before, based on *FLSN*, a family of L-systems is defined as $FLSN(\alpha)$, where $\alpha$ is a proper tile-word that generates a sequence of proper tile words, e.g, the flow-graphs of the following such tile-words generate infinite sequences of space-filling polygons: *AAA, BBB, CCC, DDD, CECECE, JAJAJA*, etc.

The L-systems given here for the *Gosper's FLowSNake* and its variants have rewriting rules that replace each letter of the alphabet by a word of length 7. Thus, there is a 7-fold increase in the number of covering units, be it of rhombi or regular hexagons. To make the generated sequence of tile-words space-filling, each generation should occupy the same area. To achieve this, coded in a top-level procedure, the sides of these tiles are reduced by a factor $\sqrt{7}$ between generations.

## 11.11.  Lock-and-Key Tiles, Tiling the Sierpiński Space-Filling Polygon

By changing the axiom and the grints in vK, the well-known space-filling polygon sequence created by the great Polish mathematician W. Sierpński, is given here as the following grinted L-system:

$$Sierpinski = (\{a, b\}, \{a \rightarrow abaa, b \rightarrow abab\}, bb).$$

The grint, $G$, of the letters is the following: $G(a) = [\text{f h f h}]$, $G(b) = [\text{f r f r}]$, where the code for the procedures f, h and r are as follows:

| to  f | to  h | to  r |
|-------|-------|-------|
| **fd** :k | **lt**  45 | **rt**  90 |
| **end** | **end** | **end** |

where "k is a scalable global variable whose value, :k, is assigned in a top-level procedure.

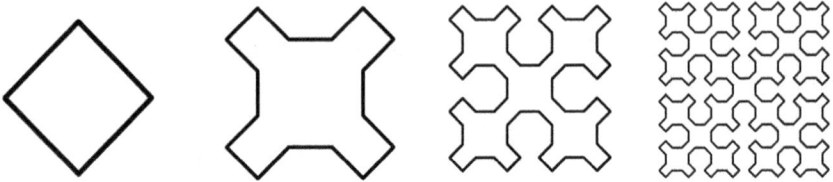

Fig. 11.18.   The initial development of the Sierpiński flow-graph sequence, rooted at 45 degrees.

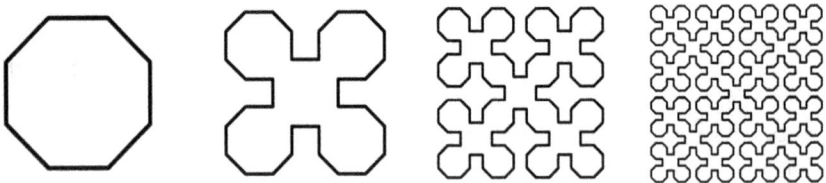

Fig. 11.19.   Tiling of the merged sequence from Figs. 11.18 and 11.19 .

As seen before with vK, a merged version of the two sequences of space-filling polygons, generated by Sierpiński from the axioms $bb$ and $aaaa$, can also be generated with the same grint, $G$, by a single and simpler L-system: $Sierpinski2 = (\{a, b\}, \{a \rightarrow ab, b \rightarrow aa\}, bb)$. This is another case of "less is more".

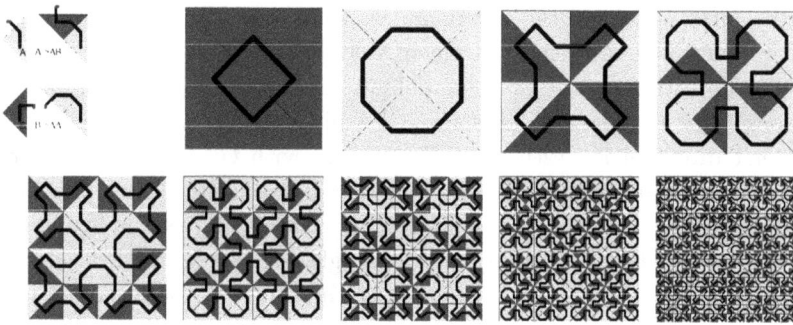

Fig. 11.20.   The complementary flow-graph sequence generated by the axiom *aaaa*.

## 11.12.   Lock-and-Key Flow-Tiles for *Sierpinski2*

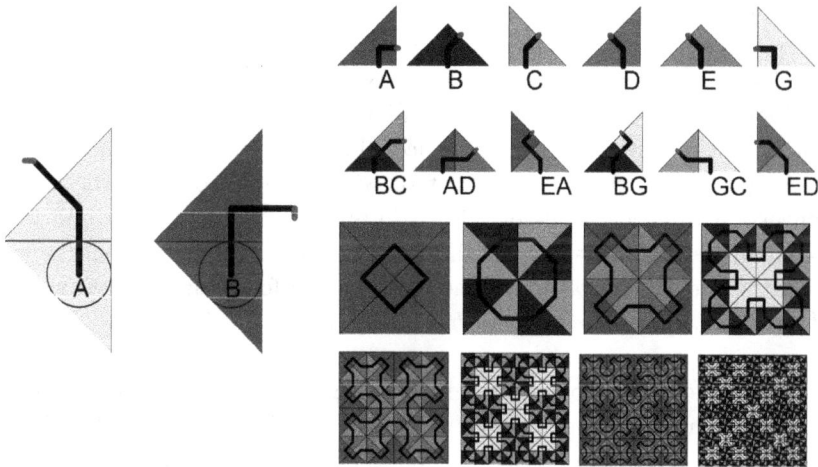

Fig. 11.21.

Figure 11.20, in its first square, shows the tile-rewriting rules of the L-system *Sierpinski2*, whose grint is enhanced now with a tile construction that is a new form of a flow-tile, called *lock-and-key flow-tile*. The requirement that flow-lines enter in and exit from points of the perimeter of the tiles no longer holds. In the lock-and-key flow-tile scheme, a flow-line can start in any designated point of the tile and may end outside the perimeter. The entry direction and the exit direction are the directions of the flow-line at the entry point and the exit point, respectively, as given by the grint of the system. The adjacency placement rule for tiles is unchanged.

For both tiles $A$ and $B$, being default rooted, the entry direction is 12 o'clock. For tile $A$, with $G(a) = $ [f h f h], after the two 45°-left turns, the exit direction is westbound. For tile $B$, with $G(b) = $ [f r f r], after the two 90°-right turns, the exit direction is 6 o'clock. Each tile, being an isosceles right triangle in their default rooting, have their hypotenuse parallel to the entry direction, and their right angle is on the left side, i.e., to the west. The entry point is placed to the centre of the inscribed circle of the right triangle making up the lower half of the tile. The value of :k in the procedure f is the length of the diagonal of this circle. This specifies the geometric proportions necessary to construct the lock-and-key tiles, $A$ and $B$, that correspond to the grint $G$. To make sure that tiles intended to be adjacent are, in fact, adjacent and without overlap, the scaled geometry of the flow-tiles with their entry and exit points, and the corresponding scaled grint has to match, as a key into its lock. The geometric details for *Sierpinski2* are displayed in Figure 11.21 (left side). This explains also why the flow-graph of $BB$ is a square and that of $AAAA$ is a regular octagon.

Figure 11.21 (right side) shows a flinted L-system, *Sierpinski3*, and an initial part of the generation sequence. The flow-graph polygon sequence of *Sierpinski3* is the same as that of *Sierpinski2*. To make the simple conversion from lock-and-key tiles to ordinary flow-tiles, the grints were found by seeing what part of the flow-lines were present in one half of each the tiles of *Sierpinski2*. The result is the following: *Sierpinski3* = $(\{a, b, c, d, e, g\}, h, aaaa)$, where $h = (a \rightarrow bc, b \rightarrow ad, c \rightarrow ea, d \rightarrow bg, e \rightarrow gc, g \rightarrow ed)$.

The functional-dependence graph of h is bipartite, which explains the fact that each generation has a set of at most three different types of tiles and that the partition sets alternate for consecutive generations. The grint for *Sierpinski3* is the following: $G(a) = $ [f r f], $G(b) = G(c) = $ [f j f], $G(d) = G(e) = $ [f h f], $G(g) = $ [f l f], where the procedures f, h, r, l and j are coded as follows:

| to f | to h | to r | to l | to j |
|------|------|------|------|------|
| fd :k | lt 45 | rt 90 | lt 90 | rt 45 |
| end | end | end | end | end |

The value of :k is determined by a top-level procedure, it represents the length of the radius of the incircle of the triangle of the tiles $A \cdots G$. The complete program for a flinted *Sierpinski3* L-system is given in the extended version of the paper.

Flinted L-systems simplify the creation of space-filling designs since carefully chosen proper tile-words as axioms generate proper space-filling tile-words. Figure 11.22 displays an example. $(EADED)^4$, a tile-word of length 20 was chosen as axiom for *Sierpinski3*. The resulting flow-graph space-fills a 12-sided polygonal region around a square.

Fig. 11.22.

## 11.13. Conclusions and Historical Remarks

This work is an updated version of the notes of the author's lectures given in the late 1970's. Since then an enormous amount of L-systems research has developed. Most significantly, the amazing achievements of the Prusinkiewicz school must be mentioned, particularly for capturing the beauty of plants through interpreted L-systems. Proving the mathematical and combinatorial properties of interpreted L-systems will keep mathematicians and theoreticians busy, as these proofs might be quite complex. Recently, J. Shallit, with collaborators, used automatic methods to prove theorems related to properties of words defined by interpreted L-systems. L-systems with 3D interpretation are even more fascinating, and the LOGO language has facilities to render images of 3D structures. This writing is self-contained, as the author intends that this subject be of interest to a wide audience and a stepping stone to many discoveries. With this in mind the some additional references are given.

## References

1. G. ALLOUCHE, J.-P. ALLOUCHE AND J. SHALLIT, Kolam indiens, dessins sur le sable aux îles vanuatu, courbe de sierpinski et morphismes de monoïde, *Annales de l'institut Fourier* **56**,7 (2006), 2115–2130.
2. M. BADER, *Space-Filling Curves: An Introduction with Applications in Scientific Computing, Texts in Computational Science and Engineering* vol. 9, Springer-Verlag, Berlin, 2013.

3. M. BARNSLEY AND S. DEMKO, Iterated function systems and the global construction of fractals, *Proceeding of the Royal Society* **A399** (1985), 243–275.

4. K. CULIK II AND S. DUBE, L-systems and mutually recursive function systems, *Acta Informatica,* **30**,3 (1993), 279–302.

5. M. GARDNER, *Penrose Tiles to Trapdoor Ciphers,* W.H. Freeman & Co, 1989.

6. D. GOČ, D. HENSHALL AND J. SHALLIT, Automatic theorem-proving in combinatorics on words, *Int. J. Found. Comput. Sci.* **24**,06 (2013), 781–798.

7. D. HILBERT, Über stetige abbildung einer linie auf ein fläschenstück, *Mathematische Annalen* **38** (1891), 459–460.

8. A. LINDENMAYER, Mathematical models for cellular interaction in development, *J. Theoret. Biology* **18** (1968), 280–315.

9. B. MANDELBROT, *The Fractal Geometry of Nature,* W. H. Freeman and Co., New York, 1982.

10. G. PEANO, Sur une courbe qui remplit toute une aire plane, *Mathematische Annalen* **36** (1890), 157–160.

11. G. PÓLYA, Über eine peanosche kurve, *Bulletin International de l'Academie des Sciences de Cracovie (Sci. math et nat. Série A),* 1913, 1–9.

12. P. PRUSINKIEWICZ AND A. LINDENMAYER, *The algorithmic beauty of plants,* Springer-Verlag, New York, 1990.

13. H. SAGAN, *Space-filling Curves,* Springer-Verlag, New York, NY, 1994.

14. D. SCHATTSCHNEIDER, *M.C. Escher: Visions of Symmetry,* Harry N. Abrams, New York, N.Y, 2004.

15. J. SHALLIT AND J. STOLFI, Two methods for generating fractals, *Computers and Graphics* **13** (1989), 185–191.

16. W. SIERPIŃSKI, Sur une nouvelle courbe continue qui remplit toute une aire plane, *Bulletin International de l'Academie des Sciences de Cracovie (Sci. math et nat., Série A),* 1912, 462–478.

17. SOFTRONICS, MSWLogo. `http://www.softronix.com/logo.html`, Acessed: 01/01/2016.

18. A. SZILARD AND R. QUINTON, An interpretation for D0L systems by computer graphics, *The Science Terrapin (Fac. of Sci. The Univ. of Western Ont.)* **4**,2 (1979), 8–13.

19. WIKIPEDIA, Logo. `https://en.wikipedia.org/wiki/Logo_(programming_language)`, Acessed 01/01/2016.

# Author Index